THE INTEGRITY OF WORSHIP

THE
INTEGRITY
OF
WORSHIP

*Ecumenical and Pastoral Studies
in Liturgical Theology*

Paul Waitman Hoon

ABINGDON PRESS
Nashville and New York

THE INTEGRITY OF WORSHIP

Copyright © 1971 by Abingdon Press

ISBN 0-687-19108-4

Library of Congress Catalog Card Number: 70-148861

Scripture quotations unless otherwise noted are
from the Revised Standard Version of the Bible,
copyrighted 1946 and 1952 by the Division of
Christian Education, National Council of
Churches, and are used by permission.

Scripture quotations noted NEB are from the New
English Bible, New Testament. © the Delegates
of the Oxford University Press and the Syndics
of the Cambridge University Press 1961. Reprinted
by permission.

SET UP, PRINTED, AND BOUND BY THE
PARTHENON PRESS, AT NASHVILLE,
TENNESSEE, UNITED STATES OF AMERICA

In memory
of my mother and father, whose love led me into Faith

CONTENTS

PREFACE

The writing of these essays was undertaken some nine years ago in the conviction that the integrity of the Church's worship[1] is decisive for the Church's life, and despite the fateful changes that have since occurred, I still hold this conviction and propose it to the reader. History, to be sure, has violently overtaken us all, and it is a great deal harder to say now what liturgical "integrity" means than it was then. In liturgy as elsewhere everything seems to have come unstuck—in a phrase of John Courtney Murray—and I frankly am relieved not to have in print what I first thought I wanted to say. Yet, the Church's life is not simply at the mercy of history. The world may indeed set the Church's agenda, as we are fond of saying, but it is God who in the Event of Jesus Christ has called the meeting. In her worship uniquely, the Church again and again hears that call. And in her reflection upon it that we speak of as liturgical theology, she cannot but obey its truth as it addresses her mind in every generation. These essays attempt to reflect upon that Event and its truth for our time, and they thus assume that only as the Church liturgically listens and reflects with integrity can her life and mission possess integrity. In this sense the need for a redefinition of liturgical integrity may be all the greater, if the more difficult.

Given this conviction, integrity would seem to require that one try to bring a measure of theological poise to the currents swirling about us. Such a stance is especially indicated in time of radical change when it is perhaps harder to know where to be conservative than revolutionary, when truthfulness is often subverted to novelty, and when liturgical reform in particular is commonly viewed as a kind of gamesmanship at which anyone may try his hand. It is quite clear, for example, that secularization today constitutes a formidable challenge to the mind of the Church liturgically as otherwise. Her response so far seems to have been uneven—at times hesitant and awkward, perhaps more often uncritically cordial. And a warning of Canon Demant some years ago, that when the Church undertakes to proclaim the Gospel in a secular idiom she must beware lest she end up proclaiming secularism in a Christian idiom, strikes home with increasing

---

[1] The title, *The Integrity of Worship*, was first suggested to me by a former colleague, Professor John Knox, whose book *The Integrity of Preaching* was published by Abingdon Press in 1957. Professor Knox has kindly allowed me to adapt his title for my own purposes.

force to me. At the risk of being misunderstood, I have to say that much liturgical reform seems misconceived to me because our reformers have brought more sensitivity to culture than theological discrimination. They have not reliably established their points of reference nor lived deeply enough with the Church's liturgical mind to avoid repeating the mistakes of their ancestors.

Now theological poise does not mean of course that one turn olympian or counter-revolutionary and stop one's ears to the realities history is reporting to us. Neither does it mean that one refuse the truth that positions of excess speak to us, nor that one miss the bus by failing to grasp the distinctive modes under which we must do our theological work in our time. Further, "poise" does not mean ignoring the peculiar tonality which resistance to change in liturgical reflection and practice often manifests. Liturgical theology, especially, is always tempted to become "fortress theology," to fasten psychologically on God as the "Great Conserver" and to slip into equating what is true with what is unchanging.[2] But poise does mean, I think, the courage to affirm continuity and tradition, a refusal to be stampeded by secularization, the chore of doing one's theological spadework, and especially a playing for the theological long run—indeed the longest run of which a man is capable.

Joining with my theological concern is also the conviction that the gathered congregation and the pastor of the congregation will continue to be central in the life of the Church in the foreseeable future. In part this conviction arises out of twenty years in the pastorate before I became transplanted into theological education—an experience I have not been able nor wanted to lay aside in preparing these studies. Even more it arises from the way I perceive history empirically to deliver the Church to us. Whatever our lamentations or doxologies over the alleged demise of the parish, the congregation will continue to be the *datum* of the Church's historical existence for a long time to come. This of course is not to say that specialized ministries and nonparochial forms of church life are not authentic or important, nor that drastic changes in the Church's institutionalized life are unwelcome. The avant-garde who are exploring new forms of ministry and new structures of church life are rightly ten years or so ahead of much of the Church, and what they are thinking and doing today, congregations will be appropriating tomorrow. The problem is, however, that the great majority of congregations are not yet even where the avant-garde were five years ago; and despite much talk about revolution as preferable to reformation,

---

[2] I am indebted for this formulation to Clement J. McNaspy, S. J., in *Our Changing Liturgy* (Image Books; Garden City, N. Y.: Doubleday & Co., 1967), p. 29.

somehow the Church must be kept obedient to her mandate, *ecclesia semper reformanda,* and theological and liturgical transition helped along.

But because the congregation in one form or other is so palpably the reality we must deal with, I also believe that all theology—including liturgical theology—is ultimately to be validated by the empirical Church as it lives and serves in culture. This is to say, I see liturgical theology as both an intellectual discipline and an expression of ecclesial, pastoral, and missionary concern. Or, to use the nomenclature of my trade, I view liturgical theology as a form of pastoral theology in the sense that it is to affirm the Church, care for the Church, judge the Church, and summon the Church to her proclamation in the world. I believe, in the words of Karl Rahner, that "theology is at the service of the preaching of the Gospel. . . . It does not regard the pastoral-theological orientation as any diminution of its strength." [3] But this orientation means in turn that liturgical theology is also to be validated by reference to what our Catholic friends speak of in a splendid phrase as "pastoral liturgy," that is, liturgy conceived and conducted as truly the people's worship so that their life in the Christian community in all its expressions is rooted and nourished in him who is their Head. To be sure, always liturgical theology is at the same time a discipline of the mind—and soul—in apprehending the truth of the Word, Jesus Christ. Yet, liturgical theology is only authentic when it is more than thought and consistently views liturgy in relation to the flesh and blood congregation and their life in the world. In short, the dialectic of thought and life is the fulcrum on which liturgical theology is to turn.

Liturgical theology, for example, is not most authentic when it is only stated propositionally within the categories of speculative theology. Yet it also is not most authentic when it consents to be turned into only experimental theology. The so-called mission theologians both warn and challenge us here. On the one hand, one feels a certain hard-nosed imperialism in their insistence that we view everything pragmatically, which those who seek that full truth which obedience to the fullness of the Gospel bestows have no alternative but to resist. On the other hand, the categories of "mission" and "praxis" they propose are much more fundamental for all forms of theological reflection than we may have understood. Their appeal is a great deal more than a passing vogue, and liturgical theologians in particular can never again think only as cerebrally as they once did. Thus while I am indebted to, and shall continue to envy, theologians of speculative temper of mind who compel us to grapple with primary axioms, I hold that liturgical theology

[3] Thomas A. O'Meara, O. P., "Karl Rahner on Priest, Parish and Deacon," *Worship,* XL (Feb., 1966).

becomes sterile when it is divorced from the Church's empirical life and when its context is not "pastoral theology" and "pastoral liturgy" in the broad sense in which I have defined them. In the words of Cardinal Montini: "Liturgy is for men, not men for liturgy."

In these essays, then, it will become evident that I take the professional theologians with a degree of realism even as I liberally draw from them. I think that some of them—and certain historical theologians and devotees of the liturgical movement in particular—have bypassed some important matters the pastor understands better than they do. In fact if I were to tip the scales one way or another in making a judgement on how we best enter into liturgical truth, it would be in favor of the parish minister. I think I have experience on my side and I also believe I have history on my side in saying this. And despite the pastor's protestations of incompetence and the criticisms I shall occasionally have to aim at him, he is often a better liturgical theologian than he knows and a more effective one than his armchair opposite numbers admit.[4] Louis Bouyer once made a biting criticism of Dom Gueranger on this point, a nineteenth century pioneer of the Roman Catholic liturgical movement. The weakness of Gueranger's conception of the proper celebration of the liturgy, Bouyer wrote, was that it "could not have become the real worship of any actual congregation of the period. It could only become the worship of that artificial monastic congregation which Gueranger had brought into existence simply to carry it out!"[5] This kind of thing also characterizes some of our contemporary professional reformers, incidentally, and it troubles me to the extent that in a number of places I have had to warn the pastor against the professionals even as in other places I have rather forcibly compelled him to listen to them.

However, precisely because the pastor has the unique opportunity to function as a liturgical theologian (this conviction will be elaborated in the second essay), he should be challenged to take theology most seriously. I believe that the pastor needs to be written up to, not down to, if such terms can be used meaningfully. That is, he should be taxed to undertake reflection upon liturgy as a most strenuous business. I do not think he should be let off easily—hence the heavy going and technical terms in some of these essays—and I do not want him to let me off easily. In my opinion too

---

[4] I often think of a comment Eric Mascall once made concerning the ill-fated revision of the Book of Common Prayer of the Anglican Church in Great Britain in 1928: "There are . . . some useful lessons we can learn from the whole sad story, and the chief one is that, in the last resort, liturgy is what the Church does and not what it is told to do." A sentence of Gregory Dix is appended in a footnote: "The good liturgies were not written; they grew!" Quoted by Martin Thornton, *Feed My Lambs* (New York: Seabury Press, 1961), p. 48.

[5] *Liturgical Piety* (Notre Dame, Ind.: University of Notre Dame Press, 1955), p. 12.

much writing about worship by free-church people especially—as too much free-church worship itself—lacks theological meat. I venture to say this even though I am quite prepared to be told that what I would like to think is meat in these essays is only gristle! But for that matter, much meat is lacking here which both the pastor and I ought to chew on, and a number of issues have had to be bypassed simply because I have not the specialty for them. One such issue consists of the problems posed for liturgy by the school of philosophers called linguistic analysts. Who is going to explore critically for us the theological statements which liturgy inevitably makes? Or who is going to help us formulate a liturgical psychology valid in our post-Freudian and post-Jungian age? What liturgical theologian, further, will take the existentialists with the seriousness they deserve? I have undertaken a few sorties in the latter two areas, but they are only that—sorties, not the plotted and sustained flight we need.

Now it may well be that this conception of liturgical theology as both an intellectual discipline and an expression of pastoral and ecclesial concern has led me to fall ineffectually between the two camps—those on the one hand who know and relish the importance of theological theory, and the practical people on the other who would bring everything before the bar of experience. Thus these essays may disappoint certain theologians who, I have observed, rather like to tie things up neatly in intellectual and historical packages. Similarly, these essays may disappoint certain pastors who want practical answers to practical problems, but quick. And I should probably warn the pastor here in particular that my practical applications of theological principle are meant to be suggestive, not exhaustive, as for example in discussing the relevance of worship in chapter 3, or the nature of liturgical language in chapters 5 and 6, or the nature of liturgical action in chapter 7. Be this as it may, I concede that I have hoped to lead clergy into thinking theologically more than they may have bargained for and to push my theological friends into thinking more practically than they may find comfortable. This part of my design is summed up in the subtitle of this book—that these are essentially pastoral studies in liturgical theology.

In following this approach I have of course taken title to my fair share of personal positions—if not outright prejudices—in liturgical matters. I believe that any theology worth the name will inevitably express not merely one's thought but one's total personality structure, including one's value systems both conscious and unconscious, and that we are foolish not to admit this more than we do. Surely the whole man—one's emotional conditioning, one's sensibilities, one's imaginative life, one's conscious memory as well as the unremembered experience one has lived through, indeed even one's body chemistry—should be expected to shape thinking. I am not a

13

mystic, for example; but I have had enough of what may be called mystic experience to know that truth indubitably lies here. And I am rather sure that my stress on the ontological character of the Word in the Christology set forth in the second essay, and on the existential character of worship in the fourth essay, reflects my subjectivity. Similarly, I find such categories as "transcendence" and "eternity" still meaningful for liturgy, and I have trouble feeling as "historicized" and "secularized" as some of my friends tell me I should be. In any case, I believe that any theological statement should reflect—for good or ill—one's full being, and that the study of worship, as worship itself, ought to declare the whole man.

But given this belief, I should perhaps account in advance for some criticism I have directed to certain of our contemporaries who validate worship exclusively out of their own secularized sensibilities. Because all of us project theology out of our inward life, we must not thoughtlessly nor vindictively throw stones at other people for feeling theology differently from the way we do. Yet not very long ago, sad-faced theologies projected out of a secularized sensibility that God was dead were the vogue. Now advancing upon us, apparently, are dionysian theologies projected out of a secularized sensibility of smiling exuberance. What happens to liturgical truth, one has to ask, if it is to be validated only by sensibilities determined by the changing moods of culture? Is there not a purchase point for thought somewhere—biblical revelation perhaps—that can save one from becoming a theological manic-depressive? In a different vein, I think we especially have to watch out in liturgical theology for our anxieties; these particularly corrupt thought. I suspect that the heavy emphasis in liturgical theology today upon the corporate nature of worship, for example, reflects both personal and cultural anxiety—as I shall try to make clear. But there are anxieties—and there are anxieties, some neurotic and some healthful. I would like to think that my chief anxiety is of the latter sort! I have called it a "holy anxiety" that God's self-disclosure in Jesus Christ shall determine worship in his Name. And on this point I have to agree with Hans Conzelmann that if this anxiety is missing, and if our own experience and the spirit of the age are made the controlling factors in reflection, then authentic theology is on the way out.[6] I have indeed worried somewhat lest this holy anxiety become the "revelation positivism" with which Dietrich Bonhoeffer charged Karl Barth, that is, the foreclosing of truth from any source except that revealed in the biblical Word, Jesus Christ. I don't really think it is. But if it is, then I can only reply with Barth that I think the Bible is still a good book and that it is

---

[6] *An Outline of the Theology of the New Testament,* trans. John Bowden (New York: Harper & Row, 1969), p. xiv.

worthwhile to take its thoughts at least as seriously as one takes one's own.

A number of factual and historical considerations also have combined with personal conviction to lead to the writing of these essays. For one thing, the mainstream free churches in the United States have not until recently paid much attention to liturgical theology, and I judge that a theological statement may be useful in helping our congregations make with greater integrity the practical decisions confronting them week by week as they plan and conduct public worship. By "free churches" I mean those denominations which do not have ecclesiastically required forms of worship but whose very freedom, so desirable and so admirable in many ways, can become a source of corruption if not informed with theological integrity. A picture of our need has been suggested by a friend, Professor Harland Hogue of the Pacific School of Religion, who estimates that out of about 300,000 Protestant congregations in the United States, the worship of probably 200,000 falls within the free-church category as I have loosely defined it.[7] A sentence of Lesslie Newbigin also quoted by Professor Hogue underscores our need: "It is one of the tragedies of the situation that the churches which have given their ministers the maximum liberty of liturgical improvisation are those which has given them the minimum training in liturgical principles." [8] Fortunately, the situation has of late changed for the better. Competent studies in the history of free-church worship have appeared, and literature is available dealing with the sacraments, the relation of worship to art and symbolism, music, architecture, and to a lesser degree with worship and mission, secularization, psychology, and Christian education. Inquiries have also been undertaken into the history and nature of the liturgical movement. Directories of worship have been updated; study manuals, new service books, and experimental orders have been published. Likewise much of the literature in liturgical theology prepared by ecumenical commissions speaks to American free churches. But Protestant statements of liturgical theology which attempt in depth to deal both theologically and practically with matters vital for the life and mission of the Church—these are wanting.

Further, certain historical breakthroughs have also strengthened my conviction that a theological analysis of integrity in worship may contribute to the renewal of the Church's life. One immediately thinks of such important developments as the rapprochement between the arts and liturgy, for example; of the crisis in communication wrought by the impact of mass media;

[7] These figures are a 1970 downward revision of those Professor Hogue originally cited in an address given in 1962 to a meeting of professors of practical theology from American and Canadian seminaries. See his monograph, "Communicating the Gospel Through Sacraments and Liturgy," *Report of the Biennial Workshop of the Association of Seminary Professors in the Practical Field* (Toronto: 1962).

[8] *South India Diary* (London: SCM Press, 1951), p. 86.

15

and the implications for worship of the mutations of cultural sensibility to which I have referred. These will require extensive comment in later essays. Here I wish briefly to identify three particular developments which hold prophetic import for the Church's life. Probably the most important is what we broadly speak of as the liturgical movement and its implications for the renewal of the Church. The perfect symbol of our situation in this respect was the promulgation by Vatican II in December, 1963, of the Constitution on the Sacred Liturgy as the first formal step in the renewal of the great Roman communion. Protestant viewers from afar may have been tempted only to smile, rapidly calculate from Trent in 1563 to Rome 1963, and say to themselves: "Hmm, 400 years, it's about time." But this is to miss the point. The point is that when Catholicism was ready to let the Holy Spirit lead her into new life, she found herself led first of all to reform her worship.[9] Now how far the liturgical movement was responsible for Vatican II, with all its far-reaching reforms, will be a matter for the historians to decide. There can be no doubt, however, about the order of priorities for the mind of the Church: the place to begin in undertaking reform is at the point where the Church's being, nature, and mission are supremely set forth— in her worship. And the significance of this should no more be lost upon the Protestant pastor than the Roman priest.

Indeed this suggests the second breakthrough—the ecumenical movement. It is now clear that whoever is going to talk seriously about the reunion of the churches is going to have to talk liturgical theology from the very first syllable, partly in the sense that points of liturgy constitute critical points of doctrine (the relation of the doctrine of the Sacraments to the doctrine of Ministry, for example), and even more in the sense that participation in common worship—specifically in Holy Communion—emerges more and more as one of the most promising bridges to union in all areas of the Church's life. In regard to the latter, J. C. Hoekendijk has remarked upon our perverseness in turning things upside down by requiring theological consensus before we find it possible to enter into communion: "Christian community is the *prius* of Christian doctrinal consenses." Communion is "learned while being practiced. . . . As long as we in fact withhold the medicine of reunion from one another, we must not expect too much from ecumenical prescriptions."[10] To me this thrust seems irrefutable. It may not seem so to

[9] Gerard Sloyan has written that the Council statement on liturgy best sums up the spirit of Pope John, and that the core of all he had hoped for in the way of *aggiornamento* is expressed in it. See *The Constitution on the Sacred Liturgy and the Motu Proprio of Paul VI, with a Commentary* by Gerard S. Sloyan (Glen Rock, N. J.: Paulist Press, 1964), p. 7.

[10] *The Church Inside Out*, eds. L. A. Hoedemaker and Pieter Tijmes, trans. Isaac C. Rottenberg (Philadelphia: Westminster Press, 1966), p. 105.

others. My point in any case is that our ecumenical time is perforce a liturgical time, and that if the pastor is going to practice his ecumenicity, he had better study his liturgy. Certainly it is arguable—if it is not already demonstrable—that the road to reunion starts more truly from altar, pew, pulpit, and font than from headquarters in Geneva or Rome, or from the telephone number of the local commission on ecumenical relations.

This ecumenical understanding of course is especially congenial to one who has had the privilege of living and working and worshiping in an ecumenical seminary such as my own; and I should record here my indebtedness to Anglican, Lutheran, and especially to Roman Catholic scholars manifest in these pages. While a free-church Protestant, I have found that Catholic authors in particular speak with truth that claims me more powerfully than those in my own tradition; hence I was not totally surprised to discover on finishing these essays that I have quoted them more often than any others. Thus while these essays are mainly directed to the free churches, I hope they will also speak to all who agree with me that our liturgical time is an ecumenical time. In liturgy as elsewhere we need to bring together both Catholic substance and Protestant principle and Protestant substance and Catholic principle.

Another breakthrough consists of the far-reaching effect upon liturgical thinking of recent studies in biblical and historical theology. In fact, some of these studies hold what some people may regard as catastrophic implications for worship as the churches today conventionally conceive it. Very simply, our traditional understanding of worship as restricted to the cultic gathering of the congregation at a designated time and place for rite and proclamation will no longer do. This is not what the New Testament means by worship. Rather, worship in New Testament terms is a comprehensive category describing the Christian's total existence, and it is to be thought of as coextensive with man's faith-response wherever and whenever this response occurs.[11] The Christian's life in its totality is a liturgical life, and liturgically it can be thought of as much missionary as cultic. Such recovered understandings of liturgy have to do with the very roots of the Church's being, and they are so radical that a new mind-set, really, is required to deal with them. I doubt whether on the whole I have succeeded in making the changeover in that I have not been able to shed earlier ways of thinking forged through the years. My predominant orientation—and most ministers will probably share this—is to think of worship as essentially cultus; I still consider this to be a valid way of thinking about worship, and this is generally the sense

[11] See Franklin W. Young, "The Theological Context of New Testament Worship," in *Worship in Scripture and Tradition*, ed. Massey H. Shepherd, Jr. (New York: Oxford University Press, 1963), pp. 89-90.

of the term "worship" as I have used it throughout this book. Yet the larger understanding of worship has at least gotten hold of me to a degree, and the reader may find it not uninteresting to wrestle through its implications with me.

A few further baselines must be mentioned. First, the reader should understand that a certain open-endedness characterizes these essays, chiefly because the essential mystery of worship, in turn inhering in the essential mystery of Jesus Christ, does not permit any final answers. In undertaking this book, my instinct led me at the outset to cast my thought in the form of a cluster of rather freewheeling essays on topics I judged to be important. I did not wish, for example, to follow the plan one often finds in writing on liturgy— a clear-cut, serial treatment of the main elements of worship such as the sacraments, preaching, rites, the Christian Year, and so forth. Nor did I feel led simply to elaborate a theology of worship in propositional outline. Rather, I have chosen to range theologically over selected problems that have emerged as important for pastor and congregation today, such as the problem of relevance, the problem of symbols and forms which I call "the language of worship," the problem of congregational participation. And now that I have finished exploring these problems—and they have finished exploring me—I am glad that I remained as open-ended as I began. A certain tentativeness in dealing with liturgical matters, I have learned, is usually wise. A remark of Ernst Käsemann to the effect that the history of the Gospel is always at the same time a history of misunderstandings, has comforted me in this regard, in that my open-endedness just may keep my misunderstandings to a minimum.

At the same time, I hope that theologically sitting loose has not meant that these essays are devoid of coherence or lacking a certain anatomy. The second essay on the theological nature of worship, for example, the fulcral essay for the entire book, sets forth in brief form a Christological way of thinking about worship which for me provides a purchase point for all theological reflection. I have come to believe that virtually all problems in liturgical theology converge in Christology. For if it is *Christian* worship we are speaking about and not merely worship in general, then if we do not get our thinking right at the point of Christology, we are not likely to get it right anywhere. On this fundamental point I may paraphrase a passage from Karl Barth to the effect that what counts most in the worship of the Church is not up-to-dateness nor progress, but reformation; that reformation, however, does not always mean to go with time, to let the current spirit of the age be the judge of what is true and false; that rather, reformation in every age means to carry out better than yesterday the Christian community's task to "sing unto the Lord a new song": "It means never to grow tired of returning not to the origin in time but to the *origin in substance* of the community." [12] I have no doubt but that the origin in substance of the Christian community and its song is simply Jesus Christ. Thus on the all-important issue of Christology, along with the open-endedness I speak of, I have also allowed myself to be just systematic enough to verify the truth of Paul Tillich's remark that one strong argument for a system is that it forces one to discover new relationships he had not suspected were there.[13] And despite the disrepute into which "systems" are supposed to have fallen, I shall be surprised if the reader, in exploring the interlocking relationship between Christology and liturgy generally, does not find this truth still to hold good.

Yet, any Christology worth consideration should be too great for one's mind to handle, and the final result in dealing with selected problems in light of the meaning of Jesus Christ is that I have been willing to be open-ended and systematic at the same time; and here I am afraid the reader will have to accept my ambivalence as best he can. Thus whereas I have previously asked him to take me seriously, now I ask him not to take me too seriously! Or rather, I ask him to take me just seriously enough to be spurred to begin his own pilgrimage into the meaning of Jesus Christ for liturgical theology, and to let the truth of the Word take him—as it has taken me—where it will, even though both of us end up where we may have had no intention of going.

Bound up with the dialectic of open-endedness and system is another baseline: acceptance of the necessity to restate identical liturgical meanings in different forms in different places. The fourth essay, on the subjective-objective character of worship, for example, in a sense continues the preceding essay on the relevance and irrelevance of worship, which in turns rests on the dialectical meaning Jesus Christ holds for liturgy as set forth in the second essay. I was led to such restatement partly because of the necessity to think dialectically about worship, and partly because of the aspect of simultaneity which authentic worship itself bears and which becomes recapitulated in one's thinking about worship. At any given moment, numerous aspects of the same reality are dancing in one's mind; and while one would like to exhaust the meaning of each as it arises, its interlocking relation with other meanings forbids. At least this has been the course of liturgical reflection with me, and I suspect most readers will find it to be the same.

Lastly, I must make explicit what doubtless has already been implicit—the frequency with which the reader will encounter dialectical patterns of thinking: that is, patterns of analysis and criticism which attempt to circumvent

---

[12] *Church Dogmatics*, IV, 1, trans. G. W. Bromiley, "The Doctrine of Reconciliation" (Edinburgh: T. & T. Clark, 1956), p. 705. Italics mine.
[13] See his *Systematic Theology* (Chicago: University of Chicago Press, 1963), III, 3.

19

the limitations imposed by the logical law of contradiction, and which try to deal with solutions to problems in terms of the truth beyond the polarities they embody. In the effort to get at the meaning of worship, one has to think bipolarly and accept the risks of walking a tightrope with truth and error on either side, even though one is perfectly sure that now and again he is going to fall off. This boundary stance may appear to be only a congenital inability to make up one's mind, or an example of the theologian's proclivity for talking out of both sides of his mouth at the same time. Yet I should report that when I originally began work on this book I had no idea I would end up having to think so dialectically. I was driven to it partly by the constraint of Christian truth vis-à-vis culture and the need to see things with something of the poise to which I have referred. I have come to feel, in the words of a church historian who also is very much a man of his age, that the Christian today must "refuse to stagger from one lopsidedness to another. 'Not only . . . but also' is a good slogan for these days. . . . There have been times when the Church has had to fight not only for faith, but for the proportion of faith, and ours may be one." [14] Most of all, I have been driven to think so dialectically by the dialectical nature of worship itself, in turn inhering in the nature of Christian revelation and quintessentially in the dialectic of the Incarnation. The dialectic of the Incarnation embodying the transcendence and the immanence of God and the divinity and humanity of Jesus Christ has become for me the pivot for all liturgical reflection. And this dialectic transposed into theological method, emerged with that kind of inevitability about it that many of us have learned to recognize as the hallmark of truth.

I am deeply indebted to many people who have had a part in helping me prepare these essays. The American Association of Theological Schools provided a fellowship grant in 1960-61 which, together with the generosity of Union Theological Seminary, enabled me to take a year's sabbatical leave for preliminary research. A number of pastors' conferences and clergy seminars have allowed themselves to be used as testing grounds for topical presentations I have altered and present here in written form. I am also indebted to the editors of the *Union Seminary Quarterly Review*, the *Andover Newton Quarterly*, and *Religion in Life* for permission to include material published in their pages. To my colleagues and students in the Union Seminary community I also am heavily indebted, especially to the late President of Union

---

[14] Gordon Rupp, *The Old Reformation and the New* (Philadelphia: Fortress Press, 1967), p. 55. Gilbert Highet also has a story about an unnamed scholar who was once asked what he judged to be the single greatest contribution of the Greeks to the world's life. He replied that the greatest contribution of the Greeks consisted of the two words *men* and *de*: "For *men* means 'on the one hand,' and *de* means 'on the other hand,' and without these two balances we cannot think truly." *The Mind of Man* (London: Oxford University Press, 1954), p. 17.

Seminary, Henry Sloane Coffin, who as teacher, friend, and mentor first awakened my interest in pastoral liturgy many years ago. I also wish to record my thanks to Mrs. Margot Biersdorf, a member of the Union Seminary community, who kindly and critically labored with me over a host of literary and structural problems. And lastly, my wife, Alice, has been a steadfast companion and helper throughout this enterprise as in all other important enterprises in my life, and I am most of all grateful to her.

In the former Latin text of the Roman Mass, there is a phrase addressed by the priest to the congregation, summoning them to their part in the celebration, that has always moved me deeply. Its opening words served for some years as the title of a journal for liturgical reform: *"Orate, frates, ut meum ac vostrum sacrificium acceptabile fiat."* In translation, these words seem to me to voice the spirit only in which we can enter into both the act of worship itself and theological reflection upon it: "Pray, brothers, that my sacrifice and yours be acceptable."

I

The Concern for Worship

This volume of essays undertakes to guide the thought of Protestant clergy and laity toward an understanding of what we have chosen to call the "integrity" of worship. The definition of the term "integrity," of course, constitutes the burden of these pages and is finally the responsibility of the author, but the reader also has a part in this task. Integrity involves the heart's motives as well as the mind's thought, and whoever would end up with a more truthful understanding of worship must muster as much honesty as he can in the attitudes he brings to reflection upon worship. To be sure, integrity means much more than honesty. Yet it at least must mean this; and it is well that those concerned for truthfulness in worship promise one another to be as least dishonest as possible in inquiring into worship.

A seminarian once suggested the kind of attitude appropriate to our task in comparing a man's decision to enter the ministry to his decision to marry. "To marry," he said, "is to choose the woman one would most like to be unhappy with, and to enter the ministry is to choose the vocation one would most like to be a sinner in." In some forms of theological inquiry a man's sins may not be disabling, but liturgy is not among them; and it is wise to lay aside as many illusions about our own virtue as we can. Here, peculiarly, spiritual things are spiritually discerned, and truth has a way of revealing itself only to those who know they are not true. The holiness of the matters one would deal with somehow becomes illumining only when we allow it first to expose our own darkness, and the weights and sins which beset us must at least be acknowledged if they cannot be laid aside.

It is so easy to corrupt reflection upon worship with our own idolatries, to subvert truth to prejudice, to deface holy things with irreverence, and to offend against charity in the name of conviction. The study of liturgy has not seldom been the refuge of the insecure, and—this may be a hard saying—one can without too great trouble detect pretensions, if not neuroses, disguising themselves as *obiter dicta*. Similarly, lurking within most of us is an

23

incurable professionalism which so easily blights the mind's vision and coarsens thought. John Whale has stripped many of us naked here: instead of putting off our shoes because the place whereon we stand is holy ground, we like to take nice photographs of the burning bush from suitable angles, or chat about the atonement with our feet on the desk instead of kneeling before the wounds of Christ.[1] Likewise our pride, even our cruelty, so often undoes us. Why is it that in speaking of worship we so enjoy pointing our finger or telling our favorite jokes? As satire these may not be out of place, but too often they reveal an ugly patronage or a forgetting of the sacredness of the matters we are dealing with. John Baillie once remarked that to believe in God is to believe that he is present in our company even as we tell one another why we believe in him, and to think about worship is itself to be a worshipping act. Only when thought is reverently "through Jesus Christ our Lord" can we hope to understand worship "through Jesus Christ our Lord." We cannot forget that the collect for cleansing, so beloved by the Church through the centuries, petitions the God unto whom all hearts are open, all desires known, and from whom no secrets are hid, to cleanse the thoughts, not of our minds but of our "hearts," that we may worthily magnify his holy name. A shrived heart is as important as a clear mind in the search for integrity in worship. The meaning of Christian worship can only be known by worshiping men.

AN INQUIRY INTO MOTIVES

Our Questionable Motives

However, this is not to say that clarity of mind is not important nor that our critical faculties may be laid aside. The Church's worship, just because it is prayer, is not to be exempt from our most critical thinking. But criticism most promisingly begins as self-criticism, and as we undertake a critique of contemporary worship in this introductory essay, let us first ask: Why are we concerned for the renewal of worship? "All our motives are mixed," an aphorism runs; "the question is, what are they mixed with?"

Possibly one answer is our boredom with the liturgical ruts into which we have fallen and our desire for something new—or perhaps for something so old it will seem new. A judgement of Claude Welch voices our malaise: the Church's life too often reveals "less the joyful song of the 'new man' than the tiresome and familiar refrain of the old captivity in which nothing has been made new." [2] So, we say, worship must be made more exciting.

---

[1] *Christian Doctrine* (London: Collins Press, 1957), p. 146.
[2] *The Reality of the Church* (New York: Charles Scribner's Sons, 1958), p. 17.

Perhaps we have read the psychologists and suppose that some "human potential" techniques can improve the situation, or the historians with their recommendation that we rehabilitate ancient forms—the "kiss of peace," for example—or the sociologists who argue for media "hot" or "cool." More likely we have become intrigued by "creative experiments" and want to try our hand. We may not quite know what to think when we read of a Catholic portrayal of the Virgin Mary as the "Juiciest Tomato of Them All," or of a Protestant jazz service at which dancers moved through the aisles hurling paper plates at the congregation bearing newspaper advertisements and biblical texts which the recipients were instructed to stand and read—this new style of worship being hailed as "important" because it "enabled the people to make interesting sounds." [3] But—and our instinct may not be unsound—perhaps we have been too stuffy in our approach to worship, we reflect. Faith is belief controlling the viscera, someone has remarked, and what we want, frankly, is worship with more visceral power.

Others of us are not so much concerned to put vitality into worship as to use worship "to turn out red-blooded churchmen" [4] and to harness its power to the program of the local church. Raising the budget, staffing the organization, winning new members, making an impact on the community—these are our aims, and we are not above using worship for our own managerial ends. Our aim here may resemble that of one congregation which advertised itself as "the liveliest church in town." The contrast between liveliness and the "Life" the Gospel speaks of may momentarily trouble us, but only momentarily, and what we want is ecclesiasticized worship with megatons of institutional power.

Another motive needing scrutiny may have to do with our free-church inferiority complex. We are not as confident about sermon-centered worship as we once were. The sacraments are increasingly important to us, but we do not quite know how to rehabilitate them. The color and drama of fancier liturgies stir our envy. And hearsay knowledge of the liturgical movement coupled with blandishments from supply-houses of colored stoles, clerical collars, and missal stands make us anxious to get our liturgical etiquette right. The spectacle arranged by a Methodist bishop who at a service of ordination decked out four district superintendents respectively in red, green, white, and purple stoles may have puzzled if not unnerved us; but expertise in using symbolism is important to our ego. Underlying our complex may also be the failure of our seminary to train us properly in worship. We had supposed

[3] Roger Ortmeyer in *The New York Times*, May 15, 1967.
[4] See the essay by Massey H. Shepherd, Jr., "Liturgy or Cult: Source or Resource?" in *Liturgical Renewal in the Christian Churches*, ed. Michael J. Taylor (Baltimore: Helicon Press, 1967).

that our legacy of "Protestant freedom" made such instruction unnecessary, but now the anxiety of our situation is coming home to us.

The obverse of our inferiority complex, however, may be a growing fondness for liturgical authoritarianism—another motive needing scrutiny. We like someone to make decisions for us, or more likely we rather enjoy making decisions for other people. The tendency of many pastors to impress a more priestly style on worship in the name of greater dignity, for example, may appear on the surface to be innocent. In reality it may be the unhealthy expression of a clerical image the minister has of himself, or has uncritically allowed his people to project upon him, which he has internalized within the depths of his own psyche. It is baffling to observe the heightening in many quarters of what has been called "Protestantism's clerical accent" at a time when Protestantism speaks so gushingly of the priesthood of all believers. The liturgical authoritarianism and fastidiousness one finds in not a few clergy may represent a subconscious defense against the growing power of the laity which the pastor professes to welcome in other spheres of church life.

Again, is our concern for integrity only a bland and bogus ecumenism because ecumenism is the vogue? To be sure, such self-deception is by no means always the case, and surely the joy with which many pastors have become caught up in the irreversible tide of Christian unity is often at the center of their concern for liturgical renewal. They have come to know with a knowledge which cannot be denied, that when the Church truly worships, her "catholic richness" becomes palpable; that the faith that unites her now and the doctrine that shall unite her in the future are penetrated to the heart as nowhere else; and that here we experience unity as well as mark the promise of its consummation. The liturgical consensus slowly but surely emerging among Catholics and Protestants as well as among Protestant denominations, the growing number of ecumenical orders restoring the unity of sermon and sacrament, the publication of journals, hymnals, and service books drawing on many traditions, ecumenical congresses on liturgy transcending denominational lines—all these and more attest to the effect of ecumenism upon our concern for liturgical reform and vice versa.

Accompanying these developments, however, is the attitude one frequently finds, that wisdom in ecumenically reconceiving worship is easily come by, that liturgical differences really do not matter very much, and that all we need is cheerily to unite in a kind of liturgical Esperanto. An illustration probably destined to become classic was found in an advertisement by one critic, describing a new type of worship center "for sale at $195 and up," consisting of a "combination table-or-altar" complete with dossal and valance, carved emblems, and paraments. "Compact and portable," in oak with veneer finished in a "neutral shade that blends pleasingly with any interior," the center can be "dismantled in two minutes and easily moved." [5] Is this a kind of crazy parable, our critic asks, a ridiculous commentary upon a facile ecumenism cheapened to fit all sorts of traditions, people, and places? Ruefully, one concludes that such items would not be offered for sale if there were not a market for them.

But we shall stop here, except to add that if this inquiry into our motives seems abrasive, then let it be remembered that worship has been classically conceived in Protestant thought as nothing less than a scene of battle with man at its focal point. "When the Word is active, evil spirits are set in motion," maintained Luther,[6] a truth as telling for one's thinking about worship as for worship itself. We should be warned here that the demonic is as much a possibility for liturgical reflection as for liturgical practice, and as each of us ponders his motives, we repeat: "integrity" must mean being as self-critical and undefensive as we know how to be.

Our Better Motives: Concern for the Edification of the Congregation

But honesty requires us to acknowledge our better as well as our worse motives. And surely most clergymen will quickly want to say, to begin with, that before their minds' eye rise up the faces of people—confirmands waiting to be taught, parents of children to be baptized, young people losing interest in the church, laymen believing and unbelieving—faces young and old, black and white, quizzical, serene, forlorn, eager, all claiming our care. In a word, the motive of pastoral concern for the congregation is surely at work, and here the pastor is on solid New Testament ground. For worship uniquely has to do with the building up of the congregation; the New Testament term is "edify" or "upbuilding" (I Cor. 14:3 ff.); and in the unequivocal if exaggerated words of Karl Barth, if edification "does not take place here, it does not take place anywhere." [7] Despite temptations to managerialism, the pastor is not wrong in seeing the relation between worship and the congregation's life, and he is entitled to be concerned that worship be "pastoral liturgy" in the sense that it strengthen and transform all their life.

A number of problems the average pastor meets every day illustrate his motivation in this respect—the question of Baptism for example. Often this sacrament is understood as only a touching ceremony with churchy overtones, with parents bringing children to be baptized as routinely as they take them

---

[5] Hugh T. Kerr, "Theological Table Talk," *Theology Today*, XIII (Jan., 1957).
[6] See Wilhelm Hahn, *Worship and Congregation*, trans. Geoffrey Buswell (Richmond: John Knox Press, 1963), p. 31.
[7] *Church Dogmatics*, trans. G. W. Bromiley, IV/2 (Edinburgh: T & T Clark, 1958), p. 638.

to be vaccinated by a doctor (and often for similar reasons). Or Baptism is understood as an individualistic experience which "religious" people are free to choose if they wish but which holds virtually no meaning for the secular man. The pastor on the other hand rightly understands Baptism as the initiatory rite into the Christian life and as the engrafting of the believer into the Christian community. How, then, can Baptism be reconceived so that its Christian meanings will command people's assent and respect? And to what extent must it be offered on the Church's own terms, require commitment from those seeking it, and be set within congregational discipline and care? In facing such a question the pastor is dealing with both congregational edification and liturgical integrity.

Again, the relation between worship and evangelism and its implications for the congregation's life troubles many a pastor. No longer can these be opposed to one another as has so often been the case. Rather, the congregation rather than the individual Christian is to be seen as the true agent of evangelism, and its worship—especially Holy Communion—as the place *par excellence* where evangelical action is beheld in its true essence. Here the Lord's saving death is proclaimed with unique power, and the life of the New Age released into the old order of decay, sin, and death. And here likewise is the pivotal reality, the Event of Jesus Christ, that saves evangelism from becoming ecclesiastical propagandizing. In short, liturgy as the showing forth of the Gospel is the heart and motive of authentic evangelism.[8] At the same time, however, "the end of the Church is not evangelism but worship. . . . The follow-up of the evangelistic task is training in worship, without which evangelism is simply abortive." [9] This is to say, worship and evangelism flow into one another. Their relation is dialectical but vital. The Constitution on the Sacred Liturgy of the Roman Catholic Church employs two memorable metaphors to convey this relation: liturgy is both the "fountain" from which the Church's evangelical power flows and the "summit" to which her activity leads.[10]

Again, the relation of worship to pastoral care is bound up with edification of the congregation. Many pastors will eagerly acknowledge their debt to the pastoral psychology movement over the past few decades, but a certain unease is mingled with their gratitude. Too often pastoral care has been conceived in individualistic and humanistic terms, especially as it takes the form of pastoral counseling. Often it is conducted independently of the Christian commu-

[8] See John A. T. Robinson, *Liturgy Coming to Life* (Philadelphia: Westminster Press, 1960), pp. 4 ff.

[9] M. A. C. Warren quoted by S. M. Gibbard, in "Christian Worship: Its Nature, Necessity and Expression," *Studia Liturgica,* I (Dec., 1962).

[10] See Walter M. Abbott, S.J., ed., *Documents of Vatican II* (New York: Guild Press, America Press, Association Press, 1966), par. 10.

nity and is indistinguishable from secular therapy. The answer to our unease, we increasingly understand, is to recover something of the classical definition of pastoral care as the extension of the same saving and healing Word that is made known in preaching and sacrament.[11] Only by seeing pastoral care liturgically and liturgical care pastorally (especially by uniting the sacraments and the rites of confession, absolution and reconciliation with pastoral care) can the congregation authentically serve and be served as a Christian congregation.[12]

Again, the relation of worship and Christian education is important for the edification of the congregation. The pastor appreciates as few others the didactic power worship can exert, and he understands why liturgy has been defined as the great "Lay Catechism," the chief "School of Faith" in which all Christians are enrolled at their Baptism.[13] He has seen with his own eyes how week in and week out, worship operates as perhaps the most powerful educative influence—for good and ill—the Church exerts. If he remembers his church history, he also knows that the Church's creeds were first formulated to teach faith liturgically, that her main catechesis was in connection with Confirmation and Holy Communion, and that the oldest formulation of the canon of the Mass was essentially a doctrinal declaration. Above all, he understands the truth of the Church's declaration through the centuries: *lex orandi* precedes *lex credendi*.[14] The rule of prayer is prior to the rule of faith. Or in free translation, worship is basic to doctrine and to instruction in doctrine.

The trouble is, however, that many congregations—and many Christian educators for that matter—seem unaware of both the educative power of liturgy and the seminal meaning liturgy holds for education. Education, rather, is thought of as confined to the church school classroom or as something that comes chiefly through involvement in mission and in life situations; and the relation of these to liturgy is not realized. It is not understood that without worship "Christian education has no heart, for here is the center of participation in Christ's invitation to join in God's mission; here is the

---

[11] See Eduard Thurneysen, A *Theology of Pastoral Care*, trans. Jack A. Worthington and Thomas Wieser (Richmond: John Knox Press, 1962), pp. 13, 15.

[12] See William A. Clebsch, and Charles R. Jaeckle, *Pastoral Care in Historical Perspective* (Englewood Cliffs, N.J.: Prentice-Hall, 1964), Parts I, IV. See also R. A. Lambourne, *Community, Church and Healing* (London: Darton, Longman and Todd, 1963), chs. VII, IX, X.

[13] See Joseph T. Nolan's essay, "The Liturgical Movement in the Roman Catholic Church," in *Liturgy Is Mission*, ed., Frank Stephen Cellier (New York: Seabury Press, 1964), p. 62.

[14] The original Latin formulation was: *Legem credendi lex statuat supplicandi*, ascribed by Tiro Prosper of Aquitania to Pope Celestine I. See the article by L. M. McMahon, "Towards a Theology of the Liturgy," in *Studia Liturgica*, III (Winter, 1964).

new life essential for joining in God's work of making all things new." [15]

But while the pastor understands how worship conveys instruction and is seminal for instruction, he also feels intensely the need for people to be instructed in worship. The fact is that ignorance of the meaning of worship is so widespread among the laity of free-church Protestantism as to be virtually disabling. A number of influences account for this ignorance of which we shall say more presently: the absence of any unifying liturgical ethos in our religiously pluralistic culture; the secularization of people's perceptions; the anti-historical bias which Sidney Mead has called "historylessness"; the subjectivism and voluntarism with which the typical laymen decides what is important to him. To have some measure of the task confronting the churches one needs only ponder the unawareness of the laity of the deeper meanings of Baptism and Holy Communion, for example, of the layman's duty really to "hear" the sermon as well as the preacher's duty to speak it, the laity's passiveness in worship generally and the sentimentality with which the sterner meanings of worship are perverted. At its best such ignorance is naïve. At its worst it is vitiating, in the manner of the woman who smilingly remarked that she went to Holy Communion for the same reason she took a walk in her garden—"to pick a pretty flower," she said, "named 'Jesus' forget-me-not.'"

Other points of pastoral concern for the edification of the congregation could be cited: anxiety as to how the Christian community can meet the wave of secularism sweeping over the modern world with a corresponding deepening of spirituality; how the prayer of the Church can be purified for the sake of its intercessory and exorcising effect in human life, a concern felt in some quarters to be naïve or out of date but which the congregation cannot evade if it is to be faithful; how authentic corporateness can be recovered that does not efface individual personhood; how liturgy psychologically makes for health and unhealth. We shall refer to these from time to time.

Concern to Relate Liturgy and Life

Important as these are, however, what most deeply troubles today's minister, we suspect, is the frightening gulf between the Church's worship and the ethical witness of her people in the world. While many clergy will frankly admit that they were not displeased with the financial and statistical prosperity their congregations have enjoyed until recently, they now see all too clearly the contradiction between more or less well-filled churches on Sunday and the immoralities of our society, between impressive statistics and the declining influence of Christianity upon the structures of culture; and in their

[15] Letty M. Russell, *Christian Education in Mission* (Philadelphia: Westminster Press, 1967), p. 122.

soberest moments they know this contradiction holds dreadful judgement for both society and the Church. Something seems to have fatally gone wrong, and one suspects that it has to do not least with the Church's worship. The powerlessness of worship to transform life is appalling, and seems to be reducing the Church to impotence. Indeed, the resistance of laymen to the Church's effort to address ethically their public as well as private life—a resistance described by a sociologist as "The Gathering Storm in the Churches" —is an indictment of the churches' liturgical failure as well as a portent of things to come.[16] This is to say, a second positive motive spurring us to inquire into liturgy is the concern that worship possess integrity in exactly the all-important sense that it be integrated with life.

Now a multitude of issues converge in this concern, and the relation of liturgy to life, or of cultus to mission as one may alternatively state it, is so complex that we shall have to approach it from a number of points of view in these essays. Only preliminary considerations can be cited here. One fundamental question must be put at the outset, however: how far should the Church's worship take as its explicit purpose the moral transformation of life? Too often this question is bypassed, and it is not understood that worship can lose integrity when it is regarded as a means to something else—even to the moral end of social action, as we shall note presently. Moreover, danger always inheres in reconceiving worship out of anxiety for the Church's impact upon the world. Dean William R. Inge remarked years ago that when the Church marries the spirit of the age, she will be left a widow in the next generation; and in our own time we have been forcefully reminded that what the Church owes the world is not her own cleverness and adaptability but obedience to the Gospel.[17]

Yet it is precisely an undoubted obedience to the Gospel which motivates our concern to bridge the gulf between liturgy and life. One has only to consider our recovered understanding of the New Testament term "worship" as meaning not only that which cultically happens at a certain time and place but as the Christian's total existence: in all his living the Christian man is a liturgical man. The meaning of "temple" as a physical place of worship, for example, has been displaced in the New Testament by the meaning of "temple" as any occasion when men are confronted by God in the risen Christ and in faith and obedience respond to him. Further, the life and work of Christ are biblically understood in terms of both worship and mission (John 6:51, 57), and cultic terms are interchangeably employed (especially by Paul) to

[16] See the book with this title by Jeffrey K. Hadden.
[17] See Karl Barth, *The Knowledge of God and the Service of God According to the Teaching of the Reformation*, trans. J. L. M. Haire and Ian Henderson (New York: Charles Scribner's Sons, 1939), p. 208.

31

apply to the totality of life, not merely to gathering for rite and cult. *Leitourgia*, whence our term "liturgy" is derived, means "service" or "work" of "the people," and is variously applied to the service of Zechariah in the temple (Luke 1:23), to the worship of Christ (Heb. 8:6) and of the Church (Acts 13:2), to collecting money for the apostolic mission (II Cor. 9:12), to the labors of the apostle Epaphroditus (Phil. 2:30), to prayer, even to Paul's impending death (Phil. 2:17). The word *thusia*, meaning "sacrifice," likewise is not confined to cultic acts but covers the whole range of ethical obedience of Christ's people (Rom. 12:1; Phil. 4:18; see also I Pet. 1:2). The term *latreia* meaning "service," also denotes the action performed by the Christian in both cultic worship and in his daily life (Matt. 4:10). In short, the thrust of our recovered understanding of the New Testament conception of worship moves us to a view of the Christian's life in its totality as *a liturgical life,* and in exploring this profound meaning (to be undertaken in later essays[18]) lies the clue to overcoming the gulf between the Church's worship and the life her laity live in the world.[19]

However, even as we cite biblical scholarship to corroborate the pastor's concern, it is crucial to understand that the New Testament always insists also upon the cultic gathering of the faithful for preaching and sacrament and prayer. Worship as cultus cannot be bleached out of the Gospel, even as the term "worship" in its general meaning is to be understood as embracing all life.[20] The very use of the terms for "church" in the New Testament, especially the term *ecclesia*, underscores the centrality of cultic worship. (Most of the approximately eighty uses of the word *ecclesia* have to do with the cultic assembly of believers.) Thus it is as much an error of reductionism simply to equate worship with service and witness in the world as it is to restrict the meaning of worship simply to cultus. In fact the New Testament illumines the meaning and locates the source of the Christian's life in the world within the life of the risen Christ meeting him in cultic worship— especially in the Eucharist—more than it derives the meaning of cultic worship from man's life in the world. Fundamentally and ultimately, these two ways of thinking about worship are a dialectic which must not be sundered, but if any priority is to be assigned to one over the other, the emphasis falls upon worship eucharistically defined.

Transposed into our present situation, the priority of worship cultically

---

[18] See especially chs. III, VII, VIII, but also *passim.*

[19] For a thorough study of biblical terminology dealing with worship, see the Introduction to Peter Brunner's *Worship in the Name of Jesus,* trans. M. H. Bertram (St. Louis: Concordia Publishing House, 1968).

[20] See R. J. McKelvey, *The New Temple: The Church in the New Testament* (London: Oxford. University Press, 1969), p. 184.

defined is to be understood as fundamental to the definition of "integrity" proposed in these essays, and only as liturgical renewal is seen as in some sense underlying other expressions of reform can both Church and world be served as the Christian is claimed to serve. Only as the renewal of the Church is seen as intensive, as requiring a liturgical deepening of its inner life even as it turns outward to the world, can the true relation between liturgy and life be established. In a moment we shall support this point with historical evidence. Here we pause only to cite the words of one of our ablest social critics: "The fullness of the Church's presence in . . . all spheres of life" awaits "the first step," "the recovery of public worship." [21] This is to say, renewal of the Church as mission is dependent upon liturgical renewal of the Church's being.

Concern for the Church

In making this fundamental point we are led to the last motive we shall cite here as underlying the pastor's concern for integrity in worship—concern for the Church. Indeed, in identifying his concern for the edification of the congregation and its life in the world, we have inevitably had to speak of the Church. Let it be clear, however, that a nervous, introverted meaning must not be read into the phrase, "concern for the Church," as if the destiny of the Church depended upon us or as if the Church needs to be saved over against the world. The Church in one sense is expendable, and often what she most needs is to cease being concerned for herself. Rather, when we say that concern for the Church underlies liturgical reform, we mean simply what the Reformers meant, *semper ecclesia reformanda*, and that reform is reliably undertaken only by those who love the Church, who live within the life of her Head, who know her mind and tradition, who pray her prayer and sing her song and serve in her name. The Church in the full magnitude of her meaning must by definition be the context within which reflection upon Christian worship is to move.

History can profitably teach us here: authentic liturgical reform has always been undertaken by people fundamentally concerned for the Church and her mission, even though the claims of culture and the needs of their generation were prominent in their minds. One thinks of Luther and of his concern to purify liturgy of corruptions and accretions, that it might be given back to the people in their own language and that as priests they might take part in the liturgical service of God; of Cranmer's great liturgical reconstruc-

---

[21] Gibson Winter, *The Suburban Captivity of the Churches* (Garden City, N. Y.: Doubleday & Co., 1961), p. 175.

tion which embodied for the English Church the meaning of the Continental Reformation; [22] of Puritanism, "of necessity a liturgical movement," [23] with its fidelity to Scripture as final authority for ecclesiology, liturgy, and doctrine; of Wesley's concern for the renewal of eighteenth century Anglicanism manifest in his liturgical innovations of field preaching, the informal prayer of Society and Class Meeting, covenant and watch night services; of Nevin and Schaff and the Mercersburg movement in the Reformed Church in America; and not least of the effect of the liturgical movement upon the renewal of the Church—both Roman and Protestant—in our time. The chronicle could be lengthened. It will suffice to say that throughout history liturgical reform and Church reform have so closely gone hand in hand that one can hardly say where the one began and the other left off. Whoever would think seriously about the reform of worship must think seriously within the context of Church.

But this is historically the case because it is first theologically the case; and if we say that whoever would think seriously about liturgy must think seriously about the Church, we must go on to say that whoever would think about either must think theologically. This would seem to be self-evident, but what we so often encounter today are people who scorn the Church or who are bereft of theological appreciation of her meaning—aesthetes and dilettantes who corrupt the reform of worship into gamesmanship because they have not grappled with the theological relation between the nature of the Church and the nature of worship. We shall examine some of their approaches and presuppositions presently. Here we explore only one aspect of this relation: the ontological meaning which worship and Church hold for one another.

Worship, let it always be remembered, involves the very being of the Church. In the transaction between God and man through Jesus Christ in Christian worship, the Church is constituted, called into being, knows and confesses her true being, and reveals her being. Indeed, worship is "the epiphany of the Church," the Church's "pre-eminent self-realization," in the words

[22] Gordon Rupp has written: "Recently the British Council of Churches called upon its members to make bold and creative liturgical experiments. So far we have not seen many, and most of them resemble the attempts to get 'brighter cricket' by widening the bat. . . . But in the British Museum you may see a manuscript of Liturgical Experiments, the mighty work which Thomas Cranmer wrought with that right hand which, one day, he thrust first into the fire. You may see there how long and hard he read, preparing his experiments over ten and it may be fifteen years, examining and comparing liturgies of the ancient Church with the new orders of Protestant Germany, and then translating and writing with a mind soaked in Scripture and the Fathers." *The Old Reformation and the New* (Philadelphia: Fortress Press, 1967), p. 32.

[23] Horton Davies, *The Worship of the English Puritans* (Westminster: Dacre Press, 1948), p. 8.

of a Protestant and of a Catholic theologian.[24] As "the public act which eternally actualizes the nature of the Church as the Body of Christ," adds an Orthodox theologian, worship "embraces, expresses, inspires and defines the whole Church, her whole essential nature, her whole life." [25] A Reformed theologian also writes: "The Church lives, not on ideas about God, but on God's grace itself, mediated by his spirit through the immemorial rites of corporate worship. . . . Apart from this, Christianity is no more than archaeology, a museum piece for antiquarians." [26] Now this conception of the relation of worship and Church may seem a high one. (To many of us it will also seem an incomplete one in that the *esse*, the being, of the Church is defined by her mission as well as her cultus, a vital point to be discussed in subsequent essays.) Nevertheless, at the minimum it becomes clear that anyone concerned for the liturgical renewal of the Church is dealing with fundamental theological realities and is challenged by fundamental theological questions.

Admittedly, to deal with these questions may seem threatening to the pastor, but let him take heart in knowing that in his concern for liturgical integrity he is working at the problem of church renewal on as deep a level as there is. Always, of course, renewal is to be seen as the gracious action of God before it is the work of man. Moreover, the Holy Spirit is revealing to us many ways in which renewal takes place—in the challenge of the agenda the world sets for the Church, in ecumenical dialogue and social action, in new forms of mission and new structures of congregational life to implement them, in creative forms of Bible study and of theological education of the laity. Yet "the fundamental problem of all revival is, How can the Church be the Church? The answer is, of course, that there are many ways. . . . Yet behind each way there is the inevitable need to express the fact that 'Ye are the Body.' . . . liturgy is quite simply the climactic expression in this world of our incorporation into Christ, . . . the best and highest example of the meaning of life in the Christian community, 'the Body of Christ at prayer.' " [27] This is to say, in worship the *esse* of the Church is re-experienced and its shape and purpose are redefined again and again. In worship the life of the congregation is established over and over in the *shalom*, the Life of the New Age Christ gives to his people. In worship the servant shape of the

---

[24] J.-J. von Allmen, *Worship: Its Theology and Practice* (New York: Oxford University Press, 1965), p. 42; Godfrey Diekmann, "The Constitution on the Sacred Liturgy in Retrospect," *Worship*, XL (Aug., 1966).

[25] Alexander Schmemann, *Introduction to Liturgical Theology*, trans. Ashleigh E. Moorhouse (London: Faith Press, 1966), p. 12.

[26] Whale, *Christian Doctrine*, p. 146.

[27] Alfred R. Shands, *The Liturgical Movement and the Local Church* (rev. ed.; New York: Morehouse-Barlow, 1965), pp. 33-34.

35

Church's mission is uniquely bestowed.[28] And surely nothing is more fundamental than these.

In summary, in his concern for worship the pastor is doing nothing less
than to help the Church know her true identity, and in this sense also Church
renewal and liturgical reconstruction go hand in hand. We best know the
nature of the Church not by speculating or reading about it but by liturgically
submitting ourselves to that Word which in proclamation, prayer, and sacrament constitutes the Church. The word orthodoxy, let it be remembered,
derives from *orthos* and *doxa*. It means "right praise" or "right worship,"
rather than "right opinion"; and a truer, more "orthodox" understanding of
the Church—as well as other theological realities for that matter—comes
through right worship as in no other way. When our worship is true, our
thought about the Church is likely to be true.

Finally, because of his very place and function as leader of a congregation
the pastor is uniquely on the growing edge of liturgical advance and has an
unmatched opportunity to be an agent of reformation. "The road to living
liturgical reform leads from the bottom upwards," not from the top down,
it has been written; [29] and whatever else "top" and "bottom" may mean,
it is a mistake to suppose that theologies imposed by the theologians or liturgies imposed by the liturgists are the first or final word. The congregation and
the pastor are the real liturgists and the real authorities. To be sure, there is
an Authority beyond authorities—the Holy Spirit known through the Word,

---

[28] Gregory Dix, in stating what he judges to be the classic fourfold "shape" of the
eucharistic liturgy as it affected the life of the Church through some fifteen centuries,
corroborates the decisive influence worship exerted upon what we would speak of today as
the Church's "mission." Exaggerated as it may seem to link ritual changes with important
social results, he writes, nevertheless, whenever "the standard rite" of the Church was
significantly altered or lost, "notable results upon the Christian *living* of those whose
Christianity has been thus impoverished," ensued. The "*ritual change can always be
historically detected before the social one.*" *The Shape of the Liturgy* (Westminster:
Dacre Press, 1945), p. xii; italics mine. Similarly, Massey H. Shepherd, Jr., in criticizing
the 1928 revision of the American Prayer Book of the Episcopal Church, writes that the
"chief failing" of the revision was "the lost opportunity to place the urgency and primary
claim of the Church's world-wide missionary responsibility at the very heart of the liturgy.
. . . The major offices of the Prayer Book, the daily services and the Holy Communion,
were left without any incisive petition for the Church's missionary task. This fact perhaps
goes far to explain the relatively poor showing of the Episcopal Church in its conviction
and support of world-wide missions when . . . compared to other Christian communions
of comparable size and resources. Of course the mission of the Church is implicit throughout the liturgy; but only here and there does it become forcefully explicit to the attention
and conscience of our worshipping congregations." *The Reform of Liturgical Worship*
(New York: Oxford University Press, 1961), pp. 65-66. See also Douglas Webster's
comments upon the Anglican Prayerbook in his essay, "The Mission of the People of
God," in *Liturgical Renewal in the Christian Churches,* ed. Michael J. Taylor.

[29] Robinson, *Liturgy Coming to Life,* p. 9.

Jesus Christ; and authentic reform requires a great deal more than taking the liturgical equivalent of congregational Gallup Polls. But "the genesis point" of liturgical reform "lies in the first instance where the [Christian] community, aware of what it is, is in contact with the epoch in which it lives." [30] Any attempt to restore integrity to worship will succeed only insofar as it is in contact with the life of the congregation in all its historical concreteness. For true reform we must still look to the equivalent of the "congregation of God's people at Corinth," as St. Paul once wrote, "each" of whom "contributes a hymn, some instruction, a revelation, an ecstatic utterance, or the interpretation of such an utterance," all aiming "at one thing: to build up the church" (I Cor. 1:2; 14:26 NEB).

A CRITIQUE OF THE LITURGICAL SITUATION TODAY

Given this inquiry into the motives bound up with our concern for worship, we turn now to look more directly at the liturgical situation of the Church today—but first, some warnings and clarifications. One observer's angle of vision will differ from another's and the following critique will inevitably reflect subjective judgements. Again, certain problems can be raised in only an introductory way. The backdrop for all liturgical reconstruction today, for example, must surely be the secularization of our culture, but only selected aspects of secularization can be considered here. Further, the methodology to be followed needs briefly to be explained. Liturgical reflection, we believe, is helpful when it is not simply theoretical but is engaged with the situation it would address. It is to be simultaneously inductive and deductive because the nature of worship itself requires this approach. By definition, worship is incarnational in the sense that the Word, Jesus Christ, becomes known as it is enfleshed in the human and the historical; and reflection upon liturgy is to recapitulate this process. As a later essay will make clear, liturgical theology has its own hermeneutics deriving from the incarnational nature of worship itself. Further, a theological understanding of the Church requires this approach. Our minds can never escape the tension in which the Church perpetually exists: the tension between the divine reality, Jesus Christ, who on the one hand ever calls the Church into being and strives to embody himself more authentically in her life, and on the other hand the palpable, human reality the Church must become in time and history. One way to describe this tension is to say that the Church is always living in two histories at the same time: her divine, sacred history—the ongoing action of God in her and through her—and her very human history being written by men and women

---

[30] Aidan Kavanaugh, "How Rite Develops: Some Laws Intrinsic to Liturgical Evolution." *Worship*, XLI (June, 1967).

of flesh and blood, living the life and speaking the language of their time, yet ever striving to translate the meaning the Word has come to hold for them into a tongue other men can speak. Without this dialectical vision we end up in liturgical docetism, or we slip into falsely equating the human character of the Church with her sinful character. Only as liturgical reflection accepts the human and historical quality of the Church can it be credible. We can never forget that the oldest definition of the Church, "the people of God," includes the noun "people"!

Thus even as we lament outright idolatries that liturgically corrupt the Gospel; even as we smile—kindly, we trust—at the paper flowers or the banal brass on the Communion table; even as we turn in disgust from the false otherworldliness and wanton aestheticism which injure worship; and even as we criticize those who lay down secular rather than Christian canons as decisive for worship—let us remember that it is not finally for us to say that these are beyond God's power to redeem for his purposes. If God was once worshiped in David's strange dance, if the esoteric speaking in tongues of the Corinthian congregation was judged by St. Paul to have place in the Christian community, if the bread in the upper room was a plain Jewish loaf and the wine of the cup the poor man's drink, surely all human things, no matter how crude, are within God's sovereignty and in his mysterious grace can be used to his praise.

Some Typical Errors—Especially the Error of Defective Forms

A number of misconceived practices which injure the integrity of worship can be described as errors rather than corruptions: the things that grate on our nerves and offend our sensibilities but are not necessarily fatal. They have to do with the *bene esse* or *plene esse*—the well-being or the full being of the Church's liturgical nature—rather than with the *esse*—the liturgical being—of the Church itself. Bad taste and insensitivity account for them more than does corrupt theology, but they nevertheless take their toll. A Saturday newspaper announces the morrow's service as "The Pause That Refreshes," or invites the public—in the words of a Hollywood actress—"Why Not Try God?" Once inside the church a visitor is enjoined, "Please wear a red bow and fill out the guest card," as eager "greeters" roll him into the hands of an aggressive usher who ostentatiously leads him to a seat, handing him a garish bulletin with smudged mimeographing bearing at the top the cliché: "Enter to worship, go forth to serve." The congregation engages in a buzz of conversational small talk while the organist competes for attention playing Liszt's "Liebestraum." The choir, wearing green vestments with taupe stoles, enters on the opening hymn in hesitation-waltz step. The minister, clad in black gown with academic hood, conspicuously takes up a position as master of ceremonies, and fetches out of his hip pocket a hand edition of the New Testament from which he will presently read a few verses as springboard for his climactic "message," preparing himself from time to time with a draught from a prominent glass of water. The opening invocation becomes a sermon with everyone's eyes closed, and the "responsive reading" which follows, with the congregation sitting, concludes with the solo, "The Holy City." Two hymns follow, concluding what is labelled on the bulletin as "I–Preparation." The service then proceeds with the offering, prefaced with an urging to present "folded money that will make Jesus smile," and the collection plates are retained at the rear of the auditorium while the ushers count the money as the minister's "morning prayer" wanders from hometown to the communists and back again. Next follows a long and pretentious anthem which stalls all movement, and the service grinds to a temporary halt. After the sermon and recessional, the benediction—laced with sentiments of the preacher's contriving—is pronounced from the rear of the church, and immediately after an "Amen" *a la* Richard Wagner, organ chimes sound "God Be with You Till We Meet Again." The service ends with a mounting crescendo of conversation competing with fortissimo organ postlude.

Such a composite of liturgical practices may not be matched in detail by similar recollections in the reader's mind, but it may suffice! It will be observed that there may not be anything outright "demonic" in such a service, and we must not conclude that the Lord has not visited and redeemed his people. While such crudities make it harder than would otherwise be the case for God to be truly worshiped, they nevertheless can be thought of as part of the earthenness of the vessel in which grace is borne, although clearly the character of the vessel is not unimportant.

A common if graver error consists of the style of verbal monologue in which the clergy (and choir?) dominate worship, and the corresponding passivity of the congregation. Important theological and psychological issues begin to arise here, such as the conception of worship as an expression of the priesthood of the people, as a celebrative action in which all participate, and as the involvement of man's whole being. As we shall note in a later essay, such issues as these are bound up with a recovery of authentic congregational action and pose what is perhaps the commonest problem clergy face today. Now let it be said that worship more or less monological can be a means of grace and is perhaps better termed an error than a corruption. But worship understood as something done rather than as something watched, as dialogue between the people and God rather than as one-way speech by the leader to the congregation, as involving all man's faculties rather than just his auditory sense—this is vital and this is what is frequently missing. Many services still deserve the indictment of a critic of a generation ago who spoke of "the uninterrupted garrulity of Protestant worship." [31]

Bound up with this common error is another—the use of defective forms of worship. By forms we mean all media employed to communicate or receive meaning, such as symbols, ceremonial acts, gestures, visual images, as well as speech and song. Taken together, these media constitute what we shall call in these essays "the language of worship," and their nature will need to be explored from several perspectives, and principles proposed for judging their validity.[32] Here we wish to specify five ways in which misconceived forms injure worship.

First, forms too often are sweet, or flat, or banal; they simply fail to grasp attention. They fail to impress as they failed to impress a Catholic layman who, in response to the question, "If in worship the salt hath lost its savor, wherewith shall it be salted?" mockingly replied, "With sugar." Man is read too pleasantly as a verbal and rational being, and the full measure of his nature has not been liturgically taken. It is not understood that he functions as a multi-sensory and "multiphasic" [33] creature, and that worship must therefore be multi-sensory and multiphasic; that its forms must engage the body, the imagination, and the emotions as well as the reason, and at the same time take into account something of the dynamics of man's subconscious as well as conscious life. Now let it quickly be said that salty effectiveness *per se* is not a maximal value in worship. One has shared in "worship experiences" with colored lights playing in rhythm with what was described as "the symphonic movement" of the service, of choirs massed in geometrical design whose renditions were accompanied with trumpets and tympani, of "celebrations" with electrically amplified guitars, clapping and swaying, and dancing in the aisles. One has little doubt that such forms were effective, although the question remains open as to whether they were Christian worship. On the other hand, the grip on man's being which liturgical forms are entitled to exert, the evocative power they should convey, and the intensity of meaning they should embody—although always within the limits of theological purpose—these are often missing. Hence the boredom which has been called the "curse" of free-church worship. Too often liturgical

---

[31] W. Johnston Ross quoted by Henry Sloane Coffin, *Communion Through Preaching* (New York: Charles Scribner's Sons, 1952), p. 2.

[32] See especially chs. V, VI.

[33] I borrow the term "multiphasic" from Joseph Sittler's Foreword to *Worship in Scripture and Tradition*, ed. Massey H. Shepherd, Jr. (New York: Oxford University Press, 1963), p. 8.

language is only prose, monodimensional, lame, unable to get at the depths of man's nature.[34]

Secondly, the language of worship is often inartistic and downright ugly. Again, this is not to say that beauty is a maximal value in worship, and the complex relation of aesthetics to liturgy—which we shall explore presently— must be borne in mind. It is far too simple to say that only what man judges to be "beautiful" is suitable for worship, and the *dictum* one often hears, that artistically only "the best" is good enough for the liturgical encounter between man and God, is dangerously misleading. One suspects that the disciples were not too concerned in the upper room for the engraving on the chalice from which the wine of eternal life was drunk, and the grammar of Peter's sermon at Jerusalem probably left something to be desired. Nevertheless, worship can in one sense be thought of as the art form of religious faith: "the projection in a specific place at a specified time of what the worshippers believe to be the nature of ultimate reality." [35] And while "ultimate reality" in Christian thought is a great deal more than Beauty spelled with a capital "B," yet we may believe that God is not displeased with the loveliest forms men can fashion through which to offer their devotion and as means he may use for his grace. Surely art in the service of liturgy may be thought of as having a quasi-sacrificial and quasi-sacramental function. While we must be always wary against the seduction of liturgy into art for art's sake, it must be recognized that man engages more readily in the dialogue of worship when its forms please his sensibilities at the same time that they are appropriate to the majesty of God.

A graver objection to forms employed in much Protestant worship today is not so much that they are weak or ugly as that they are unreal, and in a number of ways. For one thing, they are too strange or irrelevant to the actual life of the congregation to be real, or they are too familiar and too relevant.[36] Traditional forms inherited from the past, such as prayers offered in the sixteenth century language of the Tudors and Stuarts, for example, seem unreal simply because they are obsolete. We are unable to surmount their unreality simply because we do not talk or think today as the Stuarts did. Or hymn tunes cast in the semi-morbid nineteenth century harmonies of a Lowell Mason seem inane to ears toughened to twentieth century atonality. On the other hand, forms too familiar and too modern can also fail to possess reality. Because little effort is required to grasp or be

[34] See Joseph Sittler, *The Ecology of Faith* (Philadelphia: Muhlenburg Press, 1961), Appendix: "The Shape of the Church's Response in Worship."
[35] Samuel Miller, "Worship and the Arts," *Foundations*, III (July, 1960).
[36] The dialectic of relevance and irrelevance is so fundamental and takes so many forms in liturgical theology as to require an essay in itself. See ch. III, and also chs. II, V, VI.

grasped by them, the worshipper is let off too cheaply and remains unengaged with any meanings other than those he already brings. Indeed, in dealing with the question of tradition in a later essay, we shall have to argue that forms which at first sight seem to offend by their archaism often possess prototypal power to engage man's deepest nature which familiar forms do not.

In appraising the reality of forms, it is hard to know how far cultural influences conditioning man's liturgical consciousness today should be accepted and how far they should be calculatedly resisted, such as the effect of technology upon his perceptions, the incongruity of biblical thought forms with those of the Space Age, man's commitment to values of this world over against Christian otherworldliness, the historizing of his consciousness sensitizing him to the present and future more than to the past, the repugnance of discursive logic and the appeal of happening and epiphany. Given these and other influences, we can understand why critics speak of a liturgical "crisis of communication" today.

One is tempted to describe this problem as the problem of demythologizing liturgy—as many critics have done. This formulation, however, is too simplistic. The problem is better defined as the problem of demythologization and remythologization of worship, as "the re-actualization of the language of Zion." For worship is not only mythological by nature in the sense that it can only exist as figure and form, but more importantly, the proper business of liturgy is to assert Christian myths against other myths as a way of stating the Christian vision of reality. The Gospel is always involved in a war of myths for men's souls, and its language accordingly is to "orchestrate its sense of reality," in a fine phrase of Amos Wilder.

Thus the problem is best come at by asking the more fundamental question: is Christian reality most truthfully conveyed in worship when its forms are most immediately communicative, relevant, and contemporary? In formulating the question in this way, it is important to observe that we are not now inquiring first into the sense of reality the forms possess in themselves; reality in Christian worship is not to be confused with mere vitality. Rather, the sense of reality clothing forms must always be appraised in light of the larger question of Christian reality in worship in general. Otherwise it is not necessarily Christian worship we are talking about, but—as we have noted —only effectiveness of communication; and effective communication can be diabolic as well as Christian.

The answer to this question must be a discriminating "yes" and "no," and —to declare a bias—a "no" more often than is popularly understood. Much depends of course on the meaning of the phrase "Christian reality," and we shall need more fully to define this term as the Christ-Event, the Word, grasping man's life in all the depth and range of his existence. Here, it is essential to understand that forms suitable to this encounter must serve both as means of divine grace and as vehicles for human action, and that their reality must be fully judged by both dimensions. Liturgical language is to provide for divine impression as well as for human expression, for the numinous[37] as well as the human; and further, for the numinous to reveal itself in both the transparent and the obscure, in the familiar and the strange; and still further, as both immanent and transcendent. Thus, insofar as forms disserve either pole of Christian reality preliminarily understood in this way, they must be judged to fail. On the one hand, forms of contrived or vestigial numinousness which have no correspondence with the worshipper's world and time, and which he is unable to appropriate as real, simply eliminate him from the liturgical transaction. They seem quaint if not embarrassing, like a collection of old valentines found in the attic—as one critic has put it. On the other hand, if "Christian reality" is to mean that the worshiper is met by an Other encountering him with a certain fateful over-againstness, then worship whose forms render this reality too glibly is probably no longer the worship of God but of an idol.

Forms are defective, fourthly, when they require us spuriously to pretend that things are other than they are, when they do not let us call things by their true names. Certain kinds of prayer, for example, falsify God's nature and action toward his people, or falsify the situation of the people before God; they exaggeratedly demand from God more than he has promised to give, or they impressionistically meditate upon God and demand too little. Sins are confessed too dramatically or too delicately, or the evil and ambiguity of life are ignored in the name of "celebration"; the enigma of man's misery and splendor before God's awful grace is glossed over with a spiritual pep rally. Creeds likewise embody false statements, communicate false conceptions, and exact false commitments; or invitations to discipleship, casually given out, debase Christian commitment into promising to give so many dollars a week to the budget or to telephone weekly greetings to the sick. The Church's music is turned into mood music. People are exhorted to sing too loudly or too softly; Christian joy is equated with fortissimo volume, and Christian peace with a quavering humming; or the God who is as a consuming fire is dissolved into an organ tremolo. And so forth and so on.

[37] This term is from the German theologian, Rudolf Otto. In his book *The Idea of the Holy* (published in 1917), Otto coined the word "numinous" from the Latin *numen* meaning "divinity" (as "ominous" is derived from the Latin *omen*). Essentially, "numinous" means God in his unique, mysterious nature, the reality of the Divine experienced by man as absolutely different from any other reality with which man comes into relation. We shall elaborate the importance of this term in subsequent essays.

43

Indeed, such dishonesty suggests the worst aspect of defective forms: simply their unfaithfulness to the nature of God revealed in Jesus Christ and to man's situation before this God. This is to say, forms fail because they lack theological—as distinguished from aesthetic or functional—integrity. They are not kerygmatic; they do not convey or evoke the Gospel. And, as a critic has pointed out, when the signs in which the Church worships only vaguely correspond to her situation as it really is, she is on the road to illusion and her worship has become corrupt.[38]

"The resurrection of the Gospel" in our time, J. V. Langmead Casserley has said, "must necessarily be preceded by the resurrection of its proper language," [39] and the death of false liturgical forms in turn must precede such resurrection. The ideal at which liturgy aims is to provide language faithful to the Gospel in its resurrection power, that at the same time grasps the human soul in all the reality of its predicament. A sentence from George Every, reported by Amos Wilder, speaks to our need: "Of all human activities religion most involves the dramatic aspects of the life of the soul, . . . its ardors, revulsions, terrors, joys. These features of experience must be recognized in the . . . rites of faith or men will not know that the Gospel really deals with what is important to them. As Brother George Every has said of a great deal of current pallid religious art: it has all the insipidity of the secular Christmas card, 'but El Greco gives *a sense of interior experience . . . that tears at the very vitals of man.*'" [40] The vitals of contemporary man, and the searing life of the Gospel—these liturgical language must somehow bring together.

Corruptions of Function

In turning now to examine certain "corruptions" of worship as distinguished from "errors," we cross over a dividing line in our criticism. Admittedly this line is drawn arbitrarily, and to a degree we have already anticipated it. But corruptions may be said to differ from errors in that corruptions strike at the essential integrity of the Gospel itself, both in the action of worship and in man's reflection upon its meaning. Corruptions, in short, are Luther's "evil spirits set in motion" to which we have referred, and the New Testament warning to "test the spirits" must be understood to apply to the Church's liturgical life as to all else. Liturgically as in other

[38] See the article "The Nature and Role of Signs in the Economy of the Covenant," by Joseph Gelineau, Worship, XXXIX, pp. 530-50.
[39] "Event-Symbols and Myth-Symbols," *The Anglical Theological Review*, XXXVIII (Apr., 1956).
[40] *New Testament Faith for Today* (New York: Harper & Bros., 1955), p. 181. Italics mine.

ways, the truth of a violent saying of Daniel Jenkins must be borne with: it is not hard for churches to turn into "conspiracies against God." [41] And the Church must be said liturgically to conspire against God when man corrupts God's confrontation of the human soul by interposing creations of his own devising, and when he exalts these as ultimate—be they a symbol or an act, an object or a rubric, an idea or a principle.

The first corruption we may call a corruption of function: the authoritarian structuring of worship to fit preconceived ideas without primary fidelity to the nature of the God revealed in the Gospel. Types of this corruption are perpetrated by both the naïve and the sophisticated, and they cover a wide spectrum. Many pastors, for example, feel led to provide guidelines for the congregation by introducing categories into the printed order (*e.g.* "Preparation," "Offering") or by labelling hymns (*e.g.* "Hymn of Consecration"). Such structuring may not be out of place when conceived with theological integrity and a certain pastoral diffidence; but it easily becomes a mechanizing of worship in order to compel the worshipers' devotion to conform to the leader's plans. Again, the fondness of artists for manipulating congregations to conform to their own preconceptions of what a "worship experience" should be, or the presumptuousness of theologians in laying down liturgical structures with heavy-handed authority—these easily become an idolatrous imposing of man-made structures upon the sovereign nature of the Word and a violation of the integrity of the human soul to respond to the Word in a Spirit-directed way.

The psychological rigging of worship classically illustrates this type of corruption, in which attention to man and the dynamics of man's experience is made sovereign rather than the nature and action of the Word. Commonly this corruption is a compound of more or less religious humanism and shreds of theology embodied in such frank declarations that the primary purpose of worship is "to foster the religious experience"; that worship is the "experiencing" of "self as a unity or wholly" because "holiness is wholeness"; [42] that worship is "to break down inhibitions" and "expand perceptions." Man's feelings in particular are played upon, as well as his tactile senses in certain experimental liturgies, and the experience thus aroused together with discussion about it are made the content of liturgy. Such devices as "cycles" or "sequences" [43] are employed to execute this purpose;

[41] *Beyond Religion* (Philadelphia: Westminster Press, 1962), p. 100.

[42] William H. McGaw, Jr., *An Alternative Worship Service* (La Jolla, Calif.: Western Behavioral Sciences Institute, 1969).

[43] For example: "The service starts with a short sermonette of no more than five minutes. . . . Following the sermonette the congregation participates in an exercise designed to complement the sermonette. Following this experience the congregation then spends five minutes sharing not only the content of the sermon but also their personal

or "theme worship" with all parts of the service chosen to reinforce "the motif of the morning"; or such absurdities as conceiving prayer and sermon as "adagio movements within the andante phase of worship"; or the schematizing of worship into therapeutic "stages": 1) "Exposure," (2) "Diagnosis," (3) "Adjustment." [44] On reading such nomenclature, one may be pardoned for wondering whether he is in the house of God, in a group for sensitivity training, listening to a chamber orchestra, or on an osteopath's couch. Truly, the Church, too, has both its hidden and not-so-hidden persuaders.

Even as we identify this corruption, however, we need to be cautioned lest our revulsion carry us too far. In its attitude toward psychology, liturgical thought has often swung between the extremes of hostility and surrender, and we greatly need a more poised evaluation than is currently available. Integrity in worship, so far from precluding the dimension of psychology, surely requires one to take into account the contribution of this most important social science; and criticism of the psychological structuring of worship must not be understood as a denial of the need to rethink a liturgical psychology valid for our day. [45] Moreover, the human factor is always correlative with the divine factor in the transaction of worship; and the importance

---

reactions to the exercise. This sequence of sermon, exercise, and interaction is repeated three times." McGaw, *ibid.* Sometimes experimental liturgies employ the nomenclature and ethos of art rather than psychology to structure worship. For example: "First of all, the order of service of the Body has within it a threefold division. One part has to do with confession and pardon; a second with praise and witness; the third part, with offering and dedication. . . . These three divisions, like three acts in a great drama, tell the story of the life of the man who stands before God in Christ. . . . One may conceive of it as the great drama of our salvation in three acts with a prologue and epilogue. . . . Act One has two scenes. In the first the community is engaged in repentance. . . . The second scene —reconciliation—is an answer to the first. . . . Act One, then, is the rehearsal of crucifixion and resurrection. . . . If the mood of Act One is basically godly sorrow, the mood of Act Two is joy in the Lord. The players here are those who in the first act were delivered from bondage. . . . Act Two closes with a mighty affirmation of faith . . . in the form of a proclamation by the whole cast or a word of witness by one member. . . . The concluding Act . . . is a great pageant of offering. There is a double action here. . . . The first scene begins with acts of petition and supplication. . . . The second scene . . . is the presentation of the offering. . . . Act Three is a dramatic enactment of Life in the Holy Spirit. . . . After the epilogue, which may consist of a hymn . . . plus a benediction, the actors leave the stage." Joseph W. Mathews, *Common Worship in the Life of the Church* (Chicago: The Ecumenical Institute, n.d.).

[44] A variation reads: "Expose yourself to God!" "Let God develop you!" "Let God enlarge you!" The demonic possibilities of brainwashing which arise when liturgy is thus used psychologically to manipulate people are suggested by a sentence of Cliff Barrows, a musician associated with Billy Graham, in an article entitled "Musical Evangelism": "The primary purpose of music . . . is *to divest the hearer of attitudes* that would prevent his acceptance of the message that the song conveys, and *to prepare his heart and mind* for the entrance of the word of God." *Decision*, III (Dec., 1962). Italics mine.

[45] We shall assess certain insights of psychology in chs. IV, V, VII.

of man's subjective experience can never be ignored.[46] But clearly, to conceive worship primarily within the category of the psychology of man's experience is not only to subvert its purpose as the worship *of* God. It is also to risk committing liturgical suicide in that an endless train of corruptions follow from this basic corruption; for worship as the contrived fostering of experience for the sake of experience opens the door to every kind of manipulative device with only the leader of worship answerable for their legitimacy.

Theologians and liturgists, however, are hardly less guilty in forcing worship into preconceived structures, and the witness of the New Testament seems often to go unheeded:

We do *not* find in the Bible . . . an attempt to systematize . . . variety or to evaluate various types of worship over against each other. . . . There is no preference for corporate worship as against a private worship, or *vice versa*. There is no competition between a sacramental worship and a type of worship centered around the preaching of the word and prayers. There is no sign that difference between spontaneous prayer and the use of "fixed formularies" caused any controversy, although both types of prayer are evidently there. The tendency to standardize a specific type of worship . . . is alien to the Bible. . . . There is in the New Testament a greater variety of forms and expressions of worship than in the majority of divided churches and traditions today.[47]

Despite such biblical evidence, we are dogmatically told that worship always and everywhere must be "celebration" or "offering" and that all liturgical meanings must be subsumed under these categories. Or we encounter the expert who insists that a service must follow a certain order of "existential" or "evangelical" logic, or—following Isaiah 6 interpreted according to Hegel —that it is to recapitulate thesis, antithesis, synthesis. Perhaps the expert will insist that worship begin with a subjective penitential approach, or that its opening acts primarily induce fellowship, or that its first note be objective

---

[46] See ch. IV.

[47] *Report of the Theological Commission on Worship, Fourth World Conference on Faith and Order,* Faith and Order Paper 39 (Geneva: World Council of Churches, 1963), pp. 10-11. It should also be noted that Gregory Dix's thesis, that the primitive Church everywhere exhibited the same classic, eucharistic "shape of the liturgy," has been called into question by W. D. Davies: "Dix's picture of early Christian worship . . . is ridiculously dignified. . . . There is no single ordered pattern to be discerned in all this liturgical . . . activity of the Early Church. . . . The worship of the Primitive Church did not conform to a single type. Even in such a pivotal act of worship as the celebration of the Eucharist we find in the extant sources alone at last four different accounts of its institution. Dr. Vincent Taylor has examined the place of the Eucharist in the primitive communities and has convincingly argued, it would seem, that the Eucharist 'did not everywhere and always become a *central* feature in the life and worship of the primitive communities.' " *Christian Origins and Judaism* (Philadelphia: Westminster Press, 1962), p. 221.

and proclamatory; or he may insist that worship always end with an invitation to become converted or with an exhortation to mission in the world. If our expert is of the Reformed persuasion, he may argue that the sermon *must* follow directly upon the reading of Scripture, for only in this way can one be sure that preaching be true proclamation. Apparently it is not realized that such rigidity fosters the false notion that the Word is only in the sermon and not also in prayer or hymn or creed, that it is not proclaimed by the people as well as by the minister, and that this compulsive structuring lays such responsibility upon the minister as to convey the impression that he, rather than God, determines whether the Word in Scripture comes alive.

Theological obsession with the corporate character of worship transposed into arbitrary schema especially illustrates this corruption. To be sure, Christian worship theologically speaking is corporate by definition. That "the Christian unit" is the Church, not the individual,[48] is axiomatic (we shall elaborate this fundamental point in subsequent essays), and free-church worship in particular often needs to be disinfected of an unhealthy individualism. But theological insight is one thing; authoritarian liturgy which overwhelms individual personhood is another. And it is arguable whether we have not so overreacted against "pietistic individualism" that liturgical massism in the name of corporateness now threatens worship as gravely as irresponsible individualism once did. A critic writes, for example, that part of "the real cancer" in worship today is the "sub-Christian individualistic temper and outlook which, however fiercely it may be repudiated on the conscious level, still governs the basic assumptions that mould our liturgical practice."[49] Is individualism really "cancerous"? one must ask. More importantly, what does its persistence signify? The fact that man cannot subconsciously repudiate it, no matter how "fiercely" he tries, would seem to speak an important truth which liturgical theology would be wise to heed. We shall return to this question shortly.

Now let it be said that if one is going to standardize worship, it is better to do so theologically within the doctrine of the Church rather than psychologically or aesthetically. The former at least has the advantage of keeping worship more faithful to Christian revelation. Further, because the dialogue between God and man cannot be carried on without a common agreed-on language which all must speak, a corporate consensus is more or less inevitable; and this consensus is most reliable when it keeps worship always related to the nature of the Church. To protest against excessive schematizing

---

[48] See E. C. Ratcliff, "Christian Worship and Liturgy," *The Study of Theology*, ed. Kenneth E. Kirk (New York: Harper & Bros., 1939), p. 409.

[49] Neville C. Clark, *Call to Worship* (London: SCM Press, 1960), pp. 12-13.

of worship within the category of corporateness is not to advocate liturgical anarchy.

Nevertheless, perils beset all efforts to standardize liturgy, and free-church worship especially needs to be vigilant here. On a practical level, such efforts are unrealistic because they ignore the fact of variation in human temperament and the need for "liturgical spread." [50] "Rich grace" demands "full worship," [51] it has been pithily said, and the fullness of grace requires a corresponding manifoldness of ways in which man apprehends it. Further, anthropology supports common sense here. In answering the question whether individual or social prayer is prior in racial experience, Friedrich Heiler writes: "It is probable that the prayer of individuals in personal need is older than the . . . prayer of a group. . . . The formless prayer of a group goes back in the long run to a praying individual, for indeed it has always been an individual who first uttered a cry which the entire group then quite spontaneously took up." [52] We cannot expect even the modern man to renounce his own nature in this respect; he is still existential man, and he will inevitably recapitulate in his worship the individualistic cry of his ancestors.

The testimony of psychology is especially important. Jung launches perhaps the most trenchant criticism of corporateness in declaring that the very genius of Protestantism lies in its ability to expose the believer in his individuality directly to God: "The Protestant is left to God alone." Because he "is no longer shielded by walls or by communities," he is a man "*defenseless against God*," having "the unique spiritual chance of immediate religious experience." [53] Surely worship has no higher aim than to render man defenseless against God, and one must inevitably suspect anything that hinders it.

It is of exceptional interest that the existential factor cited by the psychologists has been affirmed by such theologians as Karl Barth and Dietrich Bonhoeffer. Their words must be recorded at length:

The question of the individual Christian subject has to be put, and it has to be answered with the *pro me* of faith. Without the *pro me* of the individual Christian there is no legitimate *pro nobis* of the faith of the Christian community. . . . The being and activity of Jesus Christ has essentially and necessarily the form in which

---

[50] Jaroslav Pelikan, *More About Luther* (Decorah, Iowa: Luther College Press, 1958), p. 50.

[51] P. T. Forsyth, *The Church and the Sacraments* (London: Longmans, Green & Co., 1917), p. 177.

[52] *Prayer*, trans. Samuel McComb (London: Oxford University Press, 1932), p. 15.

[53] *Psychology and Religion* (New Haven: Yale University Press, 1938), pp. 61-62. Italics mine.

He addresses Himself, not only also, but just to the individual man, . . . in which He makes common cause with the individual in his very isolation, in which His Holy Spirit speaks just to his spirit. It has been an unfortunate necessity in recent years to criticize the I-hymns which came into our hymn-books . . . and the I-piety which underlies them. Such criticism is a counterblast to the general subjectivist trend of modern Protestantism, and in face of this aberration it will constantly have to be made. But as is obvious from the . . . I-Psalms in the Bible, it can only be a relative and not an absolute criticism. It cannot try to eliminate or suppress altogether either the I-hymns or I-piety. It must be content with a limited objective. Not only is it impossible to reject as such the glance at the *pro me*, but this glance is actually necessary and commanded in . . . the Christian faith.[54]

Bonhoeffer writes:

Christ is Christ not as Christ in himself, but in his relation to me. His being Christ is his being *pro me*. . . . This personal nucleus itself is the *pro me*. That Christ is *pro me* is not an historical or an ontical statement, but an ontological one. That is, Christ can never be thought of in his being in himself, but only in his relationship to me. That in turn means that Christ can only be conceived of existentially, viz. in the community . . . *pro me*. Luther says: "So it is one thing if God is there, and another if he is there for you." . . . *Christ is the community by virtue of his being pro me.*[55]

The corruption of arbitrarily standardizing worship can in part be withstood by becoming more sensitive to the aspects of dialectic and simultaneity which worship embodies. The truth is that worship is too dynamic to be predicted even by the psychologists and too dialectical to be plotted even by the dialecticians! The relation between individuality and corporateness,

---

[54] *Church Dogmatics*, IV/1, trans. G. W. Bromiley (Edinburgh: T. & T. Clark, 1956), p. 755. Luther Reed of the American Lutheran Church also writes: "Corporate worship is more than an experience of the individual. But it must be an individual experience." *Worship: A Study of Corporate Devotion* (Philadelphia: Muhlenburg Press, 1959), p. 1.

[55] *Christ the Center*, trans. John Bowden (New York: Harper & Row, 1966), pp. 47-48, 59. Italics mine. It is noteworthy that whereas many Protestants are tending to equate authentic worship with unqualified corporateness, a number of Roman Catholic scholars are protesting this point of view. See for example Karl Rahner, S. J., *The Christian Commitment*, trans. Cecily Hastings (New York: Sheed & Ward, 1963), ch. III, "The Significance in Redemptive History of the Individual Member of the Church." Jacques Maritain also warns against "forgetting the personal character of the love which God demands . . . of each soul one by one—and not only of choirs or reciters. If our God loved only social masses praying and singing together, . . . this would have been indicated by some commandment. . . . There is only the wholly personal commandment of love: *Thou . . . thy* whole heart, *thy* whole soul, *thy* whole mind. Now neither the heart nor the soul nor the mind are social things. They are individual. . . . It is the act of faith proper to each one which is an offering pleasing to God. . . . Our love for God is always from our heart to His heart which has first loved us in our very singularity." *Liturgy and Contemplation*, trans. Joseph W. Evans (New York: P. J. Kenedy & Sons, 1960), pp. 82-84.

intimacy and awe, intelligibility and mystery, natural and supernatural, history and eternity, immanence and transcendence, world and God, *didache* and *kerygma*, sacrifice and sacrament, *gratia praeveniens* and *gratia cooperans*, spontaneity and form, art and logic, revelation and response—to name only a few polarities—is so subtle and complex as to give even the boldest theologian pause.

Likewise the aspect of simultaneity must remind us that many things can happen unpredictably in worship at the same time, or that one thing can happen many times; and it is artificial to plot these serially and to specify one as necessarily dominant over the others. Perhaps our fondness for thinking in category and sequence misleads us here. In the practical ordering of a service, for example, the pattern of Isaiah 6 is often cited as normative, in which the vision of the Lord high and lifted up in the temple inevitably impels the worshipper to confess the uncleanness of his lips and heart; and confession is accordingly insisted upon and prescribed early in the service.[56] Certainly there is abiding truth in this sequence of devotion, but one cannot mechanically transpose it into worship and assume that confession will automatically occur where we prescribe it should occur. Actually, confession can take place anywhere, and in a profound sense it is a total dimension of worship. To ask where contrition really takes place, writes Walter Lowrie, is like asking, "Where is the seat of the soul in the body?"[57] Contrition may progressively issue from, and follow after, the praise, prayer, lessons, and sermon which have stirred up the faith and penitence of the congregation. The modern man particularly may be able to experience true contrition only after his defenses have been pierced by more than the "preliminaries" with which many services perfunctorily begin.

Likewise, a service may well close in a burst of praise, for example, rather than with the act of dedication or sending to which we are commonly exhorted. Or it may open with intercession, or with an epicletic act of expectation and calling. J.-J. von Allmen remarks that such an act recognizes that the Lord is not at men's disposal: "It means that they do not control the actualization of his presence. . . . Christian worship is open to the free and sovereign action of its Lord. . . . Christ's presence springs from his grace."[58] Again, the Word can be proclaimed in the opening part of a service frequently call the "Approach," rather than restricted to the section of the service labeled "Proclamation"; and true "offering" or "communion" may be the cause rather than the result of other acts of worship.

Who is wise enough to say how or where any one of these elements can

---

[56] For example, see Mathews, *Common Worship in the Life of the Church.*
[57] *Action in the Liturgy* (New York: Philosophical Library, 1953), p. 56.
[58] *Worship: Its Theology and Practice*, pp. 29, 31.

be located with finality or used as a category under which others are to be subsumed? All order finally participates in the eschatological freedom of Christ; liturgically, as otherwise, he is "the end of the law" (Rom. 10:4). Theologians and liturgists must disavow the tyranny of preconceived structures if the Holy Spirit is freely to lead men into truth as it will. God is not at man's disposal, and the mysterious intentions of his grace cannot be presumptuously charted. The pastor will always employ his best wisdom in planning worship—yes; but over against all claims to finality in theological decision and liturgical style—including the claims made in these pages— stand the majesty and the mystery of God's Word.[59]

To a degree we have anticipated the next corruption to be identified—the using of worship primarily to achieve humanly chosen ends; but what we may call the corruption of "utilitarianism" is so widespread and takes such devious forms that it needs to be elaborated more fully. (Later essays will explore the prickly question of whether one can legitimately speak of worship as a means as well as an end.) [60] Psychologically, utilitarianism has its roots in the existential drive of man's selfhood to gather reality within his own subjectivity, and while in itself this thrust is not necessarily evil, it can easily become perverted liturgically. Culturally, the proclivity of American Protestantism for using worship for activistic ends doubtless stems in part from the pragmatism of our society. *Texne*, the ethos of practical usefulness, is so much a part of our temperament that it is not surprising that the Church's worship has absorbed it. Religiously, utilitarianism rises from the capacity for superstition that is never far from the surface of man's consciousness, and it is akin to magic in that it represents man's attempt to control the deity for human purposes. In practice, in utilitarian worship a shift in the liturgical center of gravity has taken place so that worship is viewed primarily as a means to effect changes in man and his world. Devotion is calculatingly offered with an eye to the human more than noncalculatingly to the divine. The direction,

---

[59] Music illustrates particularly well the aspect of simultaneity in the substance and language of worship, because of its unique power to convey a number of meanings at the same time. A German theologian suggests, for example, that music peculiarly combines the historical and eschatological elements in worship: a service "is not constructed in the sense that it is a logical system or a psychological process . . . unfolding rationally. . . . The crux of the liturgy is not a temporal succession but a paradoxical simultaneity. The event which is to come is already happening at this very moment when we sing . . . 'with angels and archangels and all the company of heaven.' The liturgy takes place before . . . the throne of the Lamb—there where time does not exist. We are still on the way there, and so we sing and pray the liturgy in a temporal order of succession. But we must always regard it, despite its polyphonic expression, as coming from God in . . . a spiritual unity." Gerhard Kappner, "The Church Service and Music," *Scottish Journal of Theology*, III (1959), p. 252.

[60] See chs. III, IV.

the vitality, and the purpose of worship are subverted to human ends.[61]

Forms of this corruption are legion. On a crude level they include blasphemous invitations to worship which appeal to nothing more than self-interest, and practices of worship which would be amusing were they not so pernicious. Worship as a means of "character building" and of producing "socially motivated personality," worship as a means to "self-fulfillment" and "success," invitations to worship in the vein of "come to church this week, you'll feel better, do better, live better, it's the American Way"—such are the more noxious expressions. The alliance of worship with political nationalism and its corruption into modern tribalism must especially be registered. Occasionally this perversion is clear-cut and thoroughgoing, at other times subtle or naïve though no less demonic. One author, after a survey of *What Americans Believe and How They Worship*, forthrightly declares that there is "no escape from the conclusion that, in the present world situation, America runs a grave danger from lack of attention to the spiritual core which is at the heart of her national existence. If we are to avoid this danger, democracy must become an object of religious dedication. Americans must come to look on the democratic ideal . . . as the Will of God." [62] A manifesto distributed by the official board of one congregation as an authorized statement of its "philosophy of worship" reveals how easily the Church can be infected: "We believe that the American tradition of going to church and of joining like-minded people on the Sabbath in the worship of God is an indispensable source of character and good citizenship. A God-centered philosophy is essential to our American way of life."

[61] V. A. Demant has an interesting passage distinguishing between what he calls the "purpose" and the "meaning" of worship. Worship "must be in one sense a *purposeless* act, if it is to be true worship. An action has a purpose if it is done for the sake of something else, but worship is for its own sake, or for the sake of God. That is the same thing, because any activity is doing the will of God when it is truly itself. So there is a sense in which Christian worship . . . has a meaning but no purpose; purpose means acting for a further result. Worship is the gathering up of all activities before God. In that sense it is purposeless. If we try to give it a moral or social purpose, we are destroying its nature. In the same sense, art or family relationships are also purposeless. No one would think of asking of what use is his mother. The mother is not of use; she is just there. St. Augustine once said that the essence of evil was to use the things we ought to enjoy and to enjoy the things we ought to use. The things we value for what they lead on to— those we use—are different from the things we value for their own sake—those we enjoy. He went on to say that the things to be enjoyed are God the Father, the Son, and the Holy Ghost. In worship we have this mode of valuing a thing for its own sake." See the chapter "The Social Implications of Worship," in *Worship: Its Social Significance*, ed. P. T. R. Kirk (London: The Centenary Press, 1939), pp. 107-8. See also Willard L. Sperry, *Reality in Worship* (New York: The Macmillan Co., 1925), especially ch. V, "The Kingdom of Ends," and ch. XVI, "The Social Value of Worship."

[62] J. Paul Williams (New York: Harper & Bros., 1952), pp. 367-68.

Utilitarianism is also evident in the propagandizing with which denominational bureaucracies utilize worship for "promotion" and "cultivation." "Board of Pensions Sunday" is substituted for the First Sunday in Advent, or "Rural Church Sunday" for the feast of Pentecost; or the meaning of Worldwide Communion is measured by whether or not the amount of money collected surpasses last year's record. Perhaps the humorless hand of bureaucracy was evident at its worst in a "Crusade for Morality" launched by one denomination, in which the Sundays of the year were divided into five "emphases" with "worship and sermon" tailored to fit. Sundays in the fall were pre-empted for "abstinence from beverage alcohol and personal moral regeneration," and "clean sex behavior" was laid down as the theme for Sundays in the spring!

Yet, lest we smile too patronizingly at such gaucherie, the other side of the truth is the need always to engage worship with life. When unrelated to the realities of health, citizenship, sex, world peace, racial justice, and temperance, worship has lost its claim to integrity because it has ceased to be relevant. The New Testament conception of worship as the unity of *leitourgia* and *diakonia*, of worship and service, must always be borne in mind; surely we cannot call any experience of worship authentic which leaves conduct unaffected. And as with the individual Christian, so with the congregation and the denomination. Despite an earlier remark cautioning against using worship as a "resource," a pastor is not wrong in being concerned for the relation of liturgy to the program of his parish and denomination. If Holy Communion does not stand in some kind of organic relation to the training of church school teachers, let us say; if service and sermon do not speak to a congregation's sense of mission; if Baptism and Confirmation—which have been called "the layman's ordination"—remain unrelated to Christian vocation; then worship is corrupted not by utilitarianism but by irrelevance. In one sense it is not wrong to think of worship as "the rallying act of the Church." [63]

Nevertheless, the center of gravity for liturgical reflection and decision must always remain God, the End beyond all other ends even as he is implicit in all other ends. To affirm this truth, to be sure, is not to subscribe to the theological cliché one often hears—that worship always and everywhere should be conducted *Soli Deo Gloria*, to the glory of God alone. For the *Deus* encountered in worship is never *solus* and his *gloria* always has to do with man and his life.[64] The God of Christian devotion is always a God in

---

[63] The phrase is P. T. Forsyth's.

[64] See David H. C. Read, "The Reformation of Worship," *Scottish Journal of Theology*, VIII (1955), 275 ff.

relation to man and man's world, and his glory inheres in that grace which by definition has man and his moral life as its object. Indeed, in a sense God is glorified to the extent that man is ethicized. Nevertheless, worship is first to be conceived as encounter with God; its reference is secondarily to man. While these two poles constitute a dialectic that cannot be sundered, nevertheless for liturgical theology they must remain distinguishable. They cannot be collapsed into one another any more than the "first" commandment to "love the Lord thy God" can be collapsed into the "second" commandment to "love thy neighbor." These commandments, on which hang the liturgical law and the prophets as all else, pronounce claims that "are like unto" but are not identical with one another, and they point to realities which lose their reality precisely if they are identified with one another. God is not man! There is finally a Reality that is "first" and a reality that is "second," and in the deepest sense worship must recapitulate the difference as well as the unity between them. Perhaps our concern for the corruption of utilitarianism is in the last analysis only a way of affirming the priorities of Christian truth here, and the tension as well as the unity that must exist between them.

Corruptions of Substance

The corruptions so far discussed can be loosely classified as corruptions of function rather than of substance. That is, they are destructive views of the purpose of worship and of the way in which it is ordered and conducted, rather than of the content of worship itself. However, before we turn to corruptions of substance we must consider the dialectical relation between function and substance because each profoundly affects the other, and the line between them cannot be too arbitrarily drawn. The very way in which worship is conceived and conducted, i.e., function, itself communicates substantive meaning; and the substantive content of worship likewise affects the meaning worship functionally holds.

Two terms we have previously used to describe the dialectical nature of worship, "expression" and "impression," help to clarify this relation. As "expressive," worship functions to express the faith the worshipper brings; as "impressive," worship at the same time impresses the worshipper with substantive meaning that begets or deepens faith. Thus a kind of reciprocal cycle operates in worship whereby simultaneously expression fosters impression, and impression inspires expression; and in this sense function and substance merge. Alternatively, we may say that worship as doxology—the expression of devotion—affects worship as theology—the substance of devotion; and correspondingly the theological substance of devotion in turn affects the doxological expression of devotion.

Still another way of saying this is to say that as both impression and expression, worship is always going to be kerygmatic in the sense that inescapably some gospel, some meaning, will be implicit in it and proclaimed through it. The question is not whether worship will proclaim. Rather, the question is: what gospel is experienced as being proclaimed? And because both impression and expression determine what gospel is going to come through, both must be examined in light of their fidelity to the Christian Gospel. Thus only as corruptions of function and corruptions of substance are seen in dialectical relation can one appreciate the gravity of the issues at stake. Both *what* is impressed and expressed and the *way* it is impressed and expressed are crucial.

But while expression and impression stand in dialectical relation, impression in an important sense is more fundamental: Christian worship is founded upon the divine initiative. Before the worshipper can express anything, he must first have been impressed with what God has done, is doing, and shall do.[65] This is to say, the theological substance of the Gospel is prior to his doxological response to it. He is able liturgically to love only when he knows he has first been loved. Worship can be a sacrifice he offers only when it is first seen as a sacrament God offers. Thus when worship as impression is corrupt—that is, when its substance is corrupt—all else is likely to go wrong. Corrupt impression breeds corrupt expression. Corrupt substance begets corrupt function. At stake here is nothing less than the integrity of worship— whether the people encounter the true God or an idol, whether they experience God's grace or are cheated of that grace, whether they are confirmed in truth or scandalized by error, whether—in a word—they are edified or corrupted.

This understanding of the substantive and impressive nature of Christian worship has many implications, but none more important than for the pastor. It instructs him in the responsible use of his freedom for one thing, and it reminds him that he is bound by the Gospel to conceive worship as always that which can be offered through "Jesus Christ our Lord." We sometimes hear it said, for example, that the freedom won for Protestantism by the Reformers, especially in the free churches, is "freedom to worship God as we please." Nothing is farther from the truth or farther from the intentions of the Reformers; for the passion of the Reformers was precisely that God be worshipped as he pleased to reveal himself in his Word.[66] The free

---

[65] See Roger Hazelton, *Christ and Ourselves* (New York: Harper & Row, 1965), p. 82.

[66] See Davies, *The Worship of the English Puritans*, pp. 141-42.

churchman is "free," yes, in the sense that in him and in the congregation is vested the liberty to proclaim and to respond to the Gospel in ways inspired by the Holy Spirit and consistent with Scripture; and as we have argued at length, the forms of this response can never be finally or universally fixed. But the content of the Gospel to which response is made—this is a vastly different matter. Here the integrity of the minister as servant of the Word is at stake; from this he is never free and never wants to be free. Thus it is all-important that the Christian content of the Gospel, the meaning of the Word, possess the pastor's mind and inform his liturgical thinking. We may describe this sense of being possessed by the Word by saying that the pastor must think theologically—indeed Christologically—about worship before he thinks in any other way.

But if the nature of the Gospel determines the content of worship for the pastor, so also for the people. Normally, worship is to be designed for a congregation as a Christian congregation. The Gospel binds the freedom of all; the Church is inevitably a peculiar fellowship; and thus there is inevitably a certain exclusivism in Christian worship. This is by no means to ignore the evangelical and missionary character of worship or the mixed character of any congregation assembled for worship. An absolute distinction between proclamation addressed to believers and to the world cannot be made.[67] The practice of the apostolic Church in dividing worship into the liturgy of the catechumens and the liturgy of the faithful, worship for the uncommitted and worship for the confirmed Christian, is a permanent paradigm of the situation of every congregation. (Indeed, it may well be that given the missionary situation we face today, we shall actually have to reinstitute this practice and restore the catechumenate.) Both the committed and uncommitted are always present, and for that matter both commitment and want of commitment are likewise present in the soul of every worshipper. Indeed, from one point of view there is no such thing as "a Christian congregation"; there is only a congregation of sinful people who know they are not Christian. As Karl Barth has remarked: a congregation always knows itself as a "theatre of conflict" between the true Church and the false. Moreover, liturgical perfectionism can undo us—as we have warned—and "decisions have to be taken which are not only doctrinal but existential," deciding "where we stand in the Church of God, and what, being what we are, we have to do." [68] Nevertheless, integrity is destroyed precisely at the point where worship yields

[67] See Eric James, "Worship and the Church's Mission," a mimeographed address originally given to the Convocation on Worship of The Methodist Church, April, 1966, at Baltimore.

[68] Pehr Edwall, Eric Haymann, and William D. Maxwell, eds., *Ways of Worship* (New York: Harper & Bros., 1951), p. 39.

57

to the popular notion that the people are free to worship as they please, on their own terms and not on terms of the Church's choosing. Corruption occurs when worship yields to lowest common denominators of belief and attitude, when it makes too great concessions to the cultural conditioning to which we have referred, and when, in a misconceived effort to be evangelical or missionary, it contradicts its own Gospel.

Temptations to this kind of corruption arise especially from certain values which the Church has taken over from secularism and with which it has uncritically allowed itself to become infected. Man's subjective preoccupation with himself, his conviction that he is the measure of things, that his individual freedom is prior to everything else including God, and that the ultimate source of truth lies in the dramas of his own psyche rather than in any exterior revelation—this has corrupted the Church more than it realizes.

Certainly one sympathizes with this burden of subjectivity the modern man bears, and worship of course must take account of its prophetic import. But uncritically influenced by such ideas, many ministers have slanted worship to appeal primarily to the charming pagans of which our churches are so full and in order to attract them have substituted an *ersatz* gospel for the Christian Gospel. They have not understood that to fail to conceive worship primarily for a congregation as a Christian congregation not only relaxes the demand of truthfulness which Christian worship must embody; usually it also fails in its alleged intention to evangelize the uncommitted in any vital way.

More recently, the challenge of certain mission theologians has sharpened the issue of liturgical integrity for the Church and has raised in somewhat different form the question whether worship should be designed first for a congregation as a Christian congregation. St. Paul's fourteenth chapter of First Corinthians is usually appealed to, and Paul's two references (vss. 16, 23-24 RSV) to the "outsider's" need to be able to understand what is taking place are elevated as normative for the reconstruction of worship.[69] But an examination of their exegesis matched against Paul's own thought leaves one bewildered if not suspicious. Either Paul's words do not mean what they say or his criterion is too offensive to our exegetes; for the fundamental, unequivocal criterion throughout Paul's discussion is that worship "must aim at one thing: to build up the church" (I Cor. 14:26 NEB; see also vss. 3, 4, 5, 12, 19, 22, 31). The heart of worship for Paul is "prophecy"—that is, intelligible worship as against esoteric speaking with tongues—and as such it is meant

---

[69] See for example *The Church for Others* (Geneva: World Council of Churches, 1967), p. 42; J. G. Davies, *Worship and Mission* (London: SCM Press, 1966), pp. 149-50. It is noteworthy that from the Greek word for "outsider" stems our modern word "idiot," and that Paul construes it to mean one who attends worship out of curiosity.

first "not for unbelievers but for those who hold the faith" (vs. 22 NEB). Further, it is precisely the integrity of worship addressed first inwardly to the congregation which "searches" the "outsider's" conscience and brings conviction, and causes him to "fall down and worship God, crying, 'God is certainly among you!'" (vss. 24, 25 NEB). In short, only as worship is preserved in its prophetic integrity for the community of faith does it succeed in converting the outsider; and in this respect Paul was only typical of the mind of the Church. In the apostolic era worship was conceived first not to convert the pagan but to confirm the initiated; the pagan had to undergo catechesis in order to understand and to participate, which is perhaps a paradigm for us today.

All this is to say that in a sense the Church's missionary power is in ratio to her liturgical integrity. The very contradiction which worship "through Jesus Christ our Lord" offers to the subjectivism of the individual worshiper is ultimately more missionary than the reduction of worship to appeal to man on his own terms. When the Church's liturgy possesses integrity, there is an inescapable "rupture" [70] between the Church and the world; but this rupture is itself converting. To be sure, contradiction can be so exaggerated that there is no communication of any kind, and when this happens worship is meaningless.[71] Nevertheless, to conceive worship with such theological truthfulness that the "post-Christian," "sub-Christian," or "pre-Christian" man of today is challenged by the contradiction between what he wishes to say and do in worship and what the Gospel requires of him is in the last analysis an act of both integrity and superior strategy. Authentic worship, if we only realized it, is one of the most powerful forms of mission and evangelism the Church can employ.[72] Hans Küng summarizes our point well: "If the Church wants to be a *credible* herald, witness, demonstrator and messenger in the service of the reign of God, then it must constantly repeat the message of Jesus not primarily to the world, to others, but to itself. . . . Its credibility—and no amount of energetic and busy activity can replace that vital factor—depends on its remaining faithful to the message of Jesus." [73]

Against this background, several false gospels which corrupt the substance of worship must be examined, not only because they illustrate so well our easy apostasies but also because they can serve as a foil to an attempt to

---

[70] The term is J.-J. von Allmen's.

[71] See ch. III.

[72] See the essay by Bernard Botte, "The Problem of Adaptation in the Liturgy," in *The Church in Mission*, ed. R. E. Campbell (Maryknoll, N. Y.: Maryknoll Publications, 1965).

[73] *The Church*, trans. Ray and Rosaleen Ockenden (New York: Sheed & Ward, 1967), p. 97.

restate positively the theological meaning of integrity in the following essay. For the confidence that a restatement can be made must not be abandoned despite the negativism that so far may seem to have informed our discussion. One can have such confidence, however, only insofar as the Church is willing to submit its gospels to the judgement of the Gospel. If we incur the pain of looking at our apostasies, we do so in the faith that God can make even man's apostasy to praise him, and that liturgical integrity ultimately comes from the Church's self-criticism which testifies to her anxiety that she shall live not unto herself but unto her Lord.[74]

The first false gospel we briefly analyze is a mongrel gospel with elements of naturalism, animal vitalism, and secular humanism tenuously combined with Christian truths. Christianity is reduced to a system of values, and correspondingly worship is conceived as an experience of "affirmation of values" which man is alleged to be better for thinking about. Probably this corruption has its origin partly in a theory of worship which has been popular for quite some time—worship as the recognition of God as "supreme worth," and more recently in a conception of worship as "the celebration of life" and of "the world."

This gospel is typically the gospel of "great and profound spiritual themes," and worship is understood as the "contemplation of the deeper meanings of life," as "friendly commerce with all that is good in human existence." In the typical words of a church bulletin: "Worship is a time when, through association with kindred spirits, through music, through created beauty, literature and thought, we cultivate a greater reverence for those values which give life meaning and purpose." Or in the words of a pastoral psychologist: worship consists of those "moments" in which "are celebrated the events of crucial significance in the ongoing life of the community, where the concern of all enhances and enriches the meaning of what each is living through. . . . by the joining of their separate ways into the stream of overflowing life they reinforce their better impulses by enlarging perspectives, and store up a pool of spiritual resources for each to draw upon according to his individual need." [75] (A student once remarked on hearing this definition that for him it perfectly described a Socialist Youth Rally he had attended.) Occasionally an exponent of this gospel will frankly describe it as "mystical naturalism,"

[74] See Daniel Jenkins, *The Gift of Ministry* (London: Faber & Faber, 1947), p. 27.
[75] Paul E. Johnson, *Psychology of Pastoral Care* (Nashville: Abingdon Press, 1953), p. 65. Thomas Klink also writes: Worship is any "social ceremony in a setting of solemn dignity, whereby experiences are celebrated on occasions of participation in widely valued processes." "Ecumenical Sensitivity: A Dimension of Institutional Worship," in *Pastoral Psychology*, XVIII (June, 1967).

and worship itself as becoming creature-conscious, creature-minded, creature-devoted.

More recently, under the impact of secular theologies which exalt the human and put man and his world at the center, worship has been conceived as "the celebration of the processes and products by which we live," as the "liturgical experience of communal sensitivity that I am one with my brother next to me," as "gathering together for corporate strength and encouragement, education, introspection and re-affirmation," as "the rehearsal of life as it is," as "perceiving the beauties of human existence." Indeed, one scholar has defined worship in a secular age as the *"celebration of being human* through the rehearsal of fundamental word-acts which create and reinforce unitive and *self-directive values."* [76] We shall presently comment on the way in which religious reality is often wrapped up inside human concerns, and such humanistic speech is not always to be taken at face value. Yet it is hard to escape the impression that preoccupation with the secular today often collapses worship into little more than humanism. In focusing on man rather than God it becomes eccentric, that is, literally "off-center," and it is not surprising that in turn it fosters eccentric expressions which often seem mainly to titillate the worshipper's own ego.

A variation of this mongrel gospel stresses the meanings of physical nature in worship. Celebration of the vitalities of nature displaces the life given men in Jesus Christ. The God worshipped is the only-God-can-make-a-tree deity of transcendentalist nature lovers rather than the God and Father of our Lord Jesus Christ. Christian obedience is corrupted by poetic romanticism summoning us to "sunward pilgrimages," and giving us for images of contemplation rose petals and waterfalls rather than the wounds of Christ. Budding pussy willows are equated with the Resurrection; "evensong with the birds" is substituted for the Song of the Lamb; and unity with "the hum of existence" is preferred to dying and rising with our Lord. Often nature is so exalted that worship is reduced to a kind of pantheism.

Now there is of course an obverse side to this (and the implications for liturgical theology of the doctrine of Creation will require further comment in later essays). Certainly Christian faith recognizes the revelatory meaning of nature, and its worship has traditionally embodied this recognition. It understands that the God of redemption is also the God of creation. How

---

[76] Fred M. Hudson, "Worship in a Secular Age," *Foundations*, VII (Oct., 1964), 324. Italics mine. Hudson adds: "Worship, then, is something which humans do, not as . . . a 'religious' act, but as an act which for some social grouping declares the allegiance of the whole life. . . . Its function is to unify and give perspective to all other areas of behaviour, and to disclose the worth of existence."

impoverished worship would be without Psalm 150, or St. Francis' "Canticle to the Sun," or Haydn's "The Creation"! Significantly, the canon of the Roman Mass (and the consecration prayers of many new Protestant liturgies) recognizes the divine meaning of the natural creation in the very same prayer in which is recapitulated the salvation of the world in Jesus Christ, and something deep in us would have Christian prayer be this way. Liturgical theology needs "a much more patient theology of nature," in a fine phrase of Kenneth Cragg: "Such loyalty to nature is in fact a deep loyalty also to the Incarnation. The revelatory feasibility of Incarnation presupposes the revelatory quality, in part, of all experience. . . . The 'new' or special sacredness which greets us in the Incarnate Lord employs the channels of natural sacredness." [77] Many of us would wish to subscribe to a passage from Marcel quoted by J. H. Oldham: "My deepest and most unshakable conviction is that, whatever all the thinkers and doctors have said, it is not God's will at all to be loved by us *against* the Creation, but rather glorified *through* the Creation." [78] Furthermore, in our technological society there is a danger that people will lose their sense of membership in the world of nature and become unable to conceive the God of redemption and the God of creation as one God. Much Protestant worship, with its heavy emphasis upon the spoken word, is in a less strong position here than Roman Catholicism with its symbols of palm, water, salt, oil, fire, ashes, and above all, bread and wine.[79]

Similarly, what we have called the "mongrel gospel" of vitalism and humanism can contain positive elements. We err if we do not understand that a mutation of the modern man's vision of reality seems to have occurred whereby, insofar as he is religious, the sacred is seen under the aspect of the secular, the divine under the aspect of the human, and that what appears to be only "humanism" is really much more. The sacred has not so much disappeared as shifted its focus, it has been said, and worship accordingly is to be seen as a movement not away from but toward man's experience in the world. It is to identify the transcendent in the immanent and man's experience of God in his experience of society.

The challenge of this way of thinking is self-evident, and we shall need to inquire into its implications at length. Here we shall say only that while such liturgical reorientation is unceasingly part of the Church's task, *semper liturgica reformanda*, concern for integrity must also restrain us from ig-

---

[77] "The Credibility of Christianity," *Study Encounter* (Geneva: World Council of Churches, 1967), III, 59.

[78] *Life Is Commitment* (New York: Harper & Bros., 1952), p. 99.

[79] See Jaroslav Pelikan, *The Riddle of Roman Catholicism* (Nashville: Abingdon Press, 1959), pp. 165-66.

noring the dangers. For example, it has been said with regard to the home mass now gaining in popularity that its purpose is to provoke "a renaissance of experience": "It is not so much a new way to have a Mass as a new way to have a group. It's a do-it-yourself experience with free responses to whatever a group is thinking and feeling." [80] It is significant that this comment was enthusiastically made by a Protestant to indicate the direction it is hoped liturgy will take; and indeed much Protestant worship is also developing along this line. If this hope is borne out, worship will indeed have been corrupted into a reductionized humanism, and one can understand our earlier warning of the danger of liturgical suicide.

Likewise the Church always needs to guard against uncritically appropriating the meanings of physical nature into her worship. The Christian Gospel becomes perverted into another gospel when the Creator is not distinguished from the creature, when sentiment ignores the ambiguities of nature and conceals the malevolence of the natural order in paeans of thoughtless praise, when God's providence is liturgically unrelated to his judgement and mercy, when the rhythm of the physical world is substituted for Christian death and resurrection, and above all when the life of the New Age that has come in the Event of Jesus Christ is reduced to natural vitalism. Christian worship is essentially soteriological and eschatological; and as we shall need to understand, the first Creation is to be understood in light of the New Creation, not vice versa. In the mongrel gospel so often proclaimed in the Church today, it is not understood that "between the joy of the Resurrection and the joy of an unthinking life in the sun, a great gulf is fixed." [81]

The next false gospel to be identified as threatening worship today can be described as the corruption of "aestheticism." One hesitates to use so harsh a term as "corruption," but the scope of the threat makes it hard to find another. For by "aestheticism" we mean the autonomy with which art insinuates its vision of reality into liturgy and takes captive the Christian substance of liturgy; the conscious or unconscious affirmation art commonly makes that the reality which Christianity names "God" is most authentically experienced as Beauty rather than as the Holy; the understanding of the action of liturgy as involving man's imagination and feeling more than his

---

[80] A spokesman of the Commission on the Church and Culture of the National Council of Churches, quoted in *The New York Times*, Nov. 2, 1969.

[81] A critic's remark comparing the painting of Rouault and Renoir in *The Selective Eye*, ed. Georges and Rosamond Bernier (New York: Reynal and Company, 1957), III, 60.

conscience and will; the conviction—admitted or unadmitted—which art often communicates that the essence of the experience of worship is pleasure; and the consequent acceptance of artistic canons as decisive for the substance and form of worship. However, "aestheticism" as a corruption of substance is to be distinguished from "art" as a function in liturgy, and before we analyze aestheticism more fully we must make a number of points very clear.

First, it is to be understood that it is *liturgical art* we are speaking of, not religious art in general, not Christian art in general, not Christian ecclesiastical art, to improvise classifications. Liturgical art is unique. One cannot relate art to liturgy—nor for that matter relate art to one's thinking about liturgy— in the same way that art is related to religion or can be appropriated in the life of the Church elsewhere. In liturgy, art is first the servant of the Word in its living dialogue with the human soul, and it is next servant of the worshipping community, the Church. This is to say, liturgical art by definition is kerygmatic, sacramental, sacrificial, and communal. It is bound by these canons, and the freedom the artist enjoys in expressing his individual vision elsewhere cannot prevail in liturgy. An understanding of the uniqueness of liturgical art in this sense is fundamental.

Secondly, however, the affinity between art and liturgy as ways of experiencing reality runs very deep in man's nature and must always be borne in mind (an insight to be elaborated in a later essay).[82] Both art and liturgy, for one thing, engage the symbolic faculty of man's conscious and subconscious life. They both understand man as *animal symbolicum*, as a symbol-making and symbol-using animal, in a phrase of Ernst Cassirer.[83] Man cannot become engaged with any kind of artistic expression, as he cannot become engaged in worship, without symbols. Human consciousness is metaphorical by nature; in an image of T. H. Keir, it is best thought of not as a debating hall but as a picture gallery. Thus while liturgy rejects aestheticism, it is shot through and through with symbolism.

Further, both art and liturgy regard physical matter as meaning-bearing, indeed as potentially revelatory. In fact, liturgy goes so far as to hold that the physical can be rendered sacramental through divine grace acting upon, within, and through it. The foundation of this understanding in Christian thought is simply the Incarnation: "the Word become flesh." Thus the potentiality of physical matter to convey the divine corresponds to the capacity in man's nature to respond to the divine in material form. These are basic realities for worship, and to ignore them is to violate the structure of human

[82] See ch. VI.
[83] See *An Essay on Man: An Introduction to a Philosophy of Human Culture* (New Haven: Yale University Press, 1944), p. 26.

personality and to deny the nature of divine grace. Man cannot be expected to be less sensuous in his worship of God than God has been in the creation and salvation of man.

Again, both art and liturgy perform a kind of existential and soteriological function. That is, at their best they deal truthfully with man's situation, take seriously his need to be saved from illusion about himself, and present him with a certain fatefulness of decision. They confront him with "the angels and dragons within his own being"—in a figure of R. G. Collingwood —move him to name things with their true names, and bring him to know his existence as it truly is before the Reality he may be able to call "God." The meanings life holds or fails to hold for man—his values and his illusions, his certainties and his ambiguities, his misery and his grandeur, his fate and his freedom—these are the very stuff of both art and liturgy. This is to say, both liturgy and art would render man vulnerable to the truth about himself and his predicament and would bring home to him the consequences of that truth.

Further, both liturgy and art deal with man ontologically. That is, they speak to his need "to be," and they deal in those concerns with whose ultimacy he knows his destiny to be bound. They would bring life to birth and meet death with resurrection. They would intensify vitality, refine the quality of man's being, and nerve his selfhood as he acts and is acted upon by his world. Significantly, we speak of artists as "authors," of works of art as "creations," and we assess their truth by their power to bring to birth a larger consciousness and to heighten sensibility. Similarly, worship is an experience of renewed being if it is anything, a veritable recapitulation of creation, a salvation from death into life, and a commitment to life.

Again, both art and liturgy function eschatologically—if one may strain the meaning of the term. They can bring man to cross over from lesser to fuller life. They open up dimensions of newness that were not there before. And often they make the future present with hope and with joy.

Given these affinities, we repeat: to reject the corruption of aestheticism in worship is not to deny the liturgical function of art. The "cleft" between much Protestant worship and art which prevailed until recently (and to which many congregations are still heir) was due largely to the failure to make this distinction. Rightly afraid of aestheticism, free-church Protestantism wrongly feared art. Man's nature was misread. His rationality was overestimated and his imaginative and sensuous life was underestimated. The human mind was mainly seen as a continuously working "idol factory"—in Calvin's famous phrase—and the inescapability of symbols was not understood. The relation of the divine to the natural was distorted, and spirit was opposed to matter in an unbiblical dualism.[84] Because much Protestant worship preferred to see reality opaquely rather than honestly, the shock of man's predicament which art could teach liturgy was prudishly declined. And falsely supposing that art would corrupt rather than enhance man's passion for life, much Protestant worship clung to its puritanisms and its pieties.

Now, however, the situation has largely changed, and Protestantism has, as it were, grown up into a kind of artistic awkward age. Having learned at great cost how art when exiled from man's life at one place will reappear at another, free-church Protestantism has determined that the cleft shall be overcome. From a posture of revulsion, free churches have now moved to clasp art in such vigorous embrace that while the affinities between art and liturgy are affirmed, tensions are ignored. Driven to self-criticism by the growing sophistication of the people, aware of the impact which art in its numerous forms—especially the film—exerts in our mass media culture, and eager to reassert affinities which never should have been lost, free-church Protestantism has resolved that the varnished oak pulpit and bare-walled "sanctuary," the clerical sack suit and flyspecked candlesticks, the gospel hymn and the Akron architecture, must go. For good or for ill, free-church congregations have largely abandoned their puritan legacy in a kind of cultural adolescence and, athletically overreacting as good Protestants tend to do, have undertaken to "enrich worship"—to use their favorite term—that it may be made "aesthetically exciting."

One wonders, however, how theologically discriminating this newfound enthusiasm is, especially in light of certain evidence that begins to give one pause. On its loftier levels the Church cordially merges commissions on worship with commissions on the arts rather than with commissions on faith and order, and one wonders why liturgy is yoked with art rather than with theology. On lower levels it gives *carte blanche* to commercial agencies to debase liturgy for years to come with carloads of gaudy stoles and brass appointments, of revolving altars and prefab baptismal fonts. On local levels parishes busily "beautify" Sunday services, rally or shock the faithful with "modern drama," and lure the outsider with jazz masses and liturgical dance. "Committees on the Arts" flourish more vigorously than social action cadres. "Festivals of the Arts" claim more attention than social issues on which the destiny of civilization may well hang. The polish of the choir or the hiring of the new soprano receives more concern than St. Paul's injunction that all

[84] See Howard G. Hageman, *Pulpit and Table* (Richmond: John Knox Press, 1962), pp. 111-12.

the congregation share in psalms, hymns, song,[85] and music is chosen less for its theological truth than its taste. Communion ceremonial is given more care than the discipline of the congregation in preparing for it. And proper gestures for the fraction of the loaf, or the elegance of the tray and chalice, receive more attention than the ethics of man's economic life.

Any one of these symptoms taken by itself might not be significant, but more and more it appears that in much free-church worship the reigning ethos is more aesthetic than biblical, that we have failed to say a right "no" as well as a right "yes" to art, and that we have illegitimately scrambled together aesthetic and liturgical truth. To be sure, there are exceptions to this interim appraisal, and here especially one observer's angle of vision will differ from another's. It is too soon to say with certainty to what end our new enthusiasm for art will carry liturgy. Nevertheless, liturgical thinking in many free churches is failing to distinguish between the contribution which art as function can make to worship and the substantive corruption which art, as a way of experiencing reality and as an autonomous statement of the nature of reality, projects into worship.

For art, it must be understood, finally is more than a neutral way of experiencing reality. With a certain momentum and inevitability it becomes a declaration of the nature of reality. It is in a sense revelation and it readily becomes kerygmatic, imposing its own vision, proclaiming its own gospel, breeding its own priests, raising up its own cultus, and—not surprisingly—having its own devotees; and it is for this fundamental reason that the tensions as well as the affinities between liturgy and art must be reaffirmed. The nature of Ultimate Reality reported by art is not to be equated with the nature of Reality as disclosed in Jesus Christ. *Pathos* and *Eros* are not to be

---

[85] "It is significant that the word 'choir,' *choros,* as used in the early church, referred not to a group within the congregation entrusted with certain musical responsibilities, but to the congregation itself. The terms *choros* and *ekklésia* were used synonymously in the early church. . . . The famous martyr, Ignatius, wrote to the congregation in Ephesus in the following way: 'you must every man of you join in a choir (*hoi kat' andra de choros ginesthe*) so that being harmonious and in concord and taking the keynote of God in unison, you may sing with one voice through Jesus Christ to the Father, so that he may hear you and through your good deeds recognize that you are parts of his son.' And it was Ignatius' desire that the Christians in Rome would praise God in Jesus Christ—that they might 'form a chorus in love (*en agapé choros*) and sing to the Father through Jesus Christ.' Here too, however, a clericalizing tendency soon began to manifest itself in linguistic usage. The word 'chorus' came to refer to the special priestly function in the liturgy—just as architectually speaking, the choir became the reserved 'priest-church' within the sanctuary—and it eventually became the equivalent of the word *clerus*. It is easy to agree with these who desire to restore to the word chorus the meaning it had in the early church. Every choir has its function *in* the congregation, and every choir ought to fulfill its liturgical function in such a way that the united praises of the whole church will resound in its songs." Olof Herrlin, *Divine Service: Liturgy in Perspective,* trans. Gene J. Lund (Philadelphia: Fortress Press, 1966), pp. 102-3.

equated with the Christian *Logos*. And when the nature of Reality as envisioned by art is accepted as authoritative, and the derivative assumptions on which art operates are internalized by liturgy, the polar realities in the liturgical transaction, God and man, are misconstrued and liturgy is corrupted by the false gospel of aestheticism.

For one thing, in the worship of certain free churches the fear of the Puritans has been vindicated: the God of Beauty has displaced the God of Christian revelation. The attributes of deity which Christian thought must insist upon—the personal character of God, his holiness, his active righteousness, his moral will, his judgement and mercy—are displaced by a vision of God as Beauty. The terror of God's deeds in history is made to give way to his harmony and joy. The eschatological event of Jesus Christ "shattering the backbone of history"—in Chesterton's famous phrase—is rendered into a tale of poetry and charm. "The God who acts" gives way to the God who smiles. Similarly, the man to whom such aestheticized worship is made to appeal is not first man whose soul needs redemption and whose will needs rescue; rather, he is aesthetic man whose sensibilities are to be titillated and whose imagination is to be intrigued. In this respect aestheticism has learned only too well from errors of the past. Persuaded that man is primarily a symbolic animal, it addresses man as essentially a creature of feeling and imagination. It would engage his senses and shrive him with God's beauty rather than confront his will and search him with God's holiness.

Predictably, the action of worship at its very core in turn becomes corrupted. Appreciation and impression become the proper response rather than decision. Contemplation is more fitting than commitment—"the aesthetic posture projected to cosmic ends." In a metaphor of Gerhard van der Leeuw, the right liturgical response to the thunder and lightning of Sinai is to enjoy the glow of the landscape.[86] Further, the moral character of worship often is bleached out. Because man's aesthetic sensibilities are appealed to more than his conscience and will, he is not addressed in his moral predicament by a moral God. His contrition is not evoked; his intercession on behalf of others is not claimed; and the ethical implications of worship for his life in the world are left unpronounced. Still further, the salvational nature of worship is corrupted into a kind of liturgical hedonism. The holy agony which Christian worship authentically is becomes narcoticized with aesthetic pleasure.[87] And not seldom the song of Pan is more prominent than the *Kyrie Eleison*.

[86] *Sacred and Profane Beauty: The Holy in Art*, trans. David E. Green (Apex ed.; Nashville: Abingdon Press, 1963), p. xii.

[87] Edward A. Sövik in a penetrating article entitled "The Architecture of Kerygma," writes: "As we reflect on those things we value as fine arts it seems that the more we

To be sure, when art authentically serves liturgy instead of taking liturgy captive for its own purposes, this need not happen, as we shall note shortly, and it is very important to be clear on this point. If art will subordinate its vision of Reality as Beauty to the Christian vision of God as the Holy; if art will address man not with pleasure but with that judgement and mercy that beget salvation; if art will let its love of the vitalities of existence be chastened with the paschal Life of the Gospel, then aestheticism is no problem. But to ask of art these renunciations is probably to ask it to yield up that autonomy which is definitive for its existence. The bald truth is that art in a sense always threatens liturgy; and liturgy rightly looks on art with an incorrigible suspicion simply because the polar enemy of liturgy is idolatry.

A conversation between T. S. Eliot and the German poet M. Hausmann illustrates this fundamental tension. Hausmann had voiced misgivings concerning Bach's *St. Matthew Passion* as a liturgical form. Used in this way, he contended, Bach's music is like being pleasantly told that one's brother has been killed in a concentration camp under terrible circumstances:

And now comes a friend and tells you of your brother's agony in an aria with orchestral accompaniment. What would you say to that? Could you really take the man seriously? Would not everything in you revolt . . . ? But if the aria was so wonderful and the music so glorious that you forget the horror of the crime, if the art so hid the reality that it almost ceases to be true, what kind of a role of deceit would art be playing then? And this is exactly what Bach did in the *St. Matthew Passion*. Just look at the people who attend. . . . Are they listening to an account of the Passion? Not at all; they are listening to art. Bach certainly did not intend this but he brought it about.[88]

In a quite different way, aestheticism also corrupts the Church's liturgical life by imposing a violent vision of reality reflecting the chaos and alienation

---

respect a particular work, the less likely it is that its value to us can be described in terms of delight or pleasure." Yet he must go on to add: "Now this question of delight in art is a perennial one. . . . The fact is that most art is in one way or another a pleasure. For the artist does not simply *tell* what he thinks the truth is, he celebrates it, and in a way it is this celebration that lifts art into being art." *Worship*, XL (Apr., 1966).

[88] Gerhard Kappner, "The Church Service and Music," *The Scottish Journal of Theology*, XII (1959), 248-49. It should be added that Bach was aware of this peril. Jaroslav Pelikan points out that Bach's greatness lay precisely in the consecration of his artistic talent to the Gospel. This is perhaps most clearly seen in Cantata 4: "Christ Jesus lay in death's strong bands for our offenses given; but now at God's right hand He stands and brings us life from heaven. *Therefore* let us be joyful and sing." The "therefore" is all-important, in that it locates the source of Christian song in what God has done in Jesus Christ. A comment of Joseph Sittler concerning Bach is added: "The good city of the consummation toward which his soul pressed was not Parnassus but Jerusalem; the songs which drew from him . . . the cantatas were not the songs of Pan but the songs of Zion." *Fools For Christ* (Philadelphia: Muhlenberg Press, 1955), p. 152.

of our culture, rather than the vision of Christian revelation. To be sure, one function of art is always to hold a mirror to life, and its vision of the brokenness of reality in our time testifies in a sense to its faithfulness to its task. But the function of art in helping us to see is one thing. Theological and metaphysical declarations it extrapolates from its vision and projects as the substance of liturgy are another. And because in holding the mirror to culture in our time art seems so gleefully to blaspheme or vindictively to profane, liturgy must be wary of the vision it would impose.

For example, in many quarters aestheticism of this kind corrupts liturgy with a savage vision of God as the *Gauche* whose reigning attribute is Absurdity, and who accordingly is best worshipped by self-conscious, Camus-like exercises in the bitter and the enigmatic. In aestheticized worship of this kind, God indeed does not smile. Rather, he frowns, or he stands on his head, or he gives us the back of his hand. The marks of the liturgical encounter here are commonly the surrealist gash on the altar, the abrasive chant, the eccentric aisle, the twisted crucifix of rubber hose, the gritty litany, the Service of Cryptic Communion. Reality here is not the Christian reality of God *incognitus* or *absconditus;* it is God *absurdus* or *aberratus.* Complementing this perverse vision of the Divine is a distinctive view of man as Stoic man or Kafka man, whose estrangement is to be maximized and whose hymns are to be wails. Admittedly the pathos of man's predicament is often stated with great power. There is little if any trace of liturgical hedonism—unless it be masochism. But usually there is also no note of redemption, and the will of man is left to its own nervelessness. With a kind of perverse humanism, aestheticism of this kind does not celebrate man; it simply mourns him and reduces his dialogue with God to a plucking of his own despair. If any relation between man and God is affirmed, it is the essential absurdity of the predicament of each, and the best liturgy is that which helps one most savagely to gnash his own teeth.

Now let it be said that the God of the *Gauche* may be nearer the true God than the God who smiles, and the man who gnashes his teeth may be nearer the Kingdom of heaven than he who only enjoys the biblical landscape. Further, liturgy on occasion will prefer the ugly to the beautiful as a less untruthful way of rendering the encounter between God and man in order to declare both the *tremendum* and the *fascinans* of that Holy One with whom man's destiny is bound up. One mark of the Holy, it must always be remembered, is that it repels as well as attracts; it daunts as well as fascinates. And worship whose forms offend may more authentically enable man to meet God than worship which only gives pleasure.[89]

[89] Van der Leeuw has an interesting passage on this point: "The least 'beautiful' images of the gods are wont to be the most holy. . . . A good part of them are fetishes. . . .

However, symbols which serve liturgy in this sense are one thing. Aestheticism which perverts the Christian vision of God and renders worship into an experience of absurdity and violence is another. And again, to ask that art be humble enough to be ugly in order to be holy is probably to ask the impossible. Art will hardly consent to let its creations be fetishes! In short, whether conventional or radical, the vision of Reality which art—when made sovereign—imports into liturgy, the doctrine of man on which art operates, and the kind of liturgical action which art—when allowed to be autonomous —precipitates are in perpetual tension with Christian revelation and liturgical theology.

Given the possibilities of aesthetic corruption, therefore, it is always dangerous to think and speak of worship as an "art," of the planning and conduct of worship as "the art of worship," and of forms of worship as "works of art." Liturgical integrity is easily undermined by using the vocabulary of the aesthetic so substantively. One may perhaps speak in this fashion colloquially, but always at the risk of sacrificing theological to aesthetic canons. We do best to think and speak of art in relation to worship as an adjective, not as a noun. Let it always be remembered in this connection that historically the Church has not undertaken to formulate liturgy primarily as a work of art. Its concern for liturgy has abundantly mothered artistic creation, yes; but from the primitive Church to the present, the kerygma, the Gospel, has exerted "the controlling influence on the shaping of liturgy." [90] Even in its eras of greatest artistic flowering, the Church could be quite indifferent to the artistic propriety of its liturgical forms, and the outstanding contributions to the Church's liturgical life were made by men who were not first artists but men of faith, of theological concern, and pastoral integrity who placed whatever talents they possessed at the service of the Gospel.

Above all, let us not forget the silence of the New Testament itself on the importance of the aesthetic dimension of the Christian life, and the mind of him in whose light all reflection upon the meaning of worship is ultimately to be carried on. Of that mind and of its judgement upon the aesthetic element, it has been written: Did Jesus have

---

Primitive man finds . . . the distance which separates him from the wholly other to be better expressed by the non-human or the semihuman. From the religious point of view, the Greeks ranked the xoanon, an ancient image of the god made of wood, rough and scarcely human, above the works of a Phildias or a Praxiteles. . . . The Roman Catholic knows that the most holy images of Christ, the Blessed Virgin, or other saints, blackened with age, are only rarely the most important works of art. . . . Thus it is possible for faith to prefer the ugly to the beautiful, because . . . [the ugly] better preserves the distance which separates the holy." *Sacred and Profane Beauty*, pp. 163-64.

[90] C. H. Dodd, *The Apostolic Preaching* (Chicago: Willett, Clark and Co., 1937), p. 122.

anything of what we call the sense of artistic beauty? Did he get any of that joy of taste of which our modern life makes so much? It is not an easy question to answer in a word. We may point to the special earnest purpose which filled all the life of Jesus. We may say that he who was walking on to Calvary had no time in the intenseness of his moral life for art and its luxuriousness. We may say that he was a Jew, and that it was not in the nature of his race to gather from beautiful things that happiness which they imparted to the quick-eyed Greek. . . . We may say that though Jesus made nothing of artistic beauty, yet his religion has made much of it, and out of Christianity the highest artistic life has come. We may say all of these things, and no doubt all of them have truth. But still the great impression of the life of Jesus . . . must always be of the subordinate importance of those things in which only the aesthetic nature finds its pleasure. There is no condemnation of them in that wise, deep life. But the fact always must remain that the wisest, deepest life that was ever lived, left them on one side, was satisfied without them. . . . And in its more earnest moods, in its reformations . . . [Christianity] has always stood ready to sacrifice the choicest works of artistic beauty for the restoration . . . of the simple majesty of righteousness, the purity of truth, the glory of God."[1]

The last corruption we cite can hardly be called a "false gospel." Rather, it is the Church mutilating her own Gospel and falsifying the meaning Jesus Christ holds for human life by abstracting worship into an escapist other-worldliness. In liturgy a man's worst foes are often those of his own household, and in the excising of the worldly dimension from worship we encounter what is probably the Church's worst conspiracy against God. Karl Barth once criticized worship with only the sermon and no Eucharist as "torso liturgy"; but in a profounder sense the Church's blindness to the full life man lives and the real world in which he lives truncates liturgy. What has been called the great ultimatum of this century, that unless Christianity comes alive as a sociology it will become dead as a religion, is not heard; and the gulf between worship and life we have spoken of has emerged as fateful. The harsh political realities that determine people's destiny from day to day, the racism and greed dehumanizing men, the evil of militarism threatening to turn America into a fascist state, violence and the repression of civil liberties, the claims of social and economic justice, the hurtling pace of history—such realities are ignored or their cutting edge is wrapped in liturgical platitudes. So often one comes away from worship feeling that one has indeed been taken on a kind of narcotic "trip" into another world.

However, again the complexity of issues converging here must restrain one from making premature or only emotional commitments. To recover authentic worldliness requires more than fulminations against the Church

[1] Phillips Brooks, *The Influence of Jesus* (New York: E. P. Dutton, 1879), pp. 199-201.

or turning the wine of theology into the water of sociology. Radical corruption requires a corresponding radicalness of thought, and radicalness is to be understood here as exactly the recovery of theological roots. Later we shall have to explore how one's doctrine of the Church speaks to the corruption of otherworldliness, for example. For only as "Church" is understood dialectically as both apostolic and cultic, the life of the congregation as both historical and eschatological, and their liturgical action as taking place in both time and in eternity can Christian "worldliness" be properly defined. Similarly, a profound paradox of liturgical Christology will be found to underlie thought: only when worship is both engagement and disengagement with the world as the Christ-Event interprets these to us can the gulf between worship and life be authentically bridged. On this theological fulcrum the issues must ultimately turn if torso liturgy is to be renounced and worship is to possess integrity.

Certain cultural and psychological factors, however, may be briefly identified here. The political doctrine of separation of Church and State, for one, has been misconstrued in much free-church Protestantism to mean a divorce between cultus and ethics, or as the restricting of religious claims to only the private sectors of life. The security and affluence so important to middle-class Protestantism have likewise fostered corruption in that religion is always as much the embodiment of man's value systems as of what he supposes to be his faith; and when men feel their values threatened, as today, social anxiety easily turns worship into neurotic escape. The individualism and voluntarism so characteristic of our culture also enter in here—the freedom the modern American boasts of in choosing his commitments. As he politically votes "as I please," so he elects to worship "as I please," and the pressure he can mount to divert worship from social realities and conform it to his individualism is indeed formidable. The population and vocational mobility characteristic of our culture also contributes to a spurious otherworldliness. Uprootedness is always threatening, and it is to be expected that people will turn to the Church's worship as refuge and insulation against the pain of change. Underlying these factors also is the ease with which religious ritual psychologically lends itself to corruption; man's instinct is to associate ritual psycologically with that which protects. And while this instinct can express itself in both good and bad ways, at its worst it uses liturgical ritual as retreat.

Two further factors which are at once both cultural and theological should also be noted. Despite "man's coming of age" heralded by secular theologies, man continues to be an existential animal very much concerned with his inward "I"; and God as the fulfiller of personal needs and the solver of personal problems has not disappeared as much as our radical theologians

73

would seem to have liked. In this respect, one feels that they would have done well not to advertise their own sensibilities as quite so normative and to have read the psychologists and phenomenologists of religion more carefully.[92] Rightly and wrongly, men still look to God to do for them what the world cannot do;[93] and in regard to worship, often wrongly in the sense that they would invert the cult into narcissism and therapy. Otherworldliness in this sense is preoccupation with the world of the self more than with the supernatural, but it is still a world "other" than the world of political and social reality. In fact, insofar as this latter world has caused the self's inward conflicts, to that degree it is usually shunned and the gulf left unbridged.

Secondly, the Church has not sufficiently understood man's preoccupation with the human as a covert search for the sacral; and it overreacts by taking up a stone-wall posture in which the supernatural is grimly affirmed at all costs—including the cost of evacuating worship of the human. The Church too easily forgets that "in the beginning is relation," in a phrase of Martin Buber; and it does not understand that, in our day especially, the experience of God for many people comes through man's experience of relation with man. To be sure, this assessment must be considered provisional; it is too soon to be sure that the divine will not be reduced to the human. Very real dangers lurk here, and as we have flatly remarked, liturgy cannot but insist that God is more than "man writ large." But this is not to say that God is not experienced through the human; and affirmation of the human against forces dehumanizing life must be seen as in many ways a religious affirmation. The director of the Research Institute on Communist Affairs at Columbia University has said that "what we have been witnessing is a society shaped culturally, socially, psychologically, and economically by technology and electronics. . . . Now we are moving into a phase where we are very seriously asking ourselves what people are for. The only other time that man was preoccupied with this question was in the early stage of genuine religious commitment. Then for a long, long time we forgot to ask the question." [94] Now men are indeed remembering to ask this question. As Horst Symanowski has written, Luther's famous question which unleashed

[92] For example, Paul M. Pruyser's *A Dynamic Psychology of Religion* (New York: Harper & Row, 1968).

[93] For example, see the chapters entitled "The God Who Would Not Stay Dead" and "The Role of Religion in American Society," in *What Do We Believe?* ed. Martin E. Marty, Stuart E. Rosenberg, and Andrew M. Greeley (New York: Meredith Press, 1968).

[94] Sbigniew Brzezinski, in an interview in the *Christian Science Monitor* quoted in the *Morgan Guaranty Survey*, published by the Morgan Guaranty Trust Company, New York, May, 1970.

crusades and started wars, "How can I find a gracious God?" has given place to another: "How can I find a gracious neighbor?" Symanowski continues: "How can we still live together? Man and wife, superiors and subordinates, colleagues in competitive struggle, and finally, one people with another, East and West? Here we become excited, ask questions, and seek ways. The question of a gracious neighbor has become the cardinal question of our industrial society." [95] Surely the Church must see the asking of this question as religious. In a sense the question of a gracious God and a gracious neighbor is the same question differently phrased. And only as the Church's worship translates this question and binds together the human world and the divine world can it possess integrity.

THE SOVEREIGNTY OF THE WORD, JESUS CHRIST, FOR LITURGICAL INTEGRITY

We have inquired in this essay into certain of the motives, better and worse, which may underlie the pastor's concern for the integrity of worship. We have related this concern to the renewal of the Church and made clear how one's theology of liturgy is of a piece with one's theology of the Church. We have discussed in a preliminary way the relation of worship cultically understood to worship as the Christian's life in the world. And we have criticized liturgical practice and theory with particular reference to common corruptions. A number of problems have been identified, and lines of thought leading to the topics of succeeding essays have been adumbrated: the relation of theology and liturgy, the dialectic of liturgy and life, the language of worship, the nature of liturgical action, and others.

At the same time we trust that the conviction has also emerged that liturgical reflection and reform are best undertaken by starting at the point of the sovereign claim of the New Testament Gospel. This conviction clearly does not preclude attention to such fundamental problems as those we have cited to illustrate the need for reform; and the stance of criticism we have taken up, it is hoped, will be understood both as part of the self-criticism in which the Church must always engage and as an effort to be sensitive to the culture in which the Church lives and serves. Convictions, while derived from the Gospel, must be repossessed anew in light of each new situation in which the Church historically finds itself. Nevertheless, a more positive posture must now be taken up if we would be grasped by the mean-

[95] *The Christian Witness in an Industrial Society,* trans. G. H. Kehm (Philadelphia: Westminster Press, 1964), p. 50.

ing of liturgical integrity. Reform becomes abortive if it is only reaction, and ultimately, the springs of reform lie *a priori* in the claim of the Word. In her reflection upon liturgy, the Church like Peter must hear again and again the voice of this Word calling: 'Lovest thou me?" This does not mean that Jesus Christ and his Spirit are not also speaking through the challenges the world presents to the Church as well as through the criticism the Church must make of the corruptions she finds within herself. God's chastening Word meets us both outside and inside the Church, in the world and in the Bible; and correspondingly, reform always bears both a negative and a positive aspect. As we have said, it is, in a sense, both inductive and deductive, and it is probably wise not to try to draw the line too sharply between them. Nevertheless, to let our ultimate directives be taken mainly from the contemporary situation rather than primarily from the Gospel can reduce renewal to reaction and maneuver us into the very error from which we seek to be delivered—the error of defining integrity in terms other than Christian. "All true newness comes ultimately from the Word," it has been written;[96] and in liturgy as elsewhere, obedience to the meaning of Jesus Christ comes first.

Further, only such obedience can transmute the anxiety, even the anguish, one feels in proportion to one's sensitivity to the need for renewal into something more than anxiety or sheer protest. The power of the "newness" of the Word consists not least in its strange grace whereby it transforms what would otherwise be unrelieved discouragement into hope, saves one from the bitterness that tempts to cynicism, and bestows that vision whereby things both temporal and spiritual can be truthfully discerned. This is to say, in attempting to restate the meaning of integrity for the Church's liturgical life today, we are to do what we do in worship itself: rather than fasten first on our own need, we would be grasped by the Word and obediently let it deal with us as it will. A passage from Dietrich Bonhoeffer points our way:

The way of Jesus Christ, and therefore the way of all Christian thinking, leads not from the world to God but from God to the world. This means that the essence of the Gospel does not lie in the solution of human problems, and that the solution of human problems cannot be the essential task of the Church. Of course, it does not follow from this that the Church has no task at all in this connection. We can perceive what is her legitimate task only when we have found the right point of departure. The Church's word to the world can be no other than God's word to the world. This word is Jesus Christ and salvation in His name. It is in Jesus Christ that God's relation to the world is defined.

[96] W. A. Visser 't Hooft, *The Renewal of the Church* (Philadelphia: Westminster Press, 1956), p. 91.

We know of no relation to the world other than through Jesus Christ. For the Church too, therefore, there is no relation to the world other than through Jesus Christ. . . . The proper relation of the Church to the world can . . . be deduced . . . *only* from the gospel of Jesus Christ."[7]

In conclusion, then, and as a transition to the next essay, let us define our central theological term more fully and propose what we believe to be the truest approach to rethinking the meaning of integrity in liturgy. We have interchangeably used such phrases as "the sovereignty of the Gospel," "the claim of the Word," "obedience to the Word," and other similar terms. These are all intended to say the same thing: all thought about worship and all statements about its nature must be subject to the meaning of Jesus Christ as the sovereign norm for their truth and validity. Christian worship by definition is Christological, and analysis of the meaning of worship likewise must be fundamentally Christological.

This conviction may be elaborated by variously saying that Christian worship is God's revelation of himself in Jesus Christ and man's response; that it is the dialogue between man and God through the Word; that it is Christ's priestly action kindling the priestly action of the faithful; that it is the re-enactment of *Kultmysterium*,[98] the cultic "mystery" of Christ; that it is encounter of Christ in his Real Presence with the human soul. These theological metaphors, however, are only variations of the central conviction that Christian worship is grounded in the reality of the action of God toward the human soul in Jesus Christ and in man's responsive action through Jesus Christ. A symbol of theological truth and power with which to portray this reality is the term "Word," but Word understood not as the verbal speech to which our minds so readily reduce it. Rather, the term "Word" is to be understood in its full meaning biblically, theologically—indeed metaphysically: as the living person and Event of Jesus Christ in which God discloses and communicates his very being to man, including all the sacred-human history bound up with this Event and flowing from it.

But if this be our understanding of worship, then it is also to govern our thinking about worship. Jesus Christ who is "the Given" in worship constitutes "the Given" for reflection on worship. Liturgical theology has its own hermeneutics, we may say, and it possesses integrity only when it is bound by the same Word which alone bestows integrity in worship, when

---

[97] *Ethics*, ed. Eberhard Bethge, trans. Neville Horton Smith (New York: The Macmillan Co., 1955), pp. 320-21.

[98] This term was introduced into the vocabulary of the Roman Catholic liturgical movement by Abbot Idelfons Herwegen of the Monastery of Maria Laach in Germany, in the early twentieth century. It means the basic redemptive reality of Christianity, Christ's Passion and Resurrection, as continually becoming present in the Church's worship, through which she shares in eternal salvation.

it is a mode of hearing and answering the Word as worship itself is to hear and answer. A sentence of Augustine summons us to this profoundly Christological task: "Walk by him the man and . . . thou goest. Look not for any way except himself by which to come to him. . . . I do not say to thee, Seek the way. The way itself is come to thee: arise and walk." [99]

---

[99] Quoted by H. Richard Niebuhr, *The Meaning of Revelation* (New York: The Macmillan Co., 1941), p. 191.

II

The Theological Character of Worship

Wisdom in thinking theologically about worship would seem to require at the outset that one define his terms, and in particular the systematizing term of these essays—"integrity." In all theological conversation the vocabulary one uses not only establishes parameters for thought and provides the coin of intellectual exchange; it also attunes the conversation and affects the discovery of truth. Especially in reflection upon *Christian* worship is one's choice of semantics vital. The liturgical encounter between God and man through Jesus Christ is a reality *sui generis;* and it can only be elucidated with terms of discourse appropriate to that encounter. To employ terms not organic to Christian worship itself is like trying to study chemistry with harmonics or inquiring into botany with mathematical equations. Such mischoice not only confuses thought; above all it distorts the reality one is dealing with. The primary category for defining the meaning of integrity therefore must be "theological," a term we construe to mean not merely "the science of God" in the manner of classical theology, but rather, in the manner of the Bible, as referring supremely to the self-disclosure and self-communication of *Theos,* God, in the *Logos,* the Word, Jesus Christ. We hold that only a frame of discourse bound to this term will suffice. Christian worship has its own hermeneutics, and the Word through whom worship is transacted determines our thesaurus for us.

Thus it is "integrity" understood in this theological sense, not merely integrity in general, that we are concerned with. Other than theological meanings of the term "integrity" may be helpful up to a point, but they can mislead us because they do not get at the root of the matter. "Integrity" can mean fidelity to liturgical standards formulated by an ecclesiastical commission, for example, or loyal adherence to prescribed rubrics. Or "integrity" can suggest worship that is relevant to life and able to verify itself as helpful to people. To the more scholarly inclined, "integrity" may mean using accurately such important liturgical terms as "service," "sacrament," "sacrifice," "offering." For others, especially the historically minded, "integrity" may mean steadfastly following tradition, or for the unhistorically minded, throwing tradition over. To the journeyman pastor, "integrity" can mean diligence in his craft and taking care with the practical aspects of worship. These ways of thinking are more or less helpful, but "integrity" as we propose the term means something much profounder: the conformity of one's thought to God's Word, Jesus Christ, as the integrating reality for all liturgical reflection, decision, and practice.

The dictionary definition of "integrity" as wholeness, coherence, as the structural unity of things in unbroken relation and correct proportion, is quite helpful to us here. For wholeness requires the presence of a reality with the authority and power to bring things into wholeness. Integrity exists when an integrating reality brings order out of disorder, includes and excludes, relates and connects, assigns significance, and discriminates proximateness and ultimacy. The integrating reality for Christian worship is the Word, Jesus Christ, who in his work, person, and present Spirit performs these functions and bestows upon worship and upon our thinking about worship the wholeness that alone makes it true. Thus theological integrity is to be understood Christologically. As we have remarked in a sentence that provides the theme of these essays: we can only think about worship with integrity when we first think—as we pray—"through Jesus Christ our Lord."

THE MINISTER AS LITURGICAL THEOLOGIAN

To conceive worship in this way, however, means *ipso facto* that the minister will bear the burden of a certain holy anxiety from which he is never free and from which one hopes he will never wish to be free. We are not unmindful that most ministers already suffer enough anxieties to keep them well supplied for most of their days, but anxiety that the nature of Jesus Christ shall determine the nature of the Church's worship, we would maintain, is unique. We may speak of this burden as the minister's calling to function as a liturgical theologian. And if at first sight this seems too formidable a commitment, we would reply that he cannot escape the duty—and we do not think he will wish to refuse the privilege—of functioning in this way. For in a very real sense he is already a liturgical theologian whether he accepts the title or not, and the true question is how well he is discharging his task. One cannot even begin to inquire into worship nor make a single decision about its planning or conduct without having to talk theology from the very first syllable. In taking the finger of liturgy—in the metaphor of a Dutch scholar—one has to grasp the whole fist of theology,[1] and in dealing

[1] Gerhard van der Leeuw, quoted by Howard G. Hageman, "Three Reformed Liturgies," *Theology Today*, XV (Jan., 1959), p. 507.

with worship the question is not the presence or absence of theology; rather, it is the question of how adequate one's theology is going to be.

For one thing, the matrix of worship is the Church, and the pastor's existence and vocation are set within the Church. We shall argue later in this essay that the doctrine of the Church has been excessively magnified as the primary doctrine from which to proceed in thinking theologically about worship, but this is the last thing from saying that one can think theologically about worship and not to have to think ecclesiologically. However, this is true not only theoretically and the Church is not only conceptually defined by her worship, as we have remarked earlier. Empirically, also, the Church is defined by her worship, and her character is determined by the liturgical decisions pastor and people make every day. The very setting and exercise of ministry make it so. Ministry is exercised in a definite liturgical heritage, time and place, and the pastor is dealing with the Church in the form of flesh and blood people. He cannot escape the particularity of the ecclesiological place within which he ministers, and he cannot ignore the effect upon the nature of the Church of the earthy, practical realities with which he must liturgically deal. The choosing of a hymn or the preparing of a prayer, conferring with his official board as to whether a children's sermon should be included in a service or how often Holy Communion should be celebrated, working with young people in preparing experimental liturgies or counselling parents who wish to have their child baptized—in these very practical matters the Church is formed. Such decisions inescapably compel some kind of theological answer. In a word, as he practically deals with the Church, he is functioning as a liturgical theologian.

But more than a theological understanding of the Church is at stake. The nature of ministry is also at stake, and concern for liturgical integrity inevitably raises the theological question of ministry. Traditionally, the distinctive mark of the ordained minister has been his calling to preach the Word and administer the Sacraments representatively on behalf of the congregation; and while in our day the emphasis on the minister's liturgical function in relation to his other functions is diminishing, the chief responsibility for the Church's liturgical life will almost certainly continue to be his. It must of course be remembered that emphasis upon the liturgical definition of ministry arose in an era in which the Church itself was defined in predominantly liturgical terms as the congregation of believers in which the pure Word of God is preached and the Sacraments duly administered.[2] Broadly speaking, this definition of Church controlled the definition of ministry. Today the "marks" of the Church must be redefined to match our

[2] See for example Article XIX of the Thirty-nine Articles of the Anglican Church.

larger understanding of the Church as mission, and correspondingly the definitive marks of ordained ministry must include much more than the minister's liturgical functions. Moreover, much more than in the past the ordained minister today shares the ministry of worship with the laity in various ways and within varying limits of authority. In its deepest meaning "ministry" is to be understood as inhering in the charismatic gift of the Spirit to every Christian.[3] The whole people of God minister liturgically as otherwise; and to restore this truth operationally in the life of the Church is perhaps the foremost claim upon us today.[4]

Nevertheless, final responsibility for the Church's liturgical life can hardly be withdrawn from the ordained ministry either theologically or practically. The Reformed conception of the ordained minister as one who by calling, gifts, and training is designated to serve liturgically on behalf of the congregation is still a valid conception;[5] and any ecumenical synthesis of Protestant and Catholic principles upon which union of the churches can take place will have to include the leadership of the minister as preacher and priest.[6] Practically speaking, in most congregations in the foreseeable future, the clergyman will normally be responsible for worship; and because his vocation and function will continue to be liturgical, responsibility for the integrity of worship is bound up with the integrity of ministry itself.

In a more personal sense, the minister also functions as a liturgical theologian because he is not a disembodied, angelic being, let us hope, but a fully human person who is not exempt and who does not want to be exempt from the vicissitudes and sins that beset his people, and who, in identifying with his people, learns ever more deeply of the grace God liturgically ministers through his selfhood. As a minister he is a man representatively set apart, but he is never a man set aloof.[7] Rather, he is a *theatron*, in St. Paul's phrase,

[3] See Ernst Käsemann, "Ministry and Community in the New Testament," in *Essays on New Testament Themes*, trans., W. J. Montague (London: SCM Press, 1964).

[4] See chs. VII, VIII.

[5] Typically, the *Directory* of the Presbyterian Church, U.S.A., reads: "Those ordained to the ministry of word and sacraments have entrusted to them the direction and leading of public worship." 1, 4.

[6] See Reuel L. Howe, "Theological Education and the Image of the Ministry," *The Making of Ministers*, ed. Keith R. Bridston and Dwight W. Culver (Minneapolis: Augsburg Publishing House, 1964), p. 219. Significantly, the statement on ministry of the Consultation on Church Union speaks of "the particular responsibility" of the ordained clergyman as follows: "In the worship and life of the Church the ordained ministers serve a representative function, voicing the prayers and eucharistic joy of God's people, administering the sacraments, and by God's Spirit speaking God's Word to his Church and to the world." *Digest* (Princeton, N. J.: Consultation on Church Union, Apr., 1961), III, 23.

[7] See R. E. C. Browne, *The Ministry of the Word* (London: SCM Press, 1958), p. 12.

a spectacle of a man—typical, vulnerable, mortal, bound in the same human predicament all men know but who experiences in his predicament the grace that saves and so can announce to his people the grace that can save them.[8] The confession he leads in public he has himself sorrowed over in private. The word of judgement he preaches to other men has already been heard in his own soul. The demons whose casting out he proclaims have not been alien to the inmost chamber of his own being. The hunger and thirst after righteousness met with the wine of Communion have parched his own lips. Luther once put this truth well: "I did not learn my theology all at once, but I had to search deeper for it, where my temptations took me. A theologian is born by living, nay dying, and being damned, not by thinking, reading, or speculating." [9] The pastor as liturgical theologian will understand that. His own damnations and resurrections, his vicissitudes and sorrows are those of all men, and in personally bearing these, liturgical theology becomes forged in the crucible of his own selfhood. It was said of the prayers of Endicott Peabody, the late headmaster of Groton School, that they lacked the reality of the prayers of Walter Rauschenbush because Peabody had never ministered—as had Rauschenbush—in the slums of New York's Hell's Kitchen.[10] One need not romantically seek out crucifixions to verify this truth. The equivalent of Hell's Kitchen is always there, and the note of theological reality will always sound through the pastor's liturgical ministry if he is willing to be vulnerable to it.

But not only in his identification with the human predicament, in his experience of God's grace also—indeed in his very embodiment of that grace—he may learn what it is to be a liturgical theologian. For surely the person of a man can be a "means of grace" as much as the water of Baptism or the bread of Communion. And try as we will to avoid it, and however inadmissible we may allege this way of conceiving ministry to be, the witness of grace in the minister's own character conditions his liturgical ministry as all else. Traditionally, of course, theology has declared in varying ways that ultimately the efficacy of ministry does not depend upon the grace of the minister. The Church has classically stated this position by saying that the efficacy of the Sacrament is not made or unmade by the person of him who administers it;[11] and as a way of affirming the objectivity, the sovereignty,

---

[8] I Cor. 4:9. See Daniel Jenkins, *The Gift of Ministry* (London: Faber & Faber, 1947), pp. 57 ff.

[9] Quoted by Erik H. Erikson, *Young Man Luther* (New York: W. W. Norton, 1962), p. 251.

[10] See Horton Davies, "The Expression of the Social Gospel in Worship," *Studia Liturgica*, II (Sept., 1963).

[11] See the Westminster Confession (Larger and Shorter Catechism), ch. 27, par. 3: "The grace which is exhibited in or by the sacraments rightly used is not conferred by

and the unconditioned freedom of God's grace, this will always be true. Yet, however valid this may be in theory, "it is all too true in fact that the minister is the congregation's way of access to God. His whole life is dedicated to revealing the mysteries of God to the world. We have only to look to the congregations of the Church today which are moribund to know that it depends on him whether the Holy Spirit is moving through the life of the people. The existence of a holy people . . . is within his hands." [12] Clearly, while the ministerial office as such does not give the pastor title to more virtue than any other man, functionally his calling requires him to be a man of grace; and the meaning which worship holds for his people cannot be abstracted from his person and character. To contend that the kind of man people experience the pastor to be and that the example he sets for them is of no consequence for worship is impossible. In the blunt words of Herbert Farmer: "It is of consequence, and it ought to be of consequence." [13]

If this be true, then the question of the relation of the pastor's function as liturgical theologian to the liturgical quality of his life must also be faced. The degree to which he identifies with his people, as we have said, speaks in part to this question, for such identification is to be understood as his priesthood, the intercessory living out in daily life of the priesthood he exercises at the altar. This perhaps is what the Roman Church means in saying of her priests: "They are to be aided to live the liturgical life and to share it with the faithful entrusted to their care";[14] or in the words of a British free

---

any power in themselves: neither does the efficacy of a sacrament depend upon the piety or the intention of him that doth administer it, but upon the work of the Spirit and the word of institution." It should be pointed out that this article was in part a polemical reaction against the corruption and crude externalism of Roman Catholic worship and, as all polemics, exaggerates the truth. See also Article XXVI of the Thirty-nine Articles of the Anglican Church.

[12] Alfred R. Shands, *The Liturgical Movment and the Local Church* (rev. ed.; New York: Morehouse-Barlow, 1965), p. 60. Daniel Jenkins has also written: "The personal factor cannot be left out when considering the ministry's functioning within the Church, because God's Word is a personal Word addressed by persons to persons on the most self-conscious and responsible, that is to say the most personal, level of their existence." (*The Gift of Ministry*, p. 74). And Josef A. Jungmann, quoting Karl Rahner, writes in his volume on preaching, *Announcing the Word of God* (London: Burns & Oates, 1967), p. 30: "If the concept of the Church is not to evaporate into an abstract ideal of an invisible Church, then there can be no dogma which states that the assistance of the Holy Spirit, always present in the Church, restricts the influence of human sinfulness in the leadership of the Church to their private lives, keeping quite unsullied that activity which has to be unequivocally described as the action of the Church." Rahner, "*Die Kirche in der Sunder*," in *Stimmen der Zeit*, CXL 1947), p. 170.

[13] *The Servant of the Word* (Philadelphia: Fortress Press, 1964), p. 69.

[14] Walter M. Abbott, S.J., ed., *The Documents of Vatican II*, "Constitution on the Sacred Liturgy" (New York: Guild Press, America Press, Association Press, 1966), p. 145.

churchman of a generation ago: "It is by men of grace that Christ spreads and confirms His grace in men." [15] However it be said, let it be understood that the minister is a man for others. He is to be a eucharistic man whose life, like the bread and wine of Communion, is broken and poured out, and he only does in his conduct of worship what he does all the time. Through his person and presence, whether in pulpit or marketplace, before the altar or amidst the multitudes, a liturgy is being performed in which men can meet God and God can meet man; and out of this liturgy can come the reflection that can make him a true liturgical theologian.[16]

But liturgical thinking rises out of liturgical praying as well as liturgical living. For the minister personally as for the Church corporately, *lex orandi*, the discipline of prayer, precedes *lex credendi*, the discipline of believing and reflecting. For it is assumed that the minister prays in private as in public; otherwise he is no minister, and we should be unreservedly clear on this point. However true the dialectic may be that to labor is to pray, as to pray is to labor, action and prayer are different modes of Christian existence, and it is the pastor's métier to know the difference as well as the unity between them. He will live in the truth of a spirituality which affirms the reality of communion with the divine in all his existence, yes; but he cannot be faithless to the mind of him who rose up a great while before day and departed into a solitary place and there prayed. And it is precisely out of the relation of his private life of prayer to his public ministry of worship that flows the grace that enables the pastor to function as liturgical theologian.

Is it the nature of preaching he would theologically reflect upon? Then the truth will come home to him that what he does when he is not making sermons is what gives his sermons life; that—as Bonhoeffer put it—he is claimed to speak to Christ about a brother more than to a brother about Christ; that what he is doing when he privately speaks with God for men is what enables him publicly to speak to men for God. Or is it the relation of liturgy to his congregation's life in the world? Then theological truth will emerge from the intensity and imagination with which he holds in intercessory prayer the lives of his people dispersed in their tasks in the world, as well as the world itself, and from the intercessory concern his people feel in him as they gather under his leadership to worship on Sunday. Or is the theological question the minister would grapple with the question of the nature of God, of the way the modern man is able or unable to think of

---

[15] P. T. Forsyth, *The Church and the Sacraments* (London: Longmans, Green & Co., 1917), p. 133.

[16] In a church in Annapolis, Maryland, the cloth covering the tabernacle on the altar has embroidered on it the words: "Make me Your bread, Lord. Break me up, and pass me around."

God, indeed whether he can honestly name the name "God"? The minister's discipline of prayer will be decisive in that he will be able to speak with truthfulness about God only insofar as he has spoken with God. The minister who takes prayer seriously will not find it difficult to take liturgical theology seriously. Indeed, he has already gone further toward becoming a liturgical theologian than he may know.

THE RELATION OF THEOLOGY TO LITURGY

Still further, the pastor inevitably functions as liturgical theologian because of the reciprocal relation between theology and liturgy. We have previously touched on this relation in referring to the doctrine of the Church, but let us try to restate it in a more fundamental and comprehensive way. Our starting point is the truth that the character of worship is largely derived from the character of the God who is believed in, and that the way in which we conceive God and the way we elucidate his relation with man determine our worship. The God of faith is simultaneously the God of thought and the God of devotion. Dogma—whether sophisticated or naïve—inevitably determines cultus. As man believes and thinks, so he prays. "Worship is not a happy ignorance, but a *reasonable* service,'" it has been written.[17] It is acted-out commentary upon thoughtful belief, and true belief is a condition of true devotion.

Accordingly, because worship thus embodies "theological declaration," our conception of God and its implications for worship must be stated as clearly as possible; and the task of Christian theology therefore is to impart to worship substance, purpose, and—to considerable degree—a form consistent with belief in God deriving from Christian revelation. In this sense theology may be said to exercise a genitive, critical, and conservative function toward liturgy: genitive in the sense that theological statements of the Christian understanding of God can bring to birth man's liturgical communion with God; critical in the sense that theology must distinguish truth from untruth in light of the Christian revelation of God in all its implications; and conservative in the sense that structures of theological thought—embodied in worship—can save worship from corrupting the Christian vision of God. Thus from one point of view theology exercises an independent and objective function toward liturgy. The theological objection of the Reformers to the medieval Roman Mass as a propitiatory rite classically illustrates this function. Worship as propitiation embodied a conception of God whose grace is won by man's works rather than as one whose grace is received by

[17] Roger Hazelton, *The God We Worship* (New York: The Macmillan Co., 1946), p. 6.

86

faith; and the Reformers' insight into theological truth could not tolerate liturgical error.

But the reverse is also true, and often more true than theologians will recognize or concede: liturgy underlies theology and performs something of the same genitive, critical, and conservative function toward theology as theology does toward liturgy. To be sure, the relation is always reciprocal, as we have said, and the truth of a sentence of P. T. Forsyth must always be borne in mind: "True Christian prayer must have theology in it, no less than true theology must have prayer in it. . . . Prayer and theology must interpenetrate to keep each other great." [18] Yet if one were to assign precedence to theology or liturgy, a strong case can be made for saying that liturgy is more fundamental. Historically, for one thing, Christian "theology" in the early centuries was subsumed under the category of "praise" and "liturgy." [19] Forms of worship were not devised by drawing liturgical inferences from theological statements; rather, theology only codified, as it were, the meanings of liturgical experience and stated conceptually what the Church in her worship had found to be the truth existentially. The creeds, for example, were first formulated and employed in connection with the Church's worship, and their heavy Christological emphasis only underscored in a symbolic way what Christians had found God in their experience of Jesus Christ to mean.

But this sequence was the case historically because it is first the case ontologically and phenomenologically. The action of man experiencing and doing something is prior to his reflection upon it. Of course, theological reflection can be a vital form of action; and rationality, let us hope, is part of man's psyche! Nevertheless, imagination, feeling, the action of the body and the putting forth of the will which characterize worship are more elemental modes of apprehending and expressing reality than is thought.[20] The relation of poetry to philosophy as understood by the late philosopher of religion Charles Bennett provides an analogy here. Always these must go hand in hand, but it is the poet who first catches the music of the spheres, and then the philosopher tries to fit words to the music.[21] The relation

[18] *The Soul of Prayer* (London: Independent Press, 1916), p. 78.

[19] For example, see Jean Leclercq, O.S.B., "Theology and Prayer," *Encounter*, XXIV (Summer, 1963).

[20] Gerhard van der Leeuw writes: "There is no basis for doing what theology might perhaps wish to do, and give words an exclusive or even a preferred position in the relationship of man to the 'other,' in the religious sense. . . . Words do not even represent the original form of human expression. For the first word was a gesture. . . . Gesture is not only . . . an elucidation of the word, but is its predecessor. . . . The words are secondary." *Sacred and Profane Beauty*, trans. David E. Green (Apex ed.; Nashville: Abingdon Press, 1963), p. 124.

[21] Noted by Bernard E. Meland in *Modern Man's Worship* (New York: Harper

between worship and theology is of this kind: worship also first catches the music of divine meaning, and only then can theology take up its conceptual and linguistic task. Accordingly, one must say that in its genitive function liturgy makes theology possible; it brings theology into being; it is theology's ontological ground.[22] It is also genitive in that it can infuse into theology a vitality and immediacy that otherwise may not be present. Theological statements are different after they have been liturgically rendered from what they were before. They become existential rather than intellectual statements.[23]

Liturgy also exercises a critical and conservative function toward theology in that it submits theological statements to the test of experience and confirms truth and exposes error in a way not otherwise possible. For example, when theology exaggerates the transcendence of God as "wholly Other," liturgy replies with its experience of a God whose presence is closer than hands or feet, than seeing or breathing. Or when theology affirms, as in certain sects, that God as pure spirit dispenses with sensuous media in his approach to his creatures, liturgical experience overwhelmingly answers with its sacraments and its song. Or when theology finds itself in controversy with certain heretical foes, such as Gnostics or Arians, Pelagians or Deists, liturgy rises up—as under Hilary and Ambrose and Luther and Wesley— and composes hymns to confound the enemy and to confirm the faithful. Melanchthon once said, parenthetically, that when the Church's music ceases to sound, doctrine will disintegrate; Bucer held that the Church is built around the hymn; and a Jesuit complained that Luther's hymns had damned more souls than all Luther's sermons put together! In fact, a study of the Church's liturgical music often provides a truer understanding of the Church's mind than a study of the formal writings of her theologians. If one would understand the Methodist doctrine of Holy Communion, for example, or the Puritan doctrine of *sola scriptura*, one can hardly do better than to study the hymns of Charles Wesley or Isaac Watts.

In short, the living nerve of theology is touched in liturgy, and as the parish pastor conceives, plans, and conducts worship with his people, he has an unexcelled opportunity to match theology against experience, and from experience to apprehend theology.

& Bros., 1934), p. 208.

[22] Alexander Schmemann writes: "Liturgical tradition is . . . the ontological condition of theology . . . because it is in the Church, of which the *leitourgia* is the expression and the life, that *the sources of theology are functioning as precisely 'sources.'* " "Theology and Liturgical Tradition," in *Worship, Scripture, and Tradition,* ed. Massey H. Shepherd, Jr. (New York: Oxford University Press, 1963), p. 175. Italics mine.

[23] See Vilmos Vajta, "Creation and Worship," *Studia Liturgica,* II (Mar., 1963).

But if the pastor should welcome the opportunity to think theologically about liturgy, the theologian should also welcome the opportunity to think liturgically about theology. In making this point we are indulging in a detour from the main argument of this essay and addressing a parenthesis to those whose vocation is distinctively that of theologian. But the question as to why so relatively few Protestant theologians have given to liturgy the attention they have paid to other areas of the Church's life is a critical one. The contrast between the God presented to us in much theological writing and the God we know in the actual experience of worship is often bewildering if not shattering. It seems not to be understood that God becomes real as an object of truthful knowledge only insofar as he is an object of devotion at the same time, and that a God who can be worshipped is as necessary to any adequate theology as a believable God is necessary to authentic worship.[24]

Further, one may ask whether theologians sufficiently understand how worship offers promising directions for dealing with a number of fundamental problems claiming our attention today—the truth and authority of Scripture, the nature and mission of the Church, the problem of helping the modern man apprehend the reality of the transcendent, and problems in Christology and soteriology. It has been pointed out, for example, that Scripture needs the commentary of liturgy if it is to be understood; it cannot be taken *sola scripta* if it would yield its fullest meaning. A Roman Catholic scholar has written that "the Word can never be rightly understood apart from . . . [liturgical] celebration. The reading of the Scripture that takes place in the framework of the Mass is not merely one among many types of reading the divine Word: it is the chief and fundamental type, to which all the others refer as their norm." [25] Surely the Protestant can respond to this insight and sense its implications for the congregation on the one hand and for biblical studies in a seminary on the other. Indeed it may be that the credibility of Scripture can only be renewed for the modern man in something of the same way in which the letters and gospels of the New Testament came to be experienced as true by the primitive and apostolic Church. There is little doubt that the original New Testament documents were formulated in response to the Church's liturgical needs, and that they are to be understood not simply as history or literature but as liturgy. Today, hardly less than originally, the inmost meaning of Scripture is best rendered within a "cult context."

[24] See Hazelton, *The God We Worship*, pp. 13, 158.
[25] Louis Bouyer, *Liturgical Piety* (Notre Dame, Ind.: University of Notre Dame Press, 1955), pp. 30-31. See also Alan Richardson, *An Introduction to the Theology of the New Testament* (London: SCM Press, 1958), p. 387.

Problems in Christology likewise are most susceptible of solution when approached liturgically. The Christological question, "What think ye of Christ?" can never be resolved in a liturgical vacuum.[26] The closing words of Vincent Taylor's study of *The Person of Christ* put the point well:

This investigation has shown repeatedly how worship, as well as reflection, has prompted the greatest Christian affirmations. Throughout the centuries worship has opened the eyes of men to truth concerning Christ. . . . We do not first discover who Christ is and then believe in Him; we believe in Him and then discover who He is. . . . The penalty of treating the Person of Christ as a purely intellectual problem is that He remains an enigma.[27]

It may well be that advances in rethinking and restating the meaning of Jesus Christ in our day will only be made insofar as we recapitulate the experience of the early Church, and in worship submit our minds to the truth which he uniquely imparts in his own appointed rites of fellowship, proclamation, and meal. A belief in Jesus Christ as divine, for example, a "scandal" to the modern man, is more likely to take on meaning through worship than in any other way, as indeed it originally became real to men in the post-Easter worship of the primitive Church.[28] Oscar Cullmann sums up our conviction: as the "great perception that Jesus rules as the present Lord over his Church, over the world, over the life of each individual . . . was given to the first Christians in *common worship*, above all in the common meals," so we shall likely find that "the main root of New Testament Christology is this experience in worship of Jesus as the present Lord." [29]

In his study of medieval Catholic piety, Henry Adams reports a charming legend that speaks to all who are concerned for the relation of liturgy and theology. Fra Egidio, one of the little brothers of St. Francis, was assailed by a most learned theologian with an array of profound propositions. The arguments were mighty, the logic seemingly relentless. The little brother withheld his reply until his opponent's position was fully laid out, with all its threatening implications ready like arrows to be launched at their target.

---

[26] See Roger Hazelton, *How May Protestant Worship Become Ecumenical?* (New York: Federal Council of Churches, 1947).

[27] (London: Macmillan & Co., 1958), pp. 305-6.

[28] See Raymond E. Brown, S.J., *Jesus God and Man* (Milwaukee: Bruce Publishing Co., 1967), p. 34.

[29] *The Christology of the New Testament*, trans. Shirley Guthrie and Charles A. M. Hall (Philadelphia: Westminster Press, 1959), p. 320. Dietrich Bonhoeffer, in his class-room lectures on Christology, would tell his students: "We must study Christology in the humble silence of the worshipping community." *Christ the Center*, trans. John Bowden (New York: Harper & Row, 1966), p. 27.

Then, taking a flute from the folds of his robe, he played out his theological answer in sacred song! [30]

A THEOLOGICAL CRITIQUE OF THE CATEGORY OF "WORTHSHIP"

Having defined terms in a preliminary way, and having described the pastor's calling as liturgical theologian, we now undertake a fuller statement of the substantive meaning of theological integrity. Our thought will proceed through a series of four concentric circles, narrowing down to what we believe to be the core of the matter. We shall examine in turn the category of "worth" and its etymological connection with "worthship," which, it is widely held, best serves as the point of departure for construing the meaning of Christian worship; the category of "Tradition" in its manifold meanings; the category of "Church"; the doctrine of the Trinity; and finally the Christological understanding of worship summarized in the term "Word." The points of view symbolized by the first four circles all hold truth, but the ultimate truth—in whose light they are seen to be proximate—resides in the Word; and this category will be implicit throughout our discussion as the foil against which all else is to be tested.

To begin with, the dictum widely heard that theological reflection should start with the definition of Christian worship as man's recognition of the "supreme worth of God" must be examined. The word "worship" is said to stem from the word "worthship," and worship accordingly is defined as the acknowledgement of God as supreme value and the ascription of supreme worth to him. Entire theologies—or one should more accurately say, philosophies—of worship are built upon this proposition, and up to a point this is a reliable way of thinking. Christian thought certainly acknowledges God's worth and the values in human life in which his worth immanently manifests itself. It also recognizes the incurable hunger of the human soul for that in God which satisfies man's craving for value. We remember the call of the Psalmist, "Give unto the Lord the glory *due* unto his name," and the song of Revelation, "*Worthy* is the Lamb to receive honor and glory and blessing." Yet the frame of discourse set by this term can mislead us because it does not correspond to the deepest meanings of biblical revelation; and when taken as the primary rather than as a derivative point of departure, it distorts thinking.

For one thing, the category of value in biblical thought is secondary to the categories of being, decision, and action. The Word which addresses man in worship embodies nothing less than divine Reality on which man's

[30] *Mont Saint Michel and Chartres* (Boston: Houghton Mifflin, 1904), p. 338.

being depends, and it confronts him with no less fateful a decision than that on which depends his deliverance from death into life. It bears an "either-or" character, and to conceive within the category of worth such a momentous transaction for the human soul as that which the Word proposes cannot do justice to the *logos theou* which was from the beginning, and to the decision of faith and obedience to this Word on which man's fate depends. The Word which encounters man in worship would bring him into a new order of existence. It would set before him life and death, light and darkness, blessing and cursing, with no less fateful a choice at stake than his eternal destiny. Liturgical encounter with this Word is clearly more than an exercise in discriminating and identifying value, and the fatefulness of this encounter cannot be contained within reflection resting on a dictionary etymology of verbal meanings.

Further, worship conceived as the recognition and ascription of supreme worth to God does not of itself necessarily have anything to do with the particularity of Christian revelation. And one suspects that it is the popularity of this conception which explains why much Protestant worship has become detached from its uniquely Christian foundations and corrupted into a humanistic affirmation of values, the simple celebration of life, mystical naturalism, aestheticism, and so on. Actually, worship defined as the ascription of supreme worth to God can apply to the dance of the sun worshipper or the prayer wheel of the Oriental, to the rites of a mystery cult or the thought of the philosopher, as well as to the prayer of the Christian. This is not to say that each of these may not be valid worship in its own way. It is to say that they are not, by definition, Christian. One does well to ponder a remark of Karl Barth that he whom the Christian names "God" is not to be regarded as a continuation and enrichment of the ideas which usually constitute religious thought in general about God: "He is not to be found in the pantheon of human piety." [31] The Word biblically understood does not tolerantly offer itself as one option among others in a pantheon of values. Rather, the Word consists of an event of supernatural significance which happened once and only once, in which God has acted toward man in a way in which he has acted nowhere else, and by means of a particular history which the worshipper must relive if he would know his true destiny. The Word, writes one scholar, "is a tree that has grown in the Holy Land and not a rosy glow in the atmosphere of the soul. Salvation is of the Jews." [32] It is precisely the recital of, and engagement with, a

[31] *Dogmatics in Outline*, trans. G. T. Thompson (Torchbook ed.; New York: Harper & Row, 1959), p. 36.

[32] Amos Wilder, *Otherworldliness and the New Testament* (London: SCM Press, 1955), p. 80.

particular history bound up with a particular Jew, in a particular land, at a particular time, that is the basis of Christian worship.

When made the systematizing theme for theological reflection, the category of worth can also bleach worship of the sense of mystery and adoration classically signified by the phrase "the holy," partly because this category implies that the initiative in worship lies with man. On this view, it is man who "recognizes" and "ascribes" worth. The holiness of God revealed in the Word, on the other hand, consists precisely in its initiatory and overwhelming character. God is the first agent in Christian worship, not man. Always, of course, the agency of God and the agency of man are correlative, as we shall explore in later essays; but if any agent is to assign or ascribe worth, it is God who ascribes worth to man rather than man to God. It is precisely the divine initiative undertaking to reconcile the world while we were dead in our trespasses and sins that becomes recapitulated in worship and evokes the Christian's wonder.

Still further, the anthropocentrism implicit in conceiving worship within the category of worth inevitably blurs the discontinuity between the creature and the Creator, between man and God, which Christian worship is obliged to stress. Of course, up to a point the values man generally cherishes in his experience are to be thought of as intimations of the divine; indeed they can mark and convey the divine immanence; and worship fails if it does not make connection with them. Thus a dialectic of continuity and discontinuity must be understood as operating in both the experience of worship and in our reflection upon it, as we shall need to note from time to time. Yet, Christian worship is not an exercise in escalating human values until one encounters God, nor is it simply the identifying of a supreme value amidst all other human values and calling it God. On the contrary, Christian worship presupposes a fundamental discontinuity—as well as a continuity—between man and God; and it rests upon the affirmation that the divine reality which deals with us in Jesus Christ is, in an important sense, radically different from any other kind of reality with which it is possible for man to be in relation. Christian thought has described the worshipper in this respect as being possessed by a sense of the sheer "Godness of God." [33] This tautology, strange to ears untrained to the mystical and enraptured with only what is human, may seem irrational. But so far from being irrational, it actually "signifies a meaning which any attempt to describe it in other

[33] See Herbert H. Farmer, *Revelation and Religion* (New York: Harper & Bros., 1954), p. 50. See also the essay by T. F. Torrance, "Come Creator Spirit," in *Liturgical Renewal in the Christian Churches*, ed. Michael J. Taylor (Baltimore: Helicon Press, 1967).

terms would immediately falsify," [34] because the essentially unique nature of God ultimately transcends any human language we can use about him.

To be sure, Christian worship is much more than irrational abasement before the discontinuous and the numinous; yet without the element of the irrational—or perhaps we should say, nonrational—and of the numinous, there is no true worship.[35] And one authentic mark of the Word is exactly that it confronts man in the aspect of "otherness" and "discontinuity," as well as of resemblance and affinity. It outruns our human experience even as it meets us in our experience. The unknowableness of the Word is correlative with its knowableness. Indeed we cannot speak of the "revelation" given in the Word without having to assume as the very ground of our speech that there is that which is unrevealed. "It is because God is so infinitely above the world that His coming down into the world is so wonderful," [36] it has been written; and the recapitulation of this "coming" and this "wonder"—which is very near the heart of Christian worship—the category of worth is unable to provide.

Now such language-terms as "coming," "above," and "down" are not, of course, to be taken literally, although to some people even their symbolic meaning will be offensive; and the objections commonly voiced to thinking of God as "up there" or "beyond" or "out there" make a helpful if rather obvious point. Yet one cannot eliminate such language from the gospels and still have the Gospel, for the language of distance and descent is a metaphorical way of pointing to the occurrence of *a radical event which transcended all human possibilities.*[37] Transcendence thus understood is very near the core of the Gospel, and such transcendence the category of worth is in the last analysis unable to convey. One can therefore understand how the influence of this category in much Protestant worship has contributed to the loss of a sense of the mystery and glory of God, of "God in his Godness," and the substitution instead of commerce with God as divine pal, soft father, or ethical fellow-partner. To the extent that scholars, pastors, and congregations have so uncritically absorbed ways of thinking bound up with worship understood as "worthship," much Protestant worship has become flabby rather than holy, folksy rather than numinous, hortatory rather than adoring, feminine more than masculine, and one is not surprised that it often appeals to infantile elements in human personality.

[34] *Ibid.*
[35] See D. H. Hislop, *Our Heritage in Public Worship* (Edinburgh: T. & T. Clark, 1935), pp. 285-86.
[36] Edwyn Bevan, *Symbolism and Belief* (Boston: Beacon Press, 1957), p. 76.
[37] See Reginald H. Fuller, *The Foundations of New Testament Christology* (New York: Charles Scribner's Sons, 1965), pp. 255-56.

LITURGICAL INTEGRITY AND TRADITION

A second viewpoint from which to think about worship, the category of "tradition" to which we now turn, holds a variety of meanings which must be carefully distinguished. We may begin by asking: what images come to the pastoral mind when the word "tradition" is flashed before us, and what inferences for worship may we draw therefrom? "The dead hand of . . ." one can immediately hear someone replying, or "my black leather Service Book" from another. For others the term "tradition" will evoke memories of frustrated efforts to persuade a congregation to sing hymn tunes other than "traditional" ones or to be hospitable to new ways of worship. To others "tradition" will mean recollections of a denominational assembly in which impassioned speakers pled with the brethren to be faithful to "the traditions of our fathers." Just possibly, however, "tradition" may recall a volume of church history or theology we have read, or an ecumenical service of worship we have shared in when "traditions"—plural—became gathered up into "Tradition"—singular—and a feeling for the broad, eternal-flowing stream of the Church's life swept over us. In short, a word association test would probably reveal three concentric circles of meaning which the term "tradition" holds for us: the more or less prejudiced traditions of the local congregation; the wider circle of denominational or national loyalties; and the still larger circle of the apostolic witness of the centuries of faith.[38]

A disconcerting fact emerges from this fanciful word test, however: most congregations—and pastors?—reverse the true order of the claims of tradition. Whereas Tradition in the ecumenical and apostolic sense ought to have first claim upon our minds, it usually comes last; and whereas our parochial or denominational loyalties ought to matter least—such as the singing of that favorite hymn or our psychological bondage to our denominational service book—they actually loom largest. Tradition too often suggests the customary way in which a parish serves Holy Communion more than it suggests the Apostles' Creed of all Christendom; or it suggests our Methodist or Presbyterian emphasis upon the preaching of the Word rather than, let us say, a sense of the Communion of Saints.

Now it is the largest meaning of the term "tradition" that speaks to the quest for liturgical integrity. The lesser meanings are not unimportant, as we shall note shortly, but it is Tradition—singular—understood as a universal, not a parochial reality, and as a living, not a dead thing, that speaks to liturgical integrity. Tradition is the mind of the Church universal, illumined by the Holy Spirit, investing the event of Christ the Word with interpretation

---

[38] I am indebted to David H. C. Read for this analysis. See "The Reformation of Worship," *The Scottish Journal of Theology*, VIII (1955), pp. 76 ff.

and meaning, and transmitting the continuing life of the Word through forms which declare that meaning.[39] Understood in this sense, Tradition is not a static or conservative principle but a reality of creative power which partakes of the life-giving power of the Word itself. As such it reminds us of a truth which those of us concerned for the primacy of a Christological understanding of worship must not ignore: that the Word is never proclaimed without nor uninterpreted by Tradition; it is known only through the community of faith—the Church; and it cannot be experienced in naked immediacy. In any experience of the Word, Tradition is always present and interposes itself as the medium of encounter, whether as history, as the Church, as a rite, as a written or spoken word, or as an image in the mind. In this sense Tradition may be thought of as the living manifestation of God's ongoing revelation itself, in something of the same way in which the Church may be thought of as a form of the Word's continuous self-revelation. Understood as a process or principle of perpetual incarnation, Tradition is inescapable, and liturgy belittles Tradition at the peril of disowning the source of its very life.

It is on this level of understanding that the attack on liturgical tradition mounted by certain radical theologians today is to be met. One can, indeed one must, appreciate the reasons for this attack: the loss of a sense of history caused by the unprecedented speed of change; man's alleged "coming of age" and the transferring to theology of the psychological motif of "repudiation-of-the-father"; the influence of existentialism which collapses faith into the present moment of decision; the impact of futurist-oriented theologies; and not least the Church's corruption of authentic "memory" into sentimental nostalgia and her refusal to retool her ideas and recast her images.[40] Clearly, liturgical theology will identify these signs of the times, and others, and will gladly learn from them.

But equally, liturgical theology will not be cowed by those who arbitrate the question of tradition only out of their own contemporary sensibilities. The man who would live only out of the "now" is surely as immature as he

---

[39] See A. G. Hebert, *Liturgy and Society* (London: Faber & Faber, 1935), pp. 224 ff. Tradition has also been defined by David G. Buttrick as "the whole body of churchly event and word from the time of Christ to the present." See his essay, "Renewal of Worship—A Source of Unity?" in *Ecumenism, The Spirit and Worship,* ed., Leonard Swidler (Pittsburgh: Duquesne University Press, 1967), p. 223. Dietrich Ritschl defines tradition as follows: "The various expressions of the Church's attempts to see her own past and present in the light of the presence of Christ, manifest in writings, liturgies and indirectly in forms of art, are the *tradition* of the Church." *Memory and Hope* (New York: The Macmillan Co., 1967), p. 64.

[40] See Gabriel Fackre, *Humiliation and Celebration* (New York: Sheed & Ward, 1969), chs. V, VI, VIII.

who would regress into the past; and after all, amnesia is a worse sickness than nostalgia. Man does not live by the present alone, neither does he live by the future alone, and to reject tradition is simply to dismember the self. As memory is necessary to the sanity of personality, so tradition sustains the collective personality of a people. But most of all, to reject Tradition as we have defined it is to sin against the Holy Spirit as it ever illumines the mind of the Church and invests the Event of Jesus Christ with meaning. The Spirit is as much the source of continuity, of order, and of heritage as it is of newness and freedom; and it is this truth which those who reject tradition conveniently ignore. Present-tense or future-tense theologies cannot be permitted to stake out a monopoly on the doctrine of the Spirit. The Spirit's reality is to be marked as much by what it has done as by what it is doing or shall do; and out of its richness the wise man brings forth treasures both new and old.

An understanding of tradition in this substantive sense also requires us to appreciate how traditional forms—what we have called the language of worship—can enhance worship's truth and power. However, we need to distinguish here two levels of "traditional" language: what has been described as "last year's language" whose truthfulness is self-evidently impaired, and "last milennium's language" which, while archaic, must be resmelted and respoken in the experience of the present.[41] To the former belong such forms as "yesterday's pulpit oratory," "the Emersonian meditation," the sticky anthem, the Sallman "Jesus," the fake Gothic architecture, perhaps the "Thees" and "Thous," the "didsts" and "wasts," of traditional prayer. "Millennial" language, on the other hand, denotes the master images, the visceral symbols and dynamic patterns from the past which, as Denis de Rougemont has remarked, preform those inner movements of our sensibility without which we cannot psychically or spiritually survive. Traditional forms thus understood usually possess an archetypal power and make an archetypal appeal to the submerged world of man's instinctual life where response is not so much logical as emotional and evocative; and they thereby invest the Word with meaning it would not otherwise have. As symbols which successive generations have found to speak with primitive power, they evoke depths in our nature we share with every other man. The formula of the Trinity, for example, seems to appeal to an ineffaceable tendency in the human psyche to apprehend meaning in a triune form. The aspects of eating and drinking in the Eucharist engage man's most primal appetites, and the profound water-symbolism of Baptism appeals to something aboriginal in man's

---

[41] See Amos Wilder, *The New Voice* (New York: Herder & Herder, 1969).

nature.[42] Precisely because such traditional forms possess a certain "anthropological plentitude" in their appeal to man's nature, they are not peculiar to Christianity alone but universally operate as man's intuitive way of symbolically apprehending the inmost nature of the reality with which he feels his destiny to be bound. The universal image of the God-Man, for example, is probably at least five thousand years old, and the universal symbol of the trinity may be even older.[43] Likewise such motifs as the sacred hero struggling with adversaries, the rhythms of life and death and of light and darkness, the images of marriage feasts, of breath as figuring spirit, of fire, of fatherhood and childhood, hold prototypal religious meanings.

Again, traditional forms often possess a timeless eloquence and beauty exceeding our own inventive powers. When the Christian man contemplates human mortality in light of God's eternity and would declare his faith against death, he can hardly improve upon Isaac Watts's text, "O God Our Help in Ages Past." The prayer of General Thanksgiving from the Book of Common Prayer is probably unsurpassable as an expression of Christian thanksgiving and of the motivation of the Christian life as gratitude to God for his grace. And who can excel St. Paul's benediction of the Christian peace which passes all understanding, or the poet's voice of trust in God's providence in the twenty-third psalm? Traditional forms, to be sure, must sometimes be laid aside temporarily, or reinterpreted; but the Church cannot start de novo in conceiving liturgical forms. Tradition is always present when worship possesses authentic eloquence and vitality.

Bound up with their eloquence is the paradoxical function of traditional forms in relation to time: they have power on the one hand to foster a historical awareness which restrains man from escaping the life of his time and age, and on the other, they can foster a spiritual awareness which delivers him from being too much at home in any time and age. In the last analysis it would seem the Gospel pronounces this to be the meaning of worship: to keep man in the world but to save him from being of the world, simultaneously to involve him in and to detach him from time.

One way to describe this power is to say that traditional forms perform both a stabilizing and liberating function in worship. They stabilize in the sense that they have risen out of the engagement of Christian faith with man's historical life, clothe his devotion in symbols of time and place which

---

[42] See R. S. Lee, *Psychology and Worship* (London: SCM Press, 1955), ch. VI.
[43] See Carl G. Jung, *Psychology and Religion* (New Haven: Yale University Press, 1938), pp. 56 ff. Jung believes, however, that the symbol of quaternity is more fundamental to man's conscious and unconscious life than the trinity, and that the cult of the Virgin in Roman Catholic devotion represents the collective unconscious completing the incomplete triune metaphor with a fourth member. See *ibid.*, p. 76.

orient him to the world, and require him to take seriously history and the world. In short, traditional forms historicize man's consciousness. To be sure, in their stabilizing function, traditional forms can also become demonic, especially as history overtakes their historicization! Frozen into liturgical formulas lasting hundreds, even thousands, of years, they can tyrannize man's soul with sheer archaism, idolatry, and magic against which the Church has no alternative but to rebel again and again. (The iconoclastic controversies of the Church are instructive here.) Yet, because man is a historical being and because the Word is a historical Word, this risk must be accepted if the historicity of the Gospel and the historical character of man's life are to be taken seriously. On the other hand, traditional forms liberate in that they communicate a sense of the timeless as well as the timeful. They can detach man from the immediate and turn his consciousness to things unseen and eternal. They claim him for a life that is more than his historical life. Admittedly, Protestant worship today often corrupts tradition in this sense into a sickly otherworldliness; and one can understand the reaction of those who allege that the Church's worship must stop being concerned so much with the eternal and who accordingly would abandon traditional forms *in toto*. But surely this is overreaction. Because man is a time-transcending as well as a time-immersed creature, and because the Word is both an eternal and a historical reality, the power of traditional forms simultaneously to engage man with time and to liberate him from time must not be underestimated.

To illustrate: the objection often voiced against the strangeness of ancient language must be carefully appraised.[44] This objection may mean that one finds traditional forms totally unreal; in this case they must be abandoned if communication is to take place at all. Yet their very contradiction to man's sensibilities may teach him how he is a creature of time. He listens to the seventeenth century speech of the King James Version of the Bible, let us say. He may react favorably and like it, or he may react unfavorably and prefer a contemporary translation. But in either case he is compelled to expose his sensibilities and to feel and think in terms of some time. In reaction to tradition positively or negatively, he becomes stabilized in time. On the other hand, ancient forms also have power to gather up man's conscious and subconscious mind into the ongoing self-revelation of the Word, and to liberate him to enter into the perspective of the eternal only from within which he can measure the meaning of the things of time. A church architect once made what was intended to be a complimentary remark about a church building done in contemporary style: "It is an un-

[44] For further discussion of this problem, see ch. VI especially, and also chs. III and VII.

usually satisfying building," he said, "one in which the contemporary man can feel entirely at home." Precisely! The power of the traditional as over against the contemporary is just that it can save the Christian man in any time and place from being too much at home, and by doing so locate him in his true home. It refuses to relieve him of the rigor of the Christian pilgrim and to permit him to settle down in Egypt.[45]

The dialectical power of tradition both to deliver man from captivity to time and to engage him with time, is paralleled by its power to lift the worshipper into a sense of communion with the Church universal and eternal and at the same time into an experience of solidarity with the church local and historical. The value of tradition in informing liturgy with integrity in this respect can hardly be exaggerated because worship must always communicate a sense of the universal and corporate if it is authentic. In part, tradition does this by conveying a sense of heritage and by bringing the worshipper to appropriate as his own the devotion of the people of God through the centuries. The prayer of the Church—of our Lord, of St. Paul, of Chrysostom, of Augustine, of Calvin, of Cranmer, of Donne, of Newman, of Rauschenbusch—becomes his prayer. Hymns of Greek patriarchs and German mystics, of Anglican priests and Puritan rebels, of American evangelists and Spanish monks, become his song. But tradition also has power to unite him with the faithful company of God's people beyond time and to gather him with the ten thousand times ten thousand who bow before the throne of the Lamb. In a word, tradition makes real the Communion of Saints, the Church triumphant as well as the Church militant. It uniquely bestows a sense of what T. S. Eliot has called "the backing of the dead." It confirms us in mystical union with all the faithful, living and dead, "from St. Peter and St. Paul"—as Evelyn Underhill whimsically writes—on "down to the last baptized baby." [46] Through tradition, the plentitude and splendor of the Church historical, universal, and eternal is brought home to us.

Yet, fundamental as tradition is, can we say that it is finally decisive for theological integrity in worship? The answer must be "no," because in the

---

[45] Van der Leeuw has a pregnant paragraph on this point: "Liturgy must hold to the ancient. . . . That is no romanticism or love of the archaic, but a means of attaining objectivity. In the sermon, the language of our day is spoken or at least should be. But in the liturgy . . . 'in the Church, the difference between today and yesterday must be done away with; nothing must look as though it has its origin in the present day.' . . . For this reason, when the Church goes out into the world to teach and to preach, she speaks the language of the world. But when she returns to worship and fellowship with God, she speaks the language of the liturgy, in which so many generations already have carried on their conversations with God." *Sacred and Profane Beauty*, p. 111.

[46] *Collected Papers of Evelyn Underhill*, ed. Lucy Menzies (New York: Longmans, Green & Co., 1946), p. 84.

54649

last analysis there is an indissoluble tension between the Word and tradition which cannot be cancelled out, and because a distinction in our thinking between these separate though related realities must always be made. The heart of worship is not tradition; it is Jesus Christ encountering the human soul. This encounter does not take place except through the medium of tradition, as we have said; yet tradition is a proximate, not the ultimate reality. It is witness to the Given; it is not the Given itself. Tradition is the historical flesh in which the Word incarnates itself; yet the flesh is not the Word. Tradition is the mind of the Church investing the Word with meaning and transmitting the life of the Word through that meaning; yet the Word is sovereign over the mind of the Church in a way that the mind of the Church is not sovereign over the Word. Tradition is "an answer to Jesus' whole person and mission"; yet the answer "points beyond itself to him . . . who proves his presence . . . as the resurrected and risen Lord." [47] Thus one theologically suspects and accepts tradition at the same time. One simultaneously says "no" and "yes" to its claim: "yes" because tradition is the inescapable form of the Word's expression; "no" because the Word in its fontal life transcends any form of expression.

Now it is well to remind ourselves that the very making of this judgement upon tradition is itself conditioned by tradition! Even as we assert the sovereignty of Word over tradition, our minds are "traditioned" by understandings of the Word to which we are heir. To get behind tradition to the Word is somewhat like trying to get behind a succession of causes to the first cause. Nevertheless we are not to be relieved from trying, and it is precisely the relief from trying which overreliance upon tradition so beguilingly presents, and which so quickly leads to an idolatrous captivity to something less than the Word itself as normative for liturgical theology. Protestant worship rightly needs to learn—as indeed it is increasingly learning—what Jeames Moffatt a generation ago called "the thrill of tradition," and one is grateful that the liturgical movement has inspired the churches to recover both their respective liturgical traditions and the greater catholic and evangelical Tradition running as a stream through the Church's life. The danger, however, is exactly that we will accept "the thrill" of tradition as a substitute for the numinous presence of the Word, that we shall become so enamored of tradition that the Word itself which makes tradition live is not allowed to grasp us with its sovereign immediacy. The truth of the Word requires us to test and renounce tradition as often as it leads us to accept and cherish it. Here as elsewhere the Word is both the stone which grinds to powder and the foundation stone that is the corner of the temple.

[47]Gunther Bornkamm, *Jesus of Nazareth*, trans. Irene I. McLuskey and Fraser McLuskey, with James M. Robinson (New York: Harper & Row, 1960), p. 21.

101

Thus it is on this fundamental level that the claims of tradition must be judged. On other levels, of course, criticism can also be made. Once tradition is judged to be authoritative, one faces the problem of deciding what stage of tradition one shall designate as normative—the primitive, or the apostolic, or the patristic, or the Reformed—and the problem of sifting out the ecumenical and universal elements from the parochial. The oldest is by no means the most authoritative, and Karl Barth's remark concerning "normativeness" for the form of the Church in general applies also to tradition as normative for liturgy in particular: "The question . . . cannot possibly resolve itself simply into that of conformity with any forms which are earlier in point of time. Reaction in the form of a return to any fathers is ecclesiastical romanticism." [48] Further, tradition is always to be subject to the Holy Spirit as the decisive mode of the Word's self-expression; and while the Spirit cannot be simply equated with the new, as we have said, it yet has a strange way of shattering what were thought to be the most valid forms.[49] But these comments are secondary to our main point: tradition is a penultimate, not the ultimate, reality for worship, and it cannot take the place of the Word. Man's mind cannot be relieved from the strain of offering itself to the Word with as much immediacy as possible. In appraising the meaning of tradition for worship, integrity requires that our minds still be torn by that "holy anxiety" of which we have written and not prematurely settle down into theological sleep.

LITURGICAL INTEGRITY AND THE DOCTRINE OF THE CHURCH

Much of our appraisal of tradition in thinking theologically about worship also applies to our thought about the Church, the third category to which we turn. Previously we have thought of "Church" in relation to the empirical place in which the pastor finds himself, and in relation to the congregation's need of renewal and edification. By "Church" we now mean the doctrinal nature of the Church especially, with its implications for worship. We have of course anticipated this meaning in saying that one cannot inquire into the theological nature of the Church without inquiring into the nature of worship, and in pointing out that the classical Protestant definition of the

[48] *Church Dogmatics*, IV/1, trans. G. W. Bromiley, "The Doctrine of Reconciliation," (Edinburgh: T. & T. Clark, 1956), p. 704.

[49] It has been written of the Society of Friends: "One of the conundrums for the rest of us is how a religious tradition which bears none of the outward marks of the Christian Church—neither creed nor visible sacrament—produces a quality of life which is so essentially sacramental." Eric Fenn, *How Christians Worship* (London: SCM Press, 1942), p. 14.

Church has been a liturgical one: "The visible Church of Christ is a congregation of faithful men, in the which the pure Word of God is preached, and the Sacraments be duly ministered according to Christ's ordinance, in all those things that of necessity are requisite to the same." [50] While we shall need to qualify this definition shortly, here we may say that the Church exists where certain liturgical things are done, and that it does not exist where they are not done.[51] Worship in a profound sense is the mode of the Church's being. However, insofar as this is the case and the Church is to be defined liturgically, then liturgy must also be thought of ecclesiologically. If—as we have previously stated—the Church most truly knows herself in worship, then we must now say that worship most truly knows what it is in relation to the Church.

The doctrine of the Church instructs us in the theology of worship, first, in declaring that worship is something done by the community of faith which precedes what the individual worshipper does. In a conceptual and ontological sense rather than in a time sense, because Christ's action first constitutes the Church (a point to be developed presently), worship is the Church's action before it is the individual's action. Because Christ is the true Celebrant, the Word can only be encountered by the individual through the Body of believers whom the Word has already encountered. Christ's service to his people precedes our service to him. Thus, as St. Paul makes clear, it is only in relation to the Church that Christian worship is possible, and breaches in the Church's fellowship make worship impossible.[52] The "primary liturgical entity" is the Church.[53] Hence we are not allowed to reflect upon worship—nor to conceive and conduct worship—according to our fancy. We are bound by ecclesiological realities, and integrity requires the kind of theological submission to the Church which St. Paul's word concerning Holy Communion enjoined upon the Corinthians: "For I re-

[50] Article XIX of the Thirty-nine Articles of the Church of England, in Philip Schaff, ed., *The Creeds of Christendom* (New York: Harper & Bros., 1877), III, 499.

[51] The Greek ἐκκλησία, from which the English word "Church" derives, originally had this meaning. Karl Ludwig Schmidt's essay on "The Church" in Gerhard Kittel's *Bible Key Words*, trans. and ed. J. R. Coates (London: A. & C. Black, 1950), vol. I, book II, p. 60, has the following quotation: "It is now clear that it [the word Church] must come from κυρικόν which is the common form, current in the 4th century, of the older κυριακόν, and means a place of worship (*Gotteshaus*)."

[52] See I Cor. 11:17 ff. Likewise, the Church conceived as *communio sanctorum*, the communion of the saints or fellowship of believers, "the basic conception of the Reformers," is known as nowhere else in "the sacrament of the altar." "Here is the real starting point, the authentic orientation of the Christian's life in Luther's mind." Paul L. Lehmann, *Ethics in a Christian Context* (New York: Harper & Row, 1963), pp. 63, 65.

[53] The phrase is Romano Guardini's.

103

ceived from the Lord what I also delivered to you, that the Lord Jesus on the night when he was betrayed took bread." (I Cor. 11:23, RSV). The Church "delivers" certain theological things to liturgy which we have no alternative but to "receive."

The precedence of the Church's action over the individual's suggests the next truth the Church delivers: the objectivity of divine reality as the decisive referent for worship and for thought about worship. Because the Church is brought into being by the prior agency of Jesus Christ forming himself in his people, so worship is essentially man's being met and grasped by divine reality "already there," as it were. What we commonly call "objectivity" in worship is conceptually more fundamental than what we call "subjectivity." This does not mean—as one often hears it said—that there is no place for subjectivity in worship or that subjectivity is a kind of necessary evil. This is a foolish way of thinking, and a proper understanding of the dialectic of objectivity and subjectivity is so important that we shall devote an entire essay to it.[54] But the priority of the objective does mean that worship does not rise out of man's subjective experience, is not man's subjective feeding upon his own experience, and that the test of its validity does not finally depend on man's experience. God is the first reality in worship, not man; the soul feeds on the life God gives, not on itself; and the test of worship is not our subjective reaction but whether Christ in his truth and grace is authentically proclaimed. In this light one again understands why the aesthetic and psychological exploitation of worship of which we have written, or its utilization as in certain contemporary "experiments" to foster experience for the sake of experience, are corruptions. They flow from the false assumption—hidden or acknowledged—that the first term in worship is human subjectivity. When man's subjective experience rather than the objective reality of God is made the decisive referent, liturgy—as we have said —is on the road to delusion and suicide.

The doctrine of the Church further delivers to us the corporate nature of worship. Discussion of the power of tradition to lift the worshipper out of his individuality into the universality of the Church has partly illumined this truth. But corporateness is not so much a function which tradition performs as part of the essence of the Church itself. To be sure, the corporate nature of worship can be overemphasized, as we have previously warned and shall again. The dialectic of the Body and the individual member, of Church and person, must not be unbalanced nor collapsed. At Pentecost, we are told, it was only as tongues of fire visited *each* one that they were *all* filled with the Spirit—which is a permanent paradigm of the Church. Never-

[54] See ch. IV.

theless, corporateness is of the Church's *esse* and the range of its meaning is vast.

Corporateness to begin with bears an ontological aspect. The very being of the worshipper is merged with the being of fellow worshipper through being merged with Christ. Paul Lehmann, in interpreting the nature of *koinonia*, puts this point forcefully. A sermon of Luther has been cited in which the phrase "to communicate" has been shown to mean "to go to sacrament." Lehmann continues:

"To communicate" is to be in an actual relationship with somebody in which you give yourself to him and he gives himself to you. . . . It requires . . . a redemptive ingredient. Thus, he [Luther] declares that "Christ with all saints takes on, through his love, our estate (*Gestalt*), . . . wherefore, we . . . take on his estate. . . ." "The sacrament," he [Luther] goes on, "is nothing else than a divine sign in which Christ is peculiarly declared and given to all believers," . . . just as they are, with all that they are. . . . *The wholeness of everybody in the wholeness of all.* . . . The celebration of the sacrament is the celebration of the miracle of authentic *transubstantiation*, which means, in an unforgettably vivid phrase, "through love *being changed into each other*"! [55]

In defining corporateness so radically, Lehmann only echoes the New Testament. The Greek word *koinonia* which we interpret as "communion" or "fellowship"—together with the verb and adjective deriving from it—occurs some fifty times. One feels it to rise from the very nature of the Church, not as something promoted or added on. And correspondingly one feels it to be of the *esse* of worship. As St. Paul memorably writes: "*We* being many *are* made *one.*"

Corporateness, further, is to be understood as the mutual priesthood of all believers, a conception vital for liturgical theology. For this doctrine means so much more than is commonly supposed—that each worshipper has the right to approach God directly without the intervention of any priestly medium. It means rather that every worshipper has the duty to act as priest for his fellow worshippers. Responsibility is more primary than liberty, mutuality more basic than individuality. This conception, therefore, is vital in that it assigns the action of worship to all the congregation, and thus it both raises and answers the problem we speak of as "congregational participation." The truth is that for us as for the primitive Christian community, we need no priests because the congregation consists of nothing but priests;[56] and our Protestant task is not so much the abolition of the priest-

---

[55] *Ethics in a Christian Context*, pp. 64-65. See also ch. VIII, p. 336, n. 13.

[56] The term "priest" was applied to the whole community of Christian believers through probably the second century; only afterward did it come to be applied to a designated individual.

hood—as we are wont to say—as the abolition of the laity. Functionally, there will continue to be a leader of worship, as we have written, and this leader will usually be the pastor; but theologically the pastor is no more priest than the people, and both participate in what the other does.

Thus corporateness means, next, the intercessory character of worship. We probably associate this character most readily with prayers of intercession; and indeed the presence or absence of strong, imaginative intercession is always a good touchstone of liturgical integrity. But intercession is much more. It is of the essence of worship, and it is a total dimension of worship; and without this understanding worship is false. For example, the very decision to come together to hold a service is itself an intercessory act, as the decision —overtly or by default—to absent oneself from worship has an intercessory effect. One who absents himself from worship does not so much "let the pastor down" as deal a wound to the Christian community. In a vivid phrase of one of the church fathers, he "mangles" the body of Christ.[57] Indeed, to think of worship as intercessory may be safer than to think of it as simply corporate. "Corporate" derives from "corpus" meaning "body," and too much stress on the metaphor of the "body" can imperil the outward-looking relation of worship to the Church's ministry in the world. The metaphor of "body" most consistently suggests life within the community; accordingly it can bring a congregation to look inward more than outward.[58] "Intercession" and "priesthood," on the other hand, ethically and spiritually stretch devotion outward.

But however these terms be construed, our larger point must be made clear: the Church's corporate nature determines worship to be corporate, and a recovery of integrity in this sense is surely one of the greatest challenges facing free-church Protestantism today. What it can mean to the modern man has been movingly expressed in an oration entitled "The Biography of a Soul," read by Monsignor Fulton J. Sheen at the funeral service of the journalist Heywood Broun. The oration included the reasons Broun had given for seeking admission into the Roman Catholic Church, and the last of these, on which Broun dwelt most of all, reads as follows:

To me there is nothing more ridiculous than individualism in either economics, politics or religion. I see no reason why I should have my own individual religion

---

[57] In the *Didascalia* (ch. 13): "When thou teachest command and remind the people that they be constant in the assembly of the Church; so that ye be not hindered and make smaller by a member the Body of Christ. . . . Do not deprive our Saviour of His members; do not mangle and scatter His Body." Quoted by Theodore O. Wedel in *The Coming Great Church* (New York: The Macmillan Co., 1945), p. 61.

[58] See Claude Welch, *The Reality of the Church* (New York: Charles Scribner's Sons, 1958), p. 150.

any more than I should have my own individual astronomy or mathematics. I cannot even see why almighty God should be interested in my individual prayer, or even my individual sacrifice, for to care for me apart from my fellow man is to offend against an elementary law of charity. I love my fellow man, and particularly the down and out, the socially disinherited, and the economically dispossessed. . . . I want thus a religion which has a social aspect. If, therefore, I could take this individual prayer of mine and make it one with the prayer of millions of others who believed and prayed as I do: and if I could take this individual sacrifice of mine and tie it up with the sacrifice of millions of others, so as to form a great corporate prayer and corporate sacrifice and thus to influence those who are on the fringe of that corporation, then would I feel that my individual prayer and sacrifice were pleasing to God. That spiritual corporation I believe to be the Catholic Church.[59]

The doctrine of the Church also delivers to liturgical theology certain normative structures for conceiving and conducting worship. Two primary structures are none other than those by which the Church is liturgically defined: word and sacraments. We need, however, to distinguish between uses of "word" spelled with a capital "W" and with a small "w." In its capitalized version, "Word" is to be understood as God's self-disclosure and self-communication in the total Event of Jesus Christ, as we have previously indicated. In its lowercase version, "word" is to be understood as preaching or as proclamation. "Word" in the former sense is the content of "word" in the second sense, as it is also the content of "sacrament." Sermon and sacrament are but different modes of the same Word. In each the Word gives itself, and the worshipper feeds on the Word in one as much as the other. Cyril C. Richardson, in an important essay on "Cranmer and the Analysis of Eucharistic Doctrine," clarifies this insight in explaining how the father of our English liturgies held that preaching (as well as prayer and meditation) is as "fully effectual" a way of "eating Christ's body spiritually" as participation in the Eucharist. What goes on in preaching is precisely the same thing that goes on in sacrament, and sacramental feeding is the same kind of feeding as that which preaching, prayer, and meditation provide: "The sacrament does not differ in essence from any other spiritual exercise. Just as preaching 'putteth Christ into our ears' so the sacrament puts 'Christ into our eyes, mouths, hands and all our senses.' " [60] Sacraments are therefore to be thought of as being as much proclamatory as oral preaching, and oral preaching is to be thoughtof as being as sacramental as Baptism and the Eucharist. Indeed, Augustine defined preaching as an "audible

[59] Quoted by Gerald Ellard, *Men at Work at Worship* (New York: Longmans, Green & Co., 1940), pp. xiii-xiv.

[60] *The Journal of Theological Studies*, New Series, XVI/2 (Oxford: Clarendon Press, 1965), 428.

sacrament"; and as the sacraments are acted-out sermons, so the sermon is a spoken sacrament.

Because both sermon and sacrament are modes of the same reality and are given the same intention and substance by the Word, both should therefore be regularly embodied in the main services of the Church's worship. To separate them is nothing less than the Church disfiguring, indeed mutilating herself. In a metaphor of Karl Barth: a service without both sacrament and sermon is a "torso" service. Indeed, worship without the Eucharist is a "theological impossibility." [61] Historically, in the primitive, apostolic, and patristic eras, sermon and sacrament were a unity and were not severed until the Middle Ages. The Reformers—especially Calvin—sought to restore their unity but were not wholly successful. The result has been that until recently, Roman Catholicism has generally magnified the place of the Eucharist over the sermon, and Protestantism—with notable exceptions—has magnified the place of the sermon over the Eucharist. A heartening development in our ecumenical era, due in no small measure to the liturgical movement, is the correction of these excesses now taking place. Many Protestant directories and service books have restored the unity of sermon and sacrament, and the Roman Church has re-established preaching within the Mass.[62] Free-church Protestantism, especially, is returning from its sojourn in the liturgical "wilderness;" [63] it is healthily reacting from its idolizing of preaching; and it is coming to understand that it can recover integrity in worship only when it speaks the full normative language of word and sacrament delivered unto us. The day is hopefully drawing to a close when it will be possible for a congregation to announce in a Sunday bulletin: "Holy Communion will be administered at the close of worship"!

At the same time, it is unrealistic to suppose that in the immediate future many free-church congregations will readily unite sacrament and preaching in each weekly service. Until influences of reform have had more time, a number of things can be done. The service of preaching as we

[61]Barth quoted by J.-J. von Allmen, *Worship: Its Theology and Practice* (New York: Oxford University Press, 1965), p. 156.

[62] S. M. Gibbard, writing on "Liturgy as Proclamation of the Word," cites two significant statements, the first by a distinguished Protestant, M. A. C. Warren, and the other by a prominent Roman Catholic, the late Cardinal Bea: "The sermon itself is an act of worship not to be divorced from but most clearly associated with the breaking of the bread and the blessing of the cup." "A priest who knew how to celebrate the holy sacrifice, '*fractio panis*,' but did not know how to break for the faithful the bread of the Word of God, would be only half a priest." *Studia Liturgica*, I (Mar., 1962), 7. Significantly, a virtual spate of books on preaching of the Word is now coming from Roman Catholic publishers.

[63] See J. D. Benoit, *Liturgical Renewal*, trans. Edwin Hudson (London: SCM Press, 1958), p. 35.

typically know it can be recast into a eucharistic form, so that it becomes a pre-Communion service and can at any time be completed with the sentences of institution, the prayer of consecration, and the administration of the elements. Concretely, this can mean regularly introducing the traditional Communion invitation into the early part of the service, perhaps as a call to confession; providing a form of congregational confession followed by a declaration of pardon; rehabilitating the meaning of the offering and locating it toward the end of the service as the analogue of the bringing in of the bread and wine; especially placing the main prayers of thanksgiving and intercession after the sermon and including in them elements of the traditional prayers of the Communion service itself; and perhaps moving the Communion table nearer to the congregation and conducting much of the service from it, especially the opening parts and the main concluding prayers.

The customary preaching service in free-church Protestantism, however, will only be rendered sacramental by more than mechanical changes. Proclamation itself, in its preparation and execution, must be thought of as sacramental and as eucharistic. Involved here are the pastor's and congregation's theological conception of what preaching is, the integrity with which they prepare for it, and the reverence with which this office is discharged. Such fundamentals, as well as such new forms of proclamation as dialogue preaching, congregational conversation, preaching through drama and dance, are beyond the range of the present essay. Here we shall say only that preaching in all its aspects is to be as reverently obedient to the Word as the action of the Roman priest is reverent before "the awful elevation in the Canon of the Mass." [64] Preaching is "the monstrance of the Gospel," in a memorable phrase of Henry Sloane Coffin.[65] As the Roman priest at the elevation of bread and wine holds up and shows forth—de-*monstrates*—the Word, so the preacher sacrificially and sacramentally shows forth the Word in the sermon. In a memorable phrase of P. T. Forsyth: "Preaching is offered to God and addressed to men."

A further truth delivered by the Church to liturgical theology is the relation of liturgy to mission. We have explored this relation in a preliminary way in citing the motives kindling a concern for liturgical reform, and we shall later deal with it more systematically. Here, in the context of the doctrine of the Church, we must say that because the *esse*—the being—of the Church is apostolic or missionary, so the *esse* of worship must embody apostolicity. In making this statement we now enlarge the traditional cultic

---

[64] A phrase of G. K. Chesterton quoted by Read, "The Reformation of Worship," in *The Scottish Journal of Theology*, p. 74.

[65] See his book *Communion Through Preaching* (New York: Charles Scribner's Sons, 1952).

definition of the Church as the company of faithful people in which the word is purely preached and the sacraments duly administered. Taken strictly, this definition will not suffice, not only because the historical situation which evoked it no longer prevails, but also, and more importantly, because our recovered biblical understanding of the Church as mission does not allow us to equate its existence only with visible word and sacrament; these alone are not necessarily signs of the Church's reality. Rather, in the words of Bonhoeffer: "The first demand . . . made of those who belong to God's Church is . . . that they shall be witnesses to Jesus Christ before the world. . . . This testimony before the world can be delivered in a right way only if it springs from a hallowed life in the congregation of God. But a genuine hallowed life in the congregation . . . at the same time impels a man to testify before the world. If this testimony ceases to be given, that is a sign of the inner corruption of the congregation." [66] This is to say that the Church's nature is "holy" only to the degree that it is "testimony" in the world, or as we would say today, to the degree that it is "missionary." To be the Church and to be missionary are the same thing; without the element of apostolicity one cannot think about the Church in terms of reality. But if this be true, that "the Church can exist only to the extent that it is mission," [67] then it is also true that worship can only exist when it is missionary, and liturgical theology must understand the truth of Paul's use of the terms "Church" and "temple" in Ephesians as Gerhard Delling exegetes them:

Not only is the congregation met for Worship a "dwelling place of God" in which He is present "in the Spirit" but also the community when not gathered together in one place is God's temple. . . . Hence, . . . among the dispersed members of the community a continuous service goes on in the presence of God, for the Spirit is present in all the members effecting a continuous union among them and offering uninterrupted worship in them.[68]

The missionary nature of worship bears first an ontological aspect in that it consists in the receiving and sharing of divine life. To be sure, this life is manifest in action. Yet it is important to mark ontology first because the essence of missionary action is exactly that it flows out of the eschatological life in Christ that grasps the believer. The life God gives to the Church in Christ is the life Christ gives through his people to the

---

[66] *Ethics*, ed. Eberhard Bethge; trans. Neville Horton Smith (New York: The Macmillan Co., 1955), p. 69.

[67] A quotation from W. Elert in J. C. Hoekendijk, *The Church Inside Out*, ed. L. A. Hoedemaker and Peter Tijmes; trans. Isaac C. Rottenberg (Philadelphia: Westminster Press, 1966), p. 43.

[68] *Worship in the New Testament*, trans. Percy Scott (London: Dartman, Longman & Todd, 1962), p. 21.

world. The presence of Christ in word and sacrament is the same presence with which his disciples are present in the world. However, the way in which Christ gives himself to men and the way men give themselves to Christ in worship also patterns the way the Church gives herself to the world. In worship the Church receives the shape as well as the substance of her mission. In both worship and mission the Church lives eucharistically; in both she lives sacramentally and sacrificially; and in both she lives transformingly. Douglas Webster describes this shape:

The end of all our worship is that we should be transformed into Christ's likeness and that he should be formed in us. And the end of the Christian mission is that the kingdoms of this world become the kingdom of our God and of his Christ. Transformation is part of the sacramental principle and of the missionary principle. In the Eucharist what begins as bread and wine does not remain mere bread and wine. By virtue of human prayer and divine promise something happens. Bread and wine become vehicles for Christ. There is always the process of becoming. Sinners become saints; mere men become prophets and priests, pastors and evangelists; the desert becomes a garden; water becomes wine; . . . those who were no people become the people of God. So it goes on as the hands of God touch history through Christian lives, till shame becomes glory and struggle becomes peace. The mission of the people of God is to be so completely his, that they are agents of this transformation.[69]

Many implications follow from this apostolic understanding of "Church." We shall find that perhaps the most important is the light this redefinition casts upon the question of liturgical action. For if worship partakes of the apostolic *esse* of the Church and is coextensive with the Christian's life in the world, then liturgical action must similarly be viewed as having reality only as it includes both cultic action and worldly (or ethical) action. Thus a fundamental principle operates which we may speak of as the principle of correspondence, whereby the total life of the Christian community grounds its cultic action as its cultic action grounds its worldly life. An analysis of this principle in a subsequent essay will carry us far in stating the meaning of liturgical integrity.

However, to say that the *esse* of the Church and her worship includes apostolicity is not to say that worship and mission can be so merged that cultus can be dispensed with, as certain radical interpreters of the relation of liturgy and mission suggest. While both worship and mission can in a sense be subsumed under "liturgy," i.e. "service," yet their dialectical relation is to be preserved, and the two poles of "cultus" and "mission" differentiated as "poles." The cultic gathering of Christ's people in disengagement from

[69] "The Mission of the People of God," *Liturgical Renewal in the Christian Churches*, p. 195. See ch. VIII, pp. 342-53.

their life in the world is clearly sustained in the New Testament, and the Church is cultically liturgical before it is apostolically liturgical. The imperatives "*Come* unto me" and "*Do* this in remembrance of me" theologically precede the imperative "Go into all the world."

Moreover, the nature of man and the relation of his life with God to his life in the world answer to these biblical priorities. Man is a creature of successiveness living in time and space, and only as he knows certain times and places as occasions of concentration of the Holy can all time and place be experienced as holy. The only practical way "to hallow the whole," writes C. F. D. Moule, "is to bring a token portion of it consciously to God. As with the Jewish ritual of the offering of the firstfruits to hallow the entire crop, or of the sabbath to hallow the whole week, so it is with the Christian Sunday and with specific places and actions of worship. In these is concentrated the offering of all our time and space—all our being and possessions—in praise to God." [70] We cannot forget that in our Lord's promise, "*Wherever* two or three are gathered together, *there* am I in the midst of them," the words "where" and "there" are space terms; and that his word "often" in the institution of the sacrament, "As *often* as ye do this, ye do it in remembrance of me," is a time term. Man's nature was rightly read by our Lord to be such that he needs particular places and times for communion with the divine if all his living is liturgically to show forth the divine.

These, then, are some of the key theological realities delivered to liturgy by the doctrine of the Church: the priority of the Church's worship to the individual's; the objectivity of divine reality as the decisive referent for worship; the corporate and intercessory character of worship; word and sacrament as the constitutive norm of worship; the dialectical unity of worship and mission. For purposes of analysis we have separated these serially in thought. In the end, however, they are one reality, or rather, they are to be gathered up into one reality: the Church itself as the context of both the act of worship and of theological reflection about worship.

Nevertheless, we cannot say that the doctrine of the Church is the decisive doctrine for theological integrity, and on this very important point we depart from the position of a number of liturgical theologians writing today. Perhaps our free-church temper becomes evident here, but we feel

[70] *Worship in the New Testament* (London: Lutterworth Press, 1961), p. 83. A. G. Hebert has similarly written that the presence of a church building does not mean that all other buildings—factories, shops, public houses, are the devil's: "By the existence of a house called God's House, these others are all claimed for Him. So the Lord's Day at the beginning of each week claims all the other days . . . for God's glory: and times of prayer are set apart . . . not to imply that those times only are given to God, but to claim for Him all the rest." *Liturgy and Society*, pp. 191-92.

that too much discussion of worship starts and stops with the Church, and that in thinking about worship as in the act of worship itself, the human mind can idolatrously worship the Church instead of the Lord of the Church. Ecclesiology becomes corrupted into ecclesiolatry, in a phrase of J. G. Davies.[71] Certainly it is good for every reason that the meaning of "Church" be theologically restated and that its implications for liturgy be set forth in every generation; all of us are the richer for the studies of the nature of the Church made available in our day. Yet theological emphases come and go, and changing enthusiasms must be resisted as well as appreciated. In saying this, we are well aware that it is biblical criticism and theology which have largely fostered a deepened appreciation of the centrality of the Church; and insofar as biblical truth commands us to conceive the doctrine of the Church as the context for liturgical reflection, we have no alternative but to obey. Yet cultural and psychological forces have also been at work, and while often hidden, they must be taken into account. One has the uneasy feeling that overpreoccupation with the doctrine of the Church (especially with the corporateness of the Church) may be neurotic —the theological equivalent of the contemporary retreat into collectivism, or the expression of a psychological need to be delivered from cultural estrangement and insecurity. For example, harsh strictures against individualism in the name of the Church made by certain free churchmen who see individualism only as "cancerous" strike one as obsessive; indeed they may even be compensation for free-church inferiority complexes. The fanaticism with which enthusiasts for the doctrine of the Church override the freedom of the mind to offer itself directly to the truth of Word and Spirit beyond the Church gives one pause.

In any case, the fundamental affirmation for liturgical theology is that worship is finally determined not by the Church but by the Word which is Lord of the Church. To be sure, this affirmation must always be qualified with the same qualification we have previously made with respect to tradition: in one sense we can no more get behind "Church" to the Word than we can get behind "tradition," and liturgy inevitably has to be thought of ecclesiologically. Yet the doctrine of the Church cannot be decisive for worship in the same way that the doctrine of Jesus Christ is decisive. For the Church as Christ's Body is not identical with Christ. He is the Church's life in a way that the Church is not his life. And as the Word is ontologically constitutive of the Church in experience and in history, so it is constitutive for worship and for thought about worship.

Further, as Head of the Church, the Word is sovereign over the Church

---

[71] *Worship and Mission* (London: SCM Press, 1966), p. 49.

at the same time that it is manifest in it; while Head and Body are not to be divided, neither are they to be identified. "If the Church may see itself as being not less than its Lord's body, it must not regard itself as anything more." [72] The Church is to be obedient to Jesus Christ in a way that he is not obedient to the Church, and liturgical theology is to be obedient to Jesus Christ in a way that transcends its obedience to the Church. Still further, worship is Christ's action before it is human action, and it is his action that gathers up man's action to God. We signify this truth in the definition of worship that has become virtually axiomatic: revelation and response. The former denotes the self-revealing action of Christ, the latter the action of man. But this formula also applies to our thinking about worship: theological thinking about worship is likewise a form of revelation and response, and that which reveals itself with decisiveness for theology is not the Church but Jesus Christ. As we have said, our hermeneutics is first determined Christologically, not ecclesiologically. The sovereignty of Jesus Christ for worship has been compellingly stated by Gerhard Delling in his study of New Testament worship:

Christ was its actual content; confession of faith in *Him* played a decisive part; hymns praised the salvation which was wrought through *Him*; the burning expectation of the Church looked out for *Him*. Through *Him* the old man was overcome; in *Him* the new being was bestowed; "in *Him*" the common fellowship was founded. *He* was present in the Lord's Supper; *His* spirit furnished the utterance in the life of worship; "in *His* Name" men called upon God in thanks and requests. The whole evidence seems not unimportant for reaching a judgment about the place of Jesus in primitive Christian worship. [73]

Such massive evidence is not only important for the historical scholar; it is decisive for the liturgical theologian.

LITURGICAL INTEGRITY AND THE DOCTRINE OF THE TRINITY

As we conclude this discussion of the doctrine of the Church and before we undertake a Christological interpretation of worship, certain aspects of the doctrine of the Trinity need to be considered. The character of Christian worship is fundamentally determined by the nature of God disclosed in Christian revelation; this revelation is essentially trinitarian; and in a broad sense the doctrine of the Trinity is thus an inescapable frame within which

[72] Roger Hazelton, *Christ and Ourselves* (New York: Harper & Row, 1965), p. 78. See also Hans Küng, *The Church*, trans. Ray and Rosaleen Ockenden (New York: Sheed & Ward, 1967), p. 237.
[73] *Worship in the New Testament*, pp. 119-20.

all thought about worship must move. While both worship and theological reflection upon its nature are carried on "through Jesus Christ our Lord," they are also to be carried on "in the name of the Father, and of the Son, and of the Holy Spirit." The God who encounters the human soul is one God whose being and action are manifested in three different modes: God the Father and Creator, God the Son and Redeemer, and God the living Holy Spirit. Liturgical reflection is bounded by this frame as the epitomization of the nature of the divine reality with which man is engaged in worship. As a service of Christian worship is authentic only when all its elements are reconcilable with the Trinity, so thought about worship possesses integrity only when all its elements can be related within the Trinity. The Trinity constitutes a basic morphology which cannot be violated if liturgical theology is to be Christian.

As we explore the triune character of Christian revelation as basic for thought, however, we still must understand that here, as elsewhere, the integrating reality is Jesus Christ. As it was the encounter with Jesus Christ in his sovereign meaning which originally inspired the doctrine of the Trinity, so the decisive center of liturgical theology lies not in the Trinity in general but in Jesus Christ in particular. In fact, we have to recapitulate in our thinking about worship something of the same process the early Church went through as it originally conceived the doctrine of the Trinity. For originally the Trinity was not a dogma of theology but a datum of experience, and the key to the meaning of the datum was Jesus Christ. It was his event and presence that required a doctrine of the Trinity as "monotheism revised and enlarged."[74] In Canon Leonard Hodgson's striking epigram quoted by Henry P. Van Dusen: "Christianity began as a trinitarian religion with a unitarian theology"; and it was the task of the early Church to bring its theology to match its experience.[75] The motive for undertaking this task was simply the impact of Jesus Christ: the early Christians came to name as "Father" the unitarian God they had known in Judaism because of what they had found this God to be to them in the Son. And they named as "Holy Spirit" the divine presence which dealt with them so mysteriously and abundantly because of the character they had found this presence to bear toward them in the Son. Thus it spontaneously happened that the entities, God, Christ, Spirit, became named alongside each other in continually new combinations of thought, issuing finally in what we now know as the formula of the Trinity. But the doctrine of the Trinity sprang from, and always had as its fulcrum that reality which alone could do

---

[74] Hazelton, *Christ and Ourselves*, p. 135.
[75] Van Dusen, *Spirit, Son, and Father* (New York: Charles Scribner's Sons, 1958), p. 150.

justice to the fullness of their experience of God—the Word, Jesus Christ.

It is in this sense, then, that we say that the Church's elucidation of the Trinity with Christ as pivotal is a paradigm of the way in which the Church is to set forth its liturgical theology. The meaning of Christ polarizes trinitarian thinking about worship in the same way that the Church's experience of Jesus Christ shaped its reflection upon the meaning of God. In short, we can think reliably about worship "in the name of the Father and of the Son and of the Holy Spirit" because we primarily think "through Jesus Christ Our Lord."

However, this is not to say that other than Christological conceptions of worship are necessarily false. It is possible to construct a theology of worship predominantly upon the first person of the Trinity as the constitutive element, and in one sense the affirmation of God as Creator is a theological absolute which guarantees to worship the theistic character it must have if it is to be worship at all. Belief in God as Creator and Father is essentially a decision for theism, and liturgical theology obviously has to make this decision. Otherwise there is no liturgy and no theology.

Further, attention to God as Creator must always accompany emphasis upon God as Saviour if liturgical theology is not to be warped and if worship is not to be conceived too salvationally as only an esoteric experience for the circle of the saved or of those to be saved. When the latter conception overrules, worship tends to withdraw man from his life in the created world and to impart a negativistic tone to his attitude toward it. The affirmation of the created order as good—as well as fallen—and affirmation of the divine creativity constraining man and bringing him to participate in its dynamic ongoingness cannot be set aside in worship. And it is precisely these affirmations which the first article of the Trinity contains.[76] We shall more fully explore this point presently.

Nevertheless, to ascribe primacy to the first person of the Trinity and to make theism sovereign over Christian revelation runs the grave risk of emasculating Christian worship of precisely that which makes it Christian, namely, Jesus Christ, and of bleaching out its essential Christian elements— the incarnation, the atonement, the resurrection, eschatology, the sacraments, the Church. The end result is usually some form of liturgical unitarianism with heavily anthropomorphic overtones, resting on the simple theistic generalization that worship is the response of children to a divine father who makes himself known by the signs of creation and providence. Again, while this conception of worship is not untrue, it also is not complete nor necessarily Christian.

[76] See the article "Creation and Worship," by Vilmos Vajta in *Studia Liturgica* II (Mar., 1963).

A theology of worship constructed upon the third person of the Trinity, the Holy Spirit, comes much nearer the mark, mainly because the Christian article, "The Holy Spirit"—which we may distinguish from simply "the spirit"—commits one to think in Christian terms. What religion in general calls "the spirit," as we shall note shortly, Christian faith ultimately renames "the Holy Spirit" with all the accompanying meanings Jesus Christ infuses into it. Always, of course, there is the danger that theological reflection will fail to perform this Christian renaming. When this happens, one is likely to have on his hands little more than worship as mysticism or theosophy or as vague "celebration," and the perversions these can fasten on worship are too self-evident to require comment. However, when liturgical thought understands the Holy Spirit in its inseparable relation to Jesus Christ, this doctrine can carry one far into the meaning of Christian worship.

However, it should be understood that the New Testament does not always identify the Holy Spirit as synonymous with Jesus Christ, and in one sense the Holy Spirit possesses a certain autonomy. The Holy Spirit is essentially the immanent mode of God's presence, God functionally self-communicative to human personality, God in his intimacy and potency, "God at his most empirical" in a phrase of M. B. Handspicken. Understood thus as "God in the here-and-now," the Holy Spirit enables worship to actualize the present moment of God's action toward man and to particularize the present moment of the congregation's response.[77] As God present in the aspects of intimacy and power, the Holy Spirit also informs worship with a supernatural energy[78] that at times appears to be irrational. Thus even at considerable risk, Christian thought has never desired to exclude the Holy Spirit in its manifestation as energy but has taken up the position of St. Paul, who, while warning the Corinthians against the excesses of the Spirit, nevertheless did not forbid them. Christian worship at its best has embodied the truth of a sentence of a Benedictine hymn: *Laeti bibamus sobriam ebrietatem spiritus:* "Let us joyfully taste of the sober drunkenness of the Spirit." [79]

Further, the Holy Spirit may also be thought of as the source of freedom and openness in worship in that its contemporizing action, as we have noted, enables the congregation to respond in ways appropriate to their own time and place. The forms through which the congregation respond to the Word

[77] See J.-J. von Allmen, *Worship: Its Theology and Practice,* p. 40; Wilhelm Hahn, *Worship and the Congregation,* trans. Geoffrey Buswell (Richmond: John Knox Press, 1963), p. 58.

[78] Significantly, as divine "energy" the Spirit is sometimes spoken of in Christian tradition as the "sacred semen" which impregnated the Virgin Mary, or as the male person which at Pentecost enters the female body of the Church.

[79] Probably based on Augustine's phrase: "the sober inebriation of Thy wine."

117

must be their own, and the Spirit inspires these. However, this freedom is a bound freedom. The Holy Spirit is not "a maverick principle," [80] and it is to be thought of dialectically as the source of order as well as the source of freedom. In this sense, the Holy Spirit performs both a sacramental and sacrificial function: sacramental in that it mediates the objective reality of the Word to man, and sacrificial in that it evokes and voices man's response. Von Allmen clarifies the distinction well:

> Variety is permissible only on the sacrificial side of worship, [that is, pertaining to man's response] not on the sacramental side [that is, pertaining to the substance of God's action]. [While Paul permitted the Corinthians a certain ecstasy and disorder] , in regard to the Gospel (Gal. 1:8 ff), Baptism (I Cor. 1:13 ff) and the Eucharist (I Cor. 11:17 ff), St. Paul does not tolerate any deviation from tradition. . . . On the other hand, the sacrificial side of worship can and must be flexible for . . . the Gospel, Baptism and Holy Communion . . . are given to different people, . . . Jews in Jerusalem, the people of Corinth, the people of Rome. . . . Otherwise the worship inspired by the Holy Spirit would not be a genuine encounter.[81]

Yet, while the Holy Spirit is the source of immediacy, of vitality, of freedom, and of order, its fullest meaning for liturgical theology is to be seen through the lens of Christology, and again liturgical theology recapitulates New Testament experience and reflection. While the New Testament does not always equate the Holy Spirit substantively with Jesus Christ, it predominantly understands the nature of the Holy Spirit through Christ's person, work, and presence.[82] In the earlier strata of the New Testament documents, Gregory Dix reminds us, the Spirit is conceived as the power or presence of the ascended Jesus energizing his Body the Church: " 'To walk after the Spirit' and for 'Christ to live through me' means for St. Paul

---

[80] Hazelton, *Christ and Ourselves*, p. 67.

[81] "Worship and the Holy Spirit," *Studia Liturgica*, II (June, 1963).

[82] In Matthew and Mark, the Spirit is viewed as an autonomous reality in itself, and Jesus is seen as possessed by the Spirit. In Acts, the Spirit is viewed as the personal link between the ascended Jesus and his followers. In contrast, for Paul "the *Pneuma* means the way the life of faith is lived in its relationship to God's act of salvation in Christ." Rudolf Bultmann, *Life and Death*, trans. P. H. Ballard *et al.* (London: A. & C. Black, 1965), p. 67. The *Kyrios* appears in the mode of existence of the *Pneuma*. Indeed, the Spirit can even be regarded by Paul as subordinate to the Lord. Hans Küng writes: "The encounter between the believer and '*Theos,*' '*Kyrios*' and '*Pneuma*' is ultimately one and the same encounter. . . . The Spirit is thus the earthly presence of the glorifed Lord." *The Church*, p. 166. John goes still further in relating the Spirit and Christ. As Ernst Käsemann writes: "In radical reduction John made Jesus and his witness into the sole content and criterion of the true tradition of the Spirit. . . . The Spirit is nothing else but the continual possibility and reality of the new encounter with Jesus in the post-Easter situation as one who is revealing his Word to his own and through them to the world." *The Testament of Jesus*, trans. Gerhard Krodel (London: SCM Press, 1968), p. 46.

the same thing." [83] And of the later formulas of faith, Oscar Cullmann adds that all the elements connected with the Holy Spirit are named as functions of Christ.[84] Indeed, one recognizes the Holy Spirit through Jesus Christ (John 16:13-14), and one recognizes Jesus Christ through the Holy Spirit (I Cor. 12:3). In regard to worship specifically, worship "in spirit and in truth" is bound up with the new life Jesus Christ brings.[85] And both the sacraments of Baptism and Eucharist have meaning only insofar as the Holy Spirit and the person of Jesus Christ are held together (I Cor. 12:13; John 6:52-63; I John 5:6-7).

Above all, the Christological meaning of the Holy Spirit in New Testament worship is verified by its eschatological character. That is, the Spirit's supreme office is to convey the time-transcending and qualitatively different life with God which experience of the Word brings. Christian thought denotes this office in various ways: the Holy Spirit links the Christian man with the first coming and the last coming; the Holy Spirit bestows upon the man of faith "the earnest" of the Parousia and of the final summing up of all things in Christ as the Head; the Holy Spirit constitutes the Church as an eschatological community; the Holy Spirit conveys and ratifies the eternal life man receives in the sacraments; the Holy Spirit "is the future which in virtue of the past actualizes itself in the present." [86] But always, this most important of all offices has meaning uniquely in relation to Jesus Christ. It is the event of his life, death, and resurrection which constitutes the first coming and prefigures the last coming which the Holy Spirit mediates; it is the new life in him that the Church as the community of the Holy Spirit lives; and it is the eternal life experienced in him that the Holy Spirit seals as the foretaste of the life to come. The eschatological life mediated by the Holy Spirit, whether realized or future, is unintelligible without the interpretation which Jesus Christ alone gives. In short, the Word is the fulcrum on which the meaning of the Holy Spirit in worship turns: "Worship, which exists through the Holy Spirit and because of him, is commanded primarily by Christology." [87]

LITURGICAL INTEGRITY DETERMINED BY CHRISTOLOGY

With a certain inevitability, then, the "holy anxiety" that the nature of the Gospel shall determine the nature of Christian worship brings the

---

[83] *The Shape of the Liturgy* (Westminster: Dacre Press, 1945), p. 260.
[84] *The Christology of the New Testament*, p. 2.
[85] See Delling, *Worship in the New Testament*, p. 6.
[86] Oscar Cullmann, *Early Christian Worship*, trans. A. Stewart Todd and James B. Torrance (London: SCM Press, 1953), p. 36.
[87] Von Allmen, "Worship and the Holy Spirit," in *Studia Liturgica*, II (June, 1963).

mind up frontally before *viva vox evangelii,* the living voice of the Gospel, the Word, Jesus Christ. Other approaches we have explored—worship interpreted within the categories of worth, tradition, the Church, the Trinity—are like concentric circles through which one passes to the center. However, as we undertake to state the elements of Christology we judge to be essential, let it be confessed that there is an aspect of stammering to all thinking about worship that corresponds to the mystery of the Word itself and that verifies the truth of its encounter with our minds. Here, as elsewhere, one must expect the Word to present itself to us as problematic, as not self-explanatory, and in its very mystery as able to spur us to explore larger contexts of comprehensibility.[88] Liturgical theology will always reflect this problematic character, and a certain obliquity, even a certain confusion, is the more trustworthy posture. We recall that it was after St. Paul had spoken "concerning Christ and the Church," that he added: "This is a great mystery" (Eph. 5:32). Before the mystery of the Word in liturgy peculiarly, a man's faith is usually better than his theology.

Further, the aspects of simultaneity and dialectic—present in worship itself—likewise do not permit too clear a statement of liturgical Christology. Modes of interaction between the Word and man merge into one another too profoundly and differentiate themselves too subtly to be neatly classified; and the elements we single out for analysis should be thought of as a unity. To be sure, certain Christological meanings can be expected to be higher in the hierarchy of truth than others; one must make his theological commitments, and we shall not hesitate to make ours. Yet the plethora of ways in which the New Testament itself speaks of Jesus Christ and the many ways—some forty of them—we find him liturgically named there should give one pause: Jesus as the "High Priest" whose "ascending and descending dynamism" [89] constitutes the liturgical dialogue between God and man; Jesus as the "Messiah" with its profound eschatological meanings; Jesus as the "Son of Man" with its meanings of both human representation and divine majesty; Jesus as the *Kurios* exalted at God's right hand; Jesus as "Suffering Servant" with its reference to Baptism and the Eucharist. One must speak of the liturgical meanings of Jesus Christ in many ways at the same time and mark both the unity and the difference between them.

In fact this unity and difference pose one further problem we must briefly mention: whether a serial examination of scriptural titles and categories and of the texts recording these is the best way to proceed in thinking

[88] See John McIntyre, *The Shape of Christology* (London: SCM Press, 1966), pp. 13 ff.

[89] Edward Schillebeeckx, O. P., *Christ the Sacrament of the Encounter with God* (New York: Sheed & Ward, 1963), p. 19.

Christologically about worship. We have concluded that it is not, chiefly because meanings implicit in these titles cross-refer and reappear under different thought-forms. A proof text, biblically footnoted Christology will not do. One obeys the Word, not texts; and one must try to gather up recurring meanings conceptualized now in one way, now in another. This is to say, a conceptual rather than a textual approach will be followed. Such an approach, of course, clearly entails the risk of subjectivity. It also strains the power of the mind in discriminating meaning, and not for nothing do theologians speak of "the pain of Christological thinking." [90] Even more, this procedure strains the sensitivity of one's being and exposes one's life experience and spirituality. Here again, the liturgical theologian recapitulates the experience of the early Church whose Christology was not itself part of original revelation but emerged out of the Church's total encounter with Jesus in its continuing life. Christology emerges out of all one has personally found Jesus Christ to be in worship *and* in life. "Jesus Christ," it has been wisely said, "cannot become the object of our investigation as if he were not the subject of our lives." [91]

Hence, while the following analysis bears for us the stamp of truth, and while we believe that it is supported by the New Testament and not contradictory to the light of the Holy Spirit, we are sure that much more can be said, and doubtless more clearly, that other interpreters will find other conceptualizations equally compelling, and that in the last analysis we are all unprofitable servants of the Word. Nevertheless, that which must command us is the Word itself in the mysterious sovereignty of its truth. Here is the pivot of all liturgical thinking.[92] While "Christocentricity is not a geometrical concept," as Josef Jungmann has warned,[93] yet one cannot but feel the constraint the Word pronounces upon thought to be like the instruction given to the architects engaged to rebuild the Cathedral at Coventry, England, after it was destroyed in the last war: "Design first the altar, and then build the cathedral around it." Liturgical theology uniquely understands how central Jesus Christ is for the mind's reflection as for the soul's devotion, and how his deed shapes all thought, prayer, and life.

[90] Dietrich Ritschl, *Memory and Hope* (New York: The Macmillan Co., 1967), p. 20.
[91] *Ibid.*
[92] Paul Vanbergen, in comparing the Roman Catholic Constitution on the Liturgy and the Protestant Statement in the 1966 Montreal Faith and Order Report on Worship, significantly writes that "the Christological basis of worship and the presence of Christ in worship are the two common points whose importance for a dialogue on the Liturgy must be plain to everyone." See *Studia Liturgica*, V (Spring, 1966).
[93] *Announcing the Word of God*, p. 66.

Liturgical Integrity in Light of the Incarnation

We have previously made the statement that reflection upon worship partakes of the nature of worship itself, that the meanings the Word holds for thought derive from the meanings it holds for devotion. Theology unfolds from doxology, as it were, and from what Jesus Christ liturgically discloses himself to mean as grace derives what he means theologically as truth. Liturgical theology is a mode of intellectually hearing and obeying, as worship itself is to hear and to obey. It is to attempt to comprehend rationally what one has contemplated in wonder.[94] And surely the deepest meaning the Word holds for thought is precisely the meaning with which faith adoringly names the Word, "Jesus," "Christ", for in these terms is embodied the incarnate nature of the Word which one can do no other than to speak of as "human" and "divine." The Word is both the man "Jesus" and God's anointed—the "Christ." In the words of Dietrich Bonhoeffer:

I do not know who this man Jesus Christ is unless I say at the same time "Jesus Christ is God," and I do not know who the God Jesus Christ is unless I say at the same time "Jesus Christ is man." The two factors cannot be isolated because they are not isolated. God in timeless eternity is not God, Jesus limited by time is not Jesus. Rather God is God in the man Jesus. . . . This one God-man is the starting point of Christology.[95]

This is to say, Christian worship first is profoundly incarnational; and the dialectic of *the incarnation understood as the whole Event of Jesus Christ*, not merely his birth, is to govern all thinking about worship.

Now how the Word is truly God and truly man, how the mind comprehends this and how thought is to say this is "the problem of problems," and we quickly run hard into what has been rightly called "the bankruptcy of human logic." [96] It is well to remember that the Church first perceived and declared the incarnational meaning of the Word in its common worship, not in theological speculation. Worship was the flashpoint, as it were, at which the divine *Kurios* was identified with the Jesus of Nazareth who had appeared on earth, whom the primitive Church had known, and who had been crucified and would come again.[97] While this realization came in

[94] See Paul Verghese, *The Joy of Freedom* (Richmond: John Knox Press, 1967), p. 39.

[95] *Christ the Center*, p. 46.

[96] H. M. Relton quoted by H. W. Montefiore in his essay "Towards a Christology for Today," in *Soundings*, ed. A. R. Vidler (Cambridge: The University Press, 1966), p. 150.

[97] See Cullmann, *The Christology of the New Testament*, p. 320.

other encounters with him also, it was first through the liturgical recapitulation of what Jesus had humanly done that men came to realize what God in him had divinely done. And it was through insight into what had been done in him that they came to know who he was. They found his historical life to constitute the climax of a *Heilsgeschichte*, a "holy" or "salvational" history which opened up like a key the meaning of all else, and they declared that the human life of Jesus embodied for them the fullest self-revelation of the divine that it is possible for man to experience.

However, while this incarnational understanding first arose liturgically, the Church soon undertook a different approach, partly in order to combat certain heresies encountered in its mission to non-Jewish cultures. It soon came to interpret the incarnation speculatively and to speak propositionally of two natures, culminating in the Chalcedonian formula of Jesus Christ as very God and very man, in which there is to be neither division nor confusion, neither separation nor identity. The static, separatist, and abstract character of these categories in the "two-nature" theory was in part a reaction to and reflection of Hellenistic thought with its passion for clarity, as well as a reflection of the Latin spirit with its passion for order. It dominated the mind of the Church through succeeding centuries and is commonly felt today to be a straitjacket for thought. Today theology prefers to telescope the distinguishable meanings of "divine" and "human" into a conception of the incarnation which sees God most present in Jesus at his most human: "God addressing man as a man amongst men." [98] In the words of one scholar:

The event of Christ does not mean that God simply adds manhood to what is already his own nature. . . . It means involvement, full incarnate identification with our very humanness. . . . [The incarnation is not the] . . . pinpointing or highlighting of God in human history [but] . . . God getting himself lost in history, yielding up his supernatural and superhuman attributes precisely in order to identify himself with us at the profoundest level possible. . . . The only God we know is the enmanned God. . . . It is exactly his humble presence in our midst which is the sign and seal of his power over us."[99]

However, while the meaning of the incarnation has been defined in various ways, it is crucial to understand that *the fact of incarnation itself* is always affirmed in any Christology that is faithful to biblical revelation and hence worth taking seriously. Restatement of meaning is not the same thing as denial of fact. Christian thought has never abandoned the "what" of

[98] C. Ernst in his Foreward to Schillebeeckx, *Christ the Sacrament of Encounter with God*, p. xvi.
[99] Hazelton, *Christ and Ourselves*, pp. 9, 10, 20.

123

incarnation in its various attempts to state the "how." It has known that it is true to the Gospel only when it holds steadfastly to the unity of the Word as both human and divine, as both like unto ourselves and different from ourselves. This dialectical truth underlies and undercuts all controversy. It is a "fundamental dogma." [100]

However, theology has not found it easy to preserve the dialectical unity of the incarnation because of the tendency of the human mind to be over-attracted to the humanity or the deity of the Word. Consequently, separate—and often opposing—mental attitudes appear which attach themselves respectively to one or the other of these qualities.[101] When carried to extremes in theology, these mental attitudes become Docetic and Ebionite heresies, the former emphasizing the deity of Jesus Christ at the cost of his humanity, the latter emphasizing his humanity at the cost of his divinity. When carried over into liturgical reflection, the former attitude exalts the divine, authoritative character of worship as something handed down from on high and consequently insulated from the human. It pays more heed to salvation than to creation. It tends to dehumanize worship and belittles the importance of its relevance to man and his world. It keeps worship mysterious and esoteric, even at the cost of rendering it inaccessible to the believer. The latter tendency overhumanizes liturgy and deprecates its otherworldly and soteriological nature. In the name of relevance it refuses to set places and things apart as sacred; it divinizes—sometimes sentimentally—the secular or the profane; it assigns more importance to the doctrine of creation; and it presses for points of connection between man and the Word.[102]

Now actually, these excesses are not always bad. Theological sensitivity requires one to accept the risk of error as part of the cost of wrestling with truth in dialectical form. Moreover, theological sensibility varies in different cultures and epochs. The meanings with which the Word most claims us are conditioned by the meanings of our existence we bring to it. It is quite clear, for example, that emphasis upon the humanity of the Word best matches the Lebensgefühl of the contemporary man who is less sensitive to the divine than conscious of the human, and for whom the humanization of life appears to be a sovereign claim. The ethical more than the confessional aspect of the Word claims us. And whereas Christ's priesthood was especially

[100] Karl Rahner, S.J., "On the Theology of the Incarnation," in *Word and Mystery*, ed. Leo J. O'Donovan, S.J. (Glen Rock, N.J.: Newman Press, 1968), p. 282.

[101] See Louis Bouyer, *Rite and Man: The Sense of the Sacred and Christian Liturgy*, trans. M. J. Costelloe (London: Burns & Oates, 1963), ch. I, to whom I am particularly indebted at this point.

[102] I have largely paraphrased Bouyer here.

congenial to the medieval mind, his prophethood to the Reformation, today his Kingship and Lordship appeal with greatest power. Further, what we shall speak of at the conclusion of this essay as "the fullness of the Word," the richness of the *Christus Praesens* in the manifoldness of its self-disclosure, ever humbles the mind with its power to disabuse us of predilection and to correct our error. Thus the loss of balance by pastor or theologian in bearing the tension of thinking dialectically about worship in a sense validates his fidelity to the incarnational nature of the Word and testifies to the holy anxiety from which we never want to be free.

Nevertheless, the dialectic of the incarnation must always remain at the same time a synthesis, and the loss of either pole can be fatal. At stake here in part is the nature of theological thinking in general but even more of liturgical thinking in particular. "Dialectic," it has been said, "is criticism dealing with contradictions and their solutions";[103] and it is obedience to the larger truth beyond our polarities, gathering them into a unity, that informs liturgical thinking with integrity, even though polarities must remain polarities and contradictions must remain contradictions. While the tendencies of the human mind to be overattracted to the deity or the humanity of the Word in a sense are inevitable, they yet can become perverse. On the one hand, we cannot help thinking polarly. On the other, we must think unitively.

Further, the dialectic of the incarnation is seminal for so much else. From it derive other forms of dialectic with which one must grapple if liturgical integrity is to be won; and if one does not get his thinking right here, he is not likely to get it right elsewhere. To unbalance or dismember the dialectic of the incarnation closes off paths of thought which alone can lead through difficult problems into truth. We shall discuss these derivative forms of dialectic and the problems they involve from time to time: the dialectic of the sacred and the secular, of the supernatural and the natural, of the eternal and the temporal, of the trans-historical and the historical.

However, two forms of dialectic especially important for liturgical theology need to be identified: first, what we have chosen to speak of as "the relevance and irrelevance of worship." The problem posed by people who ask in various ways, "How can worship be made relevant to our life today?" is a searching one and liturgical integrity demands an answer. We shall argue in the following essay that the problem as thus stated is wrongly formulated, but this is not to say that it is not fundamental. And the answer finally inheres in the incarnation.

[103] *Concise Oxford Dictionary* (Oxford: Clarendon Press, 1934), third edition revised by H. Fowler.

A second form of dialectic is in certain respects more generic than others: the dialectic of the transcendence and immanence of God, and the question of how this paradoxical truth shall be embodied in worship in a way that engages the worshipper truthfully. God as *Andere*, the Transcendent Other, for example, is felt not to be meaningful to the consciousness of our age, and it is said that models of distance to convey transcendence will no longer do. For example, ethereal, otherworldly plainsong or the elevated, distant altar is said to symbolize transcendence wrongly; and transcendence experienced as "God-in-the-depths" is felt to be more real than as "God-up-there." More recently, transcendence has been recast for thought in terms of "the Future." God is a real "Other," but his claim is not that of a metaphysical Yonder but of a historical Future, and the way to relate to him is not by turning the eyes "upward" but "forward."[104] Daniel O'Hanlon employs the phrase "absolute freedom" to define transcendence of this kind:

This way of thinking about God and our life of worship carries with it, it seems to me, the recovery of what could be called incarnational transcendence. If we keep firmly in our minds the fact of the incarnation and the sending of the Spirit on the Church, God's transcendence is not best understood by using models of distance, or changeless independence of the present moment of history. For us Christians the key to grasping God's transcendence must be the *absolute freedom* of his intimate presence. When time and history really become the central locus of God's action and man's response, then the unity of his immanence and transcendence can be understood more profoundly. Transcendence is the deep built-in spur to freely and creatively "go beyond," following the lead of God who in his freedom is always beyond and always calling us in faith to that hidden future which he has freely chosen for us and into which we freely move.[105]

At the same time, the danger for liturgy of what Father O'Hanlon calls theological overkill is self-evident, and what was intended to be a necessary shift in the liturgical center of gravity easily becomes only a mood of expectation or an uncritical immersion in the immanent. Probably many congregations would report that familiar folk music, the table-in-the-round, or photographic exhibits of "The World of Tomorrow" do not really engage man more truthfully with the reality of God than plainsong and the distant altar. Distance remains as important as nearness in authentic relation with the divine, and liturgical theology only falsifies the relation when it tries to speak to man's depths by removing God from the heights.[106]

[104] See for example Fackre, *Humiliation and Celebration*, p. 190.
[105] "The Secularity of Christian Worship," in *Worship in the City of Man* (Washington: The Liturgical Conference, 1966), pp. 20-21.
[106] "A psychologist must ask his clerical colleagues: Why are you prey to . . . simple solutions; why do you blur the hierarchies of transcendence and ultimacy, neglecting the

In any case, if one can think truthfully about worship only as one thinks incarnationally, then one must also think within the dialectic of the transcendence and immanence of God. The liturgical vision into which such a way of thinking can lead one has hardly been better portrayed than in the English translation of the Dutch "New Catechism":

Here then are the two pointers which, taken together, lead to the light where the purity of God's revelation is unfolded. God is free of the world, but He is still at the depths of its being. God is independent of man, but He is still bound up with man. The combination of transcendence and immanence in God is a mystery before which human reason remains powerless, though the believer recognizes that this revelation manifests God's greatness. It would no doubt be an easier solution to think of God as absorbed into the world (pantheism) or as utterly aloof (deism). But the assertion of His distance and presence at once gives revelation the very tension, grandeur and impact through which man feels that God is speaking. Our heart expands in the unfathomable mystery which lies outside the paths of our thought. It finds peace. It was made for such a God.[107]

All the polarities we have cited, however, as well as others we shall explore, ultimately inhere in the Christ-Event understood as incarnation. Their inherence is not in every case immediately visible or precise, but it is palpable for liturgy. And one can do justice to their truth, and to worship as a transaction embodying them, only when they are kept related to the dialectic of the incarnation. We shall let a passage from Bonhoeffer state for us this seminal truth:

Such pairs of concepts as secular and Christian, natural and supernatural, profane and sacred, and rational and revelational . . . [have their] original unity . . . in the reality of Christ. . . . The world, the natural, the profane and reason . . . have their reality nowhere save in the reality of God, in Christ. . . . Just as in Christ the reality of God entered into the reality of the world, so, too, is that which is Christian to be found only in that which is of the world, the "supernatural" only in the natural, the holy only in the profane, and the revelational only in the rational. . . . And yet what is Christian is not identical with what is of the world. The natural is not identical with the supernatural or the revelational with the rational. But between the two there is in each case a unity which derives solely from the reality of Christ.[108]

---

worlds of difference, represented traditionally by planes of being and classes of angels, between the levels and kinds of love; . . . why do you confuse the voices of autonomous complexes with the Pentecostal gift of tongues; how can you equate falling-in-love with coming home to the Godhead?" James Hillman, *Insearch* (New York: Charles Scribner's Sons, 1967), p. 82.

[107] *A New Catechism: Catholic Faith for Adults*, trans. Kevin Smyth (New York: Herder & Herder, 1967), p. 492.

[108] *Ethics*, pp. 64-65.

Liturgical Integrity in Light of the Word as Act

Inevitably we have anticipated the next meaning the Word holds for worship: its meaning as *Act*, as *Event*. One cannot reflect upon the incarnation at all without having to perceive it as act and correspondingly to think of liturgy as act. Indeed the incarnation cannot be understood under any other mode of meaning than that of divine and human act. However, in its divine meaning, the God who acts in the Jesus of history acts also in creation and in revelation generally. In all his manifestations God goes out of his "being-in-himself" to "being-in-action." [109] In biblical thought he is defined by active verbs more than by substantive nouns. Characteristically he is "the God who acts." The synoptic term "Word" intensely conveys this meaning. God's Word speaks through God's deeds and it acts through God's speech. In Scripture the Word of God is the work of God. In a typical sentence from the Psalms: "He spoke, and it came to be. He commanded and it stood forth." (Ps. 33:9 RSV).

However, the action of God's Word supremely comes to focus in the Event of Jesus Christ. While this Event includes God's total action in history leading up to it and flowing from it, in another sense this Event stands by itself and uniquely embodies God's action. Accordingly, liturgical Christology is the doctrine of the Event of Jesus Christ before it is the doctrine of the nature of Jesus Christ. Christ's person is to be understood through his work. To be sure, different strata in the interpretation which the New Testament itself makes of the meaning of Jesus Christ forbid assigning priorities too sharply;[110] and to say that reflection upon Jesus' work is theologically prior to reflection upon his nature is not to say that existentially his nature is experienced in worship as secondary to his action. The reality of Jesus Christ in worship is as ontological as it is actional (a crucial point to be developed shortly). Nevertheless, for purposes of thought we must understand that

The New Testament hardly ever speaks of the person of Christ without at the same time speaking of his work. . . . When it is asked in the New Testament, "Who is Christ?" the question never means exclusively, or even primarily, "What is his nature?" but first of all, "What is his function?" Therefore, the various

[109] See Fuller, *Foundations of New Testament Christology*, p. 255.

[110] Reginald H. Fuller detects three strata: the earliest Christology of Palestinian Judaism, that of Hellenistic Judaism, and the later Christology of the Gentile mission in the Graeco-Roman world. Significantly, the first interprets the meaning of Christ predominantly in functional terms reflecting the perception of Christ's meaning as inhering first in his work; and the last interprets the meaning of Christ predominantly in ontic categories reflecting a perception of Christ's meaning as inhering chiefly in his person. See *The Foundations of New Testament Christology*.

answers given to the question in the New Testament . . . visualize both Christ's person and his work. . . . Jesus himself *is* what he *does*.[111]

Or, to revert to the central term used in these essays: The Word, the *Logos*, is simultaneously *ergon*, the *verbum* simultaneously *opus*.[112]

By definition, then, authentic worship necessarily embodies this eventful character. Because its very ground is God's "being-in-action," worship cannot be defined nor take place in any other mode than action. Action is not something we seek after or something we add on to worship; rather worship itself is action. Action is the only form in which worship can exist because action is the primary mode in which the Word makes itself known. To be sure, the derivative doctrines of the Holy Spirit and the Church also define worship as action. The Holy Spirit as a dynamic mode of the divine presence contemporizes and empiricizes the action of God communicating the eschatological life of Jesus Christ to man. The Church, likewise, is to be thought of as constituted by the action of Christ among his people: "The Church," writes Barth, "as *ecclesia*, as *evocatio* or *congregatio*, is a description of an event." [113] And its action, as we have noted, always precedes man's. A true understanding of liturgical action, however, rests more fundamentally upon Christology than upon pneumatology or ecclesiology. Christ is the source of the life the Spirit bestows, and Christ similarly acts to form himself in his people before they form themselves in him.

A classical *locus* where the Christological nature of liturgical action is clearly seen consists of the imperative verbs with which Jesus institutes the cultic rite in which he uniquely discloses his meaning—the Eucharist: "Take," "eat," "drink," "do this." (Matt. 26:26-27; Mark 14:22; Luke 22: 17, 19; I Cor. 11:23-26). As commonly noted, the actional nature of worship enjoined upon man in these verbs is unmistakable. What is not so often noted, however, is that these imperatives take on meaning in light of Christ's action enjoining man's action. Man does not speak these imperatives to himself; rather, his action is evoked by, follows upon, and derives its authenticity from Christ's. The derivative nature of man's action can be fully understood only in light of the preceding action of Christ epitomized in the words: "Jesus *took* bread, and *blessed*, and *broke* it, and *gave*." [114] Man takes, eats, and drinks only because Jesus has first taken, blessed, broken, and given, as well as spoken.

Further, the cultic action of Jesus expressed and enjoined here is to be

---

[111] Cullmann, *The Christology of the New Testament*, pp. 3-4, 261.
[112] See Karl Barth, *Dogmatics in Outline*, p. 67.
[113] *Church Dogmatics*, IV/1, p. 651.
[114] Typically, in Matt. 26:26. See also Matt. 14:19; 15:35; Mark 8:6; 14:22; Luke 9:16; 24:30; John 6:11; 21:13.

seen in the larger light of his entire life and death understood as a liturgical action. And still further, the double direction of Christ's liturgical action is to be marked. On the one hand, it is clearly action toward man. On the other hand, it is action directed to God. Understood in the profoundest sense as liturgical action, the lodestar of Jesus' servant life and death is God even as it is service to man. The double direction of Christ's action in this deep sense in turn grounds man's action and determines its nature in a cultic sense. The substance of what Jesus cultically commands his people to "remember" in their action ("do this in remembrance of me") is nothing less than the total action he has manifested toward God and man in his life and his death. It is his divine-human liturgy, i.e. service, that the people are to remember and recapitulate in their liturgy. Man's action, as Christ's action, is simultaneously offered to God and to man. And in this fact of double-direction set within the full meaning of Christ's life and death as a liturgy of action lies the theological ground of man's action.

To be sure, the reality, the autonomy, and the gravity of man's action must be fully affirmed; and although Christ's action grounds man's action, their polarity must be kept polar. Man is no automaton in worship. Indeed, man's liturgical action has been described by Gerhard Ebeling as "the most active form of faith." And Karl Barth has written of the seriousness with which man's action in hearing the Word in preaching is to be taken: "In the Church to act means to *hear*, i.e. to hear the Word of God, and through the Word of God revelation and faith. It may be objected that this is too small a task and not active enough. But in the whole world there exists no more intense, strenuous or animated action than that which consists in hearing the Word of God." [115] Nevertheless, man's action is finally to be thought of as kindled by Christ's, as carried on through Christ's, and—to use a spatial metaphor—as offered up through Christ's.

The metaphor of Christ as Mediator or High Priest—so central for New Testament thought—figures this truth: the ascended and interceding Lord is none other than the human Jesus through whom man's worship is offered to God, even as through the divine Lord, God's grace simultaneously comes to man (Heb. 4:14; 10:21; 13:15, I Pet. 2:5). Or, the image of Christ as Jacob's ladder likewise figures this truth: through him the ascending action of man and the descending action of God occur.[116] Alternatively, the grounding of man's action in Christ's action can be conceptualized with the formula with which Lutheran doctrine conceptualizes the presence of Christ

[115] *The Knowledge of God and the Service of God*, trans. J. Haire and Ian Henderson (New York: Charles Scribner's Sons, 1939), p. 210.
[116] See William Nicholls, *Jacob's Ladder: The Meaning of Worship* (Richmond: John Knox Press, 1958).

in the Lord's Supper:[117] "In, with and under." The preposition "in" signifies that the divine does not despise but actually enters into our human action. The preposition "with" suggests that the divine truly joins with us in our action. The preposition "under" suggests the hiddenness of the divine action which yet is comprehended within man's action. This formula has the advantage of preserving for thought the integrity of each and of denoting the qualitative difference of each; at the same time it affirms the fulcral priority of Christ's action for man's and determines the action of worship to be "through Jesus Christ our Lord."

But by whatever formula it be said, a fundamental truth is at stake here: only as the precedence of divine action Christologically defined is affirmed, can worship as action be authentically rethought for our day. Otherwise our current stress on the people's active participation in worship can lead to the error that what we do is of first importance. Or it can lead us uncritically to accept aesthetic or psychological criteria for action. To be sure, these latter can help to provide for, even help execute, the action of the Word and the responsive action of man. As we shall note in later essays, the elements of vitality and movement which always characterize true art, for example, can be taken up and be theologically baptized and restated, and facilitate the action of worship. Similarly, a psychological understanding of the "modernity" of the modern man as partly consisting in his interest in what a thing does as distinguished from it is clearly speaks to the nature of action. Nevertheless, the starting point for thought must be the action of the Word.

One further aspect of liturgical action must be marked: its time-transcending and time-transforming character. Christian worship partakes of an action that once occurred uniquely in Jesus of Nazareth, that is occurring now, and that shall continue until the Parousia. This is to say, the action of worship takes place in more than chronological time. Or, we may say, liturgical action transcends as well as embraces time. Or alternatively, worship transforms time into its own time—"sacred time" or "liturgical time." The present tense of the verbs used by Jesus may be construed to hold this meaning: "This *is* my body.... This *is* my blood.... Wherever two or three are gathered, there *am* I." The action of worship is grounded in the past action of the Word yet contemporizing and futurizing itself.

Correspondingly, man's action answers to the time-transforming nature of the divine action with a threefold orientation. First, man's action is one of recollection of past event; that is, man remembers the historically lived

[117] Proposed by William Stählin and elaborated by Wilhelm Hahn, *Worship and Congregation*, pp. 40 ff.

life, death, and resurrection of Christ. Secondly, man's action in remembering becomes engagement with this event as present. In part, this is the meaning of the New Testament term which biblical theology has recovered for us—the term *anamnesis* translated as the "remembering" Jesus commands, but "remembering" understood not as "a . . . subjective remembering, lest we should forget, but a concrete and objective bringing back from the past into the present," [118] as re-presentation and recapitulation of past event with present reality and efficacy. Thirdly, man's action is an act of hope,[119] in turn bearing three aspects. First, hope is man's putting forth his selfhood in willed faith to meet the Word as a "foretaste" of an eternal quality of life experienced now but promissory of a fuller life to come. Secondly, hope is the act of commitment to the Word as a living reality opening up future possibilities in the actuality of human history. And lastly, the action of hope is the realization through faith of the worshipper's present worship on earth as one with the Church's worship in heaven.

In speaking in this way of the time-transforming and time-transcending character of action we are, of course speaking of the eschatological nature of worship—a topic to be elaborated presently. We are also speaking theologically more than empirically. Indeed, we conclude this discussion by stressing that all the distinctions we have made are distinctions of theology rather than of experience. In the actual experience of worship, conceptual distinctions of time merge. Likewise distinctions between divine and human action merge. It is to be understood that man's action can be a form of divine revelation at the same time that the divine revealing bears the form of human action. As Dietrich Ritschl has explained, there is in fact no such thing as an unhuman divine revelation of God to man or an undivine response of men to God.[120] While divine and human action can be separated for purposes of thought, in the experience of worship they interpenetrate. In whatever moment either is thought of as being performed, the other is nevertheless present. And only as this aspect of simultaneity is understood can one avoid the corruption of absolutizing liturgical structures of which we have previously written.

Liturgical Integrity in Light of the Historical and Trans-Historical Nature of the Word

The Word, further, possesses profound *historical* meaning which liturgical theology must try to state. In one sense, of course, the term "historical"

---

[118] A. G. Hebert, *The Parish Communion* (London: SPCK, 1937), p. 9.

[119] Theology sometimes speaks of the sacraments as they embody these three aspects of time, as *signum memorativum, signum demonstrativum, signum prognosticum.*

[120] See his volume, *Theology of Proclamation* (Richmond: John Knox Press, 1960).

is related to the term "human," whose meaning we have previously explored. The source of reality in Christian worship is not an idea nor a myth, not a dogma nor abstract truth. Rather, it is a flesh-and-blood human reality wrought into and rising out of the very texture of temporal history. It is a datable, terrestrial reality as palpable to man's historical consciousness as any other historical person or event one chooses to name, and the Christian man liturgically identifies his existence in reference to this reality. He submits to it as the fundamental datum for his being in something of the same way that the ancient Jew confirmed through the saying of the liturgical "amen" the history of his people as fateful for his destiny: his "amen" was not merely an assenting but a "knowing of oneself to be bound by what has previously been stated." [121] In its broadest meaning, the Word is likewise a statement which the divine has made of itself in history; and in the broadest sense Christian worship is similarly an "amen" pronounced in many modes through which the Christian man confirms this statement as decisive for his destiny. To be sure, today no less than originally this historical meaning is precisely the "scandal" of the Gospel: "The *skandalon*, the foolishness, lies in the fact that historically datable events ('under Pontius Pilate') . . . represent the very centre of God's revelation. . . . That was just as hard for men of that time to accept as for us today." [122] Difficult as acceptance may be, liturgical theology cannot stop short of this historical claim. Always, we are bound by the conviction that the truth of Christian revelation occurs not so much in spite of as because of a particular human history.

However, the historical meaning of the Word extends beyond the datable event of Jesus of Nazareth. In its full biblical sweep it includes the prior history of God's total action toward mankind, especially toward Israel and through Israel, converging in Jesus Christ. Therefore the historical meaning of the Word is not merely that Jesus Christ can only be understood in light of the Old Testament, as we commonly say; in a way transcending logic, the Word is *in* the Old Testament. What God did in Jesus of Nazareth he did also in patriarch and prophet, in priest and psalmist, indeed, in the act of creation as well as in the act of redemption. There is of course discontinuity as well as continuity between Old Testament and New Testament history, and again one must think dialectically. In Jesus of Nazareth, God acted in history in a way in which he has acted nowhere else, and to fail to affirm the "newness" of the "New" Covenant inaugurated in him is to fail to affirm the full meaning of his death and resurrection. Yet, "Israel itself was already a partial realization of the mystery of Christ, it was the 'Christ

[121] Delling, *Worship in the New Testament*, p. 74.
[122] Cullmann, The Christology of the New Testament, p. 327.

event' in process of coming to be;" [123] and it is this vision of the sweep of God's action in all history that the Christological titles of the New Testament referring to the pre-existence of Jesus (such as "*Logos*," "Son of God") are metaphorically meant to declare. As Tertullian exclaimed to the Oriental philosophers of his day: "Your history only goes back to the Assyrians; ours is a history from the beginning of the world." [124]

The true historical meaning of the Word, however, cannot be grasped unless it is dialectically illumined at the same time by its *trans-historical* nature also. The term "trans-historical," of course, in a sense restates the meaning of the Word we have spoken of as "time-transcending"; it also anticipates a meaning to be dealt with presently under the category of eschatology. Yet only when the dialectical relation between "historical" and "trans-historical" is seen can the boldness of the meaning of either be understood. There is, on the one hand, an irreversible, finished, historical aspect to the event of the Word which theology colloquially speaks of as its "once-for-all-ness"; and the metaphysical decisiveness it originally bore for liturgy cannot be repeated.[125] On the other hand, there is an aspect to this event which transcends history; in a sense it is eternal; and it can always and everywhere recur whenever God "decides to reveal himself to men in his only begotten Son through his Holy Spirit. This abiding presence of God's revelatory acts in history . . . is . . . *sui generis*, . . . a 'mystery.' [126] Thus, beside the historical "once-for-allness" of the Event of Christ must be set its trans-historical "ongoingness." Dialectically understood, the Christ Event is both unrepeatable and repeatable. It occurred only once; yet it occurs again and again. Historically, Jesus Christ is he who cried on the cross: "It is finished." Trans-historically, Jesus Christ is he who promises, "I am with you always," and who lives and ever makes intercession for us, the same yesterday, today, and forever.

One way in which liturgy grasps this dialectic is to employ the biblical term *anamnesis* to which we have referred, meaning "remembering." Within the action of "remembering" (aptly defined by T. F. Torrance as "sacramental memory" [127]) is embraced man's recollection of the historical Jesus on the one hand, and man's encounter with the trans-historical Word

[123] Schillebeeckx, *Christ the Sacrament of the Encounter with God*, p. 12.

[124] Quoted by W. A. Visser 't Hooft, *The Renewal of the Church* (Philadelphia: Westminster Press, 1956), pp. 50-51.

[125] See the *Report of the Theological Commission on Worship*, Fourth World Conference on Faith and Order, Faith and Order Paper 39 (Geneva: World Council of Churches, 1963), p. 12.

[126] *Ibid.*

[127] See the article by Paul Crow, Jr., "The Lord's Supper in Ecumenical Dialogue," *Theology Today*, XXII (Apr., 1965).

responding to faith now as it once did, on the other. This is to say that liturgically to "remember" is to experience the historical and eternal as brought together in Jesus Christ. That which happened in time is made the sacrament of that which is beyond time, and that which is beyond time is known through that which is of time. History is at once affirmed and transcended.

Still another way to state this truth is to say that Christian worship is bound to time and yet miraculously conquers time,[128] and its miraculous character consists in just this trans-temporalization of historical events rather than in the trans-substantiation of physical elements. The nature of time rather than of matter is mystically altered. Chronological time becomes transformed into liturgical time, and worship is to be thought of as a time miracle rather than as a substance miracle.[129] It is in this direction, parenthetically, that one looks for the bridge of ecumenical agreement that shall someday unite Protestant, Roman Catholic, and Orthodox Christian in common worship.

From the historical and trans-historical meaning of the Word, a number of implications follow, both theoretical and practical, only three of which we shall mention here. First, worship embodies integrity to the extent that it is kept in reference to the history in which God has acted to save man in a way in which he could not save himself—in the calling of Israel to be his people, in election, covenant, prophecy, and supremely in the Event of Jesus Christ in which all other acts of God are summed up. This historical matrix of salvation history is decisive for worship: *"Everything that is done in Worship, every event in the service, stands right in the movement of this salvation-history and participates in it."* [130] Thus the necessity to anchor worship in Scripture which tells this history; the importance of the liturgical structures which the Church "delivers" to us—the primacy of preaching and sacrament of which we have written; thus the necessity of the Christian Year whose time-frame converts man's time—*chronos*—into divine time—*kairos*—and recapitulates past history with present efficacy. (We shall elaborate the importance of the Christian Year in subsequent essays.[131])

---

[128] See Alexander Schmemann, *Introduction to Liturgical Theology*, trans. Ashleigh E. Moorhouse (London: Faith Press, 1966), p. 35.

[129] See Leslie Wilfred Brown, *Relevant Liturgy* (New York: Oxford University Press, 1963), pp. 42 ff.; Von Allmen, *Worship: Its Theology and Practice*, pp. 34 ff.; Theodore O. Wedel, "The Theology of the Liturgical Renewal," in Massey H. Shepherd, Jr., ed. *The Liturgical Renewal of the Church* (New York: Oxford University Press, 1960), pp. 5 ff.; Schillebeeckx, *Christ the Sacrament of the Encounter with God*, pp. 55-56, 61-63.

[130] Delling, *Worship in the New Testament*, p. 10.

[131] See chs. III, VI, VII

Secondly, worship embodies integrity to the extent that it perceives present as well as past history as revelatory of the Word and exposes man to it. Precisely because that Word which is the source of Christian worship is a historical reality, the Christian man can never be allowed to engage in worship as an escape from present history into past history. Because God has declared himself in the incarnation to be a historical God who takes history with utmost seriousness, the man who worships is to take history with utmost seriousness; and because God has impregnated history with meaning in the past, so it is pregnant with meaning now. Alternatively, we may say that "time"—thought of as a synonym for "history"—is part of the matrix of worship. Worship in a sense conquers time; yet worship is also to be embedded in time and its stuff is to be events in time. What one can *not* say about worship is what Odo Casel once mistakenly said: The purpose of "the redemption of Christ [is] . . . to pull man away from the narrowness of time and introduce him to eternity without end." [132] On the contrary, the purpose of redemption as recapitulated in worship is to make man vulnerable to time, to intensify to his consciousness the present events of his time, and to help him identify and join in God's activity in time. In short, worship not only speaks to, it is always being spoken to by, history; and it is to be conceived as a worldly or secular event in the sense that it shares in the very "complicity" with which God is historically involved with his world. [133]

Thirdly, here lies the basis for conceiving worship as missionary, as the acceptance of responsibility for "a genuine historical existence." [134] Worship possesses integrity only when the action man performs toward God in cultus is made one with the action he performs toward men in his present world. Indeed, mission is to be thought of as "the resonance of liturgy," in a fine phrase of Thomas J. Talley[135]—as the worldly life of the Christian vibrating with the same dynamism with which he has been apprehended liturgically by the action of God in the historical Word, Jesus Christ. Or, in words of Horst Symanowski: "You must realize that perhaps the most important moment in the worship service is the moment in which you leave the church. Then it is decided whether you have understood why you spent that hour behind those walls." [136]

---

[132] Quoted by Richard Paquier, trans. Donald Macleod *The Dynamics of Worship* (Philadelphia: Fortress Press, 1967), p. 113.

[133] The term is J. G. Davies', to whose book *Worship and Mission* I am indebted here.

[134] *Ibid.,* p. 106.

[135] "The Sacredness of Contemporary Worship," *Worship in the City of Man,* p. 38.

[136] *The Christian Witness in an Industrial Society,* trans. G. H. Kehm (Philadelphia: Westminster Press, 1964), p. 98.

Even as we press the importance of the historical character of the Word, however, we must revert to the full dialectic of the incarnation in concluding this discussion and mark once more the trans-historical character of the Word as well. For permeating the historicity of Jesus' earthly life is always a divine reality one can only speak of as transcending history. God is revealed to be both vulnerable and invulnerable to history, as able to become savingly engaged with man precisely because he is over against man. The "absoluteness of the 'Absolute' "—in a phrase of one scholar—underlies the "relatedness" of the Absolute to the world and history. Correspondingly, in worship man must finally be addressed by that in God which is beyond history—God in his eternity, God in his "Godness." Thus worship is finally to be as much the conquest of time as immersion in time, as much "sacred" as "secular," as much "otherworldly" as "worldly." In our day, especially, man's secularized consciousness needs to be confronted by divine reality as symbolized in the vision of Christ that was at the center of worship for the early Christians: the ascended Christ sitting at the right hand of the Father. As much absorbed with him who lived and reigned beyond history as with him who had lived in history, they rendered this vision in a host of ways, perhaps most beautifully in the prayer that is still the prayer of Christendom today, the *Sursum Corda:* "Lift up your hearts!" "We lift them up unto the Lord!" The truth of this prayer was, and still is, the purpose of Christian worship itself: to summon the hearts of the faithful to the eternal living Lord as the ultimate reality for Christian existence, and to assure the believing soul that he is as mystically present to men now in all the plenitude of his grace as he was in his earthly life.

Liturgical Integrity in Light of the Ontological Meaning of the Word

The Word holds for worship, next, *ontological* meaning, and in naming this meaning we arrive at the heart of liturgical theology. While we are by no means confident that we use this term properly, only some such term can say what any theology of Christian worship must at all costs try to say: the core of worship is God acting to give his life to man and to bring man to partake of that life. Of course one's deepest convictions emerge in such a statement, and one can name "ontology" as at the heart of liturgical theology only as one reads "life" as at the heart of the Gospel. But in naming this meaning we name that category beyond which we believe the mind cannot go in being apprehended by the Gospel; and we would hold that all other categories are subordinate to it. Rudolf Bultmann has stated our conviction clearly. Of the *Ego sum vita* of Jesus Christ, the great cry, "I am . . . life,"

137

he writes that "what is sought for everywhere is here made real." [137] Here all other meanings converge. The Word most fundamentally is the Word of Life, and the incarnation is nothing less than the life of God indwelling man and bringing man to become "a partaker of the divine nature." This life, however, is not life in a timeless, idealist sense, nor is it life in the classical mystic sense. Rather, as Bultmann adds, life comes through "adhering in faith to an historical fact and an historical person . . . and correspondingly, this life consists in the manner of an historical existence." [138] As the Word historically embodied and offered this life once, so it ever does, and in this sense the Word holds for worship ontological meaning.

This meaning is to be understood first in a metaphysical sense: in the Word is concentrated and revealed the nature of all being, and in the Word is concentrated that Reality which determines man's being or not-being. We well realize that to make this affirmation is to incur the risk of a certain reductionism, of converting the wine of theology into the water of philosophy. Nevertheless, thought cannot move on any less deep a level because one cannot read out of the Gospel the conviction that in Jesus Chist the very ontal life of the universe is concentrated and revealed, and that the transaction of liturgy has to do with this life. To be sure, the Church has declared this conviction brokenly, sometimes polemically, and in thought-forms of uneven value. One thinks of the different strata of Christology in the New Testament, for example, and of the variety of metaphors—such as the doctrine of the pre-existence of Christ—in which the ontal meaning of the Word is represented. Further, it is perhaps true that Jesus did not think of himself in this way, and that his life is declared to have metaphysical significance only by the post-Easter mind of the early Church. Nevertheless, only an interpretation of the ontal meaning of Jesus Christ suggested by such a term as "metaphysical" can do justice to his nature as the Church experienced it in its inner existence: its Gospel ineffaceably presents Jesus Christ as the source of life flowing to all creation and as the end to which all creation moves. All being, nature and cosmos as well as human life and history, is penetrated with his divine vitality—"the all-powerful torrent of life of the Logos," in a phrase of Charles Moeller—and it is as an experience of this vitality that worship in his name is to be understood.

The nativity story figures this metaphysical vision: the universe itself cannot be unmoved by so stupendous an event, and the star comes to rest over the place of Jesus' birth as the center in which all nature finds its meaning. (It is significant that the Church's liturgical year begins with this event and

---

[137] Bultmann, et al., Life and Death, p. 78. Bultmann cites the Greek: ἐγώ εἰμί . . .
[138] Ibid., p. 76.

its foretelling.) Jesus' answer on Palm Sunday to those who complained of the Messianic singing of the children in the temple, "I tell you that if these should hold their peace, the very stones would cry out," similarly marks the fatefulness of his divine life for inanimate life and for the processes of history. Again, in the moment of his death, the cosmic cycle of day and night is broken, and the extinction of his life is symbolically matched by the darkness of the physical universe. Correspondingly, in his resurrection, physical and biological realities are transfigured and the universal reign of death is shattered.

Most significantly of all, the paradigm Scripture finds best able to portray the ontal life of Christ is none other than the aboriginal story of the first Creation Christologically retold. The ontology of the Christ Event holds import so profound as to require nothing less than that the very foundations of all being be reinterpreted through him; that the life of the Word be seen as that reality by virtue of which things exist or die; and that the newness visible in all creation, the dynamism immanent in history and the universe, be understood in light of the newness of the life Jesus Christ is. In the words of Enst Käsemann: It is Jesus Christ who "brings the world back into the state of creation. . . . The last creation leads back to the first. The one who is the end also reveals the beginning." [139] The author of Colossians carries this vision to its climax:

He is the image of the invisible God; his is the primacy over all created things. In him everything in heaven and on earth was created, not only things visible but also the invisible orders of thrones, sovereignties, authorities, powers: the whole universe has been created through him and for him. And he exists before everything, and all things hold together in him.[140]

In a word, the *Ego sum vita* of Jesus Christ holds cosmic, metaphysical meaning.

Nothing less than this Christian *vita* is the "life" which Christian liturgy celebrates, and nothing less than this is the basic affirmation of liturgical theology. This is to say, liturgical theology has its roots first in the doctrine of Christ through which creation is to be understood, not in the doctrine of creation through which Jesus Christ is to be understood. This distinction is absolutely fundamental, and it speaks particularly to our situation today

---

[139] *The Testament of Jesus*, p. 51. See also the chapter by Jean Daniélou, S. J., "The Sacraments and the History of Salvation," in *The Liturgy and the Word of God* (Collegeville, Minn.: The Liturgical Press, 1959); and the article "A Comparative Study of Christian Spirituality," by Trevor Rowe, in *The London Quarterly and Holborn Review* (Jan., 1966).

[140] 1:15-17 NEB. See also I Cor. 8:6; Ephes. 1:3-10, 19-23; Phil. 2:5-11; and, of course, John 1:1 ff.; Heb. 1:1 ff.

in that it constitutes the watershed between Christian and less than Christian worship. Attempts to affirm the secular nature of worship under the rubric "the celebration of life," for example, frequently seize on the Old Testament doctrine of creation as the starting point; and from here a liturgical theology is elaborated to affirm the dynamics of history, the vitalities of the created order, and the worldly life of man. Such a starting point, it is alleged, releases thought from what is felt to be the constriction of traditional Christological categories and enlarges liturgical sensibility to celebrate all life. This view, however, aside from the glosses upon the term "life" it finds convenient to perpetrate, fatally reverses theological priorities and ends up as a corrupting reductionism. Carried to its conclusion, it fosters at best only religious liturgy, and at worst, pagan liturgy, in that it subordinates that reality which alone keeps Christian liturgy Christian, the Word Jesus Christ. The "life" which Christian liturgy delights to celebrate is indeed the life of the created world and history, yes, but life as seen *sub vita Christi*, within the life of Christ, not vice versa. The "Mass of the World" is indeed in the "Mass of the Altar," but it is there in the manner of the vision of Teilhard de Chardin:

Do you now therefore, speaking through my lips, pronounce over this earthly travail your twofold efficacious word; the word without which all that our wisdom and experience have built up must totter and crumble—the word through which all our most far-reaching speculations and our encounter with the universe are come together into a unity. Over every living thing which is to spring up, to grow, to flower, to ripen during this day say again the words: This is my Body. And over every death force which waits in readiness to corrode, to wither, to cut down, speak again your commanding words which express the supreme mystery of faith: This is my blood.[141]

Liturgical Integrity in Light of the Soteriological and Eschatological Meaning of the Word

Next, the ontological meaning of the Word is to be understood in a *soteriological* sense. The profoundest meaning of the incarnation is not that in Jesus Christ the world is affirmed as good nor that the nature of Being is disclosed. Rather, in him a saving deed is done that deals with man in his moral predicament in a way he could not deal with it himself. Embodying the "design of salvation" as "arising from the depths of the divine mind," in a phrase of C. K. Barrett,[142] the Word addresses man not as first needing enlightenment in place of his ignorance, nor as needing the vitalities of his existence to be affirmed or his imagination to be grasped. Rather, the Word

[141] Quoted from de Chardin's *Hymn of the Universe* by Talley in *Worship in the City of Man*, p. 35.
[142] See *The Pastoral Epistles* (Oxford: Clarendon Press, 1963), p. 21.

became flesh to deliver men from evil, to break the bondage of sin that enslaves the will, and to do on the cross that deed which can save from guilt, corruption, and death. Thus, as the expression of divine life, the Word is more than ontal being; rather, it is "being in action" that goes forth in judgement and mercy to save. In short, the Word is *Soter* as well as *Logos* —the Saviour into life as well as the source of life. Again, as Bultmann bluntly writes of the New Testament term ζωη: "We have life only in relation to God's act of *salvation* in Christ." [143]

Indeed, on this deep level the soteriological life of the Word must be understood as meeting man with a certain "anti" character, as counter reality,[144] as a presence over against man and as saving in its very over-againstness. In its saving action, the Word opposes man in his non-being with being, in his mortality with life, in his corruption with incorruption. It contradicts the way in which man habitually experiences himself as alive and compels him radically to redefine what he means by life. Soteriologically, the Word counters man as Christ confronted the disciples on Easter Day: "They, the disciples . . . are the ones marked out by death. . . . Those who have survived him are the dead, and the dead one is the living." [145]

Thus a certain absoluteness, a certain fatefulness, attaches to the soteriological life of the Word. Liturgical theology may perhaps compromise at other points, but not here. As encounter with the Word in which the eternal life of God is communicated to man, and man in his death is yet made a partaker of the divine nature, worship by definition is soteriological and man's situation before this Word is rightly felt to be fateful. In worship the drama of man's destiny is to take place. The ultimate choices of life are posed. The boundary between the new life in Christ and the death he now lives becomes exposed. The Ultimate Reality beyond all other realities becomes present to him. The ordinary man would probably not understand the term with which theology has gone on to speak of this fatefulness, but theology has had no alternative but to say that man's situation in the presence of the life-saving and life-giving Word is inevitably *eschatological*. In each service of authentic worship man faces that Divine Reality which would invade his existence and with which he must come to terms. The Word confronting him embodies the event on which his destiny hangs: The Lord is at hand, the Kingdom of God is nigh.

To be sure, the "present-tenseness" with which the Word fatefully con-

---

[143] See *Life and Death*, pp. 68-70. Italics mine.
[144] See Bonhoeffer, *Christ the Center*, p. 30; Josef A. Jungmann, *Pastoral Liturgy*, trans. Tonbury Wells (London: Challoner Publications, 1962), p. 337.
[145] Bornkamm, *Jesus of Nazareth*, p. 185.

fronts man is also bound up with the Word's past history; it is also bound up with the future; and the eschatological life of the Word is always to be understood simultaneously within these three dimensions. The Lord is at hand; the Lord has come; the Lord shall come. But while these three aspects —past, present and future—mark the fatefulness of worship, the greatest of these is the life the Word offers *now*. And one must say of worship of which Jesus Christ is the center what C. H. Dodd has said of the Eucharist: "The Church perpetually reconstitutes the crisis in which the kingdom of God came in history. It never gets beyond this. At each Eucharist we are *there*—we are in the night in which he was betrayed, at Golgotha, before the empty tomb on Easter Day, and in the upper room where he appeared; and we are at the moment of his coming, with angels and archangels and all the company of heaven." [146]

The ontological meaning of the Word thus understood, as also embracing soteriological and eschatological meaning—this is the fundamental hinge on which liturgical theology is to turn. Jesus Christ as life savingly offered to man is that of which thought cannot stop short; it is that beyond which thought cannot go. To be sure, the liturgical mind of the Church has conceptualized in many ways the meaning we have named "ontological"—in particular as the doctrine of the Real Presence understood not as restricted to the physical elements but as in the whole liturgical event and not least in the souls of the people. But however it be conceptualized, this ontological meaning is the integrating reality which bestows integrity upon both the act of worship and man's thinking about worship. Both liturgical experience and liturgical reflection become narrowed down to confrontation with the life-giving and life-saving action of the Word as fateful.

In affirming the fulcral place the ontological meaning the Word holds, it is critical to understand that we are not deriving this truth from speculation upon the nature of Jesus Christ. Rather, we are trying to state the essence of what Jesus Christ means in the *action* of worship to the human soul. We declare this distinction to be "critical" in face of the objection that Jesus did not make ontological statements about himself, that ontic categories are obsolete, and that in contemporary thought dynamic categories must replace those of substance. As applied to the making of theological statements about the nature of Jesus Christ, this may be the case. As applied to statements about the nature of the liturgical *encounter* between God and man transacted through Jesus Christ, this is not the case. So far from being obsolete, the ontological meaning of Jesus Christ can alone, we believe, do justice to the reality of worship. For in worship, uniquely, what the Word

[146] *The Apostolic Preaching* (Chicago: Willett, Clark & Co., 1937), pp. 163-64.

is becomes known through what the Word does: *the action of Christ makes known the being of Christ.*

The thought-forms, categories, and symbols with which the mind of the Church through the centuries has attempted to conceptualize the meaning of worship abundantly corroborate this truth. Taken together, these constitute a universal apperception that the liturgical encounter between Jesus Christ and the human soul is fundamentally a transaction of life and a salvation into life. Thus the early Church declared that the invasion of divine life into human life in Jesus Christ could be adequately recognized only by altering the way in which men commonly marked the meaning of time, and fixed "the Lord's Day" as the first day of the week on which the Christian man celebrated the Eucharist as the recapitulation of the resurrection event in which he found the source of his very existence. Similarly, Easter as the festival of divine life meeting man in his death became the supreme liturgical occasion of the Church. (Indeed, every Sunday was celebrated as Easter Day, the Day of Resurrection.) This adaptation of the calendar of course held eschatological as well as ontological meaning, for the "Lord's Day" and Easter marked the event where two aeons had met—the event of the cross and resurrection in which the world had been lifted off its hinges and the future life of the Kingdom had become present. This eschatological understanding, however, arose out of the experience by the Christian community of the new life in Christ: eschatological understanding of time was secondary to an ontological experience of life, and eschatology became an aspect of Christology—especially in St. John—rather than vice versa.

Further, the rites celebrated at Easter known as the Paschal Liturgy (which determined all later developments), beginning with the fast of Good Friday, the vigil and prayers on Saturday, Baptism and confirmation, and the festal Eucharist at Easter dawn—these likewise were a symbolic acting out of the Christian consciousness that Jesus Christ had acted to bring the believer from death into life, from sin into righteousness, from bondage into freedom, from death under the law to life in the Spirit.[147] Implicit throughout was the motif of death and resurrection whereby man entered into the new life of the new age in Christ; and in all the elements of these rites "Christ the risen Lord" stood "right at the centre." [148]

Above all, in the dominical sacraments of Baptism and the Eucharist, the ontological, soteriological, and eschatological meaning of the Word became

---

[147] See Massey H. Shepherd, Jr., "The Origin of the Church's Liturgy," *Studia Liturgica* I (June, 1962); Geoffrey Wainwright, "The Baptismal Eucharist Before Nicaea," *Studia Liturgica* IV (Spring, 1965).

[148] Cullmann, *Early Christian Worship*, p. 23.

143

concentrated. In these the believer received nothing less than "his true Christian being." [149] Baptism with its water symbolism, for example, was seen as a new creation parallel to the waters of the first creation (Gen. 1:20). Or it was conceived as a rite of "crossing," of "deliverance," a "second Red Sea" as the fathers called it, marking the dividing line between the old bondage of death and the freedom of new life in Christ, symbolized by the total immersion of the convert and by his resurrection from the waters, and by the vestment of the white robe in which he was clad. Understood as nothing less than a new birth, through Baptism life came into being that was not there before; and as Hans Conzelmann reminds us, the oldest baptismal formula had but one name: Χριστοῦ εἶναι, "in Christ." [150] Engrafted into Christ, man was made a new creature, so much so that Augustine could exultantly shout: "We are become not only Christians, but Christ. Do we understand, my brethren, the outpouring of God's grace upon us? Let us wonder and shout with gladness. We are become Christ." [151] And not for nothing—as still today—was the baptismal font called "the womb of the Church."

The Eucharist supremely embodied the ontological-salvational meaning of the Word. The very bread and wine themselves, for one thing, were typological symbols. Or rather, they were counter-symbols matching the curse upon the ground when man first lost paradise; under the transforming touch of Christ's presence, the bread and wine became signs of fertility and of new possibilities of life in the world. Further, the relating of the Eucharist to the Passover similarly symbolized deliverance from death into life; and the element of sacrifice—so central to each—was understood to signify not first death but life. Christ's death was remembered in the Eucharist as life sacrificed that life might be received. The meaning of the blood of the New Covenant likewise paralleled the meaning of the blood of the old covenant with which Moses had first sprinkled the altar as atonement for the sins of the people, and then after their response, the people themselves. In both covenants the blood meant life. And whereas the core of meaning in the old covenant was God's promise to share his Shekinah, his presence, with his people, the core of meaning in the new was Christ's promise to share his risen life with his disciples. Similarly, the aspect of the Eucharist as "eating" Christ as food, and the drinking of his blood, sometimes spoken of as "incorporation," also held ontological meaning. The presence of Christ met

[149] Dix, *The Shape of the Liturgy* p. 267.

[150] *An Outline of the Theology of the New Testament*, trans. John Bowden (New York: Harper & Row, 1969), p. 49.

[151] Quoted by Alfred R. Shands, *The Liturgical Movement and the Local Church*, p. 115.

in the Eucharist was believed to be that divine body—*corpus*—into whose very reality man is taken and without which he dies, as the children of Israel would have died but for the gift of manna in the wilderness. The bread and wine of the Eucharist were nothing less—in a phrase of Bonhoeffer—than the essential "nourishment for the new being." [152]

Most of all, in the earliest tradition which only today the Church is recovering, it was the presence of the risen Christ, not his death, that was the focal point of eucharistic devotion. He who was met in the sacrament was the living Lord who was crucified more than the crucified Jesus who had also risen;[153] and consequently joy was the predominant characteristic. As the "ceremony of resurrection," the Eucharist perpetually bestowed that life without which the believer could not live. He felt compelled to be present not from constraint of duty but because he could not exist without it. He understood himself as one whose life was lived from the life given him in Christ.

Similarly on down through the centuries, the ontological-soteriological meaning of the Word has been central in the Church's liturgical self-understanding in multitudes of ways. The varying formulations of the doctrine of the Real Presence, as we have noted, and the controversies which have raged around this doctrine are only the Church's way of theologically insisting that the very life of Christ is met and can be received in worship. The biblical and doctrinal term "mystery" applied to the sacraments has had the same intention: "mystery" means "nothing less than the *transitus*, the passage from death to life, by faith, through the cross to the resurrection. . . . The grace of Christ cannot be separated from his Person; his life *in us* is not a different thing from his life lived *among* us and for us." [154] Preaching likewise, when authentic proclamation and not merely pious address, has been felt to possess ontological and soteriological meaning. It has been understood as not merely a "message" about God but as "a third sacrament," the re-enactment of the Word's life-giving and life-saving action itself, a verification of the promise, "He who hears you hears me." Indeed it has been written: "*Christ's presence is his existence as preaching*. . . . Preaching . . . is the form of the presence of Christ to which we are bound and to which we have to keep." [155] The core of the Church's prayer also, while assuming a variety of forms, has been essentially existential prayer, that is,

---

[152] *Christ the Center*, p. 59.

[153] "The decisive Christophanies, before all the disciples, took place during a meal." Oscar Cullmann and F. J. Leenhardt, *Essays on the Lord's Supper*, trans. J. G. Davies (London: Lutterworth Press, 1958), p. 8.

[154] Lancelot Sheppard, *The People Worship* (New York: Hawthorn Books, 1964), pp. 81-82.

[155] Bonhoeffer, *Christ the Center*, p. 52. Italics mine.

prayer for life and an experience of renewed life. Whether categorized as "prophetic" or "mystical" as in the analysis of Friedrich Heiler, or composed in the traditional forms of confession, thanksgiving, intercession, petition, at its heart liturgical prayer has been man's cry for divine life; and the sign of its efficacy has been the resurrection of man to life. Not least, the reading of Scripture, especially the Gospel, has been regarded as sacramental, even as paschal; the Word buried in the printed word rises with life and feeds man's soul with a divine life other than his own. The Christian funeral similarly has been the celebration of life affirmed amidst death;[156] the Eucharist as part of the office of the dead is one of the oldest customs of the Church. Finally, the pentecostal speaking in tongues, prophecies, revelations, with which Christians from time to time have conducted their worship, have been understood as signs and gifts of the Spirit confirming the eschatological life given men in Christ.

In summary, one cannot contemplate the broad sweep of Christian worship and the manifold ways in which the Church has conceptualized its meaning without being made overwhelmingly aware of the ontological reality of Jesus Christ: the action of Jesus Christ conveys the life of Jesus Christ. Liturgical *history*, we may say, *confirms* liturgical *theology*. And *theology* in turn only *confirms* the *doxology* of faith:

When all things began, the Word already was. The Word dwelt with God, and what God was, the Word was. The Word, then, was with God at the beginning, and through him all things came to be. . . . All that came to be was alive with his life, and that life was the light of men. . . . To all who did receive him, to those who have yielded him their allegiance, he gave the right to become children of God, . . . the offspring of God himself. So the Word became flesh; he came to dwell among us, and we saw his glory, such glory as befits the Father's only Son, full of grace and truth (John 1:1-14 NEB).

The Fullness of the Word

Lastly, theological integrity requires that we apprehend—we had almost said "comprehend" but this term will not suffice—the *fullness* of the Word. This fullness may in part be thought of metaphysically, as we have explained, indeed almost mystically as the abundance of God's ontal life flowing through Christ to all creation and savingly drawing all humanity to Christ as their source and end. And liturgy, when true, joyfully recapitulates this meaning: in the words of St. John, "From his fullness have we all received, grace upon grace" (1:16 RSV); or in the words of St. Paul, "In him the

[156] See the Constitution on the Sacred Liturgy, Par. 81: "The rite for the burial of the dead should evidence more clearly the paschal character of Christian death."

146

whole fullness of deity dwells bodily, and you have come to fullness of life in him." (Col. 2:9-10 RSV).

Further, the fullness of the Word is to be thought of as conveyed within the full spectrum of symbols and doctrines which discriminate the rich meanings of Jesus Christ: prophecy, birth, life, passion, resurrection, ascension, pentecost, parousia. The reality of Jesus Christ is to be grasped not under any single discrete aspect but through all the meanings to which his name and reality are attached. From time to time one or another of the doctrines corresponding to these meanings has been given more central place in the Church's worship. The fullness of the Word is like a spectrum of many colors, and the Church has found itself liturgically beholden now by this doctrine and now by that. The resurrection and the heavenly reign of Christ have distinctively claimed the devotion of Eastern Orthodoxy; incarnation and atonement, the piety of Roman Catholicism. Pentecostal worship characteristically stresses the Holy Spirit, the second coming, and last judgement. Anglican liturgy emphasizes the doctrine of the incarnation. Until recently much Protestant free-church worship has magnified the human and historical Jesus. Such diverse emphases in liturgy surely are to be welcomed. Indeed the fullness of the Word makes them inevitable.

Yet, when an imbalance prevails, liturgy becomes impoverished. This is why the forms of worship are so important, as we have pointed out, and why the normative structures of worship become decisive. Holy Communion combined with preaching, for example, sets forth the fullness of the Word better than preaching alone. The total meaning of Christ is more faithfully conveyed. This is not to say that a service exclusively of preaching necessarily fails in this respect. It was said of Luther that in any time of the Church year in which he happened to be preaching, he proclaimed the fullness of the Word: "For him and his hearers, every day was Christmas and Good Friday and Easter and Pentecost." [157] But we are not Luthers. And whereas preaching by itself does this occasionally, sacrament and sermon together do it almost inevitably. This is why the full liturgy of Communion and sermon should be the normative liturgy of the Church. The sacrament objectively embodies the fullness of the Word better than interpretation by the preacher alone. The Mystery of Jesus Christ in the sacrament, it has been said, "is suffused with the proclamation of his final glory; the worship of the Cross on Good Friday resounds with the shouts of victory; and, on Easter Sunday, the exaltation of the Resurrection" is mingled with the

[157] Jaroslav Pelikan, Regin Prenter, and Herman A. Preus, *More About Luther* (Decorah, Iowa: Luther College Press, 1958), p. 38.

memories of Christ's death. "Every Eucharist always proclaims the whole mystery." [158]

Yet, the final mark of the fullness of the Word is its strange power to contradict all our liturgical dicta and to atone for our liturgical errors. As the Word of grace, Jesus Christ somehow completes the brokenness of our thought and speech with an abundance which the distortions we fasten upon worship would not lead one to think possible. This is why we can only gratefully apprehend—rather than comprehend—the fullness of Jesus Christ. How often have heretical theologies held sway over the worship of the Church, and yet the Word visited and saved! How often has the liturgy of the Church been in one way or another a "torso" liturgy, and yet the Lord formed himself in his Body! How often has the Church's worship crudely narrowed the meaning of the Word to only the humanity of Jesus—perhaps in a homily which exhorted us to follow him as our example, or in a Communion service which dwelt only upon his death; yet to us in our liturgical poverty the Word divinely rushed in its fullness, and the example became our salvation, the death our life! Even as the Church stammered of Christ when she ought to have spoken clearly, somehow Christ in his grace forgave our sins. The vessel of liturgy had become a broken cup; yet wells of water sprang up unto everlasting life. Thus the fullness of the Word ever forbids our making absolute judgements upon worship offered through Jesus Christ our Lord. We are never to be relieved from that holy anxiety whereby thought and devotion shall be obedient to the Word in its awful sovereignty and fullness of truth. Yet the glory of the Word is that it saves us even in our apostasy and error. Here, as elsewhere, we are justified by grace, not by works, lest any man should theologically boast.

---

[158] Bouyer, *Liturgical Piety*, p. 191.

III

The Relevance and Irrelevance of Worship

Probably the plea most strongly voiced by critics of worship today is the plea for relevance, and quite clearly a grave indictment is being presented in this widespread and often passionate cry. Prophets of social action demand a cultus more relevant to our revolutionary age, and secular theologians protest the otherworldliness that corrupts worship into escape. Church educators ask why worship does not more effectively touch the springs of character and personality, and chaplains and campus ministers seek new liturgies to communicate to young people alienated from the Church. Psychologists aware of the therapeutic power of worship ask why it does not avail to heal man's pain, and artists appeal for liturgy whose forms will grasp man's life with dramatic power. Biblical scholars complain that worship fails to restate faith intelligibly for the modern mind, and missionaries facing the problem of indigenization lament its hidebound forms. Ghetto clergy concerned for the inner city, scientists concerned for the dialogue between science and religion, historians aware of the contribution of American free churches in meeting social problems in the past [1]—from all these comes the plea for worship more relevant to man's life and world. And not least do minister and layman increasingly voice the same cry. Our situation has been pictured thus:

Too much of our . . . Church life is "strictly out of this world" not in a proper eschatological sense but in an unrelated sense. So much of our Sunday worship, our pastoral prayers, our hymns and anthems, our pulpit homilies, our sacramental ceremonies, our vested choirs and divided chancels, our processing and recessing

[1] In a study of "The Expression of the Social Gospel in Worship," Horton Davies concludes that in the early part of this century, Christianity succeeded in finding more powerful expression in the flexible free-church tradition than in churches with unchanging liturgy: "There is evidence that in the essential tension between fidelity to the historically-given nature of Christian revelation and the concern to be able to communicate relevantly to the age, a liturgical church chooses fidelity and non-liturgical churches select relevance." *Studia Liturgica*, II (Sept., 1963).

. . . is simply unrelated to reality. . . . And were it not so soporific and hypnotic, it would not be tolerated by people who are otherwise very much *in* the world.[2]

Surely the liturgical theologian must listen with ears wide open to so earnest a cry. Something has fundamentally gone wrong, and a nerve deep in the Church's life is being plucked somewhere.

THE DIALECTIC OF RELEVANCE AND IRRELEVANCE

However, the liturgical theologian must also ask that the indictment be stated more substantively, for "relevance" so often is a cliché term concealing confused thinking. Indeed one has the impression that "relevance" is like a lightning rod: it draws bolts from so many directions as to suggest intensity of feeling more than clarity of thought. For many people, apparently, "relevance" means worship that rationally communicates, that "gets through" with persuasion and intelligibility. For others it seems to mean simply what they like—worship judged artistically satisfying, for example. To others "relevance" means honest worship whose forms speak truthfully to the congregation in their particular situation. For others "relevant" worship is that which adapts to cultural changes in man's perception of himself and in his world view. For others "relevance" is synonymous with "secularity" or "worldliness"; relevant worship is that which affirms man's time and history and vigorously engages him with it. For others "relevance" consists in the power of worship to address man's conscience to social problems and to affect his conduct ethically.

These meanings are generally helpful, but their very variety suggests that unexamined assumptions are lurking somewhere, and one must ask: Is relevance understood in these ways the maximum value for liturgy today? In reply it could be argued that virtually all the meanings with which the term "relevance" is commonly invested can be matched with contrary meanings whose validity can hardly be denied; that beside the need for relevance must be set what we may call with calculated risk the need for irrelevance; and that given these terms of discourse, worship fails as often because it is insufficiently irrelevant as because it is insufficiently relevant. For example, worship as deliberate ambiguity addressed to man as *animal symbolicum*, the intentional refusal—as Baron von Hügel used to say—to get things too

[2] Hugh T. Kerr, "In But Not of the World," *Theology Today*, XV (Oct., 1958). Kerr also cites the prankish pastor in Peter de Vries' novel, *The Mackerel Plaza*, who in praying for divine help before an oncoming flood, and knowing well that his liturgically doped congregation would not register the unreality of pious phrases strung together, intoned: "May a merciful Providence deliver us from this act of Almighty God!"

clear,[3] is surely as valid as "intelligible" worship addressed to man as *homo sapiens*. Likewise worship which proclaims the Lord's controversy with his people is surely more authentic than worship as only that which people aesthetically like. And while a sense of honesty must always pervade worship, is "honesty" to be defined only by contemporary sensibility? How does one interpret for liturgy today St. Paul's sentence, for example, that "a man who is unspiritual refuses what belongs to the Spirit of God; it is folly to him; he cannot grasp it, because it needs to be judged in the light of the Spirit" (I Cor. 2:14 NEB)? Or the sentence of Hebrews: "But in them the message they heard did no good, because it met with no faith in those who heard it" (Heb. 4:2 NEB)? Again, is the Christian mythos in all its profundity to be at the mercy of man's shifting perception of himself and in turn of his shifting perception of God? Paul van Buren has said that "God" is simply "a poetic word for human relationships." Can Christian liturgy consent to be validated by this kind of late twentieth-century anthropology? Further, if we insist that worship be relevant in the sense that it be oriented toward the secular and be tested by its power to affect man's life ethically in the world, what shall we say to the claim that worship is an experience of the sacral as much as the secular, or that it is as much an end as a means—as much the "summit" toward which the life of the Church is directed as the "fount" from which her activity flows?[4] Above all, must liturgy always empirically prove itself out? How much does the plea for relevance simply express American pragmatism? Running through most of the meanings the term "relevance" commonly holds is the assumption that worship in one way or another is to "do" something to man. If so, then the question arises: how is worship thus conceived different from worship corrupted into utilitarianism, and at what point does it cross over into manipulation or magic?

We shall explore some of these questions presently. However, it will have

[3] "Never try to get things too clear. Religion can't be clear. In this mixed-up life there is always an element of unclearness. . . . If I could understand religion as I understand that two and two makes four, it would not be worth understanding. Religion can't be clear if it is worth having. To me, if I can see things through and through, I get uneasy—I feel it's a fake. I know I have left something out, I've made some mistake." Quoted in the Introduction to *Letters from Baron Friedrich von Hügel to a Niece*, ed., Gwendolen Greene (London: J. M. Dent & Sons, 1928), pp. xvi-xvii.

[4] Sect. I, par. 10 of the Constitution on the Sacred Liturgy. Part of the text reads: "For *the goal of apostolic works is that all who are made sons of God by faith and baptism should come together to praise God in* the midst of *His Church*, to take part in her sacrifice, and to eat the Lord's Supper. The liturgy in its turn inspires the faithful to become 'of one heart in love.' . . . It prays 'that they may grasp by deed what they hold by creed.'" Italics mine. This paragraph has been called "the core" of the teachings of the Roman Catholic Church on worship. See *The Documents of Vatican II*, ed. Walter M. Abbott, S.J. (New York: Guild Press, America Press, Association Press).

151

become clear that to think of worship only in terms of "relevance" is to deal simplistically with matters very complex, to risk obscuring deeper issues by stating only the surface problem, and to trap oneself into false postures at the outset in trying to understand them. In short, *the question of relevance and irrelevance*—a basic theological question—*is more fundamental than the problem of relevance,* and only the dialectical way of thinking signified by these polarities can lead one into liturgical integrity.

Dialectic, it has been said, is a method of proceeding in thought by setting opposites in juxtaposition in order to express the truth beyond each;[5] and while our wedding of "relevance" and "irrelevance" may seem contradictory and the title of this essay a misnomer startling the mind, we believe that truth can only be apprehended in this provocative way. Of course, other pairs of opposites can also illumine this approach. Polarities such as the continuity and discontinuity which authentic worship embodies, of which we have written; the contemporary vis-à-vis the traditional; meaning and mystery; or the "horizontal" in relation to the "vertical," as we colloquially say, or the "manward" in relation to the "godward"—these roughly parallel relevance and irrelevance. Further, all these formulations ultimately derive from the dialectic of the incarnation and yield their truth in its light. However, two terms often used in speaking of worship, "means" and "end," especially correspond to the polarities of relevance and irrelevance; and controversy has so swirled around these—as we have noted—and they raise so well certain basic issues that we examine them further here.

Worship as End and Means

Often we are told, for example, that man's "chief end," liturgically as otherwise, is to "love God and enjoy him forever," in the words of the Westminster Confession, and that worship must not be a "means" to anything else. We are warned against "filling station liturgy" whose purpose is to refuel man spiritually and morally, and it is insisted that worship be "an offering man makes to God without any thought of what he shall get out of it." Now it is psychologically and theologically revealing that whenever we hear people speak this way, we feel the goodness of their intentions and something deep in us responds. Yet we also feel uneasy because we sense that this view taken by itself misstates the Christian understanding of God in relation to man. God is always the God of man, and man is always the man of God, it has been said;[6] and to subtract man's existential need (i.e., "what

[5] See Paul L. Lehmann, "The Changing Course of a Corrective Theology," *Theology Today,* XIII (Oct., 1956).

[6] See Emil Brunner, *The Divine-Human Encounter,* trans. A. W. Loos (Philadelphia: Westminster Press, 1943), p. 48.

we get out of it") from the liturgical equation falsifies God's nature as the God of man and man's nature as the man of God. In Christian thought, God by definition is that reality on whom man depends for his existence, who so cares about the human predicament that through his Son he became infinitely vulnerable to it and forever involved in it, and who wills to be importuned by man amidst it. Further, God is a God involved in history, unfolding his purpose through it and needing man to share in that unfolding; and only as worship intentionally enlists man in this unfolding can it be authentic encounter with a God who has committed himself in the world. In short, liturgy must be relevant as a "means," or it is not Christian liturgy.

On the other hand—and we shall have to use this qualifying phrase rather often—worship is to be irrelevant as an "end" in the sense that it is disengagement from the world because it is engagement with a God who is infinitely more than the world. By definition, worship is the worship of God, not just a pious experience of the human. While God is experienced in the human, he is who he is in his Godness. He is free from history as well as bound to history. Further, worship is an end in that it is especially the praise of God simply because God exists and is God, a delighting in him in his own nature for his own sake. It is the adoration of God in himself as the End beyond all other ends. And from this perspective, worship viewed as a means pales into secondary or tertiary significance. One can understand why a poet exclaims:

> Hurrah for those who never invented anything;
> Hurrah for those who never explored anything;
> Hurrah for those who never conquered anything;
> But who, in awe, gave themselves up to the essence of things,
> Ignorant of the shell, but seized by the rhythm of things,
> Not intent on conquest, but playing the play of the world.[7]

Worship is not least man's giving himself up in awe to the essence of things, a sharing in the divine play that sustains and moves the world.

Correlative with the Christian understanding of the nature of God, however, is a Christian understanding of the nature of man. Liturgical theology involves a liturgical anthropology, we may say, which in turn embodies a dialectical understanding of man. On the one hand, worship no more than theology can be "thrown like a stone" into man's life, and the human reality man knows in himself and his world is rightly to be asserted vis-à-vis the divine. Man's "chief end" may be God and the enjoyment of him forever, but in being grasped by this End man does not cease being man. Even in

---

[7] Aimé Césaire, quoted by Kenneth Cragg, "This Cruciform World," *Union Seminary Quarterly Review*, XXI (Jan., 1966).

the saints' worship in heaven, we are told, it is angels with "faces" who behold the Father, and man is no faceless dehumanized being as he worships. The presumption that worship is to be relevant to man's existence is the very precondition of worship, and in one sense worship is human before it is anything else. On the other hand, the final datum of man's being is that he is more than human, and the ultimate truth about him is something a great deal more than his humanity multiplied to its nth degree. Ultimately man's nature is to be understood as "theotropic," as meant for divine reality as physical nature is drawn to the sun. While a creature of time and history, he is above all *homo imago Dei, homo orans, capax dei*, praying man capable of and made for life with God. This liturgical datum is ineffaceable in biblical anthropology. One need only recall that the fundamental anxiety of the Bible—evident in its unremitting warning against idolatry—is not that man will not worship but that man will worship something less than the God of his true being and destiny.

Now let it be said that whether the "modern" man accepts this liturgical anthropology as his own self-understanding is debatable. "Modern man's originality, his newness in comparison with traditional societies," writes Mircea Eliade in an oft-quoted sentence, "lies precisely in his determination to regard himself as a purely historical being, in his wish to live in a basically desacralized cosmos." But, Eliade continues, "to what extent modern man has succeeded in realizing his ideal is another problem." [8] It is indeed, as we shall need to observe from time to time. In any case, on this all-important point the liturgical theologian has no alternative but to accept the anthropology of the New Testament as true. One simply cannot controvert a Gospel which liturgically denotes man's capacity for sacral reality with metaphors signifying man's most primal appetites—hunger and thirst; the liturgical satisfaction of man's nature with metaphors of heavenly bread and drink; and the consummation of man's life with God in the liturgical image of a heavenly banquet.[9] This is to say, worship is authentic only when it is an end in the sense that it transposes man's historical life into an experience of eternal life, and detaches man from—at the same time that it involves him in—human meanings.[10]

[8] *Birth and Rebirth*, trans. Willard R. Trask (New York: Harper & Bros., 1958), p. ix.

[9] "The Gospel of the Kingdom is so full of sayings concerning meals, eating and drinking, hungering and thirsting, that there is not *one* element in it which is not expressed somewhere in terms of a meal metaphor." Ernst Lohmeyer, *Lord of the Temple* (Richmond: John Knox Press, 1962). p. 79.

[10] A passage from K. L. Parry presses this insight to its furthest conclusion: "It is often said that worship is a preparation for life. It would perhaps be truer to say that life is a preparation for worship. . . . Is it not the function of worship to give us a foretaste of

In light of this analysis of the dialectic of worship as "means" and "end," then, it becomes clear that to use the terms "relevance" and "irrelevance" too simply and especially without reference to the fullness of Christian revelation, cuts the nerve of thought and maneuvers us into either-or postures. Only when these polarities are kept correlative and are seen as sustaining a basic theological equilibrium can we get at the truth beyond our partial vision—the truth Peter Taylor Forsyth once conceptualized in saying that the love of God in worship is the true self-love of mankind. Indeed, if we needed any final proof of the necessity to think dialectically, it would be the predicament in which we find ourselves when we too piously say that worship must be "irrelevant" as an "end" or too belligerently say that worship must be "relevant" as a "means." For when we say that worship must be "irrelevant" as an "end," we are really saying that we can only be satisfied by this way of thinking because it alone affirms something essential in any relation with God we may have which truly honors God; and hence by our very satisfaction we are confessing that worship of this kind is for us a "means"! Correspondingly, when we say that worship must be "relevant" as a "means" in that it must achieve some change or enhancement of value congruous with the intention of God, we are declaring that worship must transcend the satisfaction of our own desire; and because it fulfills something in the being of God beyond our understanding, it is in this sense an "end"! In short, a kind of mercilessness, both theological and psychological, attaches to the dialectic of relevance and irrelevance that will not let us escape either pole if we would get at the truth.

Now, admittedly, to be subject to this mercilessness is not easy, but this is exactly the posture of tension which testifies to the "holy anxiety" of which we have written, that the Word shall be sovereign both for worship and for our reflection upon it. We shall presently try to understand this sovereignty more fully within the terms of discourse entitling this essay. We should, however, declare frankly what has doubtless become evident, that in our opinion the current passion for "relevance," if allowed to go uncriticized theologically, can undo us. The larger "question" of the meanings the Gospel holds for both "relevance" and "irrelevance" will have been bypassed. Premature and simplistic answers will entangle us. And our dilemma will be confounded by consulting only our human experience and taking our directives from it. In face of these possibilities it must be said un-

---

that life which is life indeed, of which our earthly days are at best a foreshadowing? . . . In the act of worship we strain our frail mortality to the utmost to realize the fullness of our life in God." Worship "should indeed cast its sanctifying life on every day, but life can have no higher goal than to prepare us for that supreme act of worship." From his essay entitled "Prayer and Praise," in *Christian Worship: Studies in Its History and Meaning,* ed. Nathaniel Micklem (Oxford: Clarendon Press, 1936), pp. 230-31.

equivocally that one cannot dispose of an issue so critical for worship only empirically. The meanings we humanly read into the terms "relevance" and "irrelevance" out of our own wisdom are not necessarily the right ones. A warning of Herbert Farmer concerning preaching applies to the larger issues of liturgy also: "It is not the necessities of *our* nature, even our redeemed nature, which are being satisfied in . . . preaching, but . . . the necessities of God in the prosecution of His own sovereign purpose." [11] The necessities of man, both in worship and in reflection upon worship, are proximate, not ultimate.

CERTAIN INSIGHTS FROM SECULAR THOUGHT ILLUMINING THE QUESTION OF RELEVANCE AND IRRELEVANCE

But before we explore the deepest meanings of this dialectic which can only be grasped in a Christological context, we pause to examine a number of insights from secular thought which can partially help us. Common sense, sensitivity to culture, and aesthetic and psychological awareness can provide a kind of prolegomenon to theological restatement. While we shall more fully investigate worship from these perspectives in later essays, here we may point out that the question of relevance and irrelevance clearly requires that the sociological nature of the congregation be analyzed: its identity and composition, its structure and social place, the cultural forces conditioning its liturgical consciousness, and the social and psychological legacy inherited from the past. A congregation's total life conditions its liturgical attitudes, and what people are and do when they are not worshipping is decisive for what they do when they worship.

A student of church architecture once put this point in saying that while churches are rooted in eternity, they flower in the moment, and that while those who belong to them are "children of God," they are also "particular individuals" with "a certain street address." [12] A congregation's "street address" is always crucial. The ethos of American individualism, for example, whereby the layman supposes that in liturgy as in politics or art he can "take it or leave it"—how strong is this as a conditioning factor? What is the congregation's feeling-tone for tradition—is it incurably parochial or is there a minimal flexibility one can work with? How do population mobility, time-patterns of work and leisure, and family constellations affect attitudes toward worship? Do women outnumber men at the services of worship, and if so, why? What motives really impel people to worship—habit, parish or

[11] *The Servant of the Word* (Philadelphia: Fortress Press, 1964), p. 11.
[12] Otto Spaeth, "Worship and the Arts," in *Religious Buildings for Today*, ed. John Knox Shear (F. W. Dodge Corp., 1957), p. 36.

denominational loyalty, affection for the minister, setting an example to others, community mores, family togetherness, the desire for fellowship, patriotism, middle or lower or upper class expectations? The polity and organization of the congregation—is it authoritarian, democratic, bureaucratic, and how does this spirit carry over into worship? In the congregation's cultic history, what dynamics have been at work? The hymnody on which the congregation has been nurtured, for example—has it been predominantly frontier revival, English Victorian, Social Gospel, Wesleyan, Reformed, Whittieresque, and what liturgical feeling-tone has it fostered? How ecumenical is the congregation's mind-set? Does it respond to set prayers from a prayerbook, or does it regard these as popery? Has it shared in "Living Room Dialogues" with Roman Catholics, and how does it feel about the Quakers? How does the congregation perceive the relation of worship to social witness? Is the "cadre on social action" off by itself somewhere, or does the whole congregation see itself as a "cadre" bound together by the meanings of bread and wine? Is the mayor left unprayed for by name, the question of Christian ministry raised only on Recruitment Day, the issue of race confined to Brotherhood Sunday, and the problem of affluence and poverty only glanced at in reading Deuteronomy 6 at Thanksgiving?

Such considerations—and we shall cite others—would seem to be elementary, but surprisingly often the pastor brings little critical distance in appraising relevance and irrelevance sociologically and psychologically. It should not be beneath his dignity nor beyond his skill to design a questionnaire to elicit the information he needs to provide a kind of sociological-liturgical profile of his parish. Alternatively, two or three discussions a year with a council of perceptive laymen, or an invitation to his seminary professor of liturgics or of church and community to make an annual visit of liturgical inspection (!), or an annual writing by the pastor of a twenty-page analysis of "Who comes—and fails to come—to worship, and why?"—these may help.

On a deeper level are less visible but more powerful influences culturally conditioning a congregation's liturgical consciousness in general, which speak to the question of relevance and irrelevance in particular. We shall later identify these in depth, but in illustration we cite here two influences: first, what has been called "damnation by distraction"—the disabling of people for worship by the assault of stimuli upon man's inward life and by the speed with which shifts in his attention are technically engineered, in turn destroying his identity and turning him into the "omni-attentive man" a psychiatrist has described, "one whose spine is made of plastic napkin rings." [13]

[13] Robert Jay Lifton, quoted by Amos Wilder, *The New Voice* (New York: Herder and Herder, 1969), p. 127.

Our clanging, mobile world is not hospitable to the "remembering," the concentration, the adoration, that liturgy has traditionally called for; and one is not surprised that worship requiring such inward attitudes is judged to be irrelevant and that many ministers have therefore opted for liturgy that "swings."

But the question must be raised: Should the liturgist accept at face value the nervous consciousness of the modern man and conceive "relevant" liturgy that moves with shock, speed, and variety to match his sensibilities? Or is such worship counter-productive? The question is not easy to answer, partly because liturgy by definition is action and must have movement and vitality, and partly because so much worship is stupefying and vacuous. Moreover, because the inner links of psychic continuity connecting man's experience together may have been broken, perhaps improvised, extempore liturgy arising out of the moment—in short, the "happening"—can best speak to his disconnectedness. Yet, may it not be wiser to accept the risks of nervous inattention, at least initially, and conceive worship whose calculated irrelevance may invade and succeed in halting man's frantic stream of consciousness? We tend to construe man's nature and situation too unambiguously. He is more than we rationally perceive him to be on the surface. And while relevant worship may seem to be lively worship, actually the most helpful worship may be that which seems irrelevantly to contradict the mind's excitement. Ernst Lohmeyer reminds us that "the Temple is the house of God's rest," [14] and Josef Jungmann has written that "liturgy avoids restless change; liturgy in some measure shares . . . and . . . mediates something of the peace of God to the faithful." [15] Is this perhaps the truth the layman is trying to get across to us when he, while mischoosing his language and perhaps offending us in his very mischoice, remarks that he would "like to forget the cares of the world on Sunday"? What *is* the right relation between *shalom* and the liturgical consciousness of the modern man?

A second cultural influence powerfully conditioning the worshipper is the secularity all about him which by a kind of osmosis he has more or less subconsciously absorbed. The Church was once able to proceed on the assumption that man's world view was a religious if not a Christian one, and it could liturgically appeal to him as a creature who would agree that the true end of his being was God. This is no longer an axiom by which many people live, nor is it an axiom by which many people think they want to live. However, again one must not construe the situation too unambiguously.

---

[14] *Lord of the Temple*, p. 23.

[15] *Pastoral Liturgy*, trans. Tonbury Wells (London: Challoner Publications, 1962), p. 372.

Actually, the fact may fall either way. The worshipper's secularity may be more conscious than subconscious and less real than he thinks. However, it also may be more subconscious than conscious and more real than he thinks. Indeed, he may even disguise his situation from himself and use worship pathologically by "coming to church" as a means of atoning for his guilt in feeling so secular, or as a means of repressing from consciousness his sense of lost religious identity. Congregations become secularized not only in the sense that they internalize secular values in their institutional life; they also internalize secular values in attitudes they bring to their liturgical life, and they handle their secularity in obscure, even devious ways. The scrubbed-faced, white-shirted, shoe-shined, suit-neatly-pressed layman who regularly presents himself on Sunday is not to be taken at face value. Publicly, he may be conspicuously present; privately—subconsciously—he may be wondering what he is doing there. He likely lives ninety percent of the time by secular axioms quite opposed to those he nominally declares in church,[16] and he does not cease being in church what he is elsewhere.

Doubtless one element in the worshipper's secularized consciousness is his intellectual pride and his rationalistic temper of mind. Immersed in a culture whose inmost ethos is scientific and whose technological deity is the computer, he tends to equate what is real with what is rational. Privately he may hold that the existence—not to say the nature—of the God which Christian worship speaks of is problematic. He cannot rid himself of the feeling that there is a certain infantilism to religion—especially if he has read Freud; and he is probably convinced that that university president was right who declared that all the problems of the world can be solved if men will only think. Now actually he may be much less rational and more primitive than he supposes, as we shall note presently. But surely relevance would seem to require that when the Church asks people to confess they are "miserable sinners" and that "there is no health in us," for example, the

[16] The following give one pause: "Axioms from America: 1. Truth is established only by proof, and ultimate truth is unknowable. 2. Look out for number one. If you don't, nobody else will. 3. Human nature is fundamentally sound, but needs guidance and correction to achieve fulfillment. 'Sin' is just another name for ignorance or correctible imperfection, or biological lag. 4. There is progress in history, but society may yet destroy itself. . . . 5. There always have been wars and there always will be. You can't change human nature. 6. 'God' is really a projection of man's ideals. 7. A man's religion is his own business and every man has a right to his own belief. 8. Otherworldliness is dangerous because it distracts attention from the effort to gain freedom, security and justice in this life; and anyway we know nothing about what happens after death. 9. Jesus was a good man. What we need are a lot more people like Him. Now, take Lincoln. . . . 10. Do a good turn when you can—but don't be a sucker." World Council of Churches, *Man's Disorder and God's Design: The Amsterdam Assembly Series* (New York: Harper & Bros., 1949), II, 82.

pastor should at least have bowing acquaintance with certain psychological theories to the contrary that his people are familiar with, and know what he is doing if he decides liturgically to contradict them. Or when a congregation is asked to join in the Collect for Ascension Day, the pastor should realize that many a worshipper finds it difficult to reconcile its ancient cosmology with what he has read in his morning newspaper about twentieth-century man's latest conquest of space.[17] Or the ethical concepts embodied in liturgy taken from an agrarian culture in an underdeveloped nation two thousand years ago—these the pastor must understand as striking upon many a worshipper as intellectually dubious in a technological age; that while the layman may kindly listen to the Sermon on the Mount as a charming statement of the Christian ethic, let us say, he feels that as an emancipated evolutionist he has outgrown such concepts just as he has outgrown primitive ideas of medicine or astrology. In short, relevant liturgy must recognize that the whole cultural mood of our age is against unintelligible and unintelligent demands.

Another element in the secular consciousness which can foster irrelevance in a bad sense is the layman's fear of technological and social change which psychologically induces him to want worship as retreat. Not unnaturally, he psychologically associates the Church's ritual with permanence. Here at least is one place where things are as they were and they ought still to be, he subconsciously muses to himself. Only too readily he would paraphrase the hymn: "Change and decay, all around I see. O that which changest not, abide with me." To be sure, his attitude needs discriminating appraisal; and as we have noted, the meaning of the layman's remark that he wants to "forget the cares of the world on Sunday" is ambiguous. But often he is not so much seeking the *shalom* that rightly heals his distraction as he is neurotically wishing for worship that will enable him to escape reality. Further, the Church itself in its stance and program often fosters liturgy of escape. Its ministry in general deals with only selected meanings of the congregation's life, such as personal morals, family life, the problems of youth, recreation, stewardship of money, evangelization of individuals, help to the needy, etc.; and it so compartmentalizes religion in the layman's mind that he is not to be blamed in expecting the substance of worship to be "privatized" to avoid

[17] It should be added that the author of the Ascension narrative in Acts was not setting forth a cosmology; he was using poetry, specifically the image of the cloud, a common biblical symbol for the mystery of God, to convey truth. Certain critics, Alan Richardson for example, contend that the Bible has no particular cosmology; that what we call a biblical cosmology is a medieval world view read backward into the Bible; that the problem of demythologization actually is unjustified because the Bible demythologizes itself if we will let it do so. However, while the scholar may understand this, the modern layman does not, and for him the problem of liturgical relevance is still very real.

reference to the social change swirling around him. He transfers to worship all too readily what the Church has taught him all too well elsewhere.

To withstand irrelevance as neurotic retreat from reality, worship obviously must propose to the layman the world of threatening change as the very world in which he is to live a liturgical life and propel him *into* it. That is, liturgy is to be *prospective*—what we have spoken of as "apostolic." However, this is not enough. Worship itself must also be prepared to be transformed by meanings *from* the layman's life in the world. That is, worship is also to be *recollective*. To employ a biological metaphor, worship is systolic as well as diastolic: it contracts to draw into itself man's worldly life and expands to send man into his worldly life. The very changes which threaten are to be gathered into liturgy, articulated, faced, examined, learned from, prayed about, and moved into. In a word, worship is to be informed with worldly sensitivity. It is to be an experience of intersection in which all the meanings of man's life meet before God. In a phrase of Gibson Winter, it is to be "*truly public* worship" into which all the meanings of man's life are drawn— civic, political, social, as well as familial and private.

Such considerations, then, and others which we shall explore more fully, are bound up with the pastor's knowing the "street address" of the congregation.

However, to carry forward our figure of speech, he is to know their "divine address" as well—how worship is rightly as well as wrongly irrelevant, and here theological considerations begin to join with sociological and psychological ones. For example, he may not only refuse to take their nervousness at face value; he will likely refuse to take their secularism at face value likewise; and he does not necessarily agree that worship must be demythologized in order to appeal to man's reason. Abundant evidence from the study of comparative religions, from depth psychology, and from recent reconceptions in philosophy, suggests that on the decisive levels of his being man lives by realities apprehended in ways other than by discursive thought; and to the claim that liturgically the Gospel must be demythologized, it must be replied that man himself can never be demythologized. Moreover, the power of myth, of symbol, lies as much in its obscurity as in its clarity, and often worship is only authentic when at first sight its form and substance appear to be irrelevant. Perhaps this is the meaning of Karl Barth's remark that the Church has its own "queer language," and that while the pastor is never free from his duty to address this language to Everyman, "one thing is certain, that where the Christian Church does not venture to confess in its own language, it usually does not confess at all." [18]

[18] *Dogmatics in Outline*, trans. G. T. Thompson (Torchbook ed.; New York: Harper & Row, 1959), p. 31.

The Ascension cosmology we have mentioned, for example, is probably part of the Church's queerest language. Yet it may speak more powerfully to man's nature than one supposes, and the dimension of height suggested by the cloud which received the Lord out of men's sight may deal with man more savingly than the dimension of depth currently so popular. "The purpose of worship," it has been said in an oft-quoted statement of J. A. T. Robinson,

is not to retire from the secular into the department of the religious, let alone to escape from "this world" into "the other world," but to open oneself to the meeting of the Christ in the common, to that which has the power to penetrate its superficiality and redeem it from its alienation. *The function of worship is to make us more sensitive to these depths;* to focus, sharpen and deepen our response to the world and to other people beyond the point of proximate concern.[19]

But pinned down, what do people really mean by "depths," and how adequate is this term? The question must be raised because it is arguable whether the relocation of the divine from the heights to the depths is truthful to either the nature of man or the nature of God: "By removing God from 'out there' or 'up there' to the depths, the most powerful and numinous image has been placed suddenly in the territory which was formerly the devil's dominion; and how are we to judge from whence come the impulses . . . which call from these depths? *How do we discriminate the spirits rising from the deep?*"[20] How do we indeed? By substituting Descension Sunday for Ascension Sunday, or for the *Sursum Corda*, "Lift Up Your Chins"?

A function of ritual never to be lost sight of is its power to reinstate experience people once may have had but have lost. Margaret Mead writes:

The recurrence of the ritual assures them that the feeling once was there and may come back again. This is, of course, the principal function of the rituals of family relationships—wedding anniversaries, birthday celebrations, and family reunions—and of all those ceremonies where we attempt to reconstitute ritually a feeling that exists but that may lack any immediate power of expression. It is a . . . function of ritual all over the world."[21]

To be sure, whether the ritual language of the Ascension really speaks to a feeling for its meaning that once was there, already exists, or can be induced is arguable. It may be irrevocably lost. Further, ritual used to reinstate feeling runs the risk of seeking experience for the sake of experience. However, this

[19] *Honest to God* (Philadelphia: Westminster Press, 1963), p. 87. Italics mine.

[20] James Hillman, *Insearch* (New York: Charles Scribner's Sons, 1967), p. 80. Italics mine.

[21] "Ritual Expression of the Cosmic Sense," in *Worship*, XL (Feb., 1966).

risk can be accepted if ritual is used primarily to reinstate an encounter with *Christian reality*—in this case the reality of Christ's sovereignty signified by the symbol of the Ascension. This reality is indispensable to the salvation history which Christian worship must recapitulate and without which that history is liturgically unfulfilled. Christianity has its own vocabulary corresponding to its own kerygmatic realities; ritual is part of that vocabulary; and the worshipper ever needs to learn and relearn it. Of course this language needs reinterpretation. But as Amos Wilder bluntly warns: "Transposition of the myth into . . . discursive or existential analogies is desirable provided it be recognized that every such formulation is a poor surrogate and must always again appeal back to the original." [22] Or in the even blunter words of Bonhoeffer: "This mythology (resurrection and so on) is the thing itself." [23] In short, psychology and theology unite in confirming that what at first appears to be irrelevance in worship may contribute to integrity more than we suppose. We shall have to explore this important point more fully in dealing with the language of worship in later essays.

Lastly, the "divine address" of the congregation requires worship to be irrelevant in the sense that it brings them to be subject to the mystery of their life in the mystic Body of Christ; and worship lacks integrity if this perception is missing. On the one hand, the importance of man's "street address" rightly requires liturgy to affirm his humanity. On the other hand, his "divine address" rightly requires liturgy to read his nature as something more. His instinctual "folk hunger," or as we would say in our modern idiom, his "interpersonal needs" which the communal nature of worship marks, are to be met on both a human level and a more than human level; and it is at this point that the theological nature of the Church speaks to liturgical integrity. For the Church is *convocatio* as well as *congregatio*, we remember, a company divinely called together by Jesus Christ as well as a human company assembling itself. Thus, whereas relevance requires one to analyze the *human congregation* and to appropriate into worship meanings from its human life in the world, irrelevance requires one to affirm the *divine convocation* and to appropriate meanings of its life in Christ that transcend the world. As convocation, the community is constituted by objective realities greater and other than itself which often counter human reason and taste; and it must therefore expect that divine meanings will irrelevantly contradict what men suppose to be their needs.

In sum, the dialectic of relevance and irrelevance warns us that we must always be prepared to be baffled by the contradictions it offers to both our

---

[22] *The Language of the Gospel* (New York: Harper & Row, 1964), p. 135.
[23] Quoted by E. H. Robertson in his Introduction to Bonhoeffer's *Christ the Center*, trans. John Bowden (New York: Harper & Row, 1966), p. 17.

thinking about worship and the experience of worship itself. How often have we assumed that we could choose in worship the food we supposed would feed us in our need, and found ourselves instead bidden to a table already prepared with loaf and poured-out wine. How often have we craved light on our life in the world, only to be summoned to ponder our destiny in eternity. How often have we been preoccupied with the church local, and instead found our vision turned to the Church triumphant and universal. And how often have we asked that worship bless our souls with peace, only to hear the lesson for the day calling us to a holy warfare. How often have we desired strength to overcome the world, only to learn that we are to be stoned and sawn asunder in the world. How often have we sought comfort to our sorrows, and instead found the sorrows of the world added to our own.[24] Such reversals may seem strange to men. But only such contradiction answers to realities both relevant and irrelevant that are at the very heart of the Church's worship.

A CHRISTOLOGICAL ANALYSIS OF RELEVANCE AND IRRELEVANCE

With a certain inevitability, then, we again find ourselves pressed back to a source of truth other than ourselves. Terms as important as relevance and irrelevance can neither be defined only by our own sensibilities nor accommodated to our own intellectual convenience. Our course of thought, rather, must be like that of the physicist Helmholtz, who before he could understand the nature of human vision had to do more than study the structure of the eye: he had *first* to study *the properties of light.*[25] The effort to understand man's liturgical vision of God is like that. It cannot safely be undertaken by first studying man; rather, one first studies the properties of the Light. And one may say of this Light in relation to the categories of "relevance" and "irrelevance" what has been said of the doctrine of the Presence of Christ: "The *Christus praesens* invites the Church to reverse the often-heard demand 'to make Christ relevant to the present situation.' The situation, past, present or future, is to be made relevant to him." [26] In short, again we are met with nothing less than the sovereignty of the Word. And this sovereignty, it must be expected, will strike upon us with abruptness, even offense, as marks of its truth.

---

[24] These last sentences paraphrase a passage in my memory from Evelyn Underhill.

[25] I am indebted to the late Professor Carl Michalson for this analogy. See his article "Communicating the Gospel" in *Theology Today,* XIV (Oct., 1957).

[26] Dietrich Ritschl, *Memory and Hope* (New York: The Macmillan Co., 1967), p. 64.

In inquiring into the properties of the Light, it is well not to be bound too rigidly by the categories set forth in the preceding essay—the incarnational character of the Word, its eventful, historical, and trans-historical character, and its ontological, soteriological, and eschatological character. The sovereignty of the Word forbids our conceptualizing its meanings too precisely, and these elements are to be taken as guidelines rather than as moulds for thought. Also, the properties of the Light are refracted through Church and tradition, and while the Word is sovereign over these, it is yet bound up with them. Further, one's use of the terms "relevance" and "irrelevance" will reflect shifts of meaning.[27] Given the varied ways our culture interprets these words, it must be expected that Christological meanings will correspondingly vary.

The Meaning of the Incarnation for Relevance and Irrelevance; Baptism, Preaching, Prayer

Nevertheless, underlying all meanings the Word holds for thought is its incarnational character. The Word is enfleshed in man's life; yet it comes from beyond man's life. It reveals, and it conceals. It appears; it withdraws. It enlightens; it also darkens. It gives, and it withholds. It turns toward us; it turns from us. It is born into our midst; it ascends from our midst. The veil of the temple has been rent; the Word has entered that beyond the veil. It is with us always; yet it reigns from a throne in heaven. The incarnate Word is in part that which we comprehend; even more it is that which we apprehend; still more it is that which we neither comprehend nor apprehend but which apprehends us. This is to say, both that which is revealed in the incarnation and that which is unrevealed are to determine worship. Both sayable and unsayable things are part of the Church's pearl of great price; and we are not to become desperate if in order to possess this pearl, the Church must sometimes yield up the lesser pearls of commerce with the world. It is not that the Church is irrelevantly to mumble her prayer for the sake of mumbling, as on occasion she has done; nor is it that she is to cheapen her speech into noisy slang to prove how relevant she is. Rather, it is that the Church's worship is to be that through which the Word declares itself to be the Word.

The sacrament of Baptism illustrates the dialectic of relevance and irrelevance in this fundamental sense. On the one hand, Baptism embodies meanings we are humanly to understand, appropriate, even share in bringing to pass. On the part of the baptized—or on his behalf—Baptism is an act

[27] Etymologically, the term "relevant" stems from the present participle, *relevans*, of the Latin verb *relevare*, meaning "to raise up," and it generally means "pertinence," "correspondence," "related to the matter in hand."

165

of thanksgiving for life, of dedication of life, of confession and renunciation of sin and profession of faith, of decision to become a member of Christ's Church. Humanly it is also an act of the congregation declaring its faith in Jesus Christ. It is also the congregation's remembering their own Baptism, and the accepting once more, as their own, of the baptism with which Jesus was baptized in his life and death. Further, it is the congregation engrafting a life into its own covenant life, the bestowing of personal identity in the human community signified by naming the baptized with a Christian name, and the congregation's acceptance of its responsibility for care and nurture.

Yet the action of Baptism far transcends these human meanings. Formed by Christ, the Church is more than a human congregation, and it does more than it knows. Similarly, the true agent in its action is the Spirit of God before it is the will of men. Still further, Baptism is into Christ and his death and resurrection before it is into his Church.[28] And as union with Christ, Baptism is thus a participation in the eschatological life of God himself, embodied in the Word and conveyed by the Holy Spirit. This profound meaning is exactly the climax of Baptism—the bold linking of the baptized's personal name with the names of the Holy Trinity: "Name_____, I baptize thee in the name of the Father, of the Son, and of the Holy Spirit." In this act, man's being is baptized into the triune being of God himself. Man is given his personal identity in a Christian universe. And given these profound if mystical meanings, the liturgical sign executing them must be expected to strike upon us with irrelevance as well as relevance as the Light interprets these to us.

Authentic preaching likewise embodies this dialectical character. One must, of course, distinguish different types of the Church's discourse which too often are lumped together as "preaching": *didache* meaning teaching; *paraklesis*, exhortation; *homilia*, discussion; *aedificatio*, strengthening, nurture. While one may colloquially speak of these as preaching, they all presuppose a more fundamental form of discourse: *kerygma*, preaching as proclamation or heralding of the Gospel. This is the core of liturgy. And, liable to misunderstanding as the statement may be, the aim of preaching understood in this deepest sense is by no means to be most relevant as we commonly understand this term. Rather, preaching is to be incarnational: an event through which the Word manifests itself in its fullness and grasps human life with its life.

To be sure, the Word's incarnate fullness includes its humanity. And correspondingly we may say that preaching is to be relevant in the sense

---

[28] "It is Christ that receives you, not a friendly society." P. T. Forsyth, *The Church and the Sacraments* (London: Longmans, Green & Co., 1919), p. 195.

that the humanity of the preacher is to be the vesture of the Word; in the sense that preaching rises out of and is addressed to the most human realities of life, personal and social; and in the sense that its substance is to be capable of human comprehension, and is to change human nature and the human situation. Preaching too often fails to be relevant in these ways. The humanity of the preacher is not authentically put at the disposal of the Word. Or preaching properly starts with the biblical Word but only stays there and never effectively gets into the human situation. Harry Emerson Fosdick once voiced this truth in his well-known remark that preaching for him was "pastoral counseling on a group scale." The life-situation of people and the ministry of the living Word to their life always requires relevance in this sense. Further, the preacher preaches in the confidence that his words, pastoral or prophetic, can avail. Indeed, unless preaching presses for some kind of human verdict and results in some kind of change, whether in the secret chamber of a man's soul or ethically in his worldly life, the Word in its fullness has not been served.

Yet ultimately the true preacher is Christ himself, and beyond man's human words is the Word. The Directory of Worship of the United Presbyterian Church in the U.S.A. defines preaching thus: "The preaching of the Word is that act of worship through which Jesus Christ is manifested anew to men, in terms of both the promises which the Gospel offers them and the demands which it lays upon them." [29] As manifestation of the kerygma, preaching thus is clothed with something of the mystery of the original manifestation. The Gospel's promises and demands are always more than we know or can say. Hence its substance does not necessarily lend itself to nor depend upon rational comprehension; nor is its reality to be validated by whether or not it seems on the surface to be relevant to our situation. Rather, authentic preaching embodies something of the discontinuity Jesus manifested in giving the disciples to drink of the cup as St. Luke records that act: only afterward did he explain what his action in giving it to them had meant. Or, preaching strikes with something of the same irrelevance manifest in Jesus' washing of the disciples' feet: only after he had completed his action and asked the question, "Know ye what I have done unto you?" did its profound meaning begin to dawn. As servant of the Word, the preacher likewise does not know what has been done through him, nor does the congregation know. All that both can do is to offer themselves to the mysterious sovereignty of the Word, and in this sense preaching is inevitably irrelevant. Ultimately, "in a sense the sermon does not matter; what matters

[29] *The Book of Order* (Philadelphia: Office of the General Assembly, 1967), ch. III, sec. 3 of "The Directory for the Worship of God."

is what the preacher cannot say because the ineffable remains the ineffable, and all that can be done is to make gestures toward it." [30]

The relevance and irrelevance of liturgical prayer will especially reflect the dialectic of the incarnation, for the God who speaks with man in prayer "through Jesus Christ our Lord" is both knowable and unknowable. He is closer than hands or feet, yet also the high and lofty one who inhabits eternity. He desires to be prayed to as intimately as a human "father"; yet he is "in heaven"—of a different realm of being whose difference is to be marked and hallowed before all else. He is vulnerable to our human predicament to the point of bearing in his heart the cross; yet he is God in his "Godness" to whom belong the kingdom, the power, and the glory forever and ever. He shares with us his very life; yet he is not diminished by that sharing. Indeed, he is a God needing our prayers, yet not needing our prayers.

Thus, on the one hand, the form and substance of prayer must be relevant in the sense that they be human, intelligible, and grasp the human situation in all its human reality. In Cranmer's famous sentence, prayer (as the liturgy in general) is to be "in suche a language and ordre, as is moste easy and plain for the understandyng, bothe of the readers and hearers." [31] Thus relevance means prayer in clear, simple speech, indeed in vernacular and even colloquial speech, dealing with man's everyday life in the most earthy sense. It also means "free prayer" which, in a phrase borrowed from French Christendom, adapts itself with *actualité* to the most particular situations.[32] As Isaac Watts said in making his Puritan protest against Anglican forms: "We have new sins to be confessed, new temptations and sorrows to be represented, new wants to be supplied. Every change of providence in the affairs of a nation, a family or a person requires suitable petitions and acknowledgements. And all these can never be provided for in any prescribed composition." [33]

Relevance especially requires that the Church's prayer today grasp events in man's political and social life and set these in liturgical encounter with the Word. Bidding prayers[34] and litanies of intercession are particularly

---

[30] R. E. C. Browne, *The Ministry of the Word* (London: SCM Press, 1958), p. 19.

[31] Quoted by Massey Hamilton Shepherd, Jr., ed., *The Oxford American Prayer Book Commentary* (New York: Oxford University Press, 1950), p. xi.

[32] It is noteworthy that according to Friedrich Heiler, free prayer prevailed in the life of the Church until well on into the third century. See the quotation from Heiler and the summary of his historical study in Alexander B. McDonald's study of *Christian Worship in the Primitive Church* (Edinburgh: T. & T. Clark, 1934), p. 73.

[33] From Watts's *Guide to Prayer*, quoted by Horton Davies, *The Worship of the English Puritans* (Westminster: Dacre Press, 1948), p. 105.

[34] The bidding form of prayer in which topics are solicited from or announced to the congregation is the oldest form of intercession in the Church's common worship; in

suitable in this respect, although the "pastoral prayer" traditional in free-church worship, if sensitively conceived, can serve equally well. The following pastoral prayer by S. MacLean Gilmour, offered at a service at Andover Newton Theological Seminary at a critical moment in American history in 1957, admirably illustrates relevance of this kind. The occasion was the day after the decision by the President of the United States, Dwight D. Eisenhower, to assert Federal authority in Little Rock, Arkansas, enforcing legislation of the Supreme Court declaring against segregation in public school education:

Most gracious God, who wouldst have us make intercession for all men; we pray for the President of the United States, for the officer commanding the 101st Airborne Division, for the mayor of Little Rock, Arkansas, the chief of police, the superintendent of schools, the principal of Central High School and the editors of the "Arkansas Gazette"; for nine Negro children and their white classmates; and for all men and women in Little Rock who believe in good government, the rule of law, justice, civil rights, common decency and fair play.

Confound O Lord, the great evil of ignorant men. And, since we are all involved in this ugly sin, whether in Arkansas, Washington, or Massachusetts, save us from lawlessness and discord, from arrogance and pride, that reprieved by thy mercy, baptized with thy forgiveness and renewed by thy grace, we may fulfill thy purpose in this land. Through Jesus Christ our Lord. Amen.[35]

Relevance and irrelevance in public prayer also involve the person of the minister, as we have noted. On the one hand, the minister's selfhood—his experience, mind, feeling, intuition, perception of the needs of the congregation—rightly conditions his leadership of prayer. This human dimension cannot and should not be eliminated, despite the critics of free prayer who in their enthusiasm for priestly prayer that impersonally voices the devotion of the Church would deny the minister the right to be himself as he prays. It is not understood that the very humanity of the minister can be a means of grace. On the other hand, the minister is servant of the Word in its divine character also; and heaven help him if as he prays he is only himself! The Word divinely forms the Church as *convocatio*, it must be remembered, and because the minister is a servant of Word and Church in this more than human sense, his selfhood is to be gotten out of the way. He represents

---

the early Church it was regularly cast in the vernacular; and in the historic liturgies, persons and blessings prayed for were named completely and in detail. The bidding prayer came after the Scripture readings and sermon, at the end of the synaxis after the catechumens had been dismissed. The celebrant would name a particular intention; then would follow silence; and then followed the celebrant's summary prayer in collect form. This is still the preferred place for intercession, in that intercession should follow on, not precede, instruction and proclamation. The bidding form can hardly be improved upon, and its restoration can mean much for the integrity of worship today.

[35] Reprinted in *The Christian Century*, Oct. 9, 1957.

the Church divine as well as human, universal as well as local; and prayer belongs to the Church, not to him. "He is here the organ of the essential priestliness of the Church," [36] and in this sense the last thing he is to do is to exercise his right to be himself—or as Willard Sperry once harshly remarked, "to wallow in the states of his own soul."

The very posture the minister takes up in prayer in certain traditions symbolizes this truth: in turning his back and kneeling to face the altar, he both identifies himself with and detaches himself from his people. His posture acts out his human solidarity with them at the same time that it declares his priestly function for them. Through him, as he prays, the life of the people and God's grace meet. In a word, the relevance and irrelevance of prayer are set forth.

Indeed this suggests the most important sense in which prayer is to be irrelevant: prayer is to mediate the life of God to men as well as the life of men to God. The mark of authenticity in Christian prayer is that it is offered through "Jesus Christ our Lord." It has reality through the interceding Word in its divine-human character. Thus prayer sacramentally conveys divine meaning at the same time that it apprehends human meaning. It is a means of grace as well as a human cry. Its ultimate locus is a divine "altar on high"; its true agent is a High Priest who ever makes intercession for us; and while it rises from earth, it is mingled with the prayer of angels and archangels and all the company of heaven.

Thus prayer is clothed with irrelevant mystery as well as relevant meaning. It is in a speech man can both understand and not understand. It is to be vernacular speech; it is also to be numinous speech—as incense in a bowl laid by an angel upon an altar, in St. John's unforgettable image. Indeed, prayer is even to be the absence of speech—a "silence in heaven for a space." On the one hand, prayer is to be as intelligible as the prayer the human Jesus taught his very human disciples to pray—"Our Father, who art in heaven." On the other hand, prayer is to be as numinous as the Church's "Sanctus," as its ecstatic "Amen," its paschal "Allelu-yah," its imploring "Maranatha." Indeed one must finally say of prayer in this numinous sense what has been said of the "Gloria": Here "is acknowledged that there has taken place an action not of men's possible accomplishment, a revelation not of men's conceiving, an illumination not of men's lighting, and a liberation not of men's contriving." Prayer is simply a declaration of "the presence and power of God." [37]

[36] Forsyth, *The Church and the Sacraments*, p. 135.
[37] Joseph A. Sittler, Introduction, *Worship in Scripture and Tradition*, ed. Massey H. Shepherd, Jr. (New York: Oxford University Press, 1963), p. 5.

The Meaning of Relevance and Irrelevance in Light of the Word as Historical Act

Relevance and irrelevance are also to be understood in light of the Word as act, and as a historical and trans-historical reality. Because the Word is act, worship can only exist as action, and the terms on which Jesus instituted worship declare this conception and address man on this assumption: "Come," "gather," "hear," "take," "eat," "drink," "do," "remember," "go," "love." These verbs all address man as agent and require worship to be relevant in the sense that man participate in its action. Further, the Word is a historical reality, and that which Jesus enjoins man to "remember" is the historical life he lived and the death he died. Correspondingly, man's action is to be as historical as Jesus Christ's; liturgical action is self-contradictory if its reference is not man's existence in time and history. It is to embrace the congregation's life in the world no less than Jesus Christ lived in the world. In this sense worship cannot be too relevant.

Thus relevance requires that worship be "recollective" as well as "prospective," as we have noted; that it rise out of the congregation's worldly life as well as speak to that life; and that it be "occasional" worship far more than we have understood. Worship is not to be thought of only in terms of a congregation's usual gatherings and structures. Rather, it is to be flexible, "occasioned" by a public crisis or a political decision or a moral issue, let us say, or simply by significant events in everyday experience. Correspondingly, the action the congregation performs in liturgy is to be related to the action it performs in these areas of its life. A strike in industry, a race riot, an election, a legislative hearing on a welfare bill—relevance requires that such issues be brought squarely into the Church's worship and the nature of Christian social action bound up with them be identified. Similarly, man's ordinary experience, and not simply critical and dramatic events, is to be set within worship. Here lies in part the rationale for experimental liturgies employing multi-media: fast-moving pictures projected upon the walls of the church as the congregation gathers, depicting events from man's worldly life; sound tracks recording news events, the roar of subways and airplanes, sports events, bird songs, the sirens of police cars, television commercials; the reading of the morning newspaper together with the Scripture lesson for the day; the singing of secular music and the reading of secular poetry with their peculiar power to evoke man's everyday world.

Now worship will not stop with these, but it may well start with them. Relevance in a way is a matter of imagination and tactics; and, far more than we have understood, worship may need to start with man's immediate experience and set it in dialogue with the Word. Thus the statement we

171

have quoted, that the doctrine of the Real Presence requires the Church to reverse the demand to "make Christ relevant to the human situation" and instead to make "the present situation relevant to him," may need to be *tactically* qualified. For often "the present situation" can be "made relevant to him" only when liturgy first starts with that situation. The doctrine of the Real Presence in worship must not imply a doctrine of the real absence elsewhere.[38] Only as a congregation is sensitized to the presence of Christ in their worldly life can they perceive him as present in their cultic life. We shall return to this fundamental point presently.

In one further sense, relevance under the mode of action must be identified. Because the Word embodies sacred history and conveys its action through this history, the ways in which a congregation becomes engaged with this history must be such that they can make it their own. The action of "remembering," the *anamnesis* Jesus enjoined, is one way, and on the deepest level this action mystically apprehends past history as present. There are, however, other levels of remembering that must not be lost sight of— for example "remembering" in the plain sense of "not forgetting." The retelling of "the old, old story," hearing again the best-known passages of Scripture, singing familiar hymns evoking pictorial—and emotional—associations, even the crude Christmas pageant with shepherds in bathrobes and angels with cardboard wings—these are not out of place. Despite our smiles, these remind us of an event foreshadowed in God's covenant with his people, of a child born in a crib when Cyrenius was governor of Judea, of a life lived upon the soil of Galilee, of a death died on Golgotha, of a resurrection presence meeting one named Saul on a road to Damascus. Remembered in such ways, the Word in its history illumines our history. It becomes the Jesus of Nazareth whose sisters and brothers we know, the man who was tempted in all things as we are, the friend who has called us his friends, the host who at supper shared bread and wine with his guests. To be sure, myth mingles with history as a congregation remembers in such ways. But while scholarship may doubt whether we can recover "the historical Jesus," liturgy has no doubt but that men and women and children are still grasped by the "Jesus of history." The relevance with which he meets us as we remember him forbids our believing otherwise.

The congregation can also become engaged with the sacred history of the Word through the Creed. To be sure, many clergy and congregations do not understand creeds in this way. Most often, perhaps, creeds are regarded as statements of dogma; and the Nicene Creed in particular lends itself to

[38] See Eric James, "Worship and the Church's Mission," a paper presented to the Convocation on Worship of The Methodist Church, Baltimore, April, 1966.

this interpretation, having been conceived and introduced into the Church's worship for polemical purposes. Luther, however, in retaining it in his *Formula Missae* in 1523, designated it as *sacrificium laudis*, as "a sacrifice of praise," in which the congregation rehearsed the saving acts of God. In doing so he recovered the original purpose of confessions of faith, which in the New Testament were "always" expressions of praise before the Lordship of Christ known through the Jesus of history.[39] Only in the third century did creeds come to be thought of as didactic summaries of belief. In their early form they were called a "mystery"—a "salvatory event" through which the believer participated in the very life of Christ.[40] They stated the Who of faith rather than the what of belief. Baptismal creeds from the Church's earliest days likewise bore this form, centering originally in the joyful declaration "Jesus is Lord." The Apostles' Creed is of this kind. Although not reaching its final form until the sixth or seventh century, it was a celebration of salvation events more than a statement of doctrine. Certain recent reformulations—such as that of the United Church Of Christ—are similarly an exultant setting forth of the saving acts of God in history which the congregation recites, to which it testifies, and with which it becomes re-engaged. Actually—it has been said—creeds are not tests but "festivities" of faith.

Understood thus as "story theology," the Creed can possess great power. The events it sets forth become contemporized, and its history savingly gets inside men. It is hardly coincidence that musically the Creed has inspired many of man's most lyric expressions of praise. One thinks of the Masses and Requiems of Bach, Mozart, Brahms, Verdi, Fauré. One also can understand why Calvin urged that the Creed always be sung, and why Canon Shepherd felt it should be repeated to the roll of drums and the sound of trumpets. One can further understand why an English Christian, in commenting on the dubious formula "He descended into hell" (a late addition dating from the fifth century), declared that so far from being irrelevant, this phrase holds for him exorcising power: it sets forth Jesus Christ as the Saviour who descends into the passional depths of man's nature and redeems and conquers them.[41] The power of the Creed in face of death at the funeral service, likewise illustrates this truth. It is a mistake to discard the Creed in the name of rationalism as irrelevant to modern congregations.

[39] See D. Gerhard Delling, *Worship in the New Testament,* trans. Percy Scott (London: Dartman, Longman & Todd, 1962), p. 88; Oscar Cullmann, *Early Christian Worship,* trans. A. Stewart Todd and James B. Torrance (London: SCM Press, 1953), p. 23.

[40] I Tim. 3:16 is such a creed. See also Rom. 10:8.

[41] See D. H. Hislop, *Our Heritage in Public Worship* (Edinburgh: T. & T. Clark, 1935), p. 46.

As a means of engaging the worshipper with the fateful history centering in the event of Jesus Christ, the Creed can actually be one of the most relevant acts a congregation performs.

Further, the congregation can relevantly experience the historical nature of the Word in the observance of the Christian Year. The yearly cycle of seasons and festivals re-presents Christological history, with all its dramatic rhythms of emotional intensity, and the interior meaning of this history, relived by the worshipper, can transform his life. To be sure, the precise calendar embodying this cycle should be adaptable to cultural and psychological factors, as we shall note in later essays.[42] The essential *structure* of the Christian Year, however—Advent, Christmas, Epiphany, Lent, Easter, Pentecost, Ascension, Trinity—as distinguished from its *calendar arrangement*, is sacred history in vertebrate form. Remembered through these festivals, sacred history becomes a living reality. The life Jesus Christ once lived in time mysteriously engages us in our time. That event which he was and which we remember bestows Christian significance on all our days.[43]

However, beside relevance conceptualized in these ways must also be set the necessity for irrelevance as the Word as historical event interprets its meaning to us. For the history embodied in the Word, it must be remembered, is alien to us as well as congenial to us. It is both scandal and comfort. It sets before us a cross when we would only hasten to the stable and the star. It reminds us of a covenant to which we are bound when we would only enjoy the freedom with which Christ has made us free. It bids us to an exodus when we would tarry in an upper room. It raises up a stone of stumbling when we would desire a foundation of security. To the degree that the history of the Word is set forth only in that which taste finds relevant, liturgy becomes corrupt. We may rightly say with respect to the historical meanings of the Christian Year, for example, that when they become interiorized, they can "lead the faithful to conform themselves ever *more completely* . . . to the life of God revealed in the flesh." [44] Yet it is

[42] See chs. V and VI.

[43] The introduction of the symbols of the Christian Year requires instruction of the congregation. These symbols include all that is meant by the term "propers," i.e., liturgical materials appropriate to particular occasions: the appointed lessons, psalms, prayers, the preface to the consecration prayer in Holy Communion, prescribed choral introits and responses, designated seasonal colors, etc. Perhaps the best way for a congregation to become engaged with the meanings of the Christian Year is to be taught to follow the appointed course readings in Scripture week by week, with preaching concurrently rooted in these readings. So far from the pastor finding this constrictive, he will almost certainly find it liberating. In any case his preaching will be anchored in sacred history and will take on biblical relevance that hardly comes in any other way.

[44] W. K. Lowther Clarke and Charles Harris, eds., *Liturgy and Worship* (London: SPCK, 1932), p. 201. Italics mine.

precisely the "more" beyond our desire and our obedience, even beyond our comprehension, that worship is obligated to convey. The irrelevance of the Word as that which men do not want to hear, indeed may not even be able to hear—this, too, is to be declared.

In a second, more profound sense the Word defines the meaning of irrelevance: as its miraculous freedom to convey its meaning as it will, to go beyond our desire that it be human as we are human, and to declare the fullness of its truth. Irrelevance in this sense may most of all baffle if not offend the modern worshipper, who often wishes exactly that the Word be shorn of its miraculousness; that the miracles themselves be omitted or "explained" or at least "toned down"; that the "human Jesus" or the "simple gospel" be set forth. But this is precisely what cannot be permitted in liturgical encounter with the Word in its historical character, if worship is to possess integrity. To be grasped by "the Jesus of history" is to be grasped by the divine freedom in that history, and the scandal of this paradox is exactly that to which the miracles attest:[45] Satan cast out and the sick healed; the loaves of bread multiplied many times over; the tempest stilled; the dead raised up; the crucified Jesus resurrected; the Pentecostal tongues of fire made to appear. Admittedly, how the historical embodies the miraculous is beyond rational understanding; it can only be apprehended by a decision of faith. But *it is* exactly *the purpose of worship to set before men this decision.* And when worship yields up irrelevance in this sense, and in the name of a false relevance agrees to proclaim the Word only as a simple history men can understand and whose fatefulness they can evade, it has lost integrity.

Perhaps another way to understand this is to say that irrelevance derives from the Word as a reality beyond history as well as in history, as time-transcending as well as time-involved. For worship, it always must be remembered, is response not only to what Jesus Christ once did in his historical life. It is also response to what has been divinely done in him and is still being done. The mind of the Church, to be sure, states this conviction unevenly, at times queerly; but it does not doubt but that the reality meeting us in Jesus Christ comes from the other side of history as well as in history. Thus, if we have said that liturgical action is self-contradictory when it fails to embrace historically man's world and time, now we must say that it is self-contradictory if it does not bring man to transcend his world and time. Or if we have said that relevance requires us to remember the historical Jesus whose brothers and sisters we know, now we must say that irrelevance requires

---

[45] Archibald Hunter reminds us that almost one third of the earliest, most historical gospel, St. Mark—209 verses out of a total of 661—deals directly or indirectly with miracle. See his *Introducing New Testament Theology* (London: SCM Press, 1957), ⁓ 28.

us to behold the Lamb slain from the foundation of the world who even now reigns from a throne in heaven.

Or, transposed into still different terms, if relevance in liturgy may be thought of as *ethos*, irrelevance may be thought of as *logos*. Perhaps this is the perception the early Church would convey to us in St. Luke's narrative of Jesus' rebuke to Martha and his vindication of Mary who sat at his feet and listened to his word (Luke 10:39-42). Unlike Martha who busied herself with many tasks, Mary, he said, had chosen "the one thing needful," "that better part which shall not be taken from her." Symbolically, the Word ever speaks this truth to the liturgical mind of the Church. Ultimately, only "one thing" is "needful" in the sense that without it worship cannot be worship: the posture of adoration before the Lord. This is "the better part," the superior value, because it alone apprehends reality that "cannot be taken away"—the eternal meanings of the Word transcending history and time. Now irrelevance in this sense, let it be clear, still is not to deny the world and its claims. *Ethos* and *logos* cannot be sundered. Martha and Mary will always be sisters! Liturgy as adoration, it has been written, "uses the raw materials of human experience—bread, wine, water, a book, a laugh, a tear, . . . to return the song of praise to God." In these very human realities, the world is present: "Even in the act of adoring the world is remembered, *but now it is used and transformed.*[46] Surely worship can have no higher goal. As adoration of that Word in which the world is both "remembered" and "transformed," worship embodies the dialectic of relevance and irrelevance in a way from which one is never free and never wants to be free.

But given this understanding, then the forms of worship must be expected to take on an aspect of irrelevance also. Precisely because the event of the Word initiates, sustains, and consummates our action, the means of its action will always seem over against us and as reaching beyond us. And in its trans-historical character also, because the Word is unapprehensible as well as apprehensible, the forms through which it encounters us will be both unmeaningful and meaningful. This is to say, the Word incarnates meanings to which we are to respond but to which we can never respond, and in this strange sense worship will be both relevant and irrelevant. Did we say that "liturgy" is the "people's work" and that the forms of that work must be such that we can make them our own? Yet the work we do was first done for us in a Galilean life and on a Judean cross, and through what liturgical form can we ever realize so stupendous a thing? Or did we say that we can grasp the historical Word as so present in the Church's Year that the life

---

[46] Martin E. Marty, *Second Chance for American Protestants* (New York: Harper & Row, 1963), p. 161. Italics mine.

Jesus Christ once lived in time can sanctify our time? But how vain to believe that we can ever plumb the depths of that life in which dwelt all the fullness of the godhead bodily! Or did we say that worship is to be worldly, that it is to engage us with the world with the same action with which Jesus Christ engages us? But how can we finally ever know, indeed should we even wish to know, what Christ's action in its sovereign freedom will mean? Surely liturgy must stop short of saying too firmly what any man's liturgical action is to be, whether in the gathered assembly or in the world. Here as elsewhere we are not to get things too clear. A true evangelism, D. T. Niles once said, is not so much to carry the Word to a situation as to incarnate the Word in that situation, and what "incarnation" will require is rarely given a man beforehand to know. In short, irrelevance is to be met by that Word whose depths we cannot fathom and in ways we cannot—and, dare we say, must not?—understand.

Relevance and Irrelevance Understood Ontologically and Existentially

In the preceding essay, the "ontological" character of the Word was defined as the fundamental hinge on which liturgical theology is to turn. This cumbersome phrase is simply a way of saying that Jesus Christ, in all the fullness of his being, meets man on the deepest levels of his being to bring him to partake of divine life. In essence, worship is man's cry for life and the answer of the Word to that cry: *Ego sum vita*. And clearly, on this deep level, worship is nothing if it is not relevant in the most existential sense, indeed in something of the sense in which the psychologist of religion defines the essence of religion itself: "Man's religion is the *audacious* bid he makes to bind himself to creation and to the Creator. It is his *ultimate* attempt . . . to *complete* his own personality by finding *the supreme context in which he rightly belongs*." [47] Liturgical theology would dissent from this definition in ascribing the initiative in "man's bid" ultimately to God rather than to man. It would also wish to speak of God as Redeemer as well as Creator, and it would further define the end of religion as more than the "completion" of man's "personality." It would not, however, dissent from the basic truth that authentic faith bears the marks of audacity and ultimacy, that worship as its expression represents man's passion to find "the supreme context" to which he rightly belongs, and that in this respect worship possesses a certain teleological character in its vision of the End beyond all other ends claiming man's being. One needs to translate terms, and what

[47] Gordon W. Allport, *The Individual and His Religion* (New York: The Macmillan Co., 1961), p. 142. Italics mine.

177

psychology speaks of as "man's bid" to "bind himself" to the "supreme context" of his existence, theology would speak of as "the salt God has put in our mouths that we might thirst after him"—in Augustine's metaphor—and of worship itself as nothing less than the meeting of man's thirst with the water of eternal life.

But if worship is to be relevant in this existential sense, then the Church must be able to hear and translate the ways in which man voices his cry. Sometimes man will forthrightly name his thirst as "religious" although his attempts to satisfy it take strange forms. What has been called the "wild pluralism" of religions in America pictures this truth:

Today, there are advocates of ESP, Psi phenomena, and LSD. In search of spiritual expression, people speak in tongues, enter Trappist monasteries, build on Jungian archetypes, go to Southern California and join a cult, become involved "where the action is" in East Harlem, perceive "God at work in the world," see Jesus Christ as the man for others, hope for liberation by the new morality, study phenomenology, share the Peace Corps experience, borrow from cosmic syntheses, and go to Church.[48]

Sometimes man will name his thirst in brooding ways and eloquent accents. One from whom the Church would perhaps have least expected such a naming, Bertrand Russell, has written:

The center of me is always and eternally a terrible pain—a curious wild pain—a searching for something beyond what the world contains, something transfigured and infinite, the beatific vision—God—I do not find it, I do not think it is to be found—but the love of it is my life—it's like passionate love for a ghost. At times it fills me with rage, at times with wild despair, it is the source of gentleness and cruelty and work, it fills every passion that I have—it is the actual spring of life in me.[49]

On the other hand, man often does not know his hunger to be a metaphysical hunger nor does he use the word "God" to designate the life he craves. Instead he voices his craving for the supreme context of his existence in roundabout ways. Sometimes experiences of limitation in his social and historical existence evoke his cry—when he finds his freedom bound or his power powerless or his wisdom folly, and in varying accents confesses that "I am at the end of my rope." The Church will not cunningly make capital out of his predicament. But it also will not be deterred from recognizing the theological nature of man's deepest anxieties and the ontological nature

[48] Martin E. Marty, "The Spirit's Holy Errand," Daedalus, 96 (1967), p. 113.
[49] Quoted by John C. Bennett, Commencement Address, Union Theological Seminary, May 21, 1968, from the review by Malcolm Muggeridge of The Autobiography of Bertrand Russell, 1914-1944, in The Observer Review, London, April 28, 1968.

of liturgy's answer, and it will not agree that even in his secular experience man is unable to experience sacral reality. While often the most the Church can do is to help man identify the sacral in the secular as a prolegomenon to a fuller Christian affirmation, it will not yield up the conviction that man's important questions ultimately have to do with the sacred and that the ultimate answer in one way or another is to be transposed into a liturgical answer.

Relevance also requires the Church to listen and to translate questions rising out of man's more personal existence, for here, likewise, man is only more or less able to name things with their true names. A poet has said that this temporal world is not a Sahara Desert bereft of meaning but a kind of spiritual kindergarten in which millions of bewildered children are trying to spell God with the wrong blocks. In their attitudes toward the divine symbolized by the Church and its worship, people likewise try to spell God with the wrong blocks. Thus they will say that they come to Church "to get inspiration," or to "hear something that will last me through the rest of the week," or "to feel better," or "to forget the cares of the world," or "to find peace of mind." The Church must not be put off by such crude spelling, nor, for that matter, accommodate its worship too cheaply to it. Rather, it must translate the layman's colloquialisms in terms of the deeper hunger behind them, and take hold of his misconceived speech as a handle to the truth of his nature it reveals—that man dumbly knows that his true life does not lie in himself but in a divine life other than his own. Man's "bid" for "the supreme context" of his existence is always being made if we have ears to hear, and the Church is to bring to his thirst not the vinegar of scorn but the water of life.

Relevance as sensitivity to man's passion for life, however, is not only preliminary to worship. Obviously worship itself is to be shot through and through with relevance in this sense and to be tested against it. One form of testing is to ask whether worship is properly "subjective." For as the life of the Word ontologically meeting the predicament of man, worship is inevitably subjective, and we are not wrong in thinking of it in this way. Thus the true question is not "whether worship is to be subjective or objective," as we often say, but—as we shall try to clarify in the following essay—in what way it is to be subjective and how subjectivity can be kept authentic.

To illustrate briefly: How central are prayers of confession and petition in worship? These types of prayer may be said to be existentialist in a way that other types perhaps are not: they singularly represent man's attempt to be released from secondary contexts which entrap him and to lay hold on the supreme context which secures him. Confession and petition peculiarly declare the "I" of man, and when liturgical fastidiousness belittles these

179

as "selfish" or "subjective," as over against prayer of thanksgiving, for example, man's cry for life is denied and authentic relevance is lost. Further, confession must specify sins concretely if it is to be relevant, for in essence man's sins are the lesser contexts to which he has committed himself—in short, his idolatries; and only as these are existentially named will he feel worship to deal honestly with what is real to him. Similarly, petition must grasp in living, concrete language his needs, and—yes—his "desires" and his "wants." For language at best is only a symbol of the layer upon layer of the desires with which man is trying to spell "God." However self-centered and misstated these desires may be, we can be sure that God translates them and the broken speech in which we voice them, in terms of the passion for life behind them. Hence worship is not wrong when it offers prayer of confession and petition as man's crying out for the security of the supreme context over against all lesser contexts which threaten him. Admittedly, confession and petition—in free prayer especially—easily foster an unhealthy self-preoccupation. Yet this is a risk liturgy must accept if it is to be relevant to man's situation and faithful to the God of man's situation. "Prayer is a dip into acid," Douglas Steere has remarked, and only as prayer is dipped into the acid of man's existential life is it informed with that truthfulness that is relevance.

But not only in prayer, in all elements of worship the ontological aspect is fulcral. One only needs to take a swift overview of the Church's liturgical life through the centuries—as in the preceding essay—to understand that in relevance ontologically understood we are met with reality basic for thought and aboriginal in experience. One can especially understand why Holy Communion looms so centrally and why theologies interpreting its meaning have so decisively affected the Church's life. As the generic form of liturgy, Communion supremely reveals Jesus Christ dealing with man existentially, and, in the gift of his life through bread and wine, addressing his divine self to man on the most primal levels of man's being. Significantly, both psychology and anthropology verify theology's understanding of relevance in this sense.[50] Man's instinct to eat and drink the god in the form of physical life is archetypal in both his individual and racial experience; and his appetite for life through the physical is only a paradigm of his passion—however hidden —for life to his soul. It is no belittling of Christianity to say that Jesus Christ reads man's nature in this way and promises to engage man on this level. He understands how man's instinctual vitalities are ineffaceable and universal. Thus the hunger of man and that Word which is as the bread of life are realities so ultimate that neither liturgical experience nor liturgical

[50] See chs. IV, V, VII.

reflection can go beyond them. In this elemental sense worship is nothing if not relevant.

Yet, fundamental as relevance is, the transaction in which man's cry for life is met is marked also by irrelevance, in that the Word, Jesus Christ, takes man's cry with infinitely greater seriousness than man takes it himself. The Word meets man as counter-reality, it must be remembered, as against man as well as for him and as saving in its very overagainstness. Indeed, in its resurrection "being" the Word so exposes the emptiness of man's being that Scripture does not hesitate to speak violently of men as "dead" in their trespasses and sins—as marked out as dead and the dead One as the living. Liturgical theology reads the human situation no less gravely. It understands how man is both unwilling and willing to have exposed in their falsehood the less-than-supreme contexts to which he belongs. "Worship," it has been written, "is a bold plunge into the depths of reality," an acknowledgement men make of "the deepest truth about their life, . . . the truth . . . that they cannot understand their own life except by turning to their Creator." Worship is thus "a warfare against idolatry, . . . a deliverance from the fundamental lie, . . . the lie of ultimate self-sufficiency." [51] One can hardly improve upon this definition, but the fact is that often men do not want to be delivered from the fundamental lie. They prefer the death they have chosen. There is always the life with God for which man was made; and there is the more-or-less life with God which man more-or-less acknowledges he more-or-less needs.

The ontological character of the Word ultimately allows no compromise here, and its irrelevance consists exactly in its refusal to deal with man as other than he really is and to offer itself as other than it really is. The fundamental truth and the fundamental lie are at stake, and worship must set these choices before men even though it strike upon them with offense and discontinuity. The contrast between the eternal life of the Gospel and all other "contexts-of-belonging" must be set forth. Karl Barth has asked whether it is not true that when people come to worship, they consciously or unconsciously leave behind cherry tree, symphony, state, and their daily work as possibilities somehow exhausted. It is well that this insight is put in the form of a question because the meanings of nature, of beauty, of man's political existence, of his labor are in one sense continuous with the life given us in Jesus Christ; and as we shall need to make clear, they cannot be thought of as exhausted without the relevance of worship being denied. On the other hand, in an *ultimate* sense liturgical integrity requires that the self-

---

[51] Truman B. Douglass, *Why Go to Church?* (New York: Harper & Bros., 1957), pp. 106-7.

sufficiency of all human meanings be put in question and the inadequacy of all contexts of existence less than the eternal life of God in Jesus Christ be exposed. Worship as relevance affirms the worldly meanings of man's existence; worship as irrelevance crucifies the world and summons men to count all things as loss that they may gain Christ. Its purpose finally is no less than that the reality of death to these things shall come to lie behind the believer, even if, like Lazarus, he is still to die.[52]

Relevance and Irrelevance Understood Soteriologically and Eschatologically

Understood in this way, irrelevance thus bears soteriological and eschatological meaning also. For only insofar as worship is somehow a transaction in which man's being experiences that death and resurrection which are at the heart of the Gospel does it possess integrity. In this sense worship by definition is evangelical if not evangelistic: it is to convert dead men into life. And one must say of worship in this sense what Bonhoeffer says of "the word of God" the Church must declare: "The Church's word to the world is the word of . . . the *love* of God for the world in the sending of His Son, and of God's *judgement* upon unbelief. The word of the Church is *the call to conversion*, the call to belief in the love of God in Christ, and the call to preparation for Christ's second coming and for the future kingdom of God." [53] In a deep sense worship is always a "call to conversion." And the many kinds of liturgical indifferentism so popular today, which in the name of a well-meant but misconceived secularity dull the sharpness of this call, are intolerable. In this respect, the instinct of certain free churches in regularly including in their services an "Invitation to Discipleship" is not wrong.[54] This "invitation" need not always be made verbally, and the pastor's imagination should be put to work to devise symbolic forms which present it with eloquence and power. But ultimately every service in its totality and every element within a service is to be an invitation to Christian

---

[52] See Ernst Käsemann, *The Testament of Jesus*, trans. Gerhard Krodel (London: SCM Press, 1968), pp. 16-17.

[53] *Ethics*, ed. Eberhard Bethge, trans. Neville Horton Smith (New York: The Macmillan Co., 1955), p. 321. Italics mine.

[54] One may question whether every service must mechanically include such an "Invitation" in explicit terms, for the call to conversion may be implicit rather than explicit. One may also doubt whether the precise wording of this phrase adequately poses the soteriological decision involved. The decision for or against the life of the Word is more fateful than the overtones of moralism which the term "discipleship" suggests. Yet this may be the handle with which the modern man can best take hold of the deeper realities at stake.

discipleship. Men may misunderstand or resent worship of this kind. It may strike upon them as irrelevant. But only so can worship be faithful to the fatefulness the Word holds for human life.

From worship understood ontologically and soteriologically derives the irrelevance of worship understood eschatologically. Again one is not comfortable with these ponderous terms, nor is one sure that the eschatological nature of worship should not precede its ontological and soteriological nature in the course of thought. For as eschatology is the matrix of the New Testament Gospel, so eschatology ought in one sense to be the foremost category for liturgical theology. Yet, just as the experience of the life of the Word in the early Church preceded eschatological conceptualization of it, so the property of Life which the Word as Light most essentially is, precedes any formulation of its meaning we are able to make. In any case, the illogic of worship as an event in which the Word offers its life in the present moment only through what it did once two thousand years ago and through what it shall do in the future unto the end of history must be expected to strike upon men with irrelevance! And one is not surprised that such offense is too great for certain theologies today which popularly focus upon the "now"—"Dionysian" theologies, for example, which urge us to taste and feel the world as the sovereign source of abiding meanings within the present moment of our experience.[55] Yet this eschatological meaning is exactly the truth upon which the integrity of *Christian* worship rises or falls: the Word whose life fatefully confronts man simultaneously embodies a past and a future grounded in divine reality that "was, is now and ever shall be," and it summons man to relive that past precisely in order that he may cross over into that future now. Can one think of a contradiction to the mind greater than this?

It is little wonder that the eschatological symbols conveying this truth— especially those which look to the future—seem irrelevant: the maranatha, the sanctuary beyond the veil, the tongues of the Spirit, the parousia, the last judgement and the last day, the sifting of the wheat and the burning of the tares, the angels and archangels and all the hosts of heaven, the victory over the beast, the lamb upon the throne. It is also little wonder that worship so eschatological should strike upon men as exclusive if not esoteric, and that well-meaning but uninformed people with little grasp of its profoundly eschatological character should resent its exclusivism, wish to open it to all comers, and reduce it to amiable, worldly conversation. However, because the Word whose life is fateful for man's life makes himself known on his own

---

[55] See the essay "Manifesto for a Dionysian Theology," by Sam Keen, in *New Theology No. 7*, ed. Martin E. Marty and Dean G. Peerman (New York: The Macmillan Co., 1970), p. 100.

terms, and because those who have thus come to know him have entered into another, unique realm of existence, Christian worship must inevitably be exclusive. It is the conversation of the family of Christ about strange and wondrous things. It is to be conceived first for the community of faith which has experienced these things. And the Church will always have to lay itself open to the charge of irrelevance in this sense.

Relevance as Engagement with, and Irrelevance as Disengagement from, Man's Life in the World

It becomes clear, then, that worship as man's existential cry for life and as the answer of Jesus Christ to that cry can only be conceived with integrity when it is subject to the mercilessness of the dialectic of relevance and irrelevance inhering in the Word. To be sure, none of us ever succeeds in obeying this constraint. The thoughts of our hearts are not clean enough nor the thoughts of our mind clear enough to be transparent as we ought to be transparent to the Light. Nevertheless, we are never to be relieved from its claim and from the constraint of being as least untruthful in our reflection upon its meaning as we know how to be. The force of this constraint especially comes home to us in exploring the last form of the dialectic of relevance and irrelevance to be discussed in this essay: the relevance of worship as engagement with man's life in the world and the irrelevance of worship as detachment from his life in the world. Like a theme with variations, this polarity has run through much of these essays: in identifying the gulf between worship and life as the most formidable corruption the minister faces; in inquiring how far liturgy should take as its chief purpose the moral transformation of life; in analyzing worship as an end and as a means; in explaining its "missionary" and "public" character, and in indicating how it is to be both prospective and recollective; in inquiring how worship as *ethos* is to embrace man's historical existence even while, as *logos*, it reaches beyond his historical experience.

Our point of departure consists in the life of the Word viewed in its fullness as a liturgical life. Its liturgical ontology, if we may so speak, consists in its liturgical activity. The person of Christ is known in the work of Christ. Who Jesus Christ is, is declared through what Jesus Christ does. And what Jesus Christ does is supremely a liturgy—a service, a work of ministry. In this liturgy, always and simultaneously, God serves man, man serves man, and man serves God. Conceptually, insofar as the mind can resolve these distinguishable realities into the truth beyond them, one can only employ such a concept as "Incarnation," or perhaps the symbol of "mediator" or "priest." (And parenthetically, we remember that the mind of the early

Church, as it reflected upon the liturgical meaning of Jesus Christ, habitually preferred the metaphor of "priest.") Beyond such conceptual symbols, the mind can hardly go. What must be made clear, however, is that the liturgical life of the Word consists as much in its divine service of man and its human service of God as in its human service of man. In reflecting upon relevance and irrelevance, we too often ignore the former and identify only the latter. That is, we tend to project upon worship our own human vision and construe the meaning of liturgy as mainly what man humanly does; and to a degree our common definition of "liturgy" as "the work of the people" justifies this construction.

The full truth of the incarnation, however, is that the liturgy of Jesus Christ is also the work of God. Because Jesus Christ is divine, his liturgy is a liturgy of the divine serving us; and because Jesus Christ is human, it is the liturgy of a man serving man and of a man serving God. To be sure, in its work as the divine serving us, the Word takes on human form. But the glory of the Word is exactly that its human liturgy is the liturgy of the divine emptying itself, assuming the form of a servant and for man's sake becoming obedient unto the cross. In short, the liturgical life of the Word is both human and divine; it is lived both in time and from and to eternity. It is incarnate and it is eschatological. It is secular and it is sacred. It is as a Jacob's ladder on which both worldly and otherworldly meanings ascend and descend. And only as the Church's liturgy is conformed to these properties of the Light does it possess integrity.

Understood within this light, worship is relevantly to engage man with his worldly life to the degree that the liturgical life of the Word was engaged with man and his world—which is to say, infinitely and completely. In this sense worship cannot be too worldly or, if one prefers, too missionary or too secular or too apostolic. For what more worldly liturgy can the mind imagine than the man, Jesus, serving his fellowmen with the love with which we see him living out his life? And can one conceive any liturgy more worldly than the act of a God who gave his only Son to die for the world on the cross? All things worldly, and to the most intense degree, are penetrated by that liturgy, and only when worship penetrates man's worldly life as the Word penetrates it is it authentic.

Thus if we have said that worship engages man with that Word which rescues him from all secondary contexts that entangle him, now we must say that worship possesses integrity only when it engages man with that Word whose liturgical life penetrates all worldly meanings that claim him. Or, if we have said that man comes to worship feeling that cherry tree, symphony, state, daily work are somehow exhausted, now we must say that in precisely these meanings man identifies the liturgical life he is to live in obedience to that Word whose penetration of life can never be plumbed. The worshipper's entire existence is both to be seen as worship and brought into worship; and in this deep sense worship cannot be too relevant as the engagement of man with his world.

A Roman Catholic theologian, Karl Rahner, uses the thought-forms of his tradition in which the Mass is central, to set forth this truth.[56] He pleads that his Church teach her laity—especially her youth—the meaning of the "Mass of Life" as well as of the "Mass of the Church," for only sensitivity to the sacramental quality of all life can render the life received in the Mass sacramental. Only as we daily commune with Christ in the world can we truthfully commune with him at his table. The "Mass of life" is man's perceiving Jesus Christ ever coming into his worldly life, and the celebrating of Christ's presence and death and resurrection in all "grace-bearing experiences" life brings. Especially, wherever we meet a suffering and striving and overcoming of evil, whether in man's social existence or in his own nature, there something is taking place which partakes of the sacrifice of the Cross. Thus—Rahner adds—why should not the lawyer understand his daily encounters with questions of justice in society as partaking of that act of the altar which established the New Covenant of love from which all law finally derives? Why should not the student of medicine see his fight against suffering and death as part of the divine struggle of the great Healer, and even his ultimate defeat by these as overcome in the end in him who rose from suffering and death into life? Similarly, why should not the student of language see the meaning of his secular study within light of that Word in which all things consist and which supremely can transform the sign language of the world into a song of praise to God? And why should not the workman, indeed any man who helps make the world into what it ought to be, see the exercise of his creative powers as a sharing in that New Creation wrought in the life and death of him who makes all things new?

To the meaning of liturgical relevance so movingly set forth, Protestant sensibility surely responds. For all the people of Christ, the "Mass of the Altar" and the "Mass of Life" belong together. The Word at pulpit and table is correlative with the Word in the world. Communion is "holy" at the altar because Christ's liturgy is "holy" everywhere.

But, do we seem only to pile contradiction upon contradiction to say in the same breath that the liturgical life of the Word also requires worship to disengage man from his life in the world, and that in this sense it will always be irrelevant also? If so, then let it be remembered that we are dealing with

---

[56] See *The Christian Commitment: Essays in Pastoral Theology*, trans. Cecily Hastings (New York: Sheed & Ward, 1963), pp. 146-48, 165-70.

the fundamental mystery of Christianity—the incarnation; that here we move beyond theology as logic to theology as symbol—or as song. Here the mind does not so much reason as listen. For what we have called "the dialectic of relevance and irrelevance" is but an echo of a metaphysical fugue whose contrapuntal themes, "divine," "human," flow from a source beyond our human reason in the mind of God. Our minds can only fugitively hear these themes as now they cross, now separate, now join, and then oppose. But beyond their contradiction, if we have ears to hear, we can touch that divine harmony which is from the foundation of the world.

Worship is disengagement from man's worldly life, first, because the liturgical life of Jesus Christ is more than a man serving man: it is God serving man. And to be grasped by so stupendous a truth is to be met by the holy in a way so foreign to normal sensibility that its contradiction can only strike upon men as irrelevance. The mark of the holy is God in his Godness, yes; it is also God in his humanity. The holy is God in his separateness and overagainstness; it is also God in his disclosure. It is God in his absoluteness; it is also God in his relatedness. Above all, to the eyes of faith the holy is God's lordship revealed in his servanthood. What most evokes our awe— it has been written—"is not that God is high and lifted up but that he has come to us, making our life and death his own." [57] In the "numinous" thus revealed in the servant life of Jesus Christ, Christian worship has its foundations. For not until one has trembled before this vision—that "the divine should become our footman," that the hands of God should wash our feet, break to us our bread, carry our cross—does he know what worship is, either cultically or apostolically. To be sure, this vision of the holy comes *through* a vision of *the human* and in this sense will always seem relevant also. But what stuns us with wonder is just that *reality other than human* should so costingly reveal itself through the human. Grasped by this revelation, the Church can only ever look upward in adoration, even as it looks outward to the world. And despite the risks of a false otherworldliness this vision involves, it is a risk we have no choice but to accept. In this primal, mystical sense, in the sense that worship is to engage man with the numinous beyond the world that is yet known through the world, worship is to be irrelevant.

Irrelevance in a second sense derives from this vision: the life we live in the world is truly a liturgy only when it is first conformed to the liturgy of God set before us in the Word. Only as we are detached into the form of that liturgy to which we adoringly look upward can we know the mission it lays upon

---

[57] Roger Hazelton, *Christ and Ourselves* (New York: Harper & Row, 1965), p. 95. I am indebted to Hazelton for my use of the context of this quotation as well as for the quotation itself.

us as we ethically look outward. In his life in the world, the Christian man is not his own man; he is Christ's man. His mission does not rise out of his own goodwill, nor is it shaped by his own wisdom or sustained out of his own strength; rather, it is divinely grounded in Christ's liturgy. We know how to serve at the world's table only because Christ has first served us at his. We are able to break the loaves to men because of him who has broken them unto us. We are able to wash the feet of men because Christ has washed ours. And such a liturgy, life teaches us, will always affront more than it will confirm both our own desires and the world's expectations. The reversals Christ's liturgy offers to our calculations, the offense it deals to our ambition, the freedom it bestows only on him who consents to be bound, the depths it summons us to descend to and the heights to which it raises men—these will always seem irrelevant. Such a liturgy will always keep us in the world, but such a liturgy is not given us by the world.

In a final—and once more, an eschatological—sense, worship is disengagement from life in the world in that the Christian's liturgy, as the liturgy of Jesus Christ himself, is service offered to God even as it is addressed to man. Always these two directions mark the liturgy of the Word, but while they merge in experience they are to be distinguished in thought. Jesus Christ's service to God is service of man; but through service to man the Word serves God. God is not man; and the lodestar of the liturgy of Jesus Christ is finally that realm of reality other than man one can only name "God."

So it must always be with the Church's worship also. We may express this truth in part by saying that worship is an experience of the futurity of God —that is, of God in his freedom breaking history open and drawing man to choose divine possibilities and to share in bringing these to pass. To be sure, worship understood in this way is relevant also in the sense that to experience the futurity of God is to be grasped by his activity here and now. The future invades the present; the Kingdom is in our midst; and only as man follows the stride of God in present history can he serve the future. Yet, Christian futurity is finally a quality of God, not of man; while known through history, its source is beyond history. Indeed, the unpredictability and violence with which the futurity of God breaks in upon us can only be explained by a reality other than our world and ourselves. Of that violence in its otherness, Jesus once said that it was as lightning striking from heaven. And worship is only true when normal sensibility is prepared to be stunned with a vision of the action of God like that. In this sense the liturgical situation is always as that of those who in the time of our Lord did not recognize the invasion of God in his futurity as God. After a miracle in which the future had become present through his casting out of demons, Jesus

188

had to tell men bluntly not to doubt but that "the kingdom of God is come upon you" (Luke 11:20 KJV). Our human expectations are so meager and the possibilities of God so staggering that encounter with the God who makes all things new must always be expected to strike upon men with irrelevance, whether in the liturgical casting out of demons or in drinking of the royal wine of heaven.

Lastly, irrelevance as disengagement from the world derives from the liturgy of Jesus Christ as a liturgy of eternity as well as of time. This liturgy, we are never to forget, has to do with a God who is beyond history as well as in history. It was once offered to this God; it is being offered now; and it will go on being offered to the end of time. Correspondingly, the Church's worship partakes of this eternity, and she is not wrong, even in the face of many adversaries, in declaring that man's liturgical destiny is finally in this eternal God. The paradigm of her worship in this sense is St. John's vision of the worship of the saints in heaven: the saints are they whose liturgy was once lived out in time amidst great tribulation, and they are those who now sing the liturgy in eternity before the throne of the Lamb.

Liturgical theology cannot finally renounce such otherworldly images nor stop short of the truth they affirm. And despite—or shall we not say, because of?—the irrelevance with which their truth seems to contradict man's sensibility today, perhaps more than ever they are to be thought of as part of the Church's pearl of great price. To be sure, at first sight one might suppose that of all Christian concepts the most meaningless to the modern mind is the concept of eternity. What lodgement has it in reality, it has been asked,

when all our experience, external and internal, knows only transience, the death of all that once had life? Do we experience eternity in time, except poetically—and how, if at all, could we experience it from an *historical* revelation? On what basis . . . do we speak of an eternal life, or a life after death? . . . Modern reflection finds this category meaningless.

But, our critic—Langdon Gilkey—continues:

Human awareness, feeling, and existential questioning fail to obey these methodological rules. For the question of eternity, of that which transcends passage and death, haunts the psyches of our age, shapes our behaviour and our fears, and causes our frantic efforts to perpetuate ourselves and the things we love beyond the ravages of time.[58]

[58] "Unbelief and the Secular Spirit," in *The Presence and the Absence of God*, ed. Christopher F. Mooney, S.J. (New York: Fordham University Press, 1969), pp. 60-61.

Surely the deeper truth about our life today is that men cannot live without hope of some eternal "metamorphosis of being." And surely Paul Tillich was not wrong in enjoining the pastor: "To point with inner authority to the eternal is the most relevant function men can perform today." [59]

Thus in a sense the Church must ever war against man's intoxication with time. And how impoverished liturgy becomes when excitement with a world come of age is allowed to vitiate its otherworldly character, and how woefully the liturgy of Jesus Christ is misread by a sensibility which declares that "the Church's vocation . . . has little to do with salvation in the world to come."[60] That scripture which distinguishes eternal and temporal reality and which holds that if we have hope in Christ only in this life we are of all men most miserable, cannot be so easily gainsaid. The Gospel too abundantly speaks of the Omega with the Alpha, of a Second Coming and a Last Day and the Final Glory, of the New Heaven and a New Earth, of the Lord to whom the Church is betrothed and of the marriage supper of the Lamb. The Church too fervently prays the Maranatha—"Christianity is the religion of the Maranatha: 'Come, Lord Jesus,'" Schillebeeckx has written—[61] and it gazes too raptly at him who shall come and has come. Indeed one would have supposed that the Lord's own words would have instructed us as the first disciples: "Never again shall I drink from the fruit of the vine until *that day when I drink it new with you* in the kingdom of my Father" (Matt. 26:29 NEB). No, the Church is not wrong when she longs for eternity in words whose mystery she herself does not understand: "Grant that we who know thee now by faith may after this life have the fruition of thy glorious godhead." [62] And she also is not wrong when, as Paul Claudel has beautifully reminded us, in Belgium, on the day of a child's First Communion, a bottle of precious wine is walled into a cavity for him to drink—who knows when? Perhaps when matured, or on that Day when he drinks in the Kingdom of God.

This is to say, worship is irrelevant in that it is to be worship of eschatological expectation. While it relevantly engages man with his life in this world, it ever bids him look to a city to come. It gives him food and drink

---

[59] "The Relevance of the Ministry in Our Time and Its Theological Foundation," in *Making the Ministry Relevant*, ed. Hans Hofmann (New York: Charles Scribner's Sons, 1960), p. 35.

[60] Davies, *Worship and Mission*, p. 45.

[61] *Christ the Sacrament of the Encounter with God* (New York: Sheed & Ward, 1963), p. 41. Oscar Cullmann also reminds us that the "maranatha" is the oldest liturgical prayer of the Christian community. See his *Early Christian Worship*, p. 13. Scripture references: I Cor. 16:22; Phil. 4:5; Rev. 22:20.

[62] The Collect for Epiphany season, from the *Book of Common Prayer*, the Protestant Episcopal Church, U.S.A.

that he may break the crust and share the cup with the least of Christ's brethren; it kindles a divine thirst and tells of a heavenly banquet to come. It calls him to a holy warfare and amidst his battle seals him with a peace that passes all understanding; it withholds that ultimate peace known only to those who sing the Song of the Lamb. And, if the Church as she thus worships be charged with an irrelevant otherworldliness, she cannot but assent to the charge. For her liturgy partakes of the eternal liturgy of Him who came from the Father, who goes to the Father, and who reigns with the Father. This is the metaphysical secret of the Church's life. Because she liturgically lives for eternity, she is able to transform the things of time. "The Church," it has been written, "is the only society with a fulcrum outside the world; and therefore the only one that can move the world." [63] That fulcrum is finally the irrelevance and the relevance of Christian worship.

[63] Forsyth, *The Church and the Sacraments*, p. 5.

IV

The Question of Subjectivity and Objectivity

This essay[1] should be understood as a continuation of the preceding essay in the sense that the question of subjectivity and objectivity is the question of relevance and irrelevance framed in different terms. These terms, however, pose issues of such importance and in so practical a way as to permit a certain redundancy. To what extent, for example, should worship subjectively focus man's attention upon himself and his world? Should prayer be weighted more heavily as subjective petition than as objective adoration? Should music be used to plough people up emotionally—to soothe or shock, let us say? Are the sacraments more objective than a sermon? How far should preaching be directed to the needs of the congregation and how far should it objectively expound Scripture for its own sake? Should one continue to administer Baptism when its theological meanings are unreal? Is it legitimate to design worship to foster experience—a "happening" perhaps? Is "godward" worship more authentic than "manward"? The pastor cannot avoid such practical questions nor the estimate he has to make of the effect of his answers. Hopefully, he brings to them something of the holy anxiety we have pressed upon him, and the terms with which he states his concern are usually the terms "subjectivity" and "objectivity."

DIFFICULTIES WHICH CONFUSE THE QUESTION

His situation is not made easy, however, because of the conflicting advice he is liberally given which now persuades his reason though it counters his instincts, and now confirms his instincts while leaving him theologically uneasy. He may have been told, for example, that worship objectively addressed to God is "better" than worship subjectively conceived for man; yet the evidence of transformed lives before his eyes convinces him to the contrary. Or perhaps the liturgical psychologists have persuaded him that worship

[1] Part of this essay originally appeared in an article entitled "Subjectivity and Objectivity in Public Worship," in the *Union Seminary Quarterly Review*, XIX (Mar., 1964).

must be subjective if it is to help people; yet he is quite sure worship must also be objective proclamation and that its goal is something more than therapy. Again, he may have read—likely in the literature of liturgical renewal—that Protestant worship today needs less clericalism and more congregational participation. He agrees, but on reading futher he is puzzled to be told that only thus can worship remove the people's attention from themselves and direct it to the "objective realities and events" of Christian faith. Common sense has taught the pastor that it does not turn out this way, that subjectivity usually becomes heightened to the degree that a worshipper is engaged. Again, he is troubled by the claim that worship appropriate for secular men in a secular world is best conceived as "the celebration of life." Certainly delight in the world and in the marvelous works of man must have place in worship. Yet the pastor had supposed that worship had most to do with the objective reality of God, that it was considerably more than man's experience of his world and of himself.

Further heightening the pastor's predicament are certain unsettling shifts in Protestant and Roman Catholic theology. Whereas Catholic thought once flatly declared for the objectivity of worship in the sense that the sacrament possesses efficacy independently of the attitude of the worshipper, now Catholic theologians seem to be saying that grace is effective only if it is subjectively interiorized.[2] And whereas Protestant thought once insisted on the primacy of the individual's subjective faith, now the decisive reality is said to be grace objectively mediated through the Church; and man's subjectivity is denounced as a "cancerous" individualism. The correlation of liturgical subjectivity with Protestantism and of objectivity with Catholicism which prevailed for many years is no longer tenable.

Still more confusing—and the pastor certainly is not alone here—is the variety of meanings the terms "subjectivity" and "objectivity" themselves are made to bear. Indeed in few areas of liturgical study is one made more aware of the hazards of imprecise and polemical use of language. We are variously told, for example, that worship is objective in the sense that it is the action of the Church as distinguished from the subjective act of the individual; or that worship is objective when—as in Calvinism—it stresses the scriptural proclamation of God's being and sovereignty, and subjective when—as in Lutheranism—it stresses the worshipper's faith. Frequently objectivity is equated with so-called liturgical worship, subjectivity with so-called evangelical or pentecostal worship. Art identifies objectivity as the reality behind the liturgical symbol, subjectivity as man's apprehension of

[2] See example, see Karl Rahner, *The Christian Commitment: Essays in Pastoral Theology,* trans. Cecily Hastings (New York: Sheed & Ward, 1963). pp. 143-45.

the symbol's meaning. Psychologists employ "objective" to denote the independent existence of numinous phenomena, and "subjective" to denote man's experience of these. Again, worship is said to be objective when it is "God-ward," subjective when it is "manward." In objective worship we are said to "give"; in subjective worship we "get." The former is described as "vertical," the latter as "horizontal." A variation of this analysis defines objective worship as addressed to God in his transcendence, subjective worship as the experience of God's immanence. Or, subjective worship is equated with secular or worldly worship, objectivity with the experience of the sacred.

Confusion of meanings is still further heightened by the way in which guilt is imputed by association. Thus objective worship is described as corporate worship which induces ethical concern and social reform; subjective worship is stigmatized as "pietism" selfishly concerned only with the worshipper's inward emotional states, and it is implied that when worship deliberately appeals to emotion, it is evil. Alternatively, objective worship is equated with action, subjective worship with passivity. Again, subjectivity is associated with man's imagination and sensibility as less trustworthy than objective worship engaging the will. Subjectivity as a term of reproach is fastened upon worship as individualistic justification by faith in which the sermon is prominent, and objectivity is equated with the sacramental worship of the Church catholic. The most damning use of the term "subjective" seems to be reserved for worship thought of as "experience," over against objective worship as celebration of the redemptive acts of God; though how such celebration is to be performed without a subjective experience of these acts is usually not made clear.

Such pejorative usages are fundamentally due, we believe, to the failure to understand these terms dialectically and to define them with theological precision in light of the incarnation. The meaning of "subjectivity" and "objectivity"—as all else—can only be construed within an understanding of worship as "through Jesus Christ our Lord." However, it should also be candidly said that uses of these terms seem often to reflect personal feeling almost as much as they denote aspects of worship with which thought rationally tries to deal. For example, the spleen with which some scholars equate subjectivity with emotion—"a sweaty, clammy-palmed subjectivity," it has been called—and then dismiss it as horrid, probably reveals a fear of emotion in human life and an importing of personal insecurities into the liturgical conversation. Not a little liturgical literature reveals at bottom a fear of being truly human and an ignorance of the realities of human nature the pastor deals with every day. All credit, yes, to learned men who ponder the historical and theological meaning of worship and out of their rich wisdom enlighten us. Yet one wishes that we had more people writing about the question of subjectivity and objectivity with something of Luther's "peasantness," as well as scholars who dig in the mines of liturgical history but then come up blinking strangely before the light of everyday human life. On the other hand, much writing which stresses the subjective element reveals an unhealthy, even pathological, desire to be too human. Interpretation of the awesome encounter with God of the human soul becomes an indecent concern to undress man's inward life. In the name of "humanizing" worship, psychological states are examined with an almost morbid interest, and attention to "sensations" and "reactions" is made so prominent as to represent—in a phrase of Herbert Farmer—"an abuse of the human person." If some critics deal with the question of subjectivity and objectivity with too much fear of man, others bring to it too little respect for man.

In still other ways polemic and prejudice confuse the question. Sometimes high-church people look down their noses at the uncouth subjectivity of the evangelical, one feels, in order to inflate high-church egos. Free-church people unwilling to do their historical homework, on the other hand, dismiss attempts to brace worship with objective tradition as only "antiquarianism." Or, scholars urge that worship be made more objective by recovering tradition, but then turn around and heighten the very subjectivity they deplore by too fastidious concern for historical niceties. Again, the social reform and missionary endeavor which subjective, pietist worship has historically begotten are ignored because they confound preconceptions or dilute the pleasures of overreaction. Or objectivity under the aspect of corporateness is belittled because it is uncomfortable to be stirred out of genial ways of worship of one's own breeding or choosing. Or again, the historical antecedents of subjective worship are patronizingly located in nineteenth-century evangelism, but the labor of rethinking how worship can with equal power beget faith today is declined. And so forth and so on. While the question of subjectivity and objectivity is admittedly a thorny one, one also feels here the rustling of some of the evil spirits which Luther believed worship sets in motion.

Aside from the polemical meanings these terms have been made to bear, two further sources of confusion may be identified: first, the swings of theological and cultural pendulums. The polemic launched against subjectivity in the 1950's and early 1960's, for example, doubtless represented a necessary reaction—indeed an overreaction—against the corruption of worship into psychological manipulation in earlier decades. More recently, the popularity of subjective worship as secular and existential, with its impatience with tradition, its liturgical disavowal of God as "up" or "out there," and its insistence upon involvement and vitality, represents a reaction against the objectivity of revelation of the Barthian era. Characteristically, today's slogan—so Bishop John Robinson informs us—should be: "Let the liturgy be free!"[3] Clearly, reaction breeds counterreaction, and to hold to the truth comes hard amidst attack and defense.

Confusion arises, secondly, from the failure to check statement against fact. Here, if anywhere, one would suppose, people would be wise to think empirically, but what we so often run into is armchair theory and injunction. One critic characteristically writes: "It is going to make all the difference . . . whether you accustom yourself to think of the Church service as something you prepare for man, or as an offering which in the name and in the spirit of Jesus Christ you lay upon the altar of God." Now certainly one responds to the concern that worship be theocentric. Yet surely the facts of the situation hardly let one so neatly split objectivity and subjectivity and so dogmatically set God and man against one another. Is not worship in fact only truthful when it is something prepared for man as well as for God? Similarly, the theorist we have cited who equates subjectivity with emotion and then contemptuously dismisses it would do well to look at the facts. Surely in an age when depth psychology, existentialism, and the palpable evidence of the fatefulness of emotion for human destiny require us to look at man in the full dimensions of his being as never before, one should expect that liturgy, more than most theological disciplines, would desire to do justice to man's passional nature. Thus when we are told that worship is right to the extent that it is "objective" and disavows appeal to emotion, and wrong to the degree that it is "subjective" and engages emotion, we can only conclude that reality is being sacrificed to the grinding of an axe.

All this is to say that the question of subjectivity and objectivity poses issues more important than may first meet the eye. And integrity in thinking about them must mean conscientiousness in defining terms, abjuring semantic shortcuts, refusing to impute guilt by association, and being willing to be embarrassed by the facts. It further requires the courage to realize how once firm foundations may have been sapped by presumed enemies who may turn out to be friends—the psychologists or historians, for example —and how new winds of thought, or old, may resolve controversy and freshen insight. Above all, integrity means the unease of living with dialectic, the refusal to get things too clear, and restraint in stating one's vision of the truth. The realities focused in the polarity of "subjectivity" and "objectivity" are too profound and the relationship between them is too complex to be disposed of in any high-handed way.

[3] *The Christian Century*, Nov. 12, 1969.

A PROPOSED REDEFINITION OF TERMS

Let us cut through the tangle of difficulties and try to deal with the question of subjectivity and objectivity, to begin with, by simply accepting these terms as neutral terms pointing to given realities that operate in worship in a dialectical way. Broadly speaking, "subjectivity" can designate the reality of man and "objectivity" the reality of God as the two poles of the field in which worship takes place. Such a definition would seem to be a common denominator most of us can agree on, or—to change our metaphor—familiar furniture to the mind. Thus understood, "subjectivity" and "objectivity" can be defused of the polemic often investing them and made useful for liturgical discourse. Both are clearly essential, and to be told that worship is "better" or "more authentic" when it is one or the other is seen to be absurd. As we need both a right leg and a left leg to walk, so we need the dialectic of these terms to think about worship at all.

However, everything hinges on the content we ascribe to these polarities in their givenness, how we see them related and opposed, and on how we infer principles from them to help us in making decisions. The content of these terms, as we have intimated and shall more fully explore presently, is finally to be understood in light of the Word, which is to say, theologically. However, disciplines other than theology also speak of "subjectivity" and "objectivity" and up to a point can shed light on theological reality. Philosophy, for example, speaks of "subject" as that which acts, and "object" as that which is acted upon. In this context one would wish to speak of God as "subject" and man as "object" in order to recognize the priority and initiative of the divine. Richard Paquier has put this point well: "God can be the object of our worship only if he is first the subject, that is, the one who gives us the worship. We can only offer him our service if he himself inspires and orders it first of all." [4] However, in another sense one would wish to qualify this statement, in that man is also subject and God is object because both act and are acted upon.

LIGHT CAST BY PSYCHOLOGY UPON SUBJECTIVITY AND OBJECTIVITY

The meaning of "subjectivity" and "objectivity" can also be illumined psychologically. In the vocabulary of the psychology of religion, "objectivity" broadly speaking designates a realm of numinous reality and phenomena

[4] *The Dynamics of Worship*, trans. Donald Macleod (Philadelphia: Fortress Press, 1967,) p. 4.

197

independent of man, and "subjectivity" denotes man's experience of these. This way of thinking clearly parallels the construction of these terms we have proposed, and it is not without significance that "objective" and "subjective" were first introduced into the liturgical vocabulary of American Protestantism early in this century by scholars in the field of the psychology of religion.[5] Normally, as a science, psychology only reports phenomena and stops short of making theological statements about them or drawing metaphysical conclusions from them. It does not so much investigate "religion" as an objective quantum as investigate how man experiences reality religiously. We should therefore expect what is the case—that the contribution of psychology lies in what it tells us about "the eye," i.e., the subjectivity of man, rather than about "the properties of light," i.e., the objectivity of the divine. But as long as the proximateness of this perspective is borne in mind, its value can hardly be overestimated. The psychology of liturgical care, we may say, is as important as the psychology of pastoral care, especially for those who would understand Christian worship as pastoral liturgy.

In later essays a number of insights the psychology of religion brings to worship will be dealt with: the nature and importance of man's subconscious life; the transforming power of symbols; the experience of clock time in relation to liturgical time; the function of faculties of personality in liturgical action, and others. We summarily single out here three basic answers which psychology helps us formulate to the question: What is worship viewed subjectively?

First, psychology sees worship as man's assertion of his personhood and as his effort to complete his personhood, through a relation with reality in as ultimate a form as he can grasp and be grasped by. Three elements contained within this statement need elaboration. First, worship is *"self"* assertion, that is, man's declaration of his personal, individual *"I."* While set within a community of other selves, the worshipper's own self is the agent through which numinous reality is apprehended and the central *punkt* at which numinous meaning is concentrated. Sometimes psychology exaggeratedly states this truth by saying that "man makes his gods": because he can know the divine only through his "self," he conforms his gods to his "self." In any case, psychologically speaking, worship by definition is always "self-centered."

Secondly, as self-assertion and as the attempt at self-completion, worship involves all the constituent elements of personality—those man is consciously

---

[5] See, for example, the still useful volume by James Bissett Pratt, *The Religious Consciousness* (New York: The Macmillan Co., 1921).

aware of and those he is not. Further, man embodies these elements as they have been determined by his total life history, and he cannot be expected to be in worship other than all he has lived through. Especially, it is to be observed, man's emotion as a total dimension of his personhood is engaged and must be expected to be engaged in worship. Indeed, his emotional biography, particularly as it has been shaped in his early childhood by his relation with his mother, probably conditions his worship more than any other single factor.[6] This emotional biography underlies the functioning of his other faculties, the rational mind and will, for example, in a way they do not underlie it. "All human life revolves around desire," Gordon Allport has written,[7] and the thought of the mind is only "the refined merchandise of which emotional experience may be said to be the raw product."[8] Similarly, emotion underlies the action of the will. Or more accurately, and more importantly, *emotion is a form of action*, and it is psychologically absurd to set feeling and action in opposition to one another as liturgists are fond of doing. Indeed, reality, whether oneself, or the world around us, or God, is *met* through feeling. Further, reality is *known* through feeling. Feeling performs a cognitive function. "Why are emotion and soul so intimately bound up?" James Hillman asks. "Mainly because . . . it is through emotion that we get the . . . sense of soul, . . . of our own person."[9] Still further, by emotion man *evaluates* reality. Thus Jung speaks of the "feeling function" in personality as the making of an emotionally toned evaluation of experience: "When we feel it is in order to attach a proper value to something."[10] The implications of this understanding for subjectivity in worship are enormous. They can hardly be better suggested than in the following words of Daniel Callahan, a Roman Catholic, from an article entitled "God in a Technological Society":

It is just not—in the long run—enough that religion asks significant questions and has some interesting answers, or that it takes value and community seriously and offers some guidance for the ethical and communal life. What *is*

---

[6] For a provocative treatment of this insight from a Freudian point of view, see R. S. Lee's *Psychology and Worship* (New York: Philosophical Library 1956), ch. II. See also David E. Roberts, *Psychotherapy and a Christian View of Man* (New York: Charles Scribner's Sons, 1950), ch. IV; Erik H. Erikson, *Identity and the Life Cycle: Selected Papers*, "Growth and Crises of the Healthy Personality," "The Problem of Ego Identity" (New York: International Universities Press, 1959).

[7] Quoted by Paul W. Pruyser, *A Dynamic Psychology of Religion* (New York: Harper & Row, 1968), p. 201.

[8] Bernard E. Meland, *Modern Man's Worship* (New York: Harper & Bros., 1934), p. 265.

[9] *Insearch* (New York: Charles Scribner's Sons, 1967), pp. 53-54.

[10] *Modern Man in Search of a Soul* (New York: Harcourt, Brace & Co., 1933), p. 105.

necessary in the long run is that religion be able to make men *feel* the universe in a different way; that it provide them with a consciousness of themselves and of the world around them which is unique and compelling. That is why the question of religious experience seems to me central. . . . What people seem to want most of all from religion is a total way of being, in the world and in themselves. They do not only want to be intellectually convinced of the value of religion; they also want to *feel this value* in the depths of their being.[11]

Thirdly, as man's effort to complete his personhood, worship is also a seeking after what psychology speaks of as "integration" and what biblical theology speaks of as "healing," i.e. "wholeness," which in turn can be thought of in a number of ways. Integration is man's effort, for one thing, to bring into equilibrium the ego, the id, the superego, and the ego ideal. (The relation of confession of sin and absolution will be analyzed as an illustration in a later essay.) Integration also takes the form of repair of the self as it has been emotionally wounded or as part of it has been destroyed. This pain and its repair are what we speak of as "grief." But while grief is most often thought of in relation to death, it is experienced in many ways.[12] In any congregation at any time, most people are grieving in one way or another. And the "comfort" people say they find in worship is usually their way of verifying the fact that integration in some form has taken place.

Again, integration takes the form of man's quest for "the supreme context to which he belongs," of which we have written. Here the revealing value is the "supremacy" of the "supreme context." Man craves an ultimacy which, like a magnet disposing filings into a pattern, will draw into unity the brokenness of his being. Jesus' sentence, "Let thine eye be single," answers to this quest in scriptural terms. The use of the term "simplicity" in ascetical theology (from the Latin *simplex*) points to this truth in theological terms. Dante's great line, "In His will is our peace," states it in devotional terms. Now, people may or may not be able consciously to articulate their quest. The mingled fear and courage with which they seek "the supreme context" will also render their attitudes ambiguous. But worship fails if it does not take subjectivity as man's attempt to complete his personhood, with utmost seriousness, and if it lamely or apologetically names the ultimacy of that "ultimate context" which faith declares to be "God."

The second summary answer psychology offers to the question, "What

[11] *Yale Alumni Magazine*, June, 1968, p. 21.

[12] A child's failure in school, his going off to camp, a youth's leaving for college or the armed services, homesickness, leaving a job, a broken love affair, a divorce, moving to a new location, hospitalization, a quarrel—in these and many other ways the self becomes injured and grieves.

200

is worship viewed subjectively?" follows from the first: worship is man's expression of his needs and the meeting of his needs. In this simple, elemental sense, worship only illustrates the nature of man's religious life in general as psychology understands it. Offensive as the truth may seem, worship reduced to its basic terms—as religion itself—is a form of problem-solving. In liturgy as elsewhere, man *uses* his gods to deal with his conflicts. To be sure, there are many hierarchies of needs and problems, and there are many levels of refinement in the way man liturgically uses the divine. But man's existential self-interest is ineffaceable and undeniable. We shall presently attempt to supply a theological rationale for this datum. Here we wish to point out two implications for the question of subjectivity and objectivity.

First, man only knows God through his conflicts and needs, and to deny his self-interest is to deny him the vision of God. Thus worship must always be subjective in the sense that only by affirming man's predicament can one affirm the possibility—not to say, the reality—of God. Psychology thus counters with a certain irrefutability those, for example, who hold in contempt worship as "receiving a blessing," [13] or who ridicule worship for "what we get out of it." Psychology also calls before the bar of fact those who simplistically define worship as "celebration." It has been said, for example, that "worship is essentially a celebration, not repetitious assaulting of God with prayer, and . . . as such it has the continuous notes of joy and victory." [14] Such views not only misread reality and attribute to man a situation that is not his; by short-circuiting man's existential needs they also falsify the possibility of the divine reality they would affirm. Worship, it should be understood, is manipulated by theologians as well as by psychologists!

Secondly, while psychology declares man's self-interest to be the primary datum, it distinguishes hierarchies of self-interest. In its own language, the "presenting need" is not always the true need. An important category for psychology, for example, is the category of growth, of maturation, a category which liturgical theology surely finds congenial. Both psychology and theology reject worship which fosters infantilism. Thus man's subjectivity in this respect must be both psychologically and theologically appraised. Man's presenting need may be felt as the need for security from the challenges of life which threaten him; but maturity understood as his real need requires him to be summoned to face them as part of his Christian warfare. Thus

[13] Neville Clark, quoted by Ronald C. D. Jasper in an article, "Ecumenical Liturgy," *Church Service Society Annual*, May, 1965.
[14] Louis H. Gunnemann, *Worship: A Course Book for Adults* (Philadelphia: United Church Press, 1966), p. 19.

hymns, for example, must be inspected psychologically as well as theologically for their power to help or hinder growth, for their health or their neuroticism. The first verse of the hymn, "Rock of Ages, cleft for me, Let me hide myself in thee," has been interpreted as "womb symbolism" fostering regression and appealing to the desire to withdraw into a kind of prenatal, mindless security. Such an interpretation may seem strained if not morbid to some, but it alerts us to the importance of appraising hymns—as all else in worship —in terms of the levels and kinds of self-interest they speak to.

The third contribution of psychology lies in its understanding of worship as involving the basic energies of man's being. In this respect psychology would corroborate Sabatier's remark that all religion is a prayer for life, in that psychology sees worship as an exchange of energy—as the expenditure and replenishment of the self's vitalities. To be sure, worship often fails to be this, but this is what man on the most primitive levels of his being desires worship to be. For him the "numen" is supremely that which is vital and that with which he engages his most primal vitalities—his fear, his love, his guilt, his grief, his aggression, his hope, his hunger, even his sexuality. Indeed the numen ultimately holds for him the values of life and death; and he liturgically deals with it foremost as the being whose energy sustains his life and saves him from impotence and death. The symbols "Creator," "Providence," and "Salvation" conceptualize this psychological insight theologically. "Creator" signifies the ontal life force from which man's being and life derive. "Providence" signifies the energy of the numinous in its protective and preserving function. "Redemption" or "Salvation" conceptualizes the energy of the numen as deliverance from moral or emotional threat. Truly, man does make his gods! And the prominence of these symbols in liturgy in a multitude of ways only verifies the insight of psychology that worship involves man's primal energies.

From time to time worshippers will signal this understanding in various ways. A service described by a layman as "uplifting" or "inspiring" or "stirring," for example, usually testifies that energies have been involved in some important way. Or a widow's reluctance to sit in the same pew she and her husband once shared; the seriousness with which grown men— accustomed to handle important matters in their weekday life—take on the minor tasks of ushering; the unreasoning criticism a layman will occasionally make of some liturgical incident out of all proportion to its importance; the boredom which says that worship has failed to be an experience of exchange of energy or that the worshipper is afraid to involve his significant vitalities—his guilt for example; the shelter of the back pew which postures the worshipper's ambiguity in wanting and not wanting to commit his vital "self"—these corroborate the insight of psychology that worship involves the basic energies of man's being.

A CHRISTOLOGICAL ANALYSIS OF SUBJECTIVITY AND OBJECTIVITY

Nevertheless, impressive as the answers are which psychology makes to the question of subjectivity and objectivity, they cannot in themselves be assigned ultimacy. Liturgy has its own hermeneutics, we repeat, and the content of "subjectivity" and "objectivity" is to be Christologically discerned. The trouble with investigating worship psychologically and then arguing from its data to truth is not that this procedure is necessarily wrong; it is that it is proximate rather than primary or ultimate. In order to understand the structure of the eye, we must once more study first the properties of the light. Such a study, we must warn, again requires the use of technical terms, but if we would get our logic of interpretation clear, there is no alternative.

The point of departure in restating the content of subjectivity and objectivity Christologically lies in understanding worship as the presence of Jesus Christ amidst his people. This presence ever bears the same human-divine character it once bore. It performs the same action toward God and man it once performed. And from the nexus of human and divine reality in the Word, the polarities of subjectivity and objectivity can be defined. "Subjectivity" is to be referred to all that we mean by the Word as "human," and "objectivity" is to be referred to all that we mean by the Word as "divine."

The humanity of the Word determines worship to be subjective in at least two ways. First, as the human life of Jesus was the ground of the liturgy he performed, so our humanity is the datum of the liturgy we perform. A life which concentrates all that is meant by the term "human" more perfectly than Jesus' life cannot be imagined, and we are entitled to be no less human as we worship. In making this affirmation, parenthetically, liturgical theology only puts in its own language the same truth which theology generally declares, that "knowledge of God" comes through "knowledge of self." These are correlative, as Calvin remarked: "True and substantial wisdom principally consists of two parts, the knowledge of God and the knowledge of ourselves." [15] Secondly, the direction of the liturgy performed in Jesus' life is always "manward." It is also "godward," as we shall observe shortly, that is for the "glorification of God." But in the words of the

[15] *Institutes of the Christian Religion*, trans. John Allen (6th American rev. ed.; Philadelphia: Presbyterian Board of Publication and Sabbath-School Work, n.d.), I, 46.

Creed, as it was "for us men and our salvation" that he "was made flesh, . . . died, . . . rose again," so our worship is to be no less manward.[16] By definition, the Church's worship is as much *pro* man as the Word is *pro* man.

But simultaneously, the Word also determines worship to be objective, first in the sense that Jesus' liturgical life, even in its most human character and its most manward expression, was lived unto God. Its overarching point of reference—or as we have said, its lodestar—is divine reality. Secondly, Jesus Christ addresses us as divine reality coming from outside—as well as from within—our human existence. Viewed as a liturgy, the event of Jesus Christ is as much God serving man as man serving God, and its objectivity in this sense of "otherness" is inescapable. Correspondingly, objectivity in worship consists first in the movement of man's devotion "godward," that is, to "glorify God"; and it consists also in the "confronting" nature of God's service of us and in the precedence of God's service of us to our service of him.

Broadly speaking, it is within this frame of thought deriving from the incarnation that one's mind most reliably moves in untangling the question of subjectivity and objectivity. A certain equilibrium, it will be observed, marks this frame which it is difficult to sustain. And in the following analysis, insofar as balance is lost and terms are misused as we have blamed other critics for doing, we had better confess our own sins in advance!

In any case, running like a theme through the mind's reflection upon worship in light of the incarnation is the motif of action. Because the Word is Act, we have said, worship cannot be thought of under any other mode than that of action. Correspondingly, all that we mean by "the mighty acts of God" fulfilled in the event of Jesus Christ constitutes objectivity. The divine has acted toward us independently of anything we could have done, and this action—epitomized in the verbs "foretold," "born," "suffered," "crucified," "buried," "rose," "ascended," "reigns," "shall come"—is recapitulated in worship. The person who supremely acts in worship is Jesus Christ. It is he who holds the service, and objectivity in this sense is the ground of subjectivity.

On the other hand, it is in the person of the worshipper and in the human congregation, not in a vacuum, that divine action takes place. Further, it does not take place without responsive action on our part, and

[16] I am indebted to Godfrey Diekmann in developing this point. See his article, "The Reform of Catholic Liturgy," in *Worship*, XLI (Mar., 1967). Diekmann points out that the Constitution on Liturgy of Vatican II speaks in fifteen instances of worship as "for the sanctification of man," i.e., as "manward," as well as "for the glorification of God," but that "sanctification of man" is of set purpose mentioned first.

these two elements constitute the subjectivity of worship. In the words of Louis Bouyer: one cannot "oppose 'objective' to 'subjective' piety, as if there can be any subjective piety which did not proceed entirely from the apprehension of the Mystery as offered to our faith . . . or as if there could be any extension of the Mystery to us which did not demand above all that we effectively hold ourselves ready for the reception of its living substance." [17] This is to say, it is on the action of the worshipper that the action of the Word depends for its appropriation. In liturgy, as elsewhere, in the words of Paul Tillich, "God in his self-manifestation to man is dependent on the way man receives his manifestation." [18] And in this sense subjectivity sustains objectivity.

Again, worship viewed within the category of action is objective in that the movement of worship is fundamentally toward God, and one must never hesitate to think and say this. In this sense, objectivity is the ground of subjectivity. The mind is deceived and devotion contradicts itself when any form of liturgy, cultic or apostolic, is conceived as anything less. In liturgical theology as elsewhere, lines of decision must sometimes be drawn, and this is one of them. On this "first" commandment, that worship is fundamentally toward God, hang the liturgical law and the prophets. Yet the paradox is—and how pitiless is the dialectic of the incarnation!—that liturgical movement toward God is conditioned by liturgical movement toward man. As the liturgy of our Lord's life was the service of God through serving man, so worship "glorifies" God insofar as it "benefits"—that is, "does good" to—man.[19] In short, objectivity is conditioned by subjectivity.

The historical and trans-historical nature of the Word determines objectivity and subjectivity in a number of ways. First, worship is objective in the sense that it inheres in the unique history in which God has acted to save man in a way in which he could not save himself—in the call of Israel to be his people, in election, covenant, prophecy, and supremely in Jesus Christ in whom the meaning of this history is concentrated. This sacred history penetrating man's history with its "once-for-allness" determines worship to be objective in the sense of causality: that is, it causes any response man is able to make to these events. It also determines objectivity in the sense that its morphology is to structure worship. Against worship as impressionism, as piety feeding only upon itself, as a kind of Christian yoga, as vaguely numinous states of mind, Christian worship is objectively anchored in and shaped by the historical nature of the Word.

[17] *Liturgical Piety* (Notre Dame, Ind.: University of Notre Dame Press, 1955), p. 223.
[18] *Systematic Theology* (Chicago: University of Chicago Press, 1951), I, 61.
[19] From the Latin *benefacere*, meaning "to make" or "to do" "good."

Further, objectivity consists in man's being addressed by divine reality in the Word that is beyond history and that acts to draw man beyond history. Liturgical theology cannot settle for any conception of Jesus Christ which does not affirm the divine "otherness" with which he invades human life, even though that "otherness" is limned in the most human terms. And it also cannot settle for any conception of man's response to the "otherness" of the Word which does not somehow engage man with eternal reality beyond space and time. One may apply to worship in this sense a phrase with which P. T. Forsyth once described Baptism: "The Sacrament of Destination." Worship sets before man his ultimate destiny in the eternal God and in this sense is always objective.

On the other hand, worship is man's subjective interiorization of sacred history. The worshipper, we may say, has a human history which answers to the historical nature of the Word. His human history is simply his selfhood shaped by the life he has lived, including his emotional and social history. At the risk of straining words, we may say that man's selfhood is ecologically shaped. He is the product of interaction with his total environment, and the historical structure of his consciousness, thus understood, can no more be bypassed in his worship than it can be eliminated from the liturgical life of Jesus Christ himself. In this sense worship is profoundly subjective.

Worship is also subjective in that it is to focus upon man's history both private and social. As the direction of the liturgical life of the Word was historically manward, so liturgy is the service of man as a historical being. In this sense worship is always to be interrogated as to its historical relevance and moral effectiveness, and the Church is not wrong in believing that worship is false when man's conduct in his worldly life is left unaffected. Indeed, we may say that worship by definition in this sense is social action in that it is to act upon man's social being and spur him to act in his historical existence. In this sense subjectivity means that nothing pertaining to man's historical life is outside the intention of worship.

Worship, then, as the interaction of man's personal history with sacred history and as engagement with worldly reality and eternal reality—in this dialectical understanding of subjectivity and objectivity we once more find truth. The meaning with which the Word illumines this dialectic can be grasped by reflecting upon what H. Richard Niebuhr once called "the reason of the heart" in comprehending divine revelation:

The reason of the heart engages in a . . . dialectic, and it does not really know what is in revelation . . . save as it proceeds from it to present experience and back again from experience to revelation. In that process the meaning of the revelation, its richness and power, grow progressively clearer." [20]

[20] *The Meaning of Revelation* (New York: The Macmillan Co., 1941), p. 136.

Subjectivity and objectivity are next understood in light of the ontological and soteriological nature of the Word as God's very life—*Ego sum vita*—the divine "being-in-action" rescuing man in his sin and death and bringing him to participate in eternal life. Worship in one way or another takes place on this level of reality, or it does not take place at all. Nowhere is this fulcral truth seen more clearly than in the order for Holy Communion. The Prayer of Consecration typically reads: "Hear us, O Merciful Father, . . . and grant that we, receiving these creatures . . . according to Thy Son our Savior Jesus Christ's holy institution, in remembrance of his passion, death, and resurrection, may be *partakers of the divine nature through him.*" Likewise, the sentences accompanying administration mark this ontological reality: "The body, . . . the blood of the Lord Jesus Christ *preserve thy soul and body unto everlasting life.*" Here the core of worship is stated in a way thought and speech can hardly go beyond, and whether in sacrament or sermon, authentic worship possesses this ontological character. Every service in a deep sense is a partaking of the divine nature, and every element in a service is to preserve men unto everlasting life. The same life-giving and life-saving Presence is Real in all cases. It deals with man on the deepest of all levels—life and being.

Within this context, we may say that worship is objective in the sense that the life offered in the Word is prior to and independent of man's life, and subjective in the sense that the Word welcomes, indeed requires, the answering thrust of man's selfhood if its life is to be received. This dialectic can also be stated in others terms often used: worship as "revelation and response," as "sacrament and sacrifice." Terminology does not matter too much as long as the nature of the Word is kept sovereign, the ontology of the realities involved is affirmed, and as long as one does not impute error to another if the terms used do not happen to be one's own. Far more important than semantics is the dialectical relation between God the Creator and man the creature, God the Saviour and man the sinner, God the eternal and man as mortal.

On the one hand, man does not possess within himself the eternal life of the Word. What Christian faith always finds itself obligated to say in speaking of this life is that it is a reality precedent to man and yet a reality so critical for his existence that he dies if he does not possess it. It was while man was without life that the Lord God breathed into his nostrils the breath of life. It was while we were "dead in our trespasses" that the Word which "was from the beginning" came that we might have life. And it is to man in his mingled death and life now that the Word promises an eternal life far beyond what eye hath seen or ear heard. As the recapitulation of the initiative of God in fatefully offering his life to man, worship is profoundly objective.

On the other hand, while the life of the Word is the prior term, man also is always a term, and corollary to the life of the Word is man's anxiety for his destiny and his resistance of his death. Thus subjectivity in worship is man's cry of creaturehood, of his moral pain, and of his inexpungable hunger for the ultimate and the eternal. In worship as elsewhere, "man's life is moved by the search for God because it is always moved, consciously or unconsciously, by the question about his own personal existence," [21] and subjectivity is man liturgically acting out this existential question. It is man expressing that very restlessness with which the human soul is beset until it finds life in God.

Bound up with the ontological nature of the Word is its fullness, and the Christological meaning of objectivity and subjectivity is completed within light of this category: Jesus Christ comes to man with an inexhaustible abundance of life and grace which matches man's predicament at every point of need. The vitality of the universe is concentrated in the Word: all that is, is "alive with his life" (John 1:4 NEB). "From him," "through him," "in him," "unto him," St. Paul writes, are "all things"; and from this life, St. John adds, men receive "grace upon grace." The Word, we are told, emptied itself that we might become filled. It became poor for our sakes that we might be made rich. Its life is the supreme pearl whose value fulfills all others. It pours out the cup and breaks the bread that we may eat, and still many baskets are left over. It dies, and lo, we live. In this profound—indeed metaphysical—symbolism, the divine is revealed to be that reality whose fullness of life meets man in all his need, and objectivity is just this revealing. Every form of the question man asks about his personal existence is met with the fullness of the Word. Whatever else worship may be, this fullness is its very ground and the hinge on which liturgical theology turns.

But equally, bipolar with the fullness of the Word is the hunger and thirst of man and all the ways in which he spells out the question of his existence, and this is the subjectivity of worship. All that man is not, all depletions of his self, all threats before which he cowers, all agony and shame that diminish him, all the surds of existence that break apart his being, indeed all the half-life and the death he lives—this is the subjectivity of worship. In a word, subjectivity is man's assertion of his creaturehood and mortality, the declaration of his humanity needing life. Thus subjectivity is

[21] Rudolf Bultmann, *Jesus Christ and Mythology* (New York: Charles Scribner's Sons, 1958), p. 53.

not an option to be conceded to worship; it is a necessity. It is not that we may, it is that we must so worship, and liturgical theology is dismantled when we do not understand this.

Above all, it is that God can only be truly God when we thus worship. And what we must now go on to say is that if objectivity is the ground of worship, so, also, subjectivity is the ground of worship. For when subjectivity in the sense in which we are now stating it is denied, we commit an inverted form of blasphemy: we demand that God be something other to us than he has revealed himself in Jesus Christ to be. The most essential nature God bears toward his creatures is that he is that life on which they depend, and the most essential nature of his grace is that it desires to be drawn on in its fullness. God's grace is like fire that needs fuel, it has been said, and that fuel is man's existence.[22] The God of Christian faith is always a God who is glorified exactly in the sense, and to the degree, that his grace in all its fullness is importuned by man in his humanity and need. While we may have been misinformed that God desires to be worshipped only as an "End" —and we are now using terms dangerously—the truth is that he desires to be "used" as a "means." Whereas we may have been shamed for worshipping "for the sake of what we shall get out of it," all the while God longs that we do just that. The irony of slurring the truth of subjectivity in worship is not only that it requires us to be something other than God has made us and falsely traps us into a guilt for being human; above all it denies God the right to be God.

THE VALIDITY OF WORHIP AS EMOTIONAL EXPERIENCE

Within this theological context, the vexing question of the validity of worship as "experience" can be considered. We say "vexing" because in some liturgical lexicons "experience" is a nasty term, in others a favorite. Consequently many pastors have been thrown on the defensive by attacks upon worship as experience, while others have been made suspicious by the zeal of those who rest the nature of worship upon it. Uncertain as to whether they have the right to conceive worship as experience, whether one can legitimately speak of a "worship experience" or design worship to foster experience, many clergy are caught between armchair critics on the one hand and their own pastoral instincts and perceptions on the other.

To be sure, aversion to thinking of worship as experience has much justification, such as the corruption of liturgy into psychological manipula-

[22] Amos Wilder, *Otherworldliness and the New Testament* (London: SCM Press, 1955), p. 63.

tion of which we have written. The deeper roots of our aversion, however, probably lie in the fear of idolatry, and in this we are not wrong. To think and speak of worship as "experience" holds the fatal possibility that man will come to worship his experience instead of God. He can twist the meaning and diminish the fullness of Christian revelation to conform to his own desire, trying out God for size, as it were, and he can measure the reality of worship solely in terms of his subjective reaction. Over worship no less than over the Christian life must the commandment always be written: "Thou shall not tempt the Lord thy God."

Now it may be—as certain critics argue—that the term "experience" has come to be associated with meanings so offensive that it cannot be rehabilitated for liturgical discourse. It has in fact been replaced in the vocabulary of certain theological disciplines with the term "existential." Despite its offense and ambiguity, however, liturgy can hardly manage without it simply because this term is part of the ordinary man's vocabulary which liturgy must be able to speak. Whether we like it or not, there is something ineffaceable about man's use of this term, in that it is commonly the best semantic he has for asking the question about his personal existence and apprehending the answer the Gospel holds. When man speaks of wanting worship as "experience," more often than not he is consciously or subconsciously confessing his human predicament and pointing to the fullness of life which faith receives in answer. In short, he is speaking existentially and we must not be put off by his language. Our task is to translate this term without patronage or prejudice and to understand what people are really saying in using it: that they are seeking, and have in part been found by, that Life without which they cannot live, and with which, with the sure instinct of creaturehood, they know their destiny to be bound. However awkwardly they express themselves, they are corroborating the truth that the Word ontologically meets them in their poverty with its fullness. Indeed, we have to understand that so far from desiring worship only as subjective experience, they are in fact testifying to the objectivity of worship. To desire worship as "experience" is man's way of witnessing to the reality of a history beyond his own history that invades his history, of an act that strikes upon him as fateful for his own action, of a destiny beyond his own destiny to which he is yet joined. In short, the cry for "experience" is man's cry for a salvation into a life other than his own.

Thus the undiscriminating belittling of worship as "experience" is to risk emasculating worship of reality, and at this point theology and psychology converge. To be sure, theology reserves final authority in this matter. But while the properties of the Light are sovereign, those who can instruct us about the nature of the eye, the human soul, must be heard. And man's incurable "use" of his gods, the ineffaceable assertion of his selfhood, the energy of the numinous he is always seeking, and the ways in which he bewilderedly uses the "blocks" of his experience to try to spell "God"— these enlighten and humble us. The concluding words of Jung's *Psychology and Religion* state the truth to which a Christological understanding of subjectivity and objectivity has led us:

> Religious experience is absolute. It is indisputable. . . . No matter what the world thinks about religious experience, the one who has it possesses the great treasure . . . that has provided him with a source of life. . . . Where is the criterium by which you could say that such a life is not legitimate, that such experience is not valid . . . ? Is there, as a matter of fact, any better truth about ultimate things than the one that helps you to live? . . . If such experience helps you to make your life healthier, more beautiful, more complete and more satisfactory to yourself and to those you love, you may safely say: "This was the grace of God." [23]

Probably the most difficult question, however, is not whether we will think and speak of worship as "experience." This question will probably be settled for us. The harder question is whether worship should be designed to foster experience. Any realistic answer must take into account what has previously been said about the importance of making sociological and psychological estimates of the situation of the congregation and of their motivations, of the cultural influences which enable and disable people for engaging in worship, how they experience the relation between worship and their worldly life, and the residual effect of worship. Further, any ralistic answer must affirm man's need as the point where the revelation of the Word comes to life and comes with life, and in this sense worship may well be undertaken to convict and convert, to edify and instruct, to commission and empower. Liturgy is only blind or doctrinaire when it ignores these considerations and others we will need to explore in the following essays.

To register these considerations, however, is *not* to say that worship finds its primary intention in them. They are secondary, not primary; derived, not genetic. While the minister functions as both liturgical psychologist and liturgical theologian, he first functions as theologian. Prior to any design he may have will always be the intention of the Word in its own sovereign freedom. He may be able to go quite far in predicting what "experience" will be, but ultimately it is not for him to decide what forms it will take; to do so is presumption and idolatry. The purpose of worship is not to produce experience for its own sake, as we would define experience, but faithfully and obediently to proclaim the Word. The Word, we may have

[23] (New Haven: Yale University Press, 1936), pp. 113-14.

confidence, will work its own "experience." The pastor is not wrong in understanding that the Word is known in and through man's experience. But he is on sure ground when he first understands that worship is rendered authentic not by our preconceptions but by the presence of Jesus Christ.

In somewhat the same way and on somewhat the same ground the validity of emotion in worship may be viewed. The first question again is: What does the Word in its incarnate fullness say to us? All attacks upon emotion in the name of objectivity, on the one hand, and all apologies for emotion in the name of subjectivity, on the other, must come to terms with this theological question. To be sure, the truth of psychology cannot be dismissed: "The gods cannot live without emotion" [24] because man does not live without emotion. Yet the question of emotion as part of the larger question of liturgical integrity cannot finally be decided only by looking at man, no matter with what psychological wisdom. Rather, it is to be decided by looking at man in light of the Word. Here, as elsewhere, study of the properties of the Light precedes study of the structure of the eye.

But, is it not the case that we see the fullness of life in the Word addressing man in all the range of his being, and its intention as the grasping and saving of man's passional nature as all else in him? Man as God has created him has to be thought of as less than man to the degree that any part of his being, including his emotion, is ignored or unengaged as unredeemable. And the fullness of the Word has to be thought of as less than "full"—if we may so speak—to the degree that the life it offers does not include that to which human emotion corresponds. But this is precisely what we cannot say about either the Word or about man in their engagement with one another. Put positively if technically: the ontology of the Word matches the existence of man. Jesus Christ, as life, savingly meets man in all the range of his creaturehood. There is fully in the Word that to which man's total creaturehood—including his passions—corresponds. In short, the divine as revealed in the Word can be an object of worship precisely because it can be the object of human emotion. And man can be an object of God's grace because he is an object of divine emotion.

If this seems a bold way of speaking, then let us remember that it is not more bold than Scripture itself. The truth of biblical revelation is just that a passionate God seeks the worship of passional man. That is why the Bible does not hesitate to ascribe to the God who offers us his eternal life all the symbols of emotion we ourselves know. The very anthropomorphism with which Scripture depicts the divine,[25] the whole panorama of human emotion

---

[24] Pruyser, A Dynamic Psychology of Religion, p. 146.

[25] Ian Ramsey reminds us of some of the figures under which God is represented in

attributed to the deity, and above all the full emotional life lived by Jesus Christ—these mark the divine as being as passionate as the human mind can conceive. At the same time, man's emotional nature is viewed as the core of his selfhood which the Word comes with grace to enliven and to save. Nothing pertaining to this nature is unnamed, and no part of it is beyond this grace. The biblical term for this nature is "heart," and not for nothing is "heart" named more often than any part of man's being. In the "heart," not the mind nor the will, are the energies of man's life. The most secret and fatal choices are made there. The commandments are written there. Speech and thought arise there. The new covenant is established there. The new creation comes to pass there. And eternity is known there. Truly, out of the heart are the issues of life—and of death. Here deep calleth unto deep. And only as worship recapitulates this calling is it faithful to the nature of God and of man as the Word declares them to be.

As we conclude these reflections upon the question of subjectivity and objectivity, one may have the feeling that all we have done is to repeat that both poles of worship signified by these slippery terms are necessary, and in a sense this is true. But if we have been able to state the meaning of these terms less imprecisely, and if we have perchance persuaded some critics who had not previously agreed that both are necessary, our labor of thought may not have been in vain. If we have partly enlightened others who had agreed that both are necessary but had not quite understood what they were agreeing to, and if we have been able to help the pastor make his decisions more wisely, that is still better. For it is exceedingly important to know what we mean by "subjectivity" and "objectivity," to desist from using these words polemically, and to be open to truth which disciplines other than theological can teach us. Most of all, if we have been able to relate the polarities of subjectivity and objectivity to the profound dialectic inhering in the Word, Jesus Christ, we will feel that we have gotten at the truth. For the fugal themes signified by these terms have to do with nothing less than the nature of reality as it has been disclosed to us in him in whose life we see Light. Ultimately the question of subjectivity and objectivity—as the question of relevance and irrelevance—is nothing other than the question and the mystery of divine-human reality in the incarnation itself. The sovereignty which the Word holds for the mind's reflection upon worship—as for worship itself—is the great thing, even though our minds are finally victims of its

---

the Old Testament alone: as father, mother, nurse, brother, husband, friend, warrior, shepherd, farmer, metalworker, builder, potter, fuller, physician, judge, tradesman, king, fisherman, scribe. See the essay "Talking About God: Models, Ancient and Modern," in *Myth and Symbol*, ed. F. W. Dillistone (London SPCK, 1966), pp. 76-77.

mystery. Perhaps the confusion which for so long has plagued discussion of this question, and the distemper which too often has informed it, are due to our apostasy in not offering to the Word our intellectual obedience as all else. For in both theology and devotion, let us repeat, liturgical things are Christologically discerned.

V

The Language of Worship
Part 1: The Perspectives of Function and of Psychology

The phrase, "The Language of Worship," is used in this and the following essay in a very broad sense to designate *all the means employed in worship to convey or receive meaning*. It does not denote only speech orally delivered or aurally heard. Rather, "liturgical language" denotes all objects and actions in space and time employed cultically by man's physical senses and faculties of personality to express or apprehend meaning, including oral, visual, tactile, kinesthetic, and even olfactory and gustatory media, as well as mental concepts and images. Further, all the directions and dimensions of movement in which meaning is communicated are also implied in this term. Five such dimensions can be distinguished: from God to the gathered people; from the gathered people to God; by the gathered people to one another; by the congregation to those outside the gathered community; by those outside the gathered community to those within. To construe the term "language" so liberally may seem a loose way of speaking, but a number of reasons lead us to do so.

THE IMPORTANCE OF "LANGUAGE" AS A GENERIC TERM

First, such an understanding can stretch our minds to perceive the significance of everything and anything pertaining to worship. Many a minister, we suspect, supposes he has discharged his duty to use liturgical "language" properly when he has worked hard on his sermon and gotten his grammar right, or taken care with his speech delivery and seen to it that the acoustics are good. But silence also is language. The shape of a chandelier is language. The emotional health—or unhealth—of the minister is language. The symbols on the communion table—a cross, an open Bible, a picture, flowers, the form of bread used—whether thin discs, white cubes, or brown crust—are language. Sitting and standing, the tempo in which a service is conducted, the deportment of the choir, the carpeting on the floor, the vestments of the

215

clergy, the location of the font, the illumination of the windows[1]—all these are language. Especially, the order of service (even the style of type in which it is printed)[2] is a powerful form of language. It bears the same relation to worship that a plot does to a play and largely determines the kerygmatic and didactic meaning worship holds. In short, all the media of worship are pregnant with meaning to greater or lesser degree, even if the meaning is a corruption of authentic meaning.

The Dialectic of Form and Freedom

Secondly, to conceive liturgical media as "language" may be less confusing and more authentic than other ways of thinking. An alternative term, for example, is "forms," and in one sense "language" and "forms" are identical. Yet "language" may be superior to "forms" partly because it enables us to transcend the tedious controversy over so-called formal and informal (or free) worship which so often plagues the liturgical conversation. This distinction may be useful in speaking colloquially, but it is misleading if we wish to think precisely. All worship is "formal" in the sense that forms are necessary if worship is to take place at all. And to set "formal" and "informal" over against one another is to pose issues in a wrong way and be maneuvered on to false premises in undertaking to discuss them.

The fact is, as an earlier essay made clear,[3] the necessities of man's nature require forms. They are axiomatic simply because God has not made man a disembodied being but a union of spirit and sense who can only apprehend meaning through language or form as we have broadly defined it; and what has been called the "human sensorium," i.e., the complex of man's sensory apparatus, is part of his being as created by God.[4] Equally, man's psychic nature requires forms. The symbolic nature of his conscious and unconscious

---

[1] Paul Tillich has spoken of daylight through transparent windows as "rational" light, of light through stained glass as "mystical" light.

[2] One does well to ponder what could be called the theology of typography. Often the style technically named "Cloister Black," or colloquially called "Olde English," is used. What kind of liturgical ethos does this convey? Medieval? Gothic Revival? If God is indeed dead, it has been said, perhaps we have hastened his demise by casting the Word in type more suited to the "In Memoriam" obituary column than to today's world. On the other hand, should "today's world" dictate liturgical style?

[3] See ch. I.

[4] See Walter J. Ong, S. J. *The Presence of the Word* (New Haven: Yale University Press, 1967), p. 6. This given fact of man's nature, it might be added, explains why types of worship which profess to dispense with the physical as over against the spiritual, such as that of the Society of Friends, do not really succeed. The very plainness of the Quaker Meeting House, the speaking and hearing, even the silence, the handshake at the conclusion of the meeting, depend for their meaning on man's physical senses. Likewise the bare walls and central position of the pulpit in Reformed congregations which protest against images are still images.

216

life (which we shall elaborate presently) conditions his perception of religious reality and his ability to become engaged with it. Thus sects which originated in protest against so-called dead ritual reveal an inevitable tendency to adopt ritual forms, and one may with complete propriety speak of "the ritual of non-ritualistic churches." [5] For the same reason congregations which profess to dispense with exterior physical images inevitably come to substitute mental images.[6] Forms are ineffaceable in worship because they are ineffaceable in man, and it is as false to assume that they are appropriate only for the sophisticated as it is to assume that they are appropriate only for the naïve.

Above all, the truth of the incarnation requires worship to be "formal," as we have previously noted. The truth of the incarnation is exactly that God took human "form" (Phil. 2:5-8). Scripture normatively speaks of this form as the "Word," and liturgical theology, accordingly, speaks most reliably when it derives from the category "Word" the cognate category of "language" as the generic category within which to deal with the media of worship. We least likely go wrong when we think in this biblical way. We also understand why the question whether worship will be "formal" or not is pointless. The real question is: What kinds of liturgical forms are integral to the Word as it encounters man's being, and how shall we choose and evaluate these?

However, while worship is "formal" in this root sense, we are wise not to rebuke too hastily those who protest against "formal" worship in another sense. For behind their protest is almost certainly the concern that freedom also be preserved, and in this they are not wrong. Their case would be more cogent were they to speak more precisely and use such terms as "formalism" rather than "form" and "ritualism" instead of "ritual." Nevertheless, freedom is always correlative with form. This dialectic is a datum of our experience generally and of worship in particular. Only when freedom is affirmed does meaningful form become possible. Only when form is asserted does freedom become responsible. And only when these polarities are kept in tension does worship possess integrity. For this dialectic likewise inheres in the nature of

[5] See James Bissett Pratt, *The Religious Consciousness* (New York: The Macmillan Co., 1921), p. 267.

[6] A passage from Edwyn Bevan is cited by A. G. Hebert in *Liturgy and Society* (London: Faber & Faber, 1935), p. 124, quoting a number of hymns from Bernard, Tersteegen, and Wesley abounding with Christian images. Bevan adds: "Some of these Protestants may have thought it wrong to use a material crucifix to set before their eyes the supreme self-sacrifice. But they would use all the resources of language to create in the mind a visional image exactly corresponding. . . . And if the reaction to such an image . . . was a new resolution to devote his whole person to the great Lover and to the utmost service of men . . . was there much to distinguish that from the state of mind with which a Roman Catholic rose from his knees before the crucifix or before the Blessed Sacrament on an occasion when his offering of prayer had been touched by the fire from heaven?"

217

man and God. If form on the one hand inheres in man's nature as a sensory and psychic creature, and in God's nature as revealed in the incarnation, freedom also inheres in man's volitional nature and in God's sovereign freedom on the other. Freedom is the autonomy and intention with which the self puts itself forth into encounter with another. Thus if worship cannot take place without forms any more than writing or speaking can take place without words, so worship also cannot take place without that freedom with which God and man will to meet. And thus if we say that worship is by definition "formal," we must also say that it is by definition "free."

Accordingly, it is false to assign ultimacy either to freedom or form. The paradoxical truth is that form assumes and fosters freedom as freedom begets and requires form. Prayer, for example, becomes real insofar as it provides for both. Contrary to what one might expect, often the soul is strangely liberated when its devotion is undertaken within form, as for example in participating in a set prayer. Form can provide wings without which aspiration would remain limp and unalive. It can also chasten and channel aspiration in its freedom. The Lord's Prayer, for example, has been called "the homing place" for all prayer: devotion starts from it, is guided by it, and comes to rest in it as an unsurpassable expression of all prayer. On the other hand, the freedom of God and the freedom of man in a sense are sovereign over form; and often "free prayer" by an individual or a group conveys a sense of truthfulness which set prayer does not. While our Lord enjoins the form of the Lord's Prayer, "After this manner, pray ye," its reality still depends upon devotion freely put forth by man himself. The Lord's Prayer does not pray itself; "ye" are to do the praying. So it is on the larger scale with the "Prayer of the Church" we call worship. It is precisely in the mutual relation of "freedom" and "form" that "the greatness and uniqueness" of Christian worship reside.[7] The twin injunctions of St. Paul crystallize this co-relation: "Quench not the Spirit" (I Thess. 5:19 KJV), and "let all things be done decently and in order" (I Cor. 14:40 KJV).

In one other sense form and freedom dialectically condition one another. Freedom in worship is ultimately a freedom grounded in the Holy Spirit, and this freedom in turn is qualified by the Spirit's relation to the Word, Jesus Christ. Liturgical freedom is not to be equated with man's subjectivity, much less with his personal whim or taste. Nor is it independence of Christian tradition and an uncritical borrowing from culture of whatever may be popular at the moment. Further, even when thought of as grounded in the Holy Spirit, liturgical freedom takes as its reference the revelation of Christ. To

[7] See Oscar Cullmann, *Early Christian Worship*, trans. A. Stewart Todd and James B. Torrance (London: SCM Press, 1953), p. 33.

be sure, the Holy Spirit—as we have said—is the source of vitality and spontaneity, even of ecstasy in worship. Further, as "God in the here and now," as the invasion of the Divine into the present moment of a congregation's life, the Spirit is also the source of immediacy and relevance. It is also the source of movement into the future.[8] Even so, the Spirit is always to be understood in relation to Jesus Christ, and as such it is equally the source of reason and form, and one might say even of propriety and taste. In short, the freedom of the Spirit is itself a freedom bound by Jesus Christ as its norm. It is finally a Christological freedom. Thus even as we rightly claim place for freedom in worship, we still find ourselves theologically bound by the Word. And we only demonstrate in our thought about worship what we find to be true in the experience of worship itself: form and freedom are defined as correlative by the Word. And the category of "language" deriving from the biblical meaning of "Word" comprehends both as the *sine qua non* without which neither thinking about worship nor worship itself is possible.

"Language" and "Symbol"

A third reason for conceptualizing the media of worship within the term "language" lies in its greater authenticity over against the term "symbolism" which so claims our thinking today. To be sure, in one sense "language" and "symbolism" can be thought of as identical or at least as pointing to the same realities. Such a typical definition of "symbol" as the following serves quite well to define "language" as we are using the term:

The word "symbol" is used in a strict sense as "describing something which denotes and makes present an invariable reality; that is to say, something in which there is a coming together of a material thing—a sensible phenomenon—with an immaterial and transcendent reality, whether that reality exists only in the form of an idea in the mind of the symbol-maker or in some more 'real' and objective form." [9]

[8] See chs. II, VI.

[9] Eric L. Mascall quoting A. C. Bridge in *Theology and Images* (London: A. R. Mowbray & Co., 1963), p. 10. Romano Guardini writes that a symbol originates when that which is interior and spiritual finds expression in that which is exterior and material. The spiritual element must transpose itself into material forms. While occasioned by the particular, it must rise and deal with life and the soul in the abstract. *The Church and the Catholic and the Spirit of the Liturgy* (New York: Sheed & Ward, 1935), p. 167. Paul Tillich's well-known definition is as follows: "A religious symbol . . . is material taken out of the world of finite things to point beyond itself to the ground of being and meaning. . . . As a symbol it participates in the . . . 'holy.' . . . The religious symbol participates in the holiness of that to which it points, that is, to the holy itself. Religous symbols are not holy in and of themselves, but they are holy by their participation in that

Yet, one has the impression that often the term "symbol" is not so much liturgically understood in this proper way as *felt* in an evocative way to hold meanings predominantly sensuous, emotional, or aesthetic. The term "language," on the other hand, has the advantage of suggesting meanings both sensuous and other than sensuous, and rational and moral as well as emotional and aesthetic. And it is the "other than sensuous" and the "more than emotional" elements which Protestant worship—especially in its free-church expressions—has distinctively undertaken to convey.

Now this is not to say that worship is Protestant only when it deprecates symbols or appeals only to man's rationality. This is a puritan rather than a Protestant notion; and all things considered, Protestant worship today probably needs the dynamics of a full and authentic symbolism more than it needs rationality. Yet, Protestantism also takes with great seriousness the biblical conception of God as one who reasons with his people, and the New Testament understanding of worship as *"reasonable* service"—*logikos latreia* (Rom. 12.1). It has trusted in the Word as "full of grace and truth" (John 1:14). It has stressed Paul's warning to "pray with the *mind"* as well as in the ecstasy of the spirit (I Cor. 14:15). And it has steadily contended that authentic worship must engage man's cognitive and moral faculties as well as his senses and emotions. Douglas Horton once put this point by saying that whereas the Roman Mass centers in what all can *see,* the Protestant service centers in what all can *think.*[10]

The contrast embodied in this remark is too simply put, partly because the thoughts men think in worship have a symbolic if not a visional character and they are also triggered by symbols. Such concepts as the "Kingdom of God," the "will of God," the "Trinity," the "incarnation," and "Apostles' Creed" [11] are mental symbols. And a sermon, which is capable of the highest

---

which is holy in itself. . . . They are more than signs. They not only point beyond themselves to something else; they also participate in the power of that to which they point. . . . Religious symbols open up the mystery of the holy and they open up the mind for the mystery of the holy to which it can respond." "Theology and Symbolism," in *Religious Symbolism,* ed. F. Ernest Johnson (New York: Harper & Bros., 1955), pp. 110-11.

[10] See *The Meaning of Worship* (New York: Harper & Bros., 1959), p. 47.

[11] Jean Daniélou, S.J., has an interesting reference to the way in which the term "symbol" came to be applied to the Creed. The English word "symbol" derives from the Greek prefix *syn* meaning "together," and the verb *ballein* meaning "to throw." In the earliest profession of faith preceding Baptism, from which the Apostles' Creed derived, the candidate would make a pledge, a covenant with the Lord, at the same time that he renounced Satan and his works. This "pledge"—according to the Church father John Chrysostom—was called *symbalon,* a "pact," "a coming together," and it is from this use that the term "symbol" came to be applied to professions of faith. See Daniélou's essay "The Sacraments and the History of Salvation," in *The Liturgy and the Word of God* (Collegeville, Minn.: Liturgical Press, 1959), p. 26.

reaches of intellectual meaning, is a sustained oral and auditory symbol. Further, and we repeat, man's passional and imaginative nature is part of the image of God he bears, and is as potent a means of communion with the divine as any other faculty of personality.

However, the very intensity with which we feel this to be the case can lead us to overreact and endanger the truth which Christian worship cannot yield up without losing integrity: the Word addresses man in worship as the Word of Reason and enlists the response of reason. It would appeal to man's mind and compel his most naked reflection upon it. It is something of this truth C. G. Jung was getting at in describing the present predicament of Protestantism in regard to symbols. The history of Protestantism, he writes, has been a history of chronic iconoclasm, indeed excessively so, and the alarming poverty of its symbols today has created a vacuum which man fills all too easily with perverse borrowing, especially from eastern religions. However, Jung continues:

It seems to me that it would be far better stoutly to avow our spiritual poverty, our symbol-lessness, instead of feigning a legacy to which we are not the legitimate heirs at all. We are, surely, the rightful heirs of Christian symbolism, but somehow we have squandered this heritage. We have let the house our fathers built fall into decay, and now we try to break into Oriental palaces that our fathers never knew. Anyone who has lost the historical symbols and cannot be satisfied with substitutes is certainly in a very difficult position today: before him there yawns the void. . . . What is worse, the vacuum gets filled with absurd political and social ideas. . . . But if he cannot get along with those pedantic dogmatisms, *he sees himself forced to be serious for once with his alleged trust in God,* though it usually turns out that his fear of things going wrong if he did so is even more persuasive. This fear is far from unjustified, for *where God seems closest the danger seems greatest.* . . . Just as in Christianity the vow of worldly poverty turned the mind away from the riches of this earth, so *spiritual poverty seeks to renounce the false riches of the spirit* . . . in order, finally, to dwell with itself alone, where, in the cold light of consciousness, the blank barrenness of the world reaches to the very stars.[12]

Protestantism's enthusiasm for symbolism today, more often than we know, may be a seeking after false riches of the spirit, a way of avoiding the danger of becoming serious about its alleged trust in God. And the term "language" may more unrelentingly keep it exposed to this saving danger.

"Language," it must be remembered, represents rational order superimposed upon existence. It is man's most civilized achievement, the human mind penetrating and arranging meaning to correspond most truly to reality.

[12] From Jung's *The Archetypes of the Collective Unconscious,* quoted by Joseph Campbell, *The Masks of God: Creative Mythology* (New York: The Viking Press, 1968), p. 368. Italics mine.

When we speak of our "mother" language, for example, we mark not only its genitive power; we also mark its power to correlate and differentiate intelligently our worlds of meaning.[13] "Nothing affects the significance of human existence more than the range and resource of our articulation, vocabulary, syntax and discourse," it has been said: *the language of a people is its fate.*[14] The media of liturgy broadly understood as "language" and rooted in the "Word" as fulcral are nothing less than fateful for the Christian experience of reality. P. T. Forsyth, while pleading for a sympathetic approach to art on the part of Protestantism, yet warned: "The ruling type of such a religion as that of the New Testament must be revelation and not mystery, and its vehicle must be the spoken word, which in its truth and purity is a great *act* of appeal to the intelligent will of God or man."[15]

Lastly, the category of language is preferable to the category of symbolism because it may better protect liturgy from the ever-present danger of aestheticism of which we have written.[16] To be sure, the term "language" incurs the risk of flattening both worship and one's thinking about it into verbalism—what the German calls *Wortkunst*. And the judgement of many people today—which we shall need to examine presently—that our culture has become a postliterate one in which media other than the spoken or read word are the decisive media, only underscores the risk. Yet the ardor with which Protestantism has embraced "Symbolism and the Arts," and the vigor with which Catholicism is moving to chasten its symbolism and to restore "The Liturgy of the Word,"[17] give one pause. For when "symbolism" is yoked with art and is made sovereign for the media of worship, it is not hard for the human mind to conceive the divine reality which deals with man in worship as other than the God of Christian revelation, and to allow the emotion associated with the artistic vision of reality to reduce the transaction of worship to sentimentality. "Sentimentality," it has been said, is "the evocation or seeking of emotional satisfaction divorced from reason and responsibility,"[18] and this divorce is exactly the danger which application of the category of "symbolism" to worship entails. The tendency of many

---

[13] See Arthur A. Vogel, *Is the Last Supper Finished?* (New York: Sheed & Ward, 1968), pp. 23, 107.

[14] Amos N. Wilder, *The Language of the Gospel* (New York: Harper & Row, 1964), p. 13. Italics mine.

[15] From Forsyth's *Christ on Parnassus*, p. 191. Quoted by Theodore Wedel in a brilliant article entitled "Liturgy and Art," in *Religion in Life*, XXXVIII (1969), 206.

[16] See ch. I; also ch. VI.

[17] For example, see Josef A. Jungmann's book with this title (London: Burns & Oates, 1966).

[18] Erik Routley, "The Vocabulary of Church Music," *Union Seminary Quarterly Review*, XVIII (Jan., 1963), p. 142.

people to evaluate liturgical symbols in terms of their visual beauty rather than their theology, of their emotional rather than their rational appeal, of their historical interest rather than their fidelity to the Word, illustrates this peril. When the term "symbol" is met with, why is it that many if not most people react by thinking of a visual image—the beauty of a stained-glass window, perhaps, instead of the Apostles' Creed, of a finely wrought cross more quickly than of the words of the Bible, of embroidered antependia more readily than the action of the eucharistic breaking of bread? "Symbol" so easily allows us to escape from the Christological claim of the Word into only the aesthetic or pictorial or psychological.

The concept "language," on the other hand, does not let us off so easily. It corrects our thinking with an integrity that ultimately derives from the Bible and axiomatically defines worship as essentially the dialogue which worship by nature must be. To be sure, the Bible embodies many images, "signs," and references to signs—the equivalent more of less of what we mean by "symbols." The prophets' messages are often cast in signs. The oral speech of Jesus, as well as his actions, is picturesque and parabolic. And St. Paul speaks of Christ himself as "the image of the invisible God." Likewise the nature of the Church is depicted in signs and images—some one hundred of them—more often than it is discursively defined. Central affirmations of faith are likewise rendered into magnificent and memorable pictures, as in the apocalypse of St. John. Even so, the Bible on the whole is restrained in its appeal to spatial or visual images, and it is not an accident that speaking about God is commanded hundreds of times, whereas setting up likenesses of God is forbidden *expressis verbis*. Above all the Bible prefers metaphors of speech and hearing because this category is more appropriate than the category of sight for the pilgrimage of the Christian man through time. "Sight belongs essentially to the end of the journey, when the pure in heart will see God," whereas hearing belongs to the journey itself. Christ appears transfigured before the disciples, yes. But the danger of vision is just that "men wish to linger where it was given, 'Master, it is good for us to be here, and let us build three tabernacles.'" The visional symbol "does not therefore call us forth into the future as does the Word, whose true correlative is hearing." [19]

In any case, whatever place the Bible gives to signs and symbols, they come to us first through language; and the essence of language for liturgy in turn inheres in divine reality whose being and action toward man are primordially that of Word. This "Word"—in a splendid phrase of Karl

---

[19] David Cairns, *God Up There? A Study in Divine Transcendence* (Edinburgh: St. Andrew Press, 1967), pp. 98-99.

Rahner—is "the grammer of God's Self-expression" grandly made manifest in creation and redemption. Liturgy is bound to the hermeneutics of this self-expression. It cannot escape the sovereignty of the Word nor the sovereignty of the category of language deriving from it, if it is to possess integrity.

But while the category of language holds primordial *theological* authority, this does not mean that other than theological ways of thinking are to be excluded. On the contrary, "language" enables us to enlist all the perspectives necessary for analyzing the media of liturgy at the same time that it helps us to use them responsibly. Our own everyday experience of language instructs us here. Nothing is more native to us than language, we know; indeed, our language represents the essence of our self. But only a moment's reflection reveals how the language we use, which seems so personal and autonomous, yet inheres in a vast context and is shaped by many influences. And just as we appreciate the deeper meanings of language the more we understand these influences, so we best think about liturgical language when we consult the varied contexts that shape its meaning. Further, just as a man's use of language reveals the quality of his sensibilities, the breeding of his mind, and the range of his appreciations, and just as the most cultivated man is he who uses language with greatest sensitivity and precision, so, we may say, the best liturgist is he who employs the language of worship with the greatest awareness of its varied contexts and possibilities of meaning.

We therefore turn to four such contexts or perspectives: functional utility; psychology; culture; art. The first two perspectives are explored in this essay; the perspectives of culture and art in the following essay. In exploring these perspectives we shall have as our aim a statement of principles, or at least of insights, which can sensitize us in making practical decisions in worship. The requirement of theological integrity must continue to underlie these principles, at the same time that they must be made to speak to our life today. However, simply to say that liturgical language must be theologically true and effectively relevant and stop there is like saying that all poetry must be poetic, and then refusing to say anything further about meter or style or about man's imagination as he reads and writes poetry. Substance and illustration must be provided. Further, these perspectives interlock; and while their interrelation is often complex if not baffling, it can also be illumining. Plainly, bad psychology can wreck good theology; good aesthetics can make for cultural relevance; and sociology has much to say to mechanical function. Still further, the interlocking nature of these perspectives can save one from being trapped between the protagonists of "the new" and "the old" and from being hedged in by a simplistic posing of issues. In worship, the main question is not the traditional over against the contemporary. Rather, it is the question of how truthfully liturgical language embodies God's Word and man's *Antwort* and how effectively it makes these mean what they mean. Certainly cultural contemporaneity speaks to this question, but so do insights of psychology which emphasize the importance of man's past, for example, or the illumination of art repristinating tradition. One can no more deal with liturgical language by assessing its validity in terms of "old" or "new" than he can dismiss as unimportant the etymological roots of our everyday speech on the one hand, or be indifferent to the contemporary mind-set which associates "redemption" with cashing a bond on the other.

THE PERSPECTIVE OF FUNCTIONAL EFFECTIVENESS

We look first, then, at the perspective of *functional effectiveness*. If all the media of worship be thought of as "language," decisions as to their practical use may be metaphorically likened to choosing the best vocabulary to state meaning, to spelling and punctuating properly, and to writing legibly or speaking clearly. Of themselves, these do not quite make sense or nonsense of meaning, but they greatly help or hinder. Similarly, everything functional or practical, what we speak of as "the mechanics" of worship, affects meaning. We have said, for example, that encounter with the Word must be conducted in a language the people can make their own, that only thus can the congregation function as priests. But how can a worshipper do his liturgical work if the church is so hot it puts him to sleep? Or we have stressed the eschatological meaning of worship for the congregation as the pilgrim people of God on the one hand who have here no abiding city, and its worldly meaning for their historical existence on the other as those who are sent into the world as the Father sent the Son. But how can the worshipper be engaged with his worldly existence if there is no intercessory prayer for him to pray? And what is the effect upon his sense of the eternal of rusty umbrella stands, of the smell of beef gravy drifting up from the church basement, and of the same linoleum tile in the nave he sees in the lavatory of his office on Monday? Now it is not that worship cannot be transacted in such incongruous language. It can be, and it often is; and indeed there is much to be said for deliberately worldly language. Yet, insensitivity to function makes worship stammer when it ought to articulate clearly. Or it renders worship into a kind of rude slang, suggesting a certain discourtesy toward the Divine Guest like that of Simon the Pharisee, who failed to provide the Lord with a basin of water and towel.

On the other hand, too fastidious concern for function also corrupts language and artifically separates worship from life. Too fussy seating of the people by too well-trained ushers, preludes and postludes too self-consciously dramatic, too elaborate lighting, too costly communion vessels, fancy anthems beyond the capacity of the choir, a false otherworldly hush in which the human stuff of man's ordinary life is looked at askance—these strike one as liturgical vanity. One feels that such language glorifies man more than the Father who is in heaven; and it comes closer than careless language to disabling worship because it more readily makes for idolatry. It is as if worship were transacted in the strained accents of affectation rather than in honest speech.

The perspective of function especially helps to illumine the actional character of worship. To carry forward our analogy, we may say that worship is to be conducted more in the active than the passive voice, in the indicative rather than in the subjunctive mood, and in the present tense, and that the media of worship are fateful for executing this intention. It has been said, for example, that the active or passive character of a service is determined by what happens—or fails to happen—within the first five minutes; that here the attention of the congregation is grasped or lost, the action of worship set moving or stalled. This is probably exaggeration, and many other considerations we shall examine in later essays also enter in. Nevertheless, functional factors are vital. People's minds as they come to worship are distracted and need to be vigorously grasped. Likewise as the service continues, their minds are to be understood as slow-moving, and their attention span needs to be sustained by fluidity and forwardness of movement. But often the first hymn is meditative, soft, impressionistic, or too unfamiliar to become engaged with. Or the choir uses the processional to take the most roundabout—and conspicuous?—route to its place. Or the organist unduly prolongs things with exhibitionistic elaborations. Or the minister stalls the service by mistakenly locating a period of silence too early, for which the congregation is not ready.

Similarly, pacing and tempo illustrate the importance of functional factors as they affect action in prayer. Prayer seems to require three things simultaneously from the mind of a worshipper: the physical perception of the words; comprehension of the content of meaning conveyed in the words, such as the nature of a sin being confessed; and the act of passing beyond perception and comprehension to speech or communion with God. If the tempo of the prayer is too fast, the worshipper cannot get beyond stage one or two at the most and is deprived of the fulfillment of stage three. However, if the tempo is too slow, attention is lost, the mind wanders, and exasperation or boredom sets in.[20] Tempo and movement especially affect the service of Holy Communion—pre-eminently a service of action. Here supremely the tense, voice, and mood of language are vital. Surely language cast in the present tense best expresses the divine Presence. Surely the active voice best conveys the action of the divine Host who gives man to eat and drink. And surely the indicative mood best contemporizes the promise of divine grace and man's existential response. But for that matter, preaching as well as sacrament is also action—event, and liturgical language must function to serve both.

In a quite different vein, the body, manner, and person of the minister are part of the language of worship viewed functionally, and greatly affect the meaning of worship. "The offense of the Gospel is far from being the same as the offensiveness of the preacher," a Congregational theologian has remarked,[21] and the being of the minister as it functions to help or hinder the Gospel in imparting its life is vital. A. G. Hebert, in speaking of the Christian "Mystery" as the re-presentation of the event of Christ, once wrote that man's act of remembering (*anamnesis*) is not first "a psychological but an ontological fact." [22] But plainly, the Word can be hindered from imparting its ontological life by psychological and physical realities, including the minister himself. His voice, for example, and his use of it, while not decisive, are very important. One has heard prayer led in what the minister supposed was a reverent voice but whose net effect was that of a funeral dirge. Death came through but not life. Or Scripture is dramatically declaimed as by an impressario, or read in a "stained glass voice" without any feeling of reality or commitment.

The voice, however, in turn rises out of the whole man. The minister's sense of his body, his freedom or unease in letting it be liturgically used, his emotional health signalled through the realism or diffidence with which he accepts the authority with which he inevitably impresses the congregation, and especially what we can only call the minister's "spirituality"—all these condition the tone of his voice, the tone of his being, and the tone of worship. As "language," the whole being of the minister "physicalizes meaning." It is to do the work of liturgy in something of the same way in which the philosopher at his best—in the words of Miguel do Unamuno—does his thinking in philosophy: "There are . . . people who appear to think only with their brain or whatever may be the specific thinking organ; while

---

[20] See the essay "Psychological Considerations," by E. R. Micklem, in *Christian Worship*, ed. Nathaniel Micklem (London: Oxford University Press, 1936).

[21] Daniel Jenkins, *The Protestant Ministry* (Garden City, N.Y.: Doubleday & Co., 1958), p. 78.

[22] *Liturgy and Society*, p. 65.

others think with all the body, and all the soul, with the blood, with the marrow of the bones, with the heart, with the lungs, with the belly, with the life." [23] In short—to pursue our metaphor of "tone"—defective presence in the minister injures liturgy as poor musicianship injures the intention of the composer. It is often asked, for example, whether the leader's own personal godliness makes any difference in worship if he uses the right words and observes reverent attitudes, especially if he follows a prescribed ritual. In reply it must be said that a lack of religious conviction will show through the noblest ritual. It is like the difference between the same tune played on two violins, one cheaply and carelessly made, the other a masterpiece like a Stradivarius, mellow and beautiful in tone. Sooner or later a man's essential tone will steal through.[24]

THE PERSPECTIVE OF PSYCHOLOGY

To examine language from *the perspective of psychology* inevitably leads one into difficult and complex matters, for just as one cannot take the finger of liturgy without having to grasp the whole fist of theology, so one cannot deal with liturgical psychology without having to grasp much of the psychology of religion in general. Difficulty is further compounded by the paucity of competent investigation in this field; and it would be interesting to speculate on the reasons why liturgical theologians have neglected this area.[25] We cite only one reason here: the ambivalence with which liturgical theology must say "no" and "yes" to psychology at the same time. Liturgical theology rightly understands that the perspective of psychology is proximate, not ultimate; and the perversions which psychology, when made autonomous,

---

[23] Quoted by D. H. Hislop, *Our Heritage in Public Worship* (Edinburgh: T. & T. Clark, 1935), p. 281.

[24] I am indebted to the late Albert Palmer for this analogy.

[25] The current concern with the social and missionary implications of liturgy is doubtless one reason. However, even here the psychological carry-over of liturgy is manifest. Paul W. Pruyser interestingly points out how Christian witness in the cultural and political arena borrows from the cult "psychological-liturgical forms." "Instead of processions in the church or toward it, there are marches on state houses. After clerical collars have become almost abandoned in houses of worship, they reappear in the streets to identify the agents of social change as men of God. Instead of the ancient hallowed . . . banners, there are placards . . . with the same phallic attitude of protest. . . . Coffeehouses for college youth are places where one can talk about religion and perform guitar-led hymnodies under the avuncular guidance of a young chaplain in ways that resemble the erstwhile Sunday Schools. The pull toward ritual is always present, and much of the so-called free and spontaneous activity becomes quickly stylized into a new liturgy. Sit-ins have some kinship with kneeling. Slogans are chanted. . . . Formulas for grievances take on an evocative form and are repeated in the form of litanies. The postures, the gestures, the voices, and at times the clothes worn are liturgical re-creations." *A Dynamic Psychology of Religion* (New York: Harper & Row, 1968), pp. 197-98.

has fastened on liturgy are too vivid in many people's minds to be easily forgotten.[26] Yet one cannot even begin to reflect on such important matters as the didactic power of worship, the nature of the numinous and the power of symbols, the claim of tradition, the cultural conditioning of man's liturgical consciousness, the subjective and objective character of worship and the nature of religious emotion and experience, without running head on into psychology. Additional areas could be mentioned: the dynamics in liturgy which make for infantilism or maturity and pathology or health; the reality and activity of the subsconscious; the psychology of liturgical space, of numinous sound, and of sacred time; the relation of sexuality to worship; the motor carry-over from liturgy into mission; the psychology of habit in church attendance; and especially the psychology of liturgical action. We have already touched on certain of these areas, and shall again. But clearly, while the theological perspective of the Word as Light is sovereign, a minimal psychological understanding of human personality is essential. And while these essays hardly do more than to grasp the finger of liturgical psychology, yet certain things must be grasped.

The Relativity of Liturgical Language to Personality Structure

A dictum of the Cambridge Platonist, John Smith, puts plainly one vital truth which psychology speaks to the question of liturgical language: "Such as men themselves are, such will God himself seem to them to be." Transposed into our modern situation: the meaning of all liturgical language is relative to man's personality structure and experience. Language does not mean what it is in itself; rather, its meaning is subjectively conditioned. In the idiom of the social scientist: expectations determine perceptions. "Words like 'God,' 'beauty,' 'love,' signify to the individual his own experiences and associations. . . . Each individual tends to be like Humpty Dumpty, who made words mean what he liked. We interpret words by our experience." [27]

But not only do the oral words of liturgy bear this aspect; so does the whole spectrum of liturgical language. The pastor, for example, may wish to disavow the authority of the "father figure" that attaches to his person.

---

[26] See ch. I.

[27] R. S. Lee, *Psychology and Worship* (New York: Philosophical Library, 1956), p. 50. Carrol Simcox has an amusing passage from John Buchan's *The Three Hostages*: "Has it ever struck you, Dick, that ecclesiastical language has a most sinister sound? I knew some of the words though not their meaning, but I knew that my audience would be just as ignorant. So I had a magnificent peroration. 'Will you, men of Kilclavers,' I asked, 'endure to see a chasuble set up in your market place? Will you have your daughters sold into simony? Will you have celibacy in the public streets? Gad, I had them all on their feet bellowing 'never.'" *The Words of Our Worship* (New York: Morehouse-Gorham, 1955), p. ix.

But willy-nilly he is going to impress some people as father (even as husband) simply because many people in his congregation are psychologically children; inevitably, the dynamics of transference and counter-transference are going to operate. Again, a candle on the altar may be intended to be only a candle, but inevitably it will hold for some people sexual phallic meanings. (The Church has understood this in certain of its rites.) [28] The architecture of a church-in-the round may be designed to negate clericalism, bring people together, and foster congregational participation, but to some people it will suggest a baseball stadium or communicate claustrophobia. The music of a guitar may remind an older worshipper of a campfire and marshmallows; to a college student it likely means self-expression, love, and freedom. The red wine of Communion may be intended to signify the redemptive blood of Christ; to certain people it will suggest a hospital, or even menstruation.

But if language is relative to personality structure and experience, then it must be expected to involve—at least potentially—man's total being, and here theology answers to psychology. The capacity for worship, theology holds, cannot be separated out of man's nature as a single faculty. Rather, as the adjective "all" in our Lord's command to love God with "all" the heart and mind and soul and strenth suggests, man's nature in liturgy is to be thought of holistically and so likewise is his language. The Word addresses man in the total range of his being, and in worship his whole personhood is engaged.[29] Language is multi-medial, we might almost say, because man has been created a multi-medial creature by a multi-medial God.

However, precisely because language is so relative to man's total personality structure and can be so psychologically freighted, dangers arise which theology must also defend against. The corruption of manipulation aligned with a facile humanization of liturgy is one. Worship whose primary purpose is to play on man's faculties, worship reduced to sensitivity training or group therapy, "touch-and-tell worship experiences" in which participants touch

[28] William Lloyd Warner has an interesting passage entitled "Holy Coitus and Sacred Procreation," in *The Family of God: A Symbolic Study of Christian Life in America* (New Haven: Yale University Press, 1961), pp. 373 ff., interpreting the Church's paschal rites on Easter Eve for candidates for Baptism and Confirmation. The single paschal candle with its light and fire shining amidst blackness is a male symbol dramatizing Christ's ascent from hell. The font of the waters of Baptism is the female symbol in which the priest plunges the candle impregnating through the Holy Spirit (also a male symbol of spiritual power which impregnated the Virgin) the womb of the Church. The candidates for initiation become the spiritual progeny of Christ, and cry out for and receive "the milk of the Word" and of salvation. The open tomb from which Christ rises, celebrated by the candidates' resurrection to life at Easter, is also a female symbol, and their death is a beginning, a conception into new life.

[29] See chs. IV, VII.

and then tell one another "what I like most about you"—these self-evidently lend themselves to corruption. The danger here is that experience for the sake of experience replaces encounter with the Word and that worship is made into a kind of psychological gamesmanship. The "vitals of contemporary man," of which we have written in our first essay, are always to be gotten at, but in obedience to that Word whose presence is not mere vitalism but Life. Otherwise worship can become pathological, if not demonic. As we shall understand shortly, powerful forces in the unconscious are readily triggered by the media of worship, and if the psychology of language is not kept obedient to the Word, these easily become the paws and hoofs of Pan rather than means of grace and signs of the Holy Spirit. [30]

The Function of Faculties of Personality, Illustrated in the Action of Offering

Given the importance of personality structure, obviously the pastor must be minimally knowledgeable about the interrelation of man's faculties as they condition his use of language in worship. A full, technical analysis of these is beyond our purpose. But in addition to what has been said about man's rational and emotional nature (and in addition to a fuller discussion of the psychology of action in a later essay), we must briefly identify here the functioning of man's will, his physical body and senses and kinesethic nature, his memory, his moral sense, his imagination, and especially the subconscious stratum of his personality.

As an illustration, we consider the act of offering as chiefly—but by no means exclusively—an act of the will. Here the character of worship as action can powerfully come—or fail to come—to focus. Because worship is actional by definition, it is nerveless without man in some way putting forth his will. The Church has always understood this and from the beginning cast its understanding of the volitional character of worship in the emphasis it placed upon offering. Through the first three centuries, in fact, the Christian was defined as an "offerer" and the excommunicated as those "forbidden to offer." The offertory was located at a hinge point in the service immediately after the liturgy of the catechumens, at the beginning of the liturgy of the faithful, and was dramatized in a procession originally called "The Great Entrance." In such ways the Church intended offering to dramatize the action of man's will as declarative of faith and discipleship; and its corruption today into what is often little more than the "collection" pathetically exposes our historical ignorance and our liturgical poverty.

[30] See James Hillman, *Insearch* (New York: Charles Scribner's Sons, 1967), pp. 91-92.

231

But psychology can speak to our predicament by illumining the inter-relation of the faculties of personality as they can converge here, and the many layers of meaning that offering can come to hold if we have eyes to see. Offering for one thing is a *physical motor act* executing spiritual intention. It is a means of receiving the gifts of the people and presenting them to God, and when joined to the bringing in of the bread and wine and the laying of the table, it supplies the requisites of Holy Communion. But as a motor act, the offering also embodies *kinesthetic* aspects—that is, through the action of muscles and nerves man feels and works out meaning. It involves *posture*, the taking up of a position toward divine and human realities. It involves *tactile* values. Further, it involves *speech*—and often *singing*—and *hearing*. In a sense it acts out the command of Hosea (14:2 RSV): "Take with you words and return to the Lord; say to him, 'Take away all iniquity; accept that which is good and we will render the fruit of our lips.'" The offering also involves *memory*. Gifts of providence are recalled, and Christ's sacrifical offering is remembered. Again, offering involves the *imagination* in perceiving the providential, redemptive, and ethical meaning of the symbols offered and in translating the meaning of the ceremonial in presenting them. Further, the offering has *moral* meaning. It involves what psychology calls the superego and ego ideal, and what religion calls the conscience. Moral meaning is apprehended under the aspects of *duty* in doing one's service to God or to the church or one's fellowmen; of *guilt* over the imperfect stewardship of the gifts of creation; of *propitiation* or *expiation* of one's sinfulness; of *mercy* (the term "alms" derives from the Greek *eleos* meaning compassion); of *ethical involvement* with one's fellows through the sharing of possessions and through responsible attitudes toward the secular world. The offering also involves *emotions:* feelings evoked from the past perhaps, or of *boredom*, or of *kinship* or *alienation* toward one's fellow worshippers, or toward the church; of *gratitude;* of *joy*, perhaps festal joy that can even become ecstasy; and perhaps the mingled *pain* and *pleasure* of self-denial—or self-deception. And not least, authentic offering can embody man's feeling of *awe* before the numinous and his *hunger for* identification with *the divine*, indeed even an existential *sense of* his own *destiny* in communion with God. Understood as *oblation*, for example, offering can become an acted-out expression of Augustine's classic prayer: "Thou hast made us for thyself, and our hearts are restless until they find rest in thee." Truly, virtually all the elements of an entire psychology of religion are embodied in the language of offering if one has eyes to see!

Now liturgical theology, we repeat, is not wrong in understanding offering as an action of the will and in seeing man the worshipper as an "offering being." In a sense the will is the constitutive element of personality which binds man together into a self. What a man wills and does declares the veracity of his being. We do not forget that the only liturgical command given by Jesus to the disciples was addressed to the will: "*Do* this in remembrance of me." And St. Paul summons the Christian to worship as action of the will in no uncertain terms: "Present yourselves, souls and bodies, as a reasonable, living and holy sacrifice unto God." But the will is also to be understood holistically in light of psychology. As agent it not only gathers and expresses the personality, it is conditioned by the personality; it exerts a reflexive effect upon personality, and in turn is affected by the personality. In short, the psychological constellation of man's total being is involved.

For one thing, in liturgy as elsewhere the action of the will performs an epistemological function, i.e., action bestows knowledge; and both theology and psychology unite in understanding how in a sense "he that doeth liturgically shall know." Here, as in ethics, obedience is an organ of knowledge. It has been said, for example, that "until a man has expressed his emotion, he does not yet know what emotion it is. The act of expressing it is therefore an exploration of his own emotions. He is trying to find out what these emotions are." [31] Which is to say, he is trying to find out who he is. Theology would only add: he is trying to find out who he is in relation to God. And one may well ask: In conceiving the offering, how sensitive is the pastor to ranges of knowledge the worshipper may be exploring or can be led to explore?

But future as well as past and present dimensions of meaning are also discovered by action of the will. We increasingly understand the psychological truth that "it is easier to act your way into a new way of feeling than to feel your way into a new way of acting." [32] The truth of this insight— while arguable, as we shall explore in a later essay—suggests the interlocking relation between volition and emotion; that emotion can follow on volition as well as vice versa; and that until the will is put forth, certain meanings remain unapprehended. But here again, psychology and theology unite. Not merely new ways of feeling *per se*, but new ways of emotionally experiencing the divine wait on action of the will. This is perhaps why theology insists that liturgically as otherwise we must knock that the door may be opened, that we must take and eat if we would be fed, that divine grace can only be known by him who responds to its givenness with a grace-gift

[31] R. G. Collingwood, *The Principles of Art* (Oxford: Clarendon Press, 1938), p. 111.
[32] Quoted by Howard J. Clinebell, Jr., *Basic Types of Pastoral Counseling* (Nashville: Abingdon Press, 1966), p. 171.

of his own—even though it be only his sinful self. In short, in meeting God's offering with his own offering, man can come to know God, and himself in relation to God, as perhaps in no other way.

Thus the wise pastor will put his imagination to work to rethink the act of offering. He will understand that it is to be set within the perspective of a full psychology if it is to be rehabilitated and that it must be viewed within the constellation of man's total being. Just to relocate it mechanically after the sermon, for example, or aesthetically dramatize it with loud music, or underscore its meaning as peculiarly the liturgy of the laity by having a layman offer the prayer of consecration will hardly suffice. Such functional reforms, while commendable, move on a secondary, not a primary level, and require deeper psychological understanding.[33]

The Great Importance of the Subconscious

Thus far in our discussion we have followed the traditional scheme of faculty psychology in marking the identifiable elements of human personality —the will, the mind, the body, memory—and indeed this is an almost inescapable way of proceeding. The most decisive part of man's being, however, that which conditions everything else but which strangely has received least attention from liturgical scholars, is the subliminal band of man's psyche which psychology speaks of as "the subconscious" or the "unconscious," the six-sevenths or seven-eighths of human personality which like

---

[33] We might well learn from Negro and Pentecostal congregations who kinesthetically act out offering by rising and leaving the pews, walking forward to present their gifts, circling the church in procession and returning to their seats. Or at Communion, why should not women of the congregation come forward at the time of offertory, lay the cloth and "set the table" as they do at home, and bring in bread they have baked? And cannot the equivalent of offerings at a harvest festival be much more often employed? The late Charles Gore once said that the offertory at an early Christian Eucharist resembled nothing so much as a modern harvest festival. And Josef Jungmann deduces from a mosaic floor excavated at Aquileia that in the Constantinian era men and women formed an offertory procession bringing not only bread and wine, but also grapes, flowers, a bird, even property handed over in the form of a deed or voucher. In a different vein, could the worshippers' need to confess and expiate be met by inviting them to act out a gesture of reconciliation with their brother before they present their gift, or by inviting them to lay on the altar written confessions of sins or requests for counsel or prayer? But offering needs to be rethought and rehabilitated in other services than the Eucharist. Offertory processions and actions are clearly suitable at Baptism and Confirmation. Underlying all is the pastor's duty to enlarge his people's understanding of offertory by teaching them its manifold meanings, its history, and especially its connection with their worldly life. The two chief secular realities with which worship needs to be related in our day, it has been said, are matter and power, the world of economics, science and technology, and the world of sociology and politics. How money is economic matter and social power, how bread and wine symbolize natural resources and economic power, and involve the ways in which men handle matter and politically live together, and the meaning Jesus Christ holds for these—such moral and social meanings of offering need to be taught.

the proverbial iceberg exists below the level of the conscious mind. Inevitably we have referred to the unconscious in previous essays because its reality has implications for the whole range of liturgy, including the nature of symbols, the character of the numinous, the meaning of tradition and of certain archetypal forms tradition embodies, the question of relevance and irrelevance, the presence and power of emotion in worship. The unconscious must be recognized as operative throughout worship as in all of man's life, and the pastor must liturgically reckon with it with the same seriousness with which he presumably accepts its reality in all other pastoral relationships.

All the faculties of personality, as we have said, exist in the matrix of the unconscious, but the unconscious also appears to possess a certain autonomy of its own. Further, it is omnipresent and transpersonal, and transcends space, time, history, and even individuality. In fact each individual seems to participate in a common, racial, atavistic unconscious we may speak of as the "collective unconscious"—to use Jung's term—that is, the timeless, spaceless inner man each individual shares with every other man. The sum total of the vital instinctual energies of man belongs to this deeper level and can be thought of as the libido—a kind of quantum of energy able to communicate itself to any field of human activity such as the exercise of power, hunger, hatred, religion, sexuality.[34] Aspects of both the divine and demonic appear to characterize this energy, and from the viewpoint of religion it is linked with the grasp of the "Holy Other" upon man of which Rudolf Otto has written, or with the "something more" which William James remarked in his famous statement that life is lived by millions of people as if there were "something more" decisive for their lives than sense data.

Transfer of this energy from one field to another apparently cannot be effected by the conscious mind; but when triggered by the proper agent, a transformation or redirection of energy can take place similar to the transformation of energy in the physical realm.[35] The agent of this transformation—and this is what liturgy especially must realize—is what we are calling in this essay "language." Indeed the unconscious not only responds to agents exteriorly set before it; it also appears to have at its disposal a certain symbolic language it produces from its own depths. The ever-recurring themes found in virtually all religious mythologies report this language,

[34] See the Introduction in Frieda Fordham's *An Introduction to Jung's Psychology* (Baltimore: Penguin Books, 1959).
[35] Susanne K. Langer writes that the brain is not a switchboard but a transformer. *Philosophy in a New Key: A Study in the Symbolism of Reason, Rite, and Art* (New York: New American Library, Mentor Books, 1948), p. 46.

including such motifs as initiation, death and rebirth, expiation, redemption, the figure of the redeemer-hero and his superhuman labors and sufferings, the quaternity and trinity,[36] and others.

Given the reality of the subconscious—which we have described in only a very summary fashion—it becomes clear that the language of liturgy can constitute agents of transformation of immense power affecting the profoundest forces of human personality. Correspondingly, the lameness of liturgical forms commonly used today only reveals how like a plant gone to tops—in the metaphor of one critic—liturgy has cut its roots to the dark depths of man's nature where sustenance might give us life and strength. We do not comprehend the primitive levels on which man ought to be engaged as he worships, and how his psychic vitals are as important to his soul's life as the lungs, heart, and stomach are to his body.

To be sure, each man's unconscious life is unique. It reflects especially the psychic influences of his infancy and childhood (in particular the first two years) with their significant oral, anal, and oedipal experiences. (Erik Erikson believes, for example, that man's capacity for the numinous can be traced back to the ritual of morning greeting between a baby and its mother, with its accompanying sounds, smiles, mutual touch, feeding. The mother represents to the child its first "sense of hallowed presence" which becomes a lasting part of its subconscious life.)[37] However, precisely because the relation of language to the unconscious is so psychically charged and because the conscious mind is so unable to perceive or control this relation, it also becomes clear that liturgical language can release energies both good and evil, healthy and pathological, creative and corrupt.

To illustrate: we may agree that worship is only Christian when it requires genuine sacrifice on the part of the worshipper. Anything else is a contradiction in terms, as the corollary use of the terms "worship" and "sacrifice" reveals. This sacrificial character is often denoted by the biblical term "paschal," which refers to the Passover theme of death and deliverance coming to its highest expression in the death and resurrection of Christ. This term marks the truth that the condition of life is always sacrifice; of deliverance, threat; that with the throne belongs the tomb, with the crown the cross; that he who would find life must lose it. The element of sacrifice denoted by these paschal images, each of which has reality only in dialectical

[36] Why is it the liturgical rule that "when there is more than one collect, there should be three"? See Walter Lowrie, *Action in the Liturgy* (New York: Philosophical Library, 1953), p. 205.

[37] See his essay "The Development of Ritualization," in *The Religious Situation—1968*, ed. Donald R. Cutler (Boston: Beacon Press, 1968).

relation to the other, is fundamental in Christian thought and especially in liturgy.

But worship devoid of sacrifice is also a psychological contradiction in terms. A deep truth reported by psychology is just that man's nature must always surrender up part of itself, that indeed a constant conflict must be waged within the self, if a larger self is to be won. Values possessed by the "ego," the conscious self—things that are "ego-tistic," as we say—must be sacrificed to the total self if integration of personality is to be achieved. Or alternatively, man's instinctual nature as it is identified and experienced as evil must in a sense be sacrificially offered up to, and mastered by, the ego if health, i.e. wholeness, is to be won. In a word, both theology and psychology unite in saying that the price of life is always in some sense death, that true sacrifice is always in some sense "self" sacrifice.

Questions for the pastor become, then: Does the language of worship provide for the authentic acting out of the conflict between the ego and other elements of the self within the presence of Jesus Christ? How would one evaluate the act of offering in this respect as we have previously analyzed it, or the act of confession in prayer? Do these and other liturgical forms pierce down and release forces in personality which trigger real conflict? Or instead of summoning the self to real sacrifice, do they do the exact opposite, that is, suspend rather than initiate conflict by releasing forces which falsely appease the ego or superego, and split it and the full self further apart? In short, do psychological means correspond to theological ends?

Now for the term "conflict" used above, one could substitute the term "tension," and for both psychology and religion a stabilized tension between the self and the conscience, roughly paralleled in Freudian psychology by the tension between the ego and the superego, is to be desired. The coping of the ego with the superego and the ego ideal (and also the libido) is "always a matter of relative strength between the ego and these other parties. No party can be ignored; each must have its due, in perpetual give-and-take." [38] When, for example, the tension is upset to the degree that the superego is hyperactive and tyrannizes over the ego and other elements of personality, one has on his hands neurosis or psychosis. Correspondingly, when liturgical language overstresses the cross, guilt, sin, for example, or when it confuses creaturehood with sinfulness and demands that the worshipper deny not only his sinful self but any value to his full, given self, it fosters unhealth and masochism. [39]

[38] Pruyser, A *Dynamic Psychology of Religion*, p. 311.

[39] The prayers of General Confession in the Morning Order, and of Humble Access in the Communion Order of the Anglican Church, have been criticized on this score. See the article *"Unchristian Liturgy,"* by H. A. Williams in *Theology*, LXI (Oct., 1958), p. 402.

Yet if this coping is viewed only within the milder term "tension," and the requirement of "conflict" is unmet as in language of confession that is too platitudinous, for example, man's ego, super ego, and libido remain unengaged. Worship as in some sense sacrifice does not take place, and nothing of reality occurs. (An earlier warning against placing important acts of confession too early in the service may be recalled here.) The fatal result is that man's nature is conveniently left split apart. He is not compelled to explore his full self and is left in illusion about it. He is relieved of the pain of mortal—and immortal—combat with his own soul. And not surprisingly he can become addicted to such pathological worship. Indeed, because the Church has dealt with him falsely, he may even "come to church" in order to avoid real worship, that is, real sacrifice. Thus Jung has confessed his amazement that so much of what passes for religion is a substitute for the real thing. The liturgical duplicity which hosts of people foist on themselves —and which the Church foists upon them—can only be explained, he believes, by demonic rationalizations which lead men to choose "suitable symbols invested in a solidly organized dogma and ritual" by means of which "people are effectively defended . . . against immediate religious experience." [40] "If only people could realize what an enrichment it means to find one's own guilt, what a sense of honor, and new spiritual dignity!" [41]

In somewhat the same vein, the relation of a congregation's sense of corporateness to their subconscious life may be examined, for corporateness can be benign or malign. In any sizable gathering of people, it must be remembered, it is not the unique qualities of individuals that matter most; these differentiate, not unite. What unites people psychologically are subconscious affinities or archetypes which, when evoked by appropriate language, draw them together with dynamic force and impel them to act

[40] *Psychology and Religion* (New Haven: Yale University Press, 1938), pp. 52-53.
[41] From "After the Catastrophe," in *Essays in Contemporary Events* (London: Routledge & Kegan Paul, 1947), p. 55, quoted by Charles Bartruff Hanna, *The Face of the Deep* (Philadelphia: Westminster Press, 1967), p. 96. Curiously, sometimes people devise their own language of conflict when the Church's fails. James E. Dittes offers the provocative suggestion that chatting before a service during the prelude, socializing, and sitting in the rear pews are expressions of subconscious guilt and reverence, and forms of psychological resistance which the pastor is not to take at face value but to understand on deeper levels. Dittes hypothesizes that the total ritual of getting ready and coming to church may elicit a mood of guilt-feeling appropriate to coming into God's presence; that chatting may be a temporary distraction from facing God and actually contain confession; that the rear pew may be a legitimate "refuge" and signify a faith a person feels he lacks and really wants. If true, then the pastor should not fight such signs of resistance on their own terms, but rather understand and gather the resistance into worship and acknowledge candidly that God welcomes us in our true moods whatever they may be. See *The Church in the Way* (New York: Charles Scribner's Sons, 1967), ch. IX, "Resistance in Worship: A Summary."

238

from motives which they easily disguise from themselves. These affinities and motives can in reality be evil or good, and corporateness correspondingly evil or good. But the names with which people name these motives to themselves must in any case be minimally "good" in order to be consciously acceptable. Thus psychological wisdom—not cynicism!—suggests that the frequency with which the Church appeals to such biblical metaphors as "the Body" and the enthusiasm with which it speaks of "fellowship" are not always to be taken at face value. These can disguise as well as declare. Worship, R. S. Lee has warned, can be "captured by unconscious motives which, if brought to the light of consciousness, would be seen to be quite alien, even opposed to the conscious aims of worship." [42]

For example, corporateness can subconsciously be escape. Authentic response to reality requires separation from, as well as identification with, others. Every man needs his own space if he is to keep in touch with reality, and distance is as essential as nearness. As long as hearing, confessing, and interceding are done corporately, psychiatrist Earl S. Loomis has written, it is always possible to keep reality at arm's length. He continues:

Escape may be corporate rather than individual. It may be easier, for example, to face uncertainty, shame, doubt, or guilt if others share them. There is always a danger in corporate confession, corporate reassurance, and corporate affirmation. Another's guilt makes ours less poignant, another's shame makes ours less painful, another's doubts make our own less reprehensible. But only as we come to know our *own* doubt, shame, and guilt, only as we see that in some sense ours is different and personal, is it meaningful to talk about its relation to that of others. Otherwise we and they are talking about surface experiences.[43]

Again, corporateness can be simply the oneness of the cultural tribe or political mob disguised as religious. As James Gustafson has written: "Worship may simply re-inforce a sense of common life largely grounded in non-religious loyalties." [44] The corruption of much middle-class Protestant church life into a kind of American civil religion provides an illustration near at hand. In liturgical corporateness, further, mass psychopathology can become operative as in any social grouping, depending to a large degree on the kind of language engaging the deeper levels of personality. A charismatic preacher whose insecurities lead him to identify the devils of his own fears with Communism and his angels with Americanism, can communicate sickness and foster a neurotic tribal corporateness. Likewise certain kinds of music, as in some modern experimental liturgies, can unite a congregation into a collective pagan eroticism.

[42] *Psychology and Worship*, pp. 15-16.
[43] Loomis, *The Self in Pilgrimage* (New York: Harper & Bros., 1960), p. 87.
[44] *Treasure in Earthen Vessels* (New York: Harper & Row, 1961), p. 94.

Given such possibilities, one appreciates anew the Church's wisdom in laying down as the norm of worship the language of Holy Communion and in evaluating liturgy by its fidelity to this sacrament. This sacrament appeals to man's most primitive instincts—eating and drinking. Its central symbols —bread, cup, wine, cross—hold archetypal power.[45] Its central motif— dying and rising—engages the deepest substrata of man's being. Its union of the temporal and the eternal engages man's sense of time and of the timeless—as we shall note shortly. It involves all man's nature—the subconscious, the senses, feeling, memory, mind, will. Both its ground and its goal are man's oneness with his fellows—the overcoming of estrangement and a deep reconciliation. Yet, while its multi-medial appeal evokes corporateness with great power, it is always corporateness chastened with the health and salvation of the Word.

The Mystery of Liturgical Time

The perspective of psychology speaks next to one of the deepest mysteries and problems in worship: the mystery of time. We touch this mystery in understanding that clock time of itself cannot measure meaning in worship. We often say, for example, that a service should not last more than an hour or that the sermon should not be longer than the proverbial twenty minutes; yet we know that shorter services often seem long and longer services seem short. The explanation largely lies in factors which psychologically affect one's subjective experience of time.

For one thing, apparently each person has his own private time-perspective formed by numerous influences, including such factors as his sex, his body chemistry, his mental health or sickness bound up with his life history, his cultural milieu. Time apparently passes more rapidly for women and children than for men, when barometric pressure is high rather than low, the weather cold rather than warm. Likewise significant events in one's emotional history affect the perception of time and foster a predominantly future or past orientation. The stream of conscious and unconscious life of a past-oriented person, for example, is mainly filled with materials from old experiences. These materials, however, are not confined to the actual past events themselves but subconsciously comprise "a whole complex of facts, repression, rationalizations, promises for betterment, distortions, anticipations of punishment, and all kinds of coping maneuvers." [46] Further, a culture's feeling-tone for time, the power of symbolic time-structures bequeathed from its history, the reigning ethos with which it evaluates time

---

[45] The "grail" motif, for example, runs throughout cultural history.
[46] Pruyser, A Dynamic Psychology of Religion, p. 248.

—these also affect people's time perspective. The "Frontier" or "American Dream" motifs, for example, are held by some critics to foster a future orientation; and if true, one can understand in part people's disposition to conceive the Kingdom of God mainly as a future reality, or their difficulty in liturgically appropriating the existential, present-tense reality of the Divine —what theology calls "realized eschatology." On the other hand, the collapse of cultural norms with its accompanying anxiety such as western culture seems to be experiencing today can foster nostalgia for the past and impel people to want liturgy as a kind of backward-looking fundamentalism. Or cultural collapse and anxiety can kindle a kind of desperate hope and cause people to want liturgy as utopianism or apocalypticism. We see both all about us today.

Now these are only illustrations meant to sensitize the pastor. But clearly, such perceptions of time speak on a number of levels both to practical decisions about the language of worship and to the theological principles underlying them. For example, an act of absolution for the guilt of the past is obviously vital for past-oriented individuals—and we are all such, more or less—who need to be liberated toward the future. Or creeds which distortedly interpret the kingdom of God as a future reality which has never quite arrived and for whose coming one can only strive[47] must be questioned because they tend to deprive the worshipper of a present experience of divine life now. Or music which reduces the existential "now" of Christian salvation to only the *carpe diem* hedonism of much folk music currently popular in jazz liturgies, corrupts the "fulfilled time" (*kairos*) of the Gospel into only historical time (*chronos*). Or language which fails to keep pace with cultural change must be questioned insofar as it allows man to hanker after the past in order to escape the reality of the present and the summons of the future.

Most important of all, however, is the absence in man's subconscious of a sense of clock time. Hence the recapture in dreams of past events as if they were present realities, and hence prospective or forward-looking dreams in which future realities are prehended and contemporized. Time and space seem to be "creations of our consciousness, and are relative, and the unconscious does not work according to these concepts." [48] On the deepest level of the id, as Freud remarked, time literally is not of the essence of things.[49]

[47] See for example "Affirmation of Faith" Number 3, in the 1964 *Book of Worship* of The United Methodist Church.
[48] Fordham, *An Introduction to Jung's Psychology*, p. 104.
[49] See Norman O. Brown, *Life Against Death* (New York: Random House, Vintage Books, 1959), p. 93.

The Incarnational and Ontological Character of Worship
Psychologically Understood

The importance of this understanding of the unconscious for the claim of liturgical theology that worship is a present ontological experience of the Word in its divine-human and eternal-temporal nature, can hardly be overestimated. Precisely because the unconscious transcends time and because it experiences past, present, and future simultaneously, man's being is verified as that in which the numinous historical and trans-historical Presence of the Word can become Real. The truth of theology becomes corroborated: worship as encounter with the Word takes place in more than chronological time, and in experiencing both the "once-for-allness" and the "ongoingness" of the Word through memory and faith, man can live in time and yet conquer time.[50] But in this encounter, future realities as they are prehended by acts of eschatological hope and expectation, similarly can become present. Still further, it also becomes clear how the very ontological Life of the Word can be appropriated. Precisely because man's libidinal vitalities are so decisive a part of his very being, here if anywhere the Life of the Word can be expected to engage man's life. And lastly, the saving action of the Word we have spoken of as its soteriological character can take place here in the transformation and redirection of man's primal energies. In short, when out of the depths of his nature the worshipper closes with the depths of the Word, incarnation in its dialectical aspect of time and eternity can come to pass.

Yet, all this is only possibility. For it to come to pass, the right agents of transformation, i.e. language, are necessary. And it is at this point of fusion of psychological and theological truth that certain principles governing liturgical language emerge as crucial. For one thing, it becomes clear that language must be archetypally Christian. Forms organic to the gospel in the Church's life and worship from the beginning cannot be forfeited if access to the realm of reality in Jesus Christ is to be maintained. Bernard Häring has aptly described this language as consisting of "proto-symbols" possessing irreversible meaning which seem as if by divine intent to be fixed in, or addressed to, man's most primitive nature.[51] Or language may be thought of—to borrow a technical phrase of Mircea Eliade—as "dominant recurring hierophanies," that is, as revelatory forms of superior rank and generic power able to signify a unique thing or group of things over against others. However it be described, only Christian language can bring to pass

---

[50] See ch. II.

[51] See *This Time of Salvation*, trans. Arlene Swidler (New York: Herder & Herder, 1966), p. 142.

Christian worship. Its archetypal meanings must be accepted on their own terms. The Word cannot be wrenched from the context of myths which convey its primitive, generic power—creation, covenant, exodus, servant, conflict, devil, crucifixion, resurrection, ascension, pentecost, parousia, water, bread, wine, the new song, the new city. These are not just "decorative, literary or free-floating" language one can elect or not, Amos Wilder has remarked. While its affinity with worldwide myth and folklore is obvious, it embodies vital "either-or" forms on whose presence hangs the meaning of the Gospel as Christian Gospel. Such language constitutes "the shape of the liturgy" in the profoundest sense. The language of this shape must be recast in accents appropriate to each generation, to be sure; but its Christian character must be preserved if the transactions of worship are to be informed with Christian integrity.

Especially today, when man's obsession with his exterior world has drained off his libidinal energy and when his subconscious life has been so corrupted by trivial or rapacious images, the great visceral language of the Gospel must be liturgically spoken. To paraphrase a passage of Abraham Heschel quoted by Richard Neuhaus in a memorable article entitled "Liturgy and the Politics of the Kingdom": We do not realize how much we acquire from the treasures of liturgy until we learn how to commune with the spirit of the Divine through the mythic forms which the Divine Word itself has addressed to us. The heart does better to echo the music of the New Song already sung than to play upon the broken flutes of its own devising. In short, our beliefs and our passions do not finally carry our language; our language carries our beliefs and our passions.[52] And only when language archetypally Christian informs our beliefs and our passions is liturgy possessed with Christian integrity.

A second principle which psychology and theology join in affirming is that language must be both secular and numinous if the Word is to be encountered in its full meaning. On the one hand, language which tries to wipe clean the slate of man's inward life absorbed from his age—as we shall explore in the following essay—is doomed to fail. Yet language which vests encounter only in forms deposited in his being by his age equally violates the depths of his nature. Here again liturgy must speak bilingually: on the one hand, in Egyptian or Babylonian or whatever the idiom of man's culture and time may be, and on the other in the language of Canaan.[53] The metaphor of the American Dream, for example, of which we were critical because

---

[52] *Christian Century*, Dec. 20, 1967.
[53] See Karl Barth, *Evangelical Theology*, trans. G. Foley (New York: Holt, Rinehart & Winston, 1963), pp. 182-83.

of its power to corrupt liturgical time, may need to be reconsidered precisely because it is a symbol at once numinous and secular. One must ask:

Granted all its romantic eschatology and eudaemonism and its secularized version of the Old Testament story of theocratic vocation, its march toward the Promised Land and world-mission—does this social idealism and its vital semantic have to be totally rebuked? . . . However misconstrued the components of the American Dream may be, if we wish to harness what remains of healthfulness in the vitalities of our people we should not scorn or neglect the available Christian past that still operates in such forms. . . . As the early Church wrestled with but exploited the socio-cultural myths of its world, so should we today. The American Dream and its saga and mythos represent a vast reservoir of at least moral if not Christian potentiality. Appeal to it by a poet like Benet or a statesman like Woodrow Wilson suggests its relevance, though the dangers are evidently great. Our society being what it is, no theological or religious revival will be widely significant, that does not speak to this aspect of American religious life, and not only in terms of repudiation.[54]

Our citing of this statement must not be taken to mean that liturgical renewal must embody the particular symbol of the American Dream. We would hold that the dangers are indeed too great. But it is to suggest that such language, when thus bearing numinous biblical meaning if only vestigially, and when thus embedded subconsciously in the secular life of a people, must be reckoned with. Who is to say that such language cannot be baptized with the Spirit of the Word?

A better example of numinous language that yet speaks with secular power might be the vision of the new creation in the apocalypse of St. John, with its dialectic of the beast and the Lamb, of lamentation and doxology, of cosmic struggle and cosmic victory, of the great harlot and the spotless Bride, of the bottomless pit and the New Jerusalem. Such archetypal language possesses immense paschal and soteriological power. For one thing, it saves man from illusions begotten by images "limited to shepherds peacefully keeping their flocks by night and a placid face of Jesus tacked to church school bulletin boards," [55] and truthfully identifies the devils man experiences in his own world and being. Its picture of reality matches secular reality as he consciously and subconsciously knows it. It squares with the images of race riots, atomic explosions, and psychopathic murders which daily leap at his psychic life, and leaves him in no doubt about the principalities and powers that threaten and destroy. At the same time, such lan-

---

[54] Amos N. Wilder, "Social Symbol and the Communication of the Gospel," *Christianity and Crisis*, Dec. 12, 1960.

[55] Guilford Dudley, III, *The Recovery of Christian Myth* (Philadelphia: Westminster Press, 1967), p. 36. I am indebted to chs. 2 and 3 in Dudley's book for much of the thought of this paragraph.

guage sets these within a cosmic vision and unifies man's experience of evil *and* good, of struggle *and* hope, of death *and* life. It literally and figuratively "sym-bolizes" reality; that is, it "throws" reality "together." Such archetypal language—in a phrase of Jung—provides man with "a myth commensurate with his age" at the same time that it enables the Word numinously to judge and to save.

Thirdly, liturgical language viewed in relation to man's subconscious life must be mystical in the sense that it enable him to transcend the world of space and time and be nurtured in his inmost life by the eternal Life of the Word. The unconscious, it must be remembered, transcends time. It also does not have its sovereign attachment to realities outside man; rather, it implacably turns man inward to deal with his own soul. Further, the unconscious is not a repository of only evil. It is also a realm of aspirations, dreams, and ideals which await as if in a prenatal state that agent which can bring them to birth. To be sure, how these aspirations are brought to life is clothed with mystery: "The vitalities and energies of the imagination do not operate at will; they are fountains, not machinery." [56] Yet the language of worship is to cause the fountains to gush forth. The promise of the Word is just that "whoever drinks of the water that I shall give him shall find in himself wells of water springing up unto everlasting life." The Life of the Word ever reaches out ontologically to man's primal life. Deep calleth unto deep. And in the possibility of their communion through the transforming agency of liturgical language, we touch once more that "absolute hinge" of which we have spoken on which liturgical theology is to turn. It is exactly here, where the Life of the Word is enabled to grasp man's subconscious life, that we understand anew the meaning of liturgical integrity.[57]

[56] From D. G. James's *Skepticism and Poetry*, quoted by Langer, *Philosophy in a New Key*, p. 26.

[57] Any minister to whom a parishioner has said after a service of preaching, "My, you certainly hit me between the eyes this morning," or "You put into words just what I've been thinking," or even "Thank you for the inspiring service," has probably touched this reality. Always of course, such remarks must be taken with realism, but fountains of some kind have probably been released. Especially, appreciation of the element of "feeding" in worship often appears in such remarks. When pinned down, the worshipper often cannot recall with definiteness what the minister said. He only knows that the depths of his nature have somehow been nurtured, somewhat in the way he knows his physical health has been nourished although he cannot recall what he had for lunch last Friday. Spiritually, as well as physically as in Holy Communion, man's need to consume and be fed has somehow been satisfied. Probably this need is subconsciously related to the gustatory experiences that lie at the very beginning of human life. The lasting importance of oral desires and gratifications is a fact for liturgy as for all else. See Pruyser, *A Dynamic Psychology of Religion*, p. 39; Howard J. Clinebell, Jr., *Mental Health through Christian Community* (Nashville: Abingdon Press, 1965), ch. III, "The Worship Service and Mental Health"; Lee, *Psychology and Worship*, ch. VI, "The Holy Communion."

This principle, we may add as we conclude this essay, especially speaks to liturgy today when mystical language is widely suspect if not scorned. The crisis of worship can only be solved, we are widely told, if we stop looking in a rearview mirror, forswear the mystical, transform language into rational prose, and turn man's vision from heaven to earth. But the perspective of psychology does not allow one to dismiss mystical language so facilely, because man's psychic nature as the Word deals with it is violated too deeply. Probably man's inward being has never before been so impoverished as it is today by the expenditure of his libidinal energies upon his outward physical and social world—the conquest of nature, the exploration of space, the challenge of economic and social problems in every realm. Indeed, the eruption of his primal vitalities in the upheavals of our time probably constitutes a vast psycho-historical cycle we shall have to live through for a long while to come; and it is touch and go whether the human race will be able to survive this psychic explosion without a compensating implosion. Only as there is somehow a change from outflow to inflow, some reversal of energies of the kind and magnitude which Christian worship in its mystical meaning proposes—a redirection of libidinal energies whereby man's inward life is restored with divine life in the midst of his historical life—can catastrophe be avoided. Thus Jung has written that the objective of all great religions is contained in the injunction, "Be ye not of this world." This injunction, he continues,

suggests the inward subjective movement of the libido into the unconscious. The general withdrawing of the libido creates an unconscious libido-concentration which is symbolized as a "treasure," as in the Parables of the "costly pearl" and the "treasure in the field." . . . "This field is the soul—wherein the treasure of the Kingdom of God lieth hidden" . . . a constant unity of reconciliation with God. . . . The libido concentrated in the unconscious comes from objects, from the world, whose former ascendancy it conditioned. God was then "without," whereas now He works from "within," as that hidden treasure which is conceived as "God's Kingdom." [58]

One must not be put off by Jung's technical language nor by such terms as "not of this world," "inward," "withdrawing," "hidden," "within," in this passage. Such semantic is only a way of saying that in all the rhythms of man's existence, in his outward and inward history, his war and his peace, his voyages to the stars and his analyses of his own soul, his things and his values, his labor and his sleep, his going out and his coming in—in all these is implacably set the question of his life with God. For man's soul, truly, the

[58] *Psychological Types*, pp. 309-10, quoted by Hanna, *The Face of the Deep*, pp. 129-30.

Kingdom is ever at hand. And the life of this Kingdom, which has come, comes now, and shall come, is that which the language of Christian liturgy is ever called mystically to re-present:

A worshipper at First Church in Bleak Flat, Iowa, repeats the Creed or the Te Deum. . . . He boldly asserts the presence of "Cherubim and Seraphim and all the hosts of heaven." . . . Unquestionably, he has never once encountered a cherub or a seraph, and he would flee if he did. . . . Yet the very essence of his experience on Sunday may well be a shared dream of vast cosmologies—a dream which best has power to heal. He thinks he wants an antiseptic, demythologizing of age-old imagery, to see the universe "as it is" clear as televised craters on the moon. Yet it is role, script, vast scenario which he needs. . . . Liturgy at its best is our moving, head held high or bowed low, into the mysterious drama of what God does, now. . . . We want fact but need fancy, . . . cherubim and seraphim and all the host of heaven, with sacraments and the Presence.[59]

[59] John Oliver Nelson, *Kirkridge Contour* (Oct., 1964).

247

VI

The Language of Worship
Part 2: The Perspectives of Culture and Art

To understand the cultural character of liturgical language and to incorporate it with theological integrity into the Church's worship is probably as formidable a task as the minister faces. Indeed, his task may be likened to that of Michelangelo, of whom it was said that he could not work with Carrara marble until he had first wrestled with Florentine humanity. Only by wrestling with twentieth-century humanity—urban and rural, western and eastern, black and white, educated and uneducated, young and old as the case may be—can one win through to skill in handling liturgical forms. Even more must one wrestle with influences making humanity what it is. The valence of language in liturgy as elsewhere is conditioned by man's experience of culture and the vitalities at work in it; and because culture is always changing, man's language must change. The flux of history embeds him, and correspondingly his language is in flux. Since 1934, when the second edition of *Webster's New International Dictionary* was issued, over half the words then included have dropped from common use and over one hundred thousand new words have appeared.[1] But as with man's spoken and written words, so with the whole range of his liturgical words. Forms become obsolete, meanings become displaced, subjects and predicates trade places, nouns become verbs, new terms come into being.

The all-seeing eye once suggesting God—someone has said—is now the television eye of Big Brother. The fleur-de-lis once symbolizing the Cross now suggests the Boy Scouts. Theological concepts such as "judgement" and "reconciliation" now are associated with law courts; "covenant" with real estate contracts; "election" with politics; and "conversion" with an insurance policy, a heating system, or a touchdown![2] More profoundly, basic thought-forms, indeed even certain religious archetypes, seem to have changed. Of

[1] Noted by David G. Buttrick, "Renewal of Worship—A Source of Unity?" in *Ecumenism, the Spirit and Worship*, ed. Leonard Swidler (Pittsburgh: Duquesne University Press, 1967), p. 233.

[2] For an incisive and witty treatment of the displacement of liturgical meanings, see the article by Seward Hiltner, "Iona in New Jersey," *Theology Today*, XXII (Apr., 1965).

248

man's flights into space, Paul Goodman said: "These are now our Cathedrals." Laboratories have becomes "shrines." Science performs "miracles." Electronic antennae, not angels' voices, hymn "the music of the spheres." Given such a "new firmament of symbol," one is not surprised that a scientist should dismiss today's liturgical language as "old-fashioned concepts of a misunderstood reality"; that a theologian should bewail the myopia which clings to liturgical forms as if in a void where Christendom no longer exists; or that a churchman should warn of a new Dark Age from which the Church must rescue us by repristinating forms to open our eyes once more to things eternal and unseen. Change as such, however, is no more to be feared than welcomed by liturgy. It is simply a given reality to be lived with as openly as a man changes his speech as he grows more mature, or as naturally as he learns a new language when travelling to a country other than his own.

CULTURAL INFLUENCES AFFECTING LITURGICAL LANGUAGE

It is the deeper forces in our culture, then, making man what he is and his perceptions what they are, that the liturgist must heed. One such influence is population mobility and social and vocational mobility. Unstable attachments to social groupings deprive the worshipper of nurturing face-to-face relationships which normally free one to give himself to another. For example, the coherence and supportiveness of social life experienced by the early Baptists and Methodists which carried over into their worship and made it vital and free is less real in our mobile culture. And tenuousness of social attachments inhibits the worshipper from loosing the restraints he normally uses to preserve psychological and social distance—hence the aloofness and apathy which so beset worship today. Further, the tastes of people moving up the social and economic ladder tend to become formalized—hence the emphasis upon orderliness and the absence of exuberance so marked in middle-class congregations. Again, the more socially advantaged worshipper is usually the better educated worshipper. Until recently at least, education has bred what we may call a "scientistic—as distinguished from a "scientific" —temper of mind which popularly supposes that to be truly educated is to be critical rather than appreciative, reflective rather than committed. Conditioned by this ethos, many a churchgoer approaches worship as an observer and looks on it as an experience in which his intellect is to be convinced, the sermon as more important than sacrament, and the God whom he encounters to be acknowledged as truth rather than as grace he is to close with or life he is to partake of. Now how far the rational function of language, to which we have already referred, should resist or appeal to this temper is a moot question. But while always essential, cognitive language can be disabling when it too neatly complies with the worshipper's pride in his own rationality.

Another influence making humanity what it is consists of the urban and technological environment in which most of us live. Seventy percent of the American people now live on 1 percent of the land, i.e., in the city; by 1980 we can expect at least 72 percent to live in metropolitan areas. Twentieth-century man is predominantly "technopolitan man," in Harvey Cox's well-known phrase, and his cultural life-style is a fusion of political, social, and technological components coming to focus in the city whose influences irradiate to shape his perceptions regardless of where he lives geographically.[3] Similarly, technology—the organization of knowledge for practical purposes—has so focused man's consciousness on realities of matter and time and on their practical function in his everyday world that his very dictionary and vocabulary, his thought-forms and his mental processes, have been profoundly materialized. The table of chemical elements is more real for many a worshipper today than his church's creeds. He reads *Time* more congenially than he thinks about eternity. He locates a stock quotation in the newspaper more confidently than he turns to the Epistle to the Ephesians, and he charts the orbit of a satellite more reliably than the biblical scheme of salvation.

The emergence of what has been called "Electronic Man" in our "communications era" and its import for what certain churchmen have called "the crisis of worship" particularly illustrates the impact of technology upon language. Historically, we are told, communications have developed from preliterate through literate stages to our present postliterate stage, in which typographic communication of meaning through the written or spoken word has given place to communication through multiple means, especially visual media: "Telstar casts a long shadow on typographic man. To be sure, it will not eclipse him; but it will raise up another type, 'electronic man,' whose perceptive field will be more open and less specialized."[4] It remains to be seen whether our postliterate stage is as much "post" as our prophets declare and whether on this account the crisis of worship is as "critical" as alleged. Already man seems to be as much surfeited with pictures as with words; our prophets still wish to place their dicta in print; and presumably people still use words to pray! Even so, four aspects of electronic communications affecting liturgical language need to be identified. Meaning is immediately if not instantaneously communicated rather than sequentially. The ratio of man's senses involved is larger and his involvement is correspondingly more total. Man is grasped on the depth rather than on the discursive levels of his

---

[3] *The Secular City* (New York: The Macmillan Co., 1965), p. 5.
[4] Neil P. Hurley, S.J., "Telstar, Electronic Man, and Liturgy," *Worship*, XXXIX (June, 1965).

consciousness. And a communal kind of experience—even described as "tribal"—is fostered in contrast to individualistic experience fostered by the static printed symbol.

Clearly, many things have happened since 1900 and—in the phrase of one observer—"most of them plug into walls." [5] If we may pursue the metaphor, one must ask whether liturgy has sufficiently "plugged into" the things that plug into walls. Conventional liturgy still moves programmatically, according to an "order" or "shape" as over against communications' swift simultaneity. The restfulness that belongs to the house of God contrasts strangely with the bite of television's terse "profile," its hard-hitting one-minute commercial, its tense five-minute dimension or news summary. In much Protestant worship "faith" still comes predominantly "by hearing" whereas communications media reach for all man's senses. While liturgy would rather speak five words with the mind than ten thousand words in ecstasy, impression and symbol rather than logic and argument reach for the depths of the contemporary psyche. The *pro me* of faith, even in the corporateness of worship, stands over against the tribalism of electronic collectivities.[6] To be sure, these contrasts can be overstated, as to a degree we exaggerate them for illustration, but they are real.

Two further elements in man's *Lebenswelt* may be cited here, although they partly anticipate the most massive influence of all, secularization, we shall consider shortly: the sheer dynamism of our culture and the pragmatism accompanying it. By "dynamism" we mean not so much man's outward activity as the restlessness of his mind and spirit, the thrust of his attention forward, the change in his values from static *a prioris* to openness, and the displacement in his thinking of categories of substance by categories of process. Man today has been aptly described as *homo perturbatus*—man perturbed, experimenting in all directions,[7] goal-oriented with his eyes to the future, seeing himself not so much as a person who has arrived as a person on the way. As pragmatic man, "questioning has become the piety of his thinking." [8] He sees the world not as a unified metaphysical system but as "a series of problems and projects," in a phrase of Cox. He is more interested in asking how things can be brought to be than in affirming what already is.

---

[5] It is estimated that today's six-year-old child has spent 3,000 to 4,000 hours watching television before he enters first grade—more hours of instruction than he will receive from college professors while earning a bachelor's degree. And by the time he graduates from high school he has clocked 15,000 hours of television time compared with 10,800 hours of school time.

[6] The phrase is Karl Barth's. See ch. I.

[7] See J. C. Hoekendijk, "Discussion: Technology, Theology and the Christian Faith," *Union Seminary Quarterly Review*, XXI (May, 1966).

[8] *Ibid.*

"Ortho-praxy" has replaced "ortho-doxy" as the slogan of his mentality: the right response to reality is to use it rather than to reverence it. In short, *homo sapiens* has become *homo perturbatus; homo orans* has become *homo faber*. The implications for liturgy of this reading of man's nature are profound, as a scientist suggests:

The generation of knowledge and the use of technology are so much a part of the style and self-image of our own society that men begin to experience themselves, their power and their relationships to nature and history in terms of open possibility, hope, action. . . . The symbolism of such traditional religious postures as subservience, fatefulness, destiny and supra-rational faith begin then to seem irrelevant to our actual experience. They lose credibility.[9]

Secularization

But the foremost influence making humanity what it is—implicit throughout our discussion—is the secularization of man's experience and selfhood: the profound "breach" in the "feeling-tone" of our generation whereby we have moved away from inherited meanings and values bearing religious sanction, to attention to ourselves, our world, and our own time.[10] The term "secularization," we know, derives from the Latin *saeculum*, meaning "generation" or "age." Popularly defined, it is the progressive emancipation of human life from religious and metaphysical control, the "loosing of the world from religious and quasi-religious understandings of itself, the dispelling of all closed world-views, the breaking of all supernatural myths and sacred symbols. . . . Secularization is man turning his attention away from worlds beyond and toward this world and this time. . . . It is what Dietrich Bonhoeffer in 1944 called 'man's coming of age.' "[11]

Generally speaking, Christian thought has welcomed secularization at the same time that it has taken care to distinguish between *secularization* as a historical process and *secularism* as a philosophy of life which, over against religious faith, seeks to organize man's life as if God did not exist. The former has been hailed as an expression of God's action in history liberating man to come of age, as an affirmation of the worldly and the human which Christendom in its otherworldly epochs has denied, and as a recovery of authentic insight into the nature of God as a secular God who is immanently involved in man's historical life. In these respects secularization has indeed challenged the Church to let her mind be searched by meanings of the Gospel which she had not realized before were so centrally there—meanings

---

[9] E. G. Mesthene, *The New York Times*, Jan. 18, 1969.
[10] See Bernard E. Meland, *The Secularization of Modern Cultures* (New York: Oxford University Press, 1966), pp. 3, 10.
[11] Cox, *The Secular City*, p. 2.

which, if appropriated, can enable the Church to address and to be addressed truthfully by the age.

A Warning Against the Danger of Secularism

However, before we explore these meanings more fully we should acknowledge a bias and raise what we hold to be a warning. One must ask whether Christian thought has not shown more ingenuity than wisdom in staking so much on the semantic distinction between "secularization" and "secularism," and whether the New Testament Gospel really permits the Church to accept the gospel of secularization so eagerly. Actually, man's experience of secularity does not conform to distinctions of semantics as neatly as people assume; and the built-in momentum of secularization in its practical effect becomes a secularism striking more destructively upon man's consciousness than the Church cares to admit. It is all very well—in the words of one interpreter— to hail secularization as a historical process, "a mature this-worldliness that seizes from religion the responsibility for making life livable," and then to explain that "secularism is to secularization as a product is to a process, . . . the transformation of a secular sensitivity into a dogma that declares itself to be an exhaustive and closed reading of the human situation." [12] The fact is, however, that the process becomes the product more easily and terribly than the apostles of Bonhoeffer seem to understand.

A book review by Robert Jay Lifton, professor of psychiatry at Yale University, entitled "The Bomb as an Object of Worship," may put our warning for us. Nuclear technology with its unimaginable power would seem to epitomize better than almost anything else the mature this-worldliness with which secularized man seizes from religion the responsibility for making life livable. But what secularization *really* does to man's consciousness is classically seen in a man such as the physicist J. Robert Oppenheimer, in whose personality a tragic fusion took place between his very being and the nuclear power he helped bring into existence. The context for understanding Oppenheimer, Lifton writes, is really a theological context—that of a new attitude toward transcendence that has come to pass, a living by "nuclear grace" that is a pseudo-religion, indeed the worship of destructive power. He continues:

We bring to the Bomb . . . attitudes characteristic of those held toward *a deity*. Awed by its destructive power, we feel insignificant in relation to it and view it as *capable of unlimited creation* as well. We then disqualify ourselves from raising questions about its . . . *absolute authority*, and in fact come to depend

[12] Gabriel Fackre, *Humiliation and Celebration* (New York: Sheed & Ward, 1969), p. 22.

upon it for periodic *miracles* and everyday sustenance. *This pseudo-religion*—let us call it nuclearism—is ubiquitous. . . . Given man's exposure for the first time to an *apocalyptic* device of his own making, together with his strong impulse toward *transcendence*, . . . it seems that the yearning for nuclear *grace* is universal. . . . We are obsessed with the life and deeds of J. Robert Oppenheimer because we sense he has something to reveal to use about *our spiritual vulnerability.* . . . I believe that Oppenheimer shared and even exemplified our nuclear disorder, and was then *crucified* by true *believers* terrified and enraged at having their *deity* questioned. While he was immersed in nuclearism, he was made a hero; and when he began describing a vision beyond nuclearism, he became a dishonored *heretic.* . . . Perhaps Oppenheimer . . . came to view *the bomb as our savior,* as a force that "would shake mankind free from parochialism and war." Perhaps that illustration was necessary to a man in his position. In any case *a tragic fusion* took place between Oppenheimer and the instrument he so heroically and selflessly guided into existence, a fusion that became profoundly unsettling to him. . . . When he said that physicists had known *sin,* I suspect he was referring not only to the external evil of Hiroshima but to this internal man-bomb fusion—to physicists having lived in a state of nuclearism.[13]

One will note Lifton's language: it is the language not so much of ethics as of a theology of the demonic. Indeed it is almost a liturgical theology of the demonic. Verily, when secularization is allowed to cast out of man's consciousness the spirit of religion and its responsibility for making life livable, we should not be surprised to find it inhabited by seven deadlier spirits.

Thus in the current chapter of the Church's ongoing dialogue with culture, one feels that we may have conceded too much too soon and failed to see that secularization is not the unmixed blessing the Church so often claims. Is it straining things to say that the convenient distinction between "secularization" and "secularism" may in fact be a device the Church uses to avoid the discomfort of judging and of being judged by culture, and a blind for ignoring the fateful possibilities inherent in the emancipation of human life from a religious self-understanding? That it may be a theological defense mechanism to rationalize our fear of offending man by pronouncing his pride sin rather than virtue, of scandalizing him by naming God "God" as a Reality over against man as well as for him?[14] That it may be a

---

[13] From *The New York Times,* June 28, 1970. Italics mine. © 1970 by The New York Times Company. Reprinted by permission.

[14] Paul Tillich wrote of his decision to adhere to the use of "that aboriginal word, 'God'" as follows: "Going back through four decades . . . I remember the conference of Religious Socialists in Germany in the year 1924. Our movement . . . tried to heal the catastrophic split between the churches and labor in most European countries. It was my task to elaborate adequate concepts from the theological, philosophical and sociological sides. This meant that I had to replace traditional religious terms, including the word 'God,' with words which would be accepted by the religious humanists which belonged to our movement. After I had finished, Martin Buber arose and attacked what he called the

subconscious repression of the erosion of faith whereby we have lamely traded eternity for time? To be sure, from one point of view the ardor with which the Church has hailed secularization and the ingenuity with which it has sought correspondence between it and secular elements in its own Gospel can be interpreted as a wise discerning of divine signs in history's times. But from another point of view one feels it as a syndrome of theological insecurity, the Church's way of saying—unconsciously perhaps—that she does not really know her own mind, that she trembles to put forth her will, and that she does not wish to bear the anguish of living out the *full* dialectic of her being: to refuse to be of the world even as she is in the world.

One reason leading us to raise this warning is the difficulty secular theologians find in correlating secularization and liturgy. It is revealing that the Church has best come to terms with secularization in such areas as social ethics or the relation of Christianity to technology and the arts, and that it has been rather less than successful in the realm of worship and prayer. The explanation is that the acid test of any theological view is always what it is able or not able to say about prayer, and how truthful of the Gospel its affirmations appear when transposed into worship. Here the nerve of faith is uniquely exposed. Here faith-commitments have to be unequivocally made and their implications existentially faced. And the difficulty experienced in correlating secularization with Christian worship suggests that when secular theologies are forced liturgically to declare themselves, faith is confounded by what they breed. The following statement typifies the ease with which secularization becomes liturgically collapsed into secularism:

The affirmation of the ultimate significance of human existence and denial of traditional concepts of transcendence necessarily imply that prayer must be rethought or dispensed with. . . . Prayer has no transcendent referent, nor does it provide access to any external powers. . . . [Nor can worship be conceived] . . . as the attribution of worth to a transhuman reality. . . . Worship, like prayer, would have a purely anthropocentric character—celebration and enjoyment of human existence in both its individual and corporate expressions. And piety would be an act by which man nurtures and celebrates human relationship. . . . The context would be the human dimension, and that alone." [15]

Such a prospect is not encouraging. It suggests that the affinity between the Gospel and secularization may not be as native as we have supposed,

---

'abstract facade' I had built. With great passion, he said that there are some aboriginal words like 'God,' which cannot be replaced at all. He was right and I learned the lesson." "Martin Buber—1878-1965," *Pastoral Psychology*, XVI (Sept., 1965).

[15] R. Kysar, "Toward a Christian Humanism," *The Christian Century*, May 21, 1969.

that the tension between them is more radical than we have pretended, and that the menace of secularism is more real than we have understood. Actually, an appraisal of the meaning of secularization for the liturgical life of the Church yields a mixture of both promise and peril, which we shall need to explore still further in the following essay.

Positive Meanings of Secularization for Liturgical Language

But with this warning, the positive meanings of secularization for liturgy and language must be gratefully appropriated. Man's feeling of liberation, for one thing, allows him as a creature come of age to cast away enforced "postures of subservience." He need not tiptoe so much in the presence of God any more; he can be himself and shout and sing and dance. Aware of his own powers and sensitive to divine vitalities at work in his world, he can respond with pleasure to it, press his muscles upon it, liturgically affirm and use it, and insist that its meanings be integrated with his prayer.

Again, because secularization has helped man better to understand authority, he can rightly question, even help shape the declarations which liturgical language inevitably makes. "Authority" for the secularized man, it has been said, "is not a given reality any longer but resides in relationships. . . . In order to be able to give authority to any conclusion or event, the recipient must have had some part in its establishment. . . . Experience of the truth is a *sine qua non* for acceptance of the truth." [16] The Church is the better for having had to come to terms—if reluctantly—with this redefinition of authority, and the worshipper is the more mature for having claimed it. Her creeds, therefore, he shall help rewrite. Her hymns he shall choose and compose. Her proclamation he shall both criticize and have part in.[17] Again, the pragmatism absorbed from his age can open him to try out new and venturesome forms of worship. To be sure, his attitudes here are often ambivalent, as we shall note shortly. Yet his quizzical inquiry into the "how" of things, the spirit of "play" [18] he brings to laboratory, classroom, and

[16] Albert H. van den Heuvel, *The Humiliation of the Church* (Philadelphia: Westminister Press, 1966), p. 82.

[17] The demand for verification operative in the secular "feedback principle" has been transposed into worship in such ways as after-church sermon seminars, congregational debates, dialogue preaching, lay participation in preparation of the sermon, new-member inquirer-groups, etc.

[18] This trait has been well described as follows: "Play is one of the most striking features of technology. Ask a man in basic research what he is doing and he is likely to say that he is 'playing around.' . . . Men 'tinker' with machines. . . . The game element in technology is liberating because it hints at something very human inside technology. . . . There is a peculiarly human excitement attendant not only upon a psychological discovery but also on a successful organization of a technological operation such as orbiting a man

factory, the attitude of sitting loose to things to see what may happen, of enterprise and quiet excitement—this can be fruitful for finding new liturgical wineskins. To be sure, one does not tinker with worship in an irresponsible way. But man is nothing if he is not—in Huizinga's phrase— *homo ludens*, a playing animal, and a liturgy is nothing if it is not sacred play. Until recently, many Protestants—especially white middle-class ones— could hardly be imagined thinking of worship in such terms; they had seemed alien. But as one observer has put it, now we have discovered that we're all a little jazzier than we thought we were; hence the possibility of conceiving new forms plastic to the "ortho-praxy" of our time. While we shall have to continue to argue that liturgy as "ortho-doxy"—"right praise"— must finally be sovereign for man's encounter with the Word, yet modern man is not going to stop being modern and his pragmatism must be taken seriously.

The affirmation of the world as good and of man's place in it as divinely meant to be good is probably the most important contribution of secularization to reflection upon liturgical language. To be sure, free-church worship hardly turned its attention away from this world as bad as much as some of the devotees of the new worldliness would have us believe. (One need only examine the hymnals of many free-church denominations, especially hymns of the Social Gospel going back to the early decades of the century, to be aware of this.) Nevertheless, the "mystique of a false otherworldliness" has corrupted much Protestant worship. "The deliberate cultivation of an otherworldly atmosphere," in the words of a perceptive critic, has made worship "too different from the rest of life." He continues:

At the heart of the false mystique about worship is a mistaken notion of things spiritual. We have forgotten that God is a worldly God and that the way to worship Him is not by escaping this world but by approaching it in the dimension of depth. . . . All that is depends upon God and is created good. . . . One does not meet God by escaping from time and space. . . . A Christian meets God within this world by coming to a deeper understanding of the nature of the world itself and what God is doing in it. . . . To be truly spiritual is to be truly worldly.[19]

One can hardly improve upon this as a positive statement of what secularization can teach the Church; and we need to explore its implications for liturgical language at some length. For example, the very place and time of worship—which are themselves a form of language—may need to be

---

around the world. Technology has to do with the exterior world, but it is a creation of the mysterious interior which is man himself." Walter J. Ong, S.J., "Ideas of Technology: Commentary," in *Technology and Culture* (Fall, 1962), pp. 561-62.

[19] James F. White, *The Worldliness of Worship* (New York: Oxford University Press, 1967), pp. 79, 81-82.

rethought. Cannot the living room or kitchen of a home—as in the "House Church" movement [20]—be appropriate for sermon and sacrament celebrating the presence of the Word in the world of family and neighborhood life? And cannot worship take place where people engage in sports together, camp outdoors together, share in artistic creation, study and work together, face social crises together? [21] The mobile and pluriform social groupings characterizing contemporary life require that the settings of worship likewise be mobile and pluriform if worship is to "flesh out" man's worldly experience.

Further, must the Church's main services of worship be confined to Sunday? The question is not as easy to answer as some people suppose because "The Lord's Day"—the Day of Resurrection eschatologically fulfilling the Jewish "Sabbath"—holds profound archetypal and theological meanings. In the early Church, we recall, Sunday as the day of the Eucharist was the source of the Christian man's existence. Moreover, while in one sense there are no holy times (and places) in Christian thought in that Christ's presence, whenever it meets man, is itself the Temple, yet biblical thought assigns profound significance to symbols of time; and to yield up the claim that "The Lord's Day" is to be kept normatively holy for worship in the Lord's name can diminish its power to punctuate all time as holy. As George M. Gibson has written: "There is an element of self-delusion in those who think they are more constant in their memorials if they neglect the anniversaries." [22] On the other hand, a secular chronology has displaced the Christian chronology as the temporal benchline of existence for millions of people. Industrialization with its patterns of shorter workweeks and longer weekends may simply require the congregation to worship at a time other than Sunday if there is to be any congregation at all. More importantly, the Church's willingness to make such a concession ungrudgingly can signify the Church's intention that its worship be worldly. Thus midweek worship in urban communities is increasing. In small-town and semi-rural communities, worship is held on Friday and Saturday nights when the people come to shop. Decisions as to the time of worship as a sign of integration with man's worldly life are particularly the kind of decision pastor and people should sensitively work out together.[23]

[20] See Ernest Southcott, *The House Church* (pamphlet); John A. T. Robinson, *On Being the Church in the World*; the publications of the Iona Community, Scotland; of the World Council of Churches. Much of the literature on groups in the church also speaks to this need.

[21] A participant in the march on Selma, Alabama, in 1965, described the experience as "the greatest worship experience of my life."

[22] *The Story of the Christian Year* (Nashville: Abingdon Press, 1945), p. 75.

[23] Jaroslav Pelikan has noted another creative attempt to bring the rhythm of liturgy into the tempo of everyday life, charmingly expressed in the title of a Roman Catholic

To overcome the mystique of a false otherworldliness especially requires a different genre of language cast in hymn and prayer and visual art appropriate to our urbanized culture and congruous with the everyday language men speak. Two examples may be cited. In a "Service of thanksgiving for Agriculture, Industry, and Commerce," conceived by the Rev. Michael Appleyard of Salisbury, Rhodesia, the following hymn by R. G. Jones was sung.

God of concrete, God of steel,
God of piston and of wheel,
God of pylon, God of steam,
God of girder and of beam,
God of atom, God of mine,
All the world of power is Thine!

Lord of cable, Lord of rail,
Lord of motorway and mail,
Lord of rocket, Lord of flight,
Lord of soaring satellite,
Lord of lightning's vivid line,
All the world of speed is Thine!

God of Turk and God of Greek
God of every tongue men speak,
God of Arab, God of Jew,
God of every racial hue,
God of Laos and Palestine,
All the world of men is Thine!

Lord of science, Lord of art,
Lord of map and graph and chart,
Lord of physics and research,
Lord of Bible, Faith of Church,
Lord of sequence and design,
All the world of truth is Thine!

God whose glory fills the earth,
Gave the universe its birth,
Loosed the Christ with Easter's might,
Saves the world from evil's blight,
Claims mankind by grace divine,
All the world of love is Thine! [24]

book: *Cooking for Christ: The Liturgical Year in the Kitchen* (published in 1949 by the National Catholic Rural Life Conference in Des Moines, Iowa). A collection of recipes drawing on the traditions of a dozen nationalities, the book describes certain foods invented for special Christian days and seasons.

David J. Randolph of the United States, sensitive to the world of sport which is so much a part of the consciousness of secular man today, especially of youth, has written the following prayer of petition entitled "A Surfer's Prayer." While more suitable for a distinctive gathering of youth than for conventional services, it yet suggests the kind of worldly sensitivity and imagination liturgy needs.

> God, we pray for surf.
> If it be your will
> Let the swells roll
> Over a sea of glass.
> Dark in the distance
> Let me see that ribbon of perfection,
> Signal of the big wave.
> Lord, let me catch this wave.
> You know I've paddled hard to get here,
> Waited long to find it.
> Help me judge it, Lord,
> Just right,
> Not too soon . . .
> Not too late . . .
>
> When it starts
> To drive me along
> Down the mountain of water
> Let me get up quickly
> Cutting neat
> And balancing trim
> Give it the power to take me all the way.
> Hearing the coming tear of the wave,
> Feeling the kick of the surf,
> My whole body throbbing with the thrill of it
> I am at my best:
> Clean, strong,
> Carried by *your* wave,
> This *is* where you want me,
> Isn't it, Lord?
>
> But Lord, if the surf is down
> Help me to be up anyway,
> Not tempted to trade an ocean of love
> For a puddle of lust.
> Not exchanging the long ride of life
> For the quick and easy lift of drugs.
> Don't let me misjudge the big wave of life and
> Be carried along to the second best.
> Help me to help others,
> To keep my eyes open and my board under control,

To watch out for bathers. . . .
When it is time for me to leave the water,
To go home, or to school
Or maybe to war,
Help me to go responsibly
And with dignity.
God, don't let me wipe out
In the muddy waters of selfishness
But keep me honest and clean
Until that day comes
When I may hang ten
In the kingdom of heaven,
Through Christ our Lord, Amen.[25]

After all, we need to remember that Jesus spoke in popular Aramaic, not in Hebrew; that St. Paul used *koine*—popular, not classical, Greek; that St. Francis and Dante wrote not in Latin but in Tuscan vernacular; and that in New Testament worship the ordinary guitar was probably the main musical instrument. (The word "guitar" derives from the Greek *kithara*, a harp or lyre usually with six strings. It is referred to in I Cor. 14:7; Rev. 5:8; 14:2; 15:2.)

Similarly, architecture and interior decoration as liturgical language must also in one way or another declare the worldliness of worship. To be sure, they must also numinously declare something more, as we shall make clear presently; plywood and plastic tile can hardly be said to be very numinous although they are most certainly worldly! Yet, if architecture is always to be evangelical in the sense that it is to state for human life the meaning of God revealed in Christ, architecture cannot abstract this meaning from man's everyday world; meaning must be stated relationally because the God of Christian faith is always God in relation to his world. Therefore a proper architectural language, in the judgement of one critic,

will assert that God's life among men is merged with their life as a human society. The implication is that our church buildings must not be exotic, heavenly, and unworldly places, but that instead they should be forthright, reasonable, earthy places, no more lavish than our houses and schools . . . and our other community gathering places. Indeed, it is important that of all places the church should have the character of earthiness, reality, and humility.[26]

Thus, it has been suggested, worship areas should be designed with dimensions of a basketball court so that they can be used for play, or in the

[25] From *Ventures in Worship*, edited by David James Randolph, pp. 39-40. Copyright © 1969 by Abingdon Press.
[26] Edward A. Sövik, "Images of the Church," *Worship*, XLI (Mar., 1967).

manner of a Japanese tearoom in which conversation and informal human relationships can be facilitated. Indeed some critics go even farther in carrying this conception to what they feel to be its logical conclusion: construct no church building at all. If God is essentially a worldly God and if the Church is essentially mission, then ministry should be conducted without erecting any special building. Trailer units, storefronts, high-rise apartments will do.

In any case, the world with which God is in relation is this world of the latter third of the twentieth century, not the world of Catholic France in the 1300's nor of Puritan New England in the 1800's nor of Anglican Britain in the 1800's nor of free-church America in the early 1900's. The language of Gothic, Puritan, neo-Gothic, and American Akron architecture may have been authentic in its time, but the language of today is that of reinforced concrete, steel, contoured surfaces, simplicity of line, and honesty of fabric. This does not mean that a church building is to imitate the local telephone company or consent to be a chummy ranch house with a neon spire on top. The banal language of certain "modern" churches or the strained language of certain "far out" experiments probably seems as spurious to the contemporary man as the archaic language of earlier epochs. Yet, if worship is to have integrity, architecture must somehow reach out and gather the world into man's worship instead of gathering him out of the world. There is such a thing as "The Architecture of Kerygma," [27] and one must never forget that the Christian *kerygma* is a very worldly *kerygma* indeed.

Some Guiding Principles

Given this brushstroke analysis of secularization and its implications for language, how shall the minister proceed? In part, by using his common sense and taste. "Technopolis" is a universal cultural style, we have said? Dynamically, yes; practically, no. A culture contains subcultures, and it does not develop at a uniform rate into a single sensibility and style. Hence decisions as to liturgical language will discriminate. "The Lord's My Shepherd" is still a more meaningful hymn to a Vermont farmer than "God of Concrete, God of Steel"; and language appropriate for Greenwich Village probably will not appeal in Little Rock, Arkansas. Knowing "the street address" of one's congregation is still important. Of course this does not mean that one fights a holding action against history; but it does mean that there are cultures in which language is properly conservative and properly contemporary, and common sense is to mark the difference. Similarly the factor of "liturgical spread" must be in one's thinking. Given the

[27] The title of a fertile essay by Edward A. Sövik in *Worship*, XL (Apr., 1966).

varieties of age, taste, and cultural conditioning in congregations, why should not Protestantism devise the equivalent of Roman Catholic "devotions," different services in different idioms at different times? One simply makes calculated judgements here, but always cooperatively with one's people.

Further, taste applies, although with proverbial difficulty. Shall one advertise the encounter with Jesus Christ in his Passion as a "bash" as one congregation mistakenly did on Palm Sunday? This, one feels, is the Church overreacting with secular slang, somewhat like the adolescent who manfully swears in public to conceal the insecurities he feels in private. On the other hand, certainly taste in liturgical language is not to be equated with propriety, even with dignity. The disciples dipped bread in the same dish with our Lord at the Last Supper, we are told; St. Paul, while critical, did not forbid the Corinthians their unseemly ecstasy; and if one has to choose, Pentecost is probably better described as a "bash" than as a solemnity. Considerations of psychology also join with considerations of culture in the matter of taste. As a mild example, the four-letter word "hell" combines psychological, cultural, and theological meanings. Dropped from the creeds of certain denominations as theologically questionable and historically dubious, the phrase "He descended into hell," [28] can yet speak in liturgy with exorcising power. We have previously referred to the scholar who confessed that for him this formula sets forth Christ as the Saviour who descends into the dark depths of man's passions, draws them unto himself, and cleanses and redeems them.[29] A true taste requires from liturgy a certain violence on occasion, a certain disinhibition as well as decorum.

The Minister's Theological Stance: The Affirmation and the Negation of Culture

Far more important than these, however, is one's theological stance. The "holy anxiety" we have enjoined, that the nature of the Gospel shall determine the nature of worship is still the only safe if precarious way to proceed. If the context of culture poses the most formidable challenge the pastor faces, it does so because it engages him exactly at the point of his greatest sensitivity—the point of theological integrity. But his anxiety must be expected to be still further heightened because of the dialectical meaning of the Word in whose light integrity in turn is defined. Because the Word whose incarnation as historical reality requires man to live a historical existence and to worship as a man of his *saeculum*, the pastor will say "yes" to the claim of culture. Because the Word as divine Reality transcending history summons man to worship as a person meant for an eternal

---

[28] A late addition to the Apostles' Creed dating from the fifth century.
[29] D. H. Hislop.

life beyond time, the pastor will say "no" to culture. "There can be no simple affirmation of the world which does not at the same time require its negation," it has been finely said;[30] and this is exactly the Christological boundary stance the pastor will take up.

A more homely way to describe this stance is to emply the dialectic of an earlier essay and say that the pastor will take risks of both relevance and irrelevance in using liturgical language; and he will not commit theological overkill in either direction.[31] Risks of relevance must be taken on the one hand, not only because man's language changes with the flux of history. More importantly, the Word as historical event has once and for all historicized liturgy and thereby requires us to update liturgical language to correspond to the reality of man's cultural situation. In the words of the theologian Charles Davis, the Word has determined the Christian life to be not "a timeless relation with God"[32] but conditioned by time. Further, the Holy Spirit as the Word present in the here and now of time is at work and is simply to be trusted and invoked. Further, the Church herself lives in perpetual exodus, and her very nature as defined by Word and Spirit summons liturgy to move into newness. Indeed, in the last analysis, our striving to make language relevant is the way in which the Church is to act out her own eschatological cry, *Donec veniat*, "Behold him who comes," and her liturgical prayer, *maranatha*, "Come, Lord." In this deeper sense the effort to update liturgical language with relevance is itself an act of eschatological trust and hope. In a pungent phrase which Jürgen Moltmann applies to Baptism, liturgy is to be "ahead of itself."[33]

It must not be expected that updating language to make it relevant will come easily in most congregations. A baffling ambivalence will probably be met, and some of the psychological and social factors we have referred to must be borne in mind. Man's pragmatism may dispose him to search

[30] Roger Hazelton, *Christ and Ourselves* (New York: Harper & Row, 1965), p. 133.

[31] In doing so, parenthetically, he does well to remember that liturgical language develops sociologically, that it follows certain stages of evolution; and as he makes theological decisions he will try to stand off and objectively locate himself in this process. There seems first to occur the stage in which the community of faith articulates its religious consciousness in the idiom of its own epoch. Secondly, the epoch and its language reacts upon the community and begins to secularize the community's religious consciousness —even producing an identity crisis, perhaps followed by conservative counter-reaction. Finally, the community's authority structure enters in to moderate the crisis and to edit the liturgical forms the community has assumed. Where are we today? The answer is unclear, though likely at stage two. If this be the case, the danger of conservative over-reaction must be weighed against the danger of secular corruption. See Aidan Kavanagh, "How Rite Develops," *Worship*, XLI (June, 1967).

[32] Quoted by Clement J. McNaspy, S.J., *Our Changing Liturgy* (Image Books; Garden City, N. Y.: Doubleday & Co., 1967), p. 27.

[33] *Theology of Hope* (New York: Harper & Row, 1967), p. 326.

for new wineskins, and rationally he may welcome change; subconsciously, however, he may resent it. People are creatures of emotional memory; inherited archetypes operate which embody a kind of bequeathed numinousness; and memory functions both personally and corporately to render people conservative. Change also threatens their subconscious conception of God as the great Conserver, a conception characteristic of all religions; and this existential feeling brings people to have the "habit of seeing what is constant as religious and of presuming that what is religious ought to be constant." [34] The inertial power of habit must also be reckoned with. While there are positive as well as negative values to habit, "evidently those for whom regular church attendance is a lifelong habit are less likely to recognize the broader moral implications of their faith than those for whom active involvement in the church represents a departure from past patterns of action." [35] In a sense, habit blinds, and ethical insensitivity has its parallel in liturgical conservatism. Indeed, as we have noted, the inherent conservatism of liturgy can become demonic.

Yet at the same time people crave change to make liturgy relevant to their world. The uppermost question being asked by laymen today as revealed in a poll, in 1967, of five thousand Roman Catholic priests in the United States was: "How great a connection is there between religion and the lives people live today?" [36] And as the words of the scientist we have quoted remind us, the incredibility of traditional liturgical postures out of touch with today's world must somehow be overcome. A musician has pointed to one path to authentic relevance by pleading for a liturgical music which will cease trapping the modern man into a pious lie; and the first duty of pastor and musician in liberating him into integrity is in turn to ask what the experience of worship today is to be:

If it is to give a man a feeling of infinity or eternity or the world beyond—an experience of man approaching God that is unique at that moment—then a new attempt at transcendentalism will evolve and probably a new archaicism. . . . Or is the experience to be one of just praising God with the finest of man's creation? If so, then a new package-aesthetic results. If, on the other hand, the liturgical experience is to be primarily the communal sensitivity that I am one with my brother next to me and that our song is our common twentieth-century response to God's word here and now coming to us in our twentieth-century situation, it will be something quite different. We will not expect to find the holy in music by archaicism, but in our own twentieth-century idiom. We will

[34] Aelred Baker, quoted by McNaspy, *Our Changing Liturgy*, p. 29.
[35] Gerhard Lenski, *The Religious Factor* (Anchor Books ed.; Garden City, N. Y.: Doubleday & Co., 1963), pp. 189-90.
[36] Helen Dance, "Has Jazz a Place in the Church?" *Saturday Review of Literature*, July 15, 1967.

seek to share our common experience without looking for a false . . . aesthetic that simulates union with God because it seems superhuman. There is no supernatural music—not of the past, nor of the present, nor of the future.[37]

Does this mean that music is to foster a "communal sensitivity" by accepting electronic man at face value, borrowing communications techniques and tribalizing congregations into what has been called an "electronic circus of the spirit"? Hardly, although a view of worship as basically an experience of communal sensitivity in twentieth-century idiom could lead to such a conclusion. But if this plea states the case for relevance too simply, it is not wrong in asking that liturgy take risks, see our twentieth-century situation for what it is, and speak the language of our time.[38]

But risks of irrelevance must also be taken, and the claims of culture require a responsible "no" as well as a sensitive "yes." The *Lebensgefühl,* the feeling for life of the contemporary man, must be negated as well as affirmed. His judgement that traditional postures are incredible may well be premature, and the norm of his sensibilities and the idiom of his age are not the last word. Indeed, the awkwardness with which liturgy accommodates itself to secularization may well be a sounder stance than first meets the eye. At its best such awkwardness is a form of obedience to the fullness of the Word which alone can ensure to worship the integrity which makes it Christian. The Word whose reality is sovereign for worship is divine as well as human, let it be remembered, trans-historical as well as historical, otherworldly as well as worldly. Life lived in relation to the Word, while "not a timeless relation with God," yet in the twentieth century or any other century is liturgically to transcend time. While the worshipping Christian is a secular man of a particular age, he also is a spiritual member of a new race, of the people of God, of the communion

[37] Rembert Weakland, "Music as Art in Liturgy," *Worship,* LXI (Jan., 1967).

[38] It is salutary to remember that much of what we today regard as "sacred" music has its origin in secular idiom. Gerhard van der Leeuw writes: "The well-known, common chorale form originated with the French troubadours, and was used by the German Meistersinger for all possible purposes, but above all for the service of love. . . . It is at first a brutal shock to us to discover that the wonderful Passion melody, which has become dear to our hearts through Bach's *St. Matthew Passion,* and which we can only think of in connection with the words of Paul Gerhardt—'O Sacred head, sore wounded' . . . originally belonged to a *Minnelied:* 'My heart is all confusion, this did a maiden sweet.' . . . Luther composed his famous Christmas hymn, 'From Heaven High I Come to You,' to an old riddle in verse, 'From foreign lands I come to you.' The same development holds true for the hymn tunes which derived from Gregorian chant. Josquin Deprés, Obrecht, and Palestrina wrote Masses on secular themes: for example, on the theme of *'L'homme armé'*; others used the song which is still sung today, *'Sur le pont d'Avignon.'* . . . The splendid spiritual cradle song from Bach's *Christmas Oratorio,* 'Schlafe, mein Liebster,' was originally a song by which lust tried to tempt the young Hercules." *Sacred and Profane Beauty,* trans. David E. Green (Apex ed.; Nashville: Abingdon Press, 1968), pp. 220-21.

of saints whose life transcends all *saecula*. The language with which he conducts the dialogue with divine reality will correspondingly bear "a mysterious density" [39] transcending any contemporary idiom if it is to mark his citizenship as in heaven. The ultimate source of liturgical integrity, in short, is not man and his culture. Rather, it is a resurrected, ascended, and interceding Lord in whose eternal priesthood the Church shares, in whose name the Church calls "Lift up your hearts," and to whom the Christian replies "We lift them up *unto the Lord.*" To paraphrase a cryptic and hyperbolic passage from Eric Mascall: there is no possibility of our producing a more relevant way of worshipping God than that which has always existed. The most relevant way of worshipping God that has ever existed—or ever will exist—is going on in heaven now, and Christ is doing it. All we can hope to do is to express more clearly what worship always has been and always will be in his name.[40]

Now we would once more remind the pastor that considerations other than theological also encourage him to take risks of irrelevance. The archetypal nature of man's subsconscious life requires forms that are more than culturally credible. Man's libidinal need of mystical language that disengages him from his world and returns his energies in upon his own soul cannot be suppressed. His conscious and subconscious life needs as much to be decontaminated of, as engaged with, contemporary cultural images. In this respect we must heed today's poets, dramatists, and painters who, in speaking to fundamental life situations, revert to numinous myths which secularists allege are no longer congenial—"the fall," "exodus," "deluge," "apocalypse," "messiah," "pilgrimage," "resurrection," and others. Man's incurable hunger for the nonrational and the sacred, his capacity for "oceanic wonder" evident in his interest in divination, the occult, the astrological and the psychedelic, suggest a need for more than the idioms of our time. The necessity to counter the demonic mysticism of worldly principalities and powers with the numinous power of "the holy"— this claims the pastor also.[41] But these are secondary to his fundamental theological stance.

[39] The phrase is Louis Bouyer's.

[40] "The Social Implications of Worship," in *Worship: Its Social Significance*, ed. P. T. R. Kirk (London: Centenary Press, 1939,), pp. 90-91.

[41] A liturgical event in a suburban area of New York City where the use of drugs had become destructively rampant in the public schools is illumining. A Catholic priest, gravely concerned, worked with law enforcement agencies, public school administrators, and also sought to educate his youth and their parents about the problem. But he also set aside one weekday on which he asked his congregation to stay home from work and to gather for a Day of Fasting and Prayer, with frequent Masses celebrated with moral and intercessory intention. Only the numinous power of Christ, he felt, could match the power of the diabolic in such a situation.

And, if the tension of this stance at times threatens to undo him, then let him further remember that the relation of liturgical language to culture is reciprocal: if language is influenced by culture, culture is also to be influenced by language and not least by "irrelevant" language. The historical nature of the Word is to historicize language, to be sure, so that men can express their human situation in worship truthfully; but the eternal nature of the Word is also to "eternalize" language, as it were, so that divine reality can grasp man savingly. In short, language is not only expressive; it also is impressive.[42] It not only evokes the human; it is also to invoke the divine. If we need on the one hand "fresh forms of statement . . . to set forth ancient facts and encounters," [43] we need also numinous forms of statement to produce fresh facts and encounters which the Word in its mysterious grace can bring to pass.

Given the reciprocal relation between language and culture, then, only as liturgy accepts the risks of irrelevance as well as of relevance can it authentically serve culture as the Word claims it to do. Worship cannot consent, for example, to be contained within the category so popular today, "communication"; rather, liturgy must resist the secularism inherent in this category and adhere to its own hermeneutic. While useful in speaking colloquially of worship, the concept "communication" is reductionistic; it suggests that liturgical language has mainly an empirical and practical function. It fails to grasp the purpose of liturgy as man's effort to say more than he means, on the one hand, and as God's intention to address man with more meaning than man can understand or wishes to understand on the other. On the one hand, "in liturgy we say much more than we mean; we say what we might say were we better men, what we hope we mean, confessing that we are not sure what we mean." [44] And on the other hand, that which is unrevealed in the Word defines liturgy as well as that which is revealed. Mystery is to clothe meaning. The Word is in part that which we comprehend; even more it is that which we apprehend; still more it is that which we neither comprehend nor apprehend but which apprehends us. Thus liturgy is captive to unsayable as well as sayable things, and its language is *finally* to be that through which God declares himself to be God.[45]

Only in such strange accents of irrelevance, we believe, can liturgy speak

[42] See chs. I, III, VII.

[43] Joseph Sittler, *The Ecology of Faith* (Philadelphia: Muhlenberg Press, 1961), p. 96.

[44] Richard Neuhaus, "Liturgy and the Politics of the Kingdom," *The Christian Century*, Dec. 20, 1967.

[45] See ch. III.

truth to culture as it needs to be spoken to. In the metaphor of polyphonic music Bonhoeffer used to signify the transcendence and immanence of God: only as liturgy in its aspect of irrelevance sustains the "otherworldliness" of the divine as the great *cantus firmus*, the underlying melody of man's existence, can worldly meanings be gathered and woven into that metaphysical fugue which alone can declare their truth or their evil. Thus our boasted secularization—the "loosing of the world from religious and quasi-religious understanding of itself, the breaking of all supernatural myths and supernatural symbols, man turning his attention away from worlds beyond and toward this world and time"—this the language of liturgy must finally put into question. It must be seen as coming perilously near to a secularism which feels any reality beyond man to be nonexistent. The cultural predicament threatening man which liturgy must defend against has been described as follows:

In a culture in which a world-order [i.e., a transcendent religious order] is imagined or affirmed, the life-order of a people is thought to be consonant with it, or in some sense a response to it. When the notion of a world-order vanishes, the only order that remains is what Karl Jaspers has called the "life-order"—that is, the accepted rhythm of routine activities and of objectives which serve an accepted purpose in society. . . . Disassociation . . . from the notion of an ultimate cosmic order underlying all such activities [brings man] . . . to think and move within a sphere of knowledge and purpose which is expressive of immediate cycles of cause and effect, and nothing more.[46]

The cause-and-effect existence which widely seems to be man's condition today, the accepted rhythm of routine activities he feels more and more oppressing him—these cannot be countered with liturgical language cast only in accents of relevance the world understands on its own terms. Language must negate as well as affirm. Otherwise our predicament will only grow worse and inability to experience the divine fatal. If language only affirms God as "a worldly God," if it never delivers man "from time and space," if it only declares that "to be truly spiritual is to be truly worldly"— in short, if language does not mystically summon man to a life other than his worldly life which liturgy marks in its great, strange symbols—then we shall indeed become of all men most miserable. So far from worshipping God "by approaching the world in the dimension of depth," secularized man will have become crippled for worshipping God at all—in depths or heights.

Thus, if we have said that a proper architectural language will be earthly, reasonable, forthright, continuous with man's worldly environment, then now we must say that it must be discontinuous also, an anti-environment

---

[46] Meland, *The Secularization of Modern Cultures*, pp. 68-69.

bestowing a foretaste of heaven, a numinous space summoning man to lift up his heart on high. If we have said that one path to liturgical interity is to employ a twentieth-century music that rises out of the experience of communal sensitivity that I am one with my brother next to me, then now we must say that there is another path which begins not with our communal experience but in adoration of the Word. It is a music "related to the Logos and saturated with it," [47] and it is sung with the tongues of men and of angels. Or, if we have said that "there is no supernatural music—not of the past, nor of the present, nor of the future," then now we must say that there is an eternal music which in all ages it is the joy of liturgy to sing. It is the music of past, present, future—all gathered into that one eternal song of those who kneel before the throne of God: "Glory be to the Father, and to the Son and to the Holy Ghost. As it was in the beginning, is now, and ever shall be, world without end. Amen."

THE PERSPECTIVE OF ART

Affinities and Tensions Between Liturgy and Art

Our discussion of language from the perspective of art assumes at the outset that the pastor functions as a liturgical artist as well as a liturgical theologian, and an earlier warning against conceiving worship as an "art" does not mean that aesthetically one can remain a philistine. A remark attributed to Ananda Goomaraswamy, that an artist is not a special kind of man but that every man is a special kind of artist, peculiarly applies to a pastor, in part because he is a man but even more because he is a pastor. To a degree the affinities between *art and liturgy* we have previously identified set his special task[48]—their mutual dependence on symbol, their view of matter as revelatory, their power to grasp man existentially and renew his life, and others. Even more, affinities between *art and religion* also enter in. While liturgical art is unique—as we shall presently explain —the "special" responsibility of the minister rises also out of his awareness of the affinity between religion and art in man's nature in general.

For one thing, both religion and art affirm *man's relation with nature as fundamentally good* and as a source of grace. The "created" order Christianity celebrates, the world and all that is therein, the artist also affirms: the "self-identification of the artist with his natural environment . . . is primordial; it harks back to the time before time was, when the

---

[47] Olof Herrlin, *Divine Service: Liturgy in Perspective*, trans. Gene J. Lund (Philadelphia: Fortress Press, 1966), p. 151.
[48] See ch. I.

morning stars sang together and all the sons of God shouted for joy. . . . Our common creaturehood before God in the world which God loves—this is a Christian statement of the truth on which all metaphor, image, or melody is premised and made possible. It is truth to be rejoiced in, celebrated, by both art and faith." [49] Further, both art and religion deal with *reality in* light of what they believe to be *its ultimate unity,* and with man's craving for an experience of this unity. No artistic experience and no religious experience are finally satisfying unless they somehow speak to man's intuition that there is *wholeness of meaning* at the heart of things, and unless they embody—even if temporarily by negation—the persuasion that this is ultimately a universe, not a multiverse.[50] Again, both art and religion deal with *reality as "given."* Both experience reality as received more than as achieved; both declare their visions to be "inspired"; and both agree that "revelation" is not too strong a term to describe the summit of such experiences. To be sure, both religion and art also experience reality as concealing; but even its mystery is felt in a sense to be disclosure.

But the "given," further, is also experienced with *immediacy.* In a phrase of Von Ogden Vogt, both art and religion are "dissatisfied with second-hand reports of reality." What matters supremely is reality as it breaks into the here and now, and art—as religion—may be said to have its own realized eschatology. "A poem," a critic has said, "delivers a version of the world; it *is* the world for the moment." [51] The experience of immediacy, further, can become an experience of *engagement.* The test of good theatre, for example, is always whether it involves, not merely whether it entertains. This seems to be the meaning of the adjective "living" as used in the current description "living theatre." In recent years plays have been written with no ending; and the measure of the engagement the author is seeking is that it is left to the audience to determine how the play shall turn out. At their best both art and religion press for this kind of involvement. Further, the experience of immediacy and engagement can culminate in a kind of *communion.* In speaking of T. S. Eliot's greatness as a poet, Edith Sitwell has written that "here we have a man who has talked with

[49] Roger Hazelton, A *Theological Approach to Art* (Nashville: Abingdon Press, 1967), pp. 136-37.

[50] See Von Ogden Vogt, *Modern Worship* (New Haven: Yale University Press, 1927), pp. 31 ff. Dated as this book is in certain respects, I am indebted to Vogt for a number of insights into the nature of art, especially for his reflection upon unity, style, movement, rhythm.

[51] Charles. N. Fiedelson, Jr., *Symbolism and American Literature,* p. 57; quoted by Guilford Dudley III, *The Recovery of Christian Myth* (Philadelphia: Westminster Press, 1967), p. 60.

fiery angels, and with angels of a clear light and holy peace, and who has 'walked among the lowest of the dead.' " [52] One will note the mystical language Dame Edith employs: it is the language of religion as man communes with another world, and it marks the mystical element common to both art and religion when intense engagement with reality becomes internalized. This element similarly characterizes the realm of music. A businessman once described the impact of Beethoven's music upon him as "a panoramic, mystical experience." He added, "it was Beethoven's Ninth Symphony that taught me of the everlasting joy at the heart of Reality." In somewhat the same vein, the late Archbishop Söderblom liked to speak of Bach as "The Fifth Evangelist." Significantly, both art and religion resort to a term whose religiousness alone can denote this mystical element: in a phrase of the choreographer Agnes de Mille, the art experience "is a state of *grace.*" Lastly, both art and religion are *creative.* Or to use a more vital term, both are *genitive.* That is, they have power to beget, they involve travail, they bring to birth, and in a sense they possess their own children. Works of art are rightly spoken of as "creations"; and in turn they have power to create and renew.[53] And in religion, likewise, the categories of conception, of birth and rebirth, of resurrection and of life, are central.

Such affinities explain why art and religion throughout history have been so closely bound together that one can hardly say where one begins and the other leaves off. But this is the case historically because it is first the case anthropologically and phenomenologically. The affinity between art and religion in the human consciousness is primordial. And as we have remarked earlier, that pastor has gone far toward functioning as a liturgical artist who understands that the stuff of man's religious life and the stuff of his artistic life are at bottom much the same.

Given these affinities, the question will naturally arise: How can liturgical language be made good art? But tempting as this way of thinking may be, this question taken by itself is the wrong question wrongly put. It ignores the tensions as well as affinities between liturgy and art; and what makes the minister a "special" kind of artist is precisely his awareness of these tensions as requiring from him a right "no" to art as well as a responsible "yes."

[52] From *Aspects of Modern Poetry,* p. 251, quoted by R. G. Collingwood, *The Principles of Art* (Oxford: Clarendon Press, 1939), p. 27.

[53] The character of art as creation was perfectly captured in a remark of the scientist Heisenberg, reported by Julian Huxley. Heisenberg played to a group of scientists Beethoven's "Opus 111," and then said: "If I had not existed, someone else would have discovered the Uncertainty Principle: but if Beethoven had never existed, we should not have had this great piece of music. That is the difference between science and art." See Huxley's essay, "Ritual in Human Societies," in *The Religious Situation—1968,* ed. Donald Cutler (Boston: Beacon Press, 1968), p. 699.

Liturgical art, it must always be remembered, is unique. It is to be distinguished from religious art in general, from Christian art in general, and from Christian ecclesiastical art—to cite the classifications proposed in an earlier essay. One cannot assign to art the same authority nor unite it with liturgy in the same way that art can be combined with the life of religion or accepted in the life of the Church elsewhere. Art must be subject to liturgy's own hermeneutic, and ultimately to its semantic, deriving from the sovereignty of the Word. For while the mind of Jesus Christ penultimately does not deny, it ultimately does not affirm the category of the artistic as decisive for man's life with God. Thus the language of liturgy can be said to possess integrity only when art is baptized, as it were, with the theological meaning of the Word as decisive. And thus no matter how good an artist the minister may be, if he misunderstands worship Christologically he ends up misstating *Christian* worship aesthetically. Or, put positively, integrity in the use of aesthetic language derives from integrity in theological hermeneutic. Hence to ask simply, "How can liturgy be made good art?" is the wrong question because it reverses theological and aesthetic priorities, subverts liturgy to aesthetics, and opens the door to the corruption of idolatry which threatens the Church's worship in every generation. Art stands in relation to Christian worship as an adjective, not as a noun.

The nature of this temptation to corruption has been defined in an earlier essay,[54] and we shall not elaborate it again here. In essence, corruption derives from accepting as authoritative for liturgy the vision of ultimate reality which art would impose, the assumptions about man upon which art operates, the kind of liturgical action which art—when made sovereign for liturgy—fosters, and the purpose of worship which art—when made autonomous—would lay down. Art and liturgy, it should be understood, are not only *ways of experiencing reality*. They are also distinctive *visions of reality*; they become *declarations of the nature of reality*; they consequently *prescribe the nature of man's response to reality*. Art no less than liturgy—as we have said—can come to proclaim its own *kerygma*, impose its own statements, breed its own priests, claim its own devotees, and develop its own cultus. In the words of Josef Jungmann: "In art there seems to be a kind of centrifugal force, a tendency to break loose from the holy foundation of humble divine worship and to become an end in itself." [55]

One further tension between liturgy and art has to do with the role of the artist and thus speaks directly to the minister's "special" responsibility:

[54] See ch. I.

[55] Quoted by J. O. Cobham, "Sunday and Eucharist," in *Studia Liturgica*, II (Mar., 1963).

in liturgy the artist is first the servant of the Word in its living dialogue with the human soul, and he is next servant of the worshipping community. Hence the subjectivism and individualism appropriate to the artist's function elsewhere will not suffice in liturgy. By definition liturgical art must be communal; its language is to constitute a *koinonia* language suitable for the believing community—the Church. In art in general or in religious art, the artist may portray his own vision without regard to its effect upon others. Not so in liturgy. Here the artist takes on an ecclesial ministry and his role is diaconal. Indeed it is nothing less than sharing the priestly ministry of Christ in his body. In the words of Father Gelineau, the French musician and liturgical scholar:

In the celebration of Christian worship it is Christ who is expressing Himself in His visible Body, the Church. The message which art should transmit is not that of any individual man, no matter how great his genius or profound his mind. . . . The composer puts his art at the disposal of the community. . . . It is not his place, by claiming a sincerity which is but psychological, to provide the community with "his" music, nor to propose "his" sentiments, nor to impose "his" idiom. No one can produce work which is truly liturgical in spirit unless he has first meditated on the Beatitudes, unless he has appreciated the richness of evangelical poverty, unless he understands that the supernatural glory of Christmas is that of a *kenosis* and that the brightness of Easter shines forth from the Cross. The richness of liturgical art is not that of the senses, nor of the intelligence, but that of charity.[56]

As a special kind of artist, the minister is claimed by no less a vision than this. His first obedience is to the Word; his second is to the Christian community.

The Contribution of Art: The Principle of Unity

But from within this stance a number of insights of art are to be appropriated by liturgy, transmuted into theological principles, and brought to bear on liturgical language. Admittedly, to perform this transmutation is not easy, as our own efforts will make clear! This sense of strain, however, is exactly the predicament in which the minister must find himself if his holy anxiety that the nature of the Gospel shall determine the nature of worship is to carry through into liturgical practice. Bold as it may seem, the minister is to do nothing less than to change the water of aesthetics into the wine of theology. Even as he thinks about worship artistically, he still thinks first "through Jesus Christ our Lord."

[56] Joseph Gelineau, S.J., *Voices and Instruments in Christian Worship*, trans. Clifford Howell, S.J. (Collegeville, Minn.: The Liturgical Press, 1963), p. 216.

The first generic principle which liturgy accepts from art can be thought of as the *principle of unity*, under which two derivative principles, also borrowed from art, can in turn be subsumed. The second generic principle may be spoken of as the *principle of vitality*, likewise germinal for a number of insights art can provide. Taken together and theologically redefined, these two principles constitute a dialectical perspective the minister can find helpful in conceiving the language of worship. Of course the dialectic of unity and vitality is not restricted to art nor to theology. In man's experience generally—as we have noted—form and freedom are data of his existence. And secular thought often speaks of Classicism and Romanticism, of Tradition and Vitalism, although with differing modes of meaning.

The principle of unity to which we now turn inheres in the shared concern of art and religion to speak to that in man which craves wholeness and order—a craving which, in its fullest metaphysical implications, constitutes a decision about the nature of ultimate reality. In a sentence of Alec Robertson: "The artist in me insistently tells the priest in me that there is an ultimate point at which all things become one." [57] To be sure, art on occasion chooses to speak of chaos rather than unity, of the deviant, the disordered, the broken—especially in our time. Yet one feels that such expressions are a kind of lament for lost unity, that they "mask the norm under the mode of the deviant," in a phrase of Roger Hazelton; that the artist would not trouble so to portray disorder unless he cared intensely about order; indeed that in his negating he is affirming. While art no longer speaks of "harmony" or "significant form" as it once did, one feels that its brokenness yet signals its desire to participate as it can in the holistic quality of all createdness, that its alienation is a yearning for reconciliation. Form, unity are still the very grammar and ground of art.

But again, unity as understood by art cannot be taken by itself. It must be transposed into liturgy under the meaning of the Word. Both art and religion speak to man's craving for unity, we have said, through the experience of reality as "the given"; but "the given" reality for liturgy is Jesus Christ in whom—in St. Paul's daring phrase—"all things hold together" (Col. 1:17 RSV). The principle of unity as it operates in liturgy is therefore grounded in much more than the "harmony" or the "meaning" or the "form" or "*Gestalt*" which art speaks of. Rather, unity is grounded in the Christ-Event whose truth defines its meaning for both the language of liturgy and for our reflection upon it.

Up to a point, the nature of unity thus defined can be stated within the criterion St. Paul lays down for the integrity of worship in First Corinthians:

---

[57] *Contrasts: The Arts and Religion* (London: SCM Press, 1947), p. 10.

"Let all things be done decently and *in order* (14:40 KJV). "Order" as the opposite of chaos is in turn grounded by Paul in the nature of God revealed in Jesus Christ who is "the author" not "of confusion" but of "peace" (I Cor. 14:33). Unity, however, is to be further understood soteriologically. The term *symbolos*, whence derives our word "symbol" and which to a degree is a synonym for "language," is used in the New Testament as *the opposite of diabolos*: whereas the "dia-bolic" is that which sunders, throws apart, "symbol" unites, brings together. The unifying power of "symbol" or "language" in liturgy, therefore, has meaning chiefly in reference to the saving act of Jesus Christ in defeating the diabolic forces which divide and destroy,[58] and to the sovereignty of him who is "the head over all things" (Eph. 1:22 RSV).

Still further, unity is to be redefined in relation to the Church. The unity of "man's common creaturehood in the world which God loves" which art rejoices in is to be transposed into forms which restate unity ecclesially. Liturgy is always grateful, yes, for the power with which art celebrates the manifold vitalities of human life and extrapolates from them a vision of wholeness, as for example in its moving portrayals of "The Family of Man." But liturgy also marks the difference between the penultimate "unity of creation" which both religion and art affirm and the ultimate "unity of redemption" which St. Paul sees Christologically limned in the Church: God "has put all things under his feet and has made him the head over all things for the church, which is his body, the fullness of him who fills all in all" (Eph. 1:22-23 RSV). The unity Christ bestows upon his Church partakes of that reconciliation Christ has effected at the heart of reality; and the unity of the Church in turn is a paradigm of the eschatological unity toward which all creation moves.

Liturgy therefore accepts the vitalities art celebrates, and liturgical language accepts the unity art extrapolates from them insofar as art permits these to be redefined with meanings of the Word, and insofar as art serves the Christian community in its total life in witnessing to these meanings. Liturgy declines, however, to permit art to declare its own vitalities, its own vision of them and its own statements about them to be decisive for liturgical forms. Rather, liturgy insists that forms first be congruous with the Christian *kerygma* and that the unity informing them declare the nature of God revealed in Jesus Christ.

Given this content of the term "unity," what then does it mean for the minister to function as artist-theologian? To begin with, he will understand that the principle of unity holds differing hierarchies of importance for

---

[58] Noted by J.-J. von Allmen, *Worship: Its Theology and Practice* (New York: Oxford University Press, 1965), p. 264.

language, see its meaning from different angles, and transpose it by various devices into different genres of language. On the crucial level of theological theory, for example, he will review language dealing with creation in light of language bound to Christ's redemption. Art may propose language, for example, which simply "celebrates life" or "the creation" or the "world," as in much secularized worship today. In light of the reconciliation wrought by Jesus Christ at the heart of reality, however, or in light of the cosmic Christ who is head over all things, unity as understood in the secularized language of art must be inspected carefully. Does it face the reality of the diabolic? Does it gloss over crucifixion? Does it convey the soteriological promise of the Word to make life whole? Does it have any vision of the eschatological unity toward which, in Christ and his Church, all creation moves?

However, unity theologically understood also requires from the minister a certain humility and magnanimity to enlist the vision of art in grasping man's total life—his secular experience as well as his sacred, his life in the world as well as his life in the *ecclesia,* the realm of nature and the realm of grace, the vitalities of existence and the Life of the Gospel, and to set all within that *Symbolos,* that Word which has power to overcome the *diabolos* and bring all things together. Certain kinds of experimental language employed today illustrate and can be tested by this principle. The language of architecture as in the Matisse Chapel in Vence, or Corbusier's church in Ronchamps, are shot through and through with Christological and ecclesial meaning; at the same time they communicate a vibrant vitality, even gaiety, and beautifully blend nature and grace, the goodness of the world and the joy of the altar. The graphic arts of Mary Corita Kent likewise unite the secular and the sacred, as does the poetry of Gerard Manley Hopkins set as hymn. Experimental language only aesthetically contrived and uncentered in the Word and the *ecclesia,* on the other hand, and expressing only the performer's vitality and individuality does not suffice.

In a different vein, unity requires liturgy to recapitulate what we have spoken of as the fullness of the Word as it engages the full man.[59] Worship centering in Holy Communion and using varied art forms to execute theological purpose illustrates this well. In many older orders for Holy Communion, the death of Christ dominated devotion to the exclusion of other aspects of his fullness. In most updated liturgies, however, the notes of creation, advent, incarnation, and especially resurrection and parousia are also embodied. At the same time a large range of aesthetic forms is used to engage the full range of man's faculties: ceremonial, speech, song, hearing, seeing, taste, dance, image.

[59] See chs. II, IV, V.

The Principle of Style

Understood from a different angle, unity requires attention to what art speaks of as "style" in order that different genres of liturgical language not compete with nor contradict one another. Style, we know, is a distinctive way of doing or saying something and is a necessity in all art. It is the imparting of a singular impression to one's articulation of experience, the including of certain things and the excluding of others in accord with preconceived intention. Thus we speak of literary styles, architectural styles, and so on. Correspondingly there are liturgical styles, and just as style unifies and sustains the aesthetic experience, so it shapes the liturgical experience. As such, liturgical style is a powerful means of purchase upon the consciousness. It can take the mind and spirit, indeed, the body and emotions, and set them upon a fateful course of movement. But style also liturgically frees as well as claims. While it can halt the random flow of impressions and fasten men's consciousness, it can liberate the soul at the same time to rid itself of the multiple and fortuituous, to renounce one thing for the sake of another, to gather itself in the venture of prayer, and to rise from the lesser to the more inclusive meaning.[60]

But further, style holds hierarchies of importance as it impresses unity on liturgy. On one level, style simply means consistency, as for example in using the vernacular and idiomatic in contrast to the traditional and classic. The liturgical experience is made to falter, for example, when the minister randomly mixes "Yous" and "Thous" in the same prayer. On the level of denomination and tradition, style also means—let us say—that one will not mix the austere style of a Genevan Psalter service with the spontaneous informality of the Pentecostal, or that if one does so, one will know what one is doing and do it discriminatingly. Confused liturgical styles usually foster a confused liturgical experience. On another level, style requires that language not contradict itself in the sense that ceremonial, architecture, music, posture, speech are to be bound together by a minimal unity. When the "Ave Maria," a Catholic hymn to the Virgin, is sung as an anthem in a Puritan meeting house, the language of music contradicts theological meaning as expressed in the ethos of architecture. When choral vestments are those of English medieval choir boys in a suburban church-in-the-round filled with technopolitan man, visual language contradicts architectural language as well as cultural sensibilities. Or when the Psalter is read or the "Gloria Patri" is sung by a congregation seated, the passive language of posture contradicts what ought to be vigorous theological action of praise.

[60] I am indebted to Romano Guardini for this phrasing.

Yet, important as style is, there are qualifications to what we have said. Too fastidious attention to style can make for liturgical prissiness, and in many situations worship cannot take place at all except at the cost of contradiction. Churches cannot be torn down overnight nor investments in vestments be scrapped! Yet the larger point we trust is clear: unified style makes for liturgical integrity.

The Principle of Proportion

Concern for unity can also be implemented by another derivative principle the minister can appropriate from art: the principle of proportion. Understood as the right distribution of meaning and emphasis through line, color, volume of sound, tempo, mass, etc., aesthetic proportion has its counterpart in liturgical proportion. To be sure, disproportion also has place in both art and liturgy. A properly balanced service is by no means always the maximum value. Good worship can be roughhewn. Moreover, calculated disproportion is sometimes called for. Perhaps an ethical distortion has taken place in the public conscience and a grave social crisis must be dealt with, or a theological distortion has taken place in the congregation's mind and only corrective liturgical distortion can counter its effect. Nevertheless, one can only use language wisely to serve intentional disproportion when one is first sensitive to liturgical proportion.

Proportion means for one thing preserving a balance between order and variety in the elements of a service. On the one hand, the elements are often an unassembled potpourri with no frame or motif unifying them. On the other hand, they are often so tightly bound together that the worshipper is theologically and psychologically overwhelmed. So-called theme worship in which every single part of the service is made to reinforce a selected theme illustrates the latter. The wisdom of the Church in distinguishing the "ordinary," i.e. "fixed," from the "proper," i.e. "variable," parts of the service should instruct the pastor here. Proportion means, further, something of a blending of the mysterious and the intelligible. Currently, Holy Communion in some congregations is celebrated as a lively "family meal" in reaction to the somber stuffiness which has so often characterized it in the past, and its homey, human aspects are stressed. But often the meal is uninformed with any numinous meanings, and the congregation is left with the impression that worship is largely folksiness. Proportion also means —as we have noted earlier—that worship ideally includes both the preached and the sacramental Word. Without both, one has on his hands the liturgical disproportion Karl Barth described as "torso liturgy."

In a different vein, proportion as an expression of unity requires careful

279

estimates of how much verbal or visual or musical language a congregation can accept and still find meaningful. One has attended services which were nothing but words, words, words. Or one has seen churches in which crosses were carved into the end of every pew, stencilled on the walls, mounted on altar and reredos, wrought into stained glass, woven into paraments, pointed on tile, worked into chandeliers, and perched on steeple. Or one has participated in services in which, in addition to hymns, anthems, chants, prelude and postlude, every spare second was filled with organ music—in the manner of "Muzak, Muzak, Muzak everywhere." Such excesses betray insensitivity to proportion and cheapen meaning.

But proportion likewise requires careful estimates of the emphasis which the respective elements in a service are to receive and of how emphasis should be made. For example, probably the chief reason people come to church is to pray; but the minister allows little place for prayer and instead magnifies the place of his sermon. Or again, only snippets of Scripture are read which in turn are mainly "geared" to the "message of the morning." Disproportion is also evident in the mislocating and faulty execution of various acts of worship. A dramatic anthem is placed so that it strikes upon the people as a psychological climax which its theological importance does not warrant. The Creed, which ought to receive substantial emphasis as a joyous rehearsal of the savings acts of God and which best comes as the people's climactic response to the reading of the Gospel or to the preaching of the Word, is obscurely tucked into an unimportant place. Or the "collection"—as we have noted earlier—is placed to bear the meaning of "offering" where it really cannot.

In these and other ways liturgical language is made to misspeak because sensitivity to proportion and style is wanting; and the end result is injury to, if not loss of, that basic unity liturgy must have if it is to be informed with integrity.

But once more, unity is much more than good craftsmanship in using aesthetic style and proportion. These must finally be seen theologically within the meaning of that Word in whose fullness "all things hold together." It is unity understood in this all-important sense that must shape the liturgical experience. Ultimately, art can only serve liturgical integrity when it is transposed into language that declares the nature of God as revealed in Jesus Christ. And we must say of art in this sense what art at its best says of itself—in the words of the American musician Robert Shaw: "The main responsibility of the artist is not to himself but to the composer." The true composer of Christian liturgy is the Word, Jesus Christ, and the responsibility of all who deal artistically with liturgy is first to him.

The Principle of Vitality

The second generic principle, the principle of vitality, likewise inheres in affinities art and liturgy share, among them appreciation of the vitalities of the created world and existence, of which we have written. Further, both art and liturgy address the vital center of man's being and deal fatefully with his inner life. They reach for that inmost self in man by which his existence is determined, and engage those faculties in the exercise of which he is most conscious that he is alive—his passions and his imagination. To borrow a phrase from Paul Tillich, they would expose man to "the shock of being" and deal with him existentially. Further, both art and liturgy share a common vitality in their power to prophesy. In an oft-quoted passage, R. G. Collingwood writes:

The artist must prophesy not in the sense that he foretells things to come, but in the sense that he tells his audience, at risk of their displeasure, the secrets of their own hearts. . . . The reason why they need him is that no community altogether knows its own heart; and by failing in this knowledge a community deceives itself on the one subject concerning which ignorance means death. . . . Art is the community's medicine for the worst disease of the mind, the corruption of consciousness.[61]

The bitter visions art often depicts, the judgements upon human evil it can declare, the shock therapy to man's consciousness it can administer—surely liturgy responds to these. Indeed, one would like to think of liturgy as deserving at its best the remark a friend made to Rouault: "You paint as one who exorcises." Further, art and liturgy are vital in their power to redeem man into a better life. They can bring goodness to birth that was not there before. They can enhance man's existence and turn him to a new future. And not least, both art and liturgy can function to bring man to engagment, even to communion with reality in a way so vital that one can speak of it as priestly. The vitality of aesthetic experience resembles that of the religious experience in that it "lifts the veil from the common" and offers "access to depths of reality." [62]

But again, merely to identify affinities is not enough. One must identify tensions also, and the term "vitality" must itself be redefined in light of the Word whose ontological life is the hinge on which liturgy turns. And that Life, in the words of Paul Minear, "is as different from what usually passes for life as being is from nonbeing." [63] While liturgy does not belittle the vitalities of creation and understands with St. Paul how nature in one

---

[61] *The Principles of Art*, p. 336.
[62] Hazelton, *A Theological Approach to Art*, p. 104.
[63] "Adam and the Educator," *The Christian Scholar*, XXXIX (Mar., 1956).

sense precedes grace, the Resurrection Life it celebrates as decisive for all else is of a different order of being from natural vitalism. "Life" as understood by liturgy is life *from* Christ, *in* Christ, *through* Christ, *for* Christ, *to* Christ, to use the New Testament's prepositions. And as Life in the Spirit, it is a "pneumatic existence" in which God assures the believer of eternal life in the present and in the future also.[64]

Further, the vital self for which liturgy reaches is not simply man's existential self which filters all meaning through his imagination and impressions. The self the Word would bring alive in liturgy is man's full self including especially his will, through which in turn his whole self is committed to losing itself for Christ's sake and the world's. To be sure, the personal *pro me* can never be ignored by liturgy, as we have made clear. Yet, vitality in Christian worship is infinitely more than the narcissistic heightening of selfhood; in a deep sense it is the loss of consciousness of self.

Further, while liturgy prophesies to man the secrets of his heart, the life into which it would redeem him is not so much salvation from "the corruption of consciousness" as it is salvation from sin and guilt and death. Life as the Gospel understands it is more than renewal of coarsened sensibilities or a cure for the mind's self-deception. Rather, it is a paschal death and resurrection from all the untruth and evil that entomb man. Similarly, the future to which liturgy would turn man is not simply a subjective optimism or secular hopefulness, but that future which belongs to Jesus Christ and his Kingdom in life and in history. And lastly, the divine reality which liturgy in its priestliness makes accessible to man is not merely "a people's treasured meanings"[65] and common values freshly appreciated. Rather, reality in Christian worship has to do with the royal priesthood, the chosen race gathered in Jesus Christ. Reality is the eschatological Life of a New Covenant, of a sanctuary not made with hands, whose High Priest "reflects the glory of God and bears the very stamp of his nature, upholding the universe by his word of power" (Heb. 1:3 RSV). In a word, again the water of an aesthetic understanding of vitality must be changed into the wine of a Christological understanding of Life. Only so can art serve the language of liturgy with integrity.

The Principle of Truthfulness

Given this understanding, how does the principle of vitality function to shape the language of worship? First, it requires that liturgical forms at all costs speak truthfully to the depths of man's being, that the first considera-

---

[64] See Hans Küng, *The Church*, trans. Ray and Rosaleen Ockenden (New York: Sheed & Ward, 1967), p. 167.

[65] Hazelton, *A Theological Approach to Art*, p. 104.

tion not be simply whether their beauty pleases but whether they confront man with reality and resurrect him to life. When a cross is only felt to be "lovely" or a prayer is experienced as first "beautiful," liturgical language has probably lost its kerygmatic vitality. It is not that language is deliberately to offend nor that the worshipper is perversely to be denied the pleasure of beauty. Indeed, beauty can powerfully convey and reinforce the presence of the Holy. Rather, pleasure is secondary to truthfulness because truthfulness alone leads from illusion into reality and from death into life. In this sense liturgy shares the prophetic function of art in that it would deliver man from all that is escapist, compel him to stare at realities in his own heart and to name things with their true names. But truthfulness in liturgical language goes beyond art's prophetic function and seeks more than to bring man to knowledge of himself. Rather, truthfulness in liturgy means the truth of man's existence as it is before the wrath and pity of God and as it is saved and claimed by Jesus Christ. Liturgical language—as art—exorcises, yes; but it is more concerned for the Presence which comes to inhabit man's soul, bestowing upon him Life and calling him to a new future, than for the demons in his consciousness it would drive out. In speaking truth to man's life, liturgical forms cannot let man remain a narcissist and only fasten his gaze emptily upon himself. Rather, forms must both judge and save. They must both prophesy and redeem. They are not merely "medicine" for the mind; they are as wine and blood nourishing the soul.

The Principle of Movement

The principle of vitality also requires that liturgical language be language of movement, of action. Of course, the perspectives of psychology and culture as well as the perspective of aesthetics also cast light on the meaning of vitality in this sense. As we have noted, movement in worship must be analyzed in light of man's psychological nature—his sense of time, for example—and in light of his sensibilities as culture affects them—his mobility, his pragmatism, his orientation toward the future. Yet art in its feeling for vitality brings a unique understanding of movement from which liturgy can profit. We typically speak of the movements of a symphony or of a dance or of the acts of a play, for example. The design and color of a picture similarly convey movement, as does the flow of motion in a statue or in the arrangement of the columns of a building. Often we conceptualize this feeling for movement by speaking of "the dynamic quality of art"; and in thus speaking we mean that a work of art so embodies movement that it moves us. Indeed, critics see this element as fundamental to all art and as partaking of a prototypal vitality sometimes spoken of as *sacer ludus*, the sacred play between man and the divine. Significantly, the most primitive

283

form of art is the dance, and "the dance reflects the movement of God, which also moves us upon the earth." [66]

But movement as comprehended by art is again to be redefined in liturgy. It has been written:

Religious acts are not merely expressive acts or reactions to sacred stimuli. They are themselves *charged with numinous power* whose discharge or use must be carefully guided by norms which are attuned to sacred realities. . . . *Liturgical skills are to the energies of the Holy what artistic skills are to the raw materials of nature.*[67]

Transposed into Christian terms, the "sacred reality," "the Holy" normative for worship, is the Word; the "energies of the Holy" which liturgical language is to serve are the action, the movement of the Word; and the "numinous power" with which language is charged partakes of the life of the Word. In short, if we know art to be vital when its movement moves us, we know liturgy to be vital when its language moves us with the movement of God in the Word, Jesus Christ.

Broadly speaking, this divine movement can be conceptualized—as we have previously explained [68]—under three aspects which liturgical language must convey: past, present, and future. The meaning of the Word is that God's action is always prior to man's; what he has done in Christ underlies what he is doing now and shall do; and liturgical language must unequivocally say this. Thus the nature of the call to worship, for example, even the grammar and mood in which it is cast, should proclaim the movement of God who has sought and found man, before it voices the movement of man's search for God. But more, the present-tenseness, the immediacy and accessibility of God's vital movement toward man now, language is also to declare. The paradigm of all liturgical language in this sense—figuratively as well as literally—is the immediacy of the great invitation: "Behold, I stand at the door and knock." Again, the dimension of the future is also to inform the movement which liturgical language conveys. The vitality of the Word has been given; it is offered now; it also summons man into the future as challenge and as promise.

Now it is from within this trifold understanding of movement that the pastor can appreciate and appropriate much that art speaks to us. The sense of the present tense, of the active and indicative mood which we have said should inform liturgical language, surely finds echo in the concern for

[66] Van der Leeuw, *Sacred and Profane Beauty*, p. viii.
[67] Paul W. Pruyser, *A Dynamic Psychology of Religion* (New York: Harper & Row, 1968), p. 189. Italics mine.
[68] See ch. II. See also ch. VIII.

284

revelation in the present moment so characteristic of art today, in the feeling that what matters most is reality as it breaks into the here and now. Continuities with the past have been weakened and the significance of experience lies in its "nowness"—hence the "happenings" and "epiphanies" and "extemporizations" all about us. Surely the pastor can imaginatively find ways to borrow and transpose movement into liturgy in this sense that can counter its programmatic character and save its language from the rigor mortis we so often feel.

But the dimension of the future can also help him understand the very newness of artistic experiments in worship today as itself a sign of the movement of God drawing us into newness. To be sure, the novel *per se* is not necessarily Christian futurity, and it often leads liturgy astray. Yet, will it seem strained to say that liturgical jazz may be uniquely able to convey the eschatological nature of the Word? Jazz is a vital medium for hosts of people. It is an idiom of our time whose changing accents psychologically lead today into tomorrow. And its very improvisation and spontaneity, whereby the jazz musician creates anew as he plays, can partake of the vitality of Him who makes all things new.

But traditional as well as fresh kinds of language also convey vitality as movement into the future. The orientation of a church building toward the east requires the Christian to act out his hope and face that future when Christ the Dayspring from on high will manifest himself. Likewise the eschatological image of the icon—"an incredible attempt to cause what the Spirit seeks to transfigure to 'show through' here and now"—evokes the future. In fact, "is not the icon, like preaching of the Gospel, an impossibility overcome?" [69]

But the future as the action of Christ in the world in which the Christian man is to join—liturgical language is also to convey movement in this sense. It has been said, for example, that movement in the service of Holy Communion is to culminate in two climaxes: the moment of consecration and the moment when the communicant is "dis-missed," that is, literally "sent" into his future in the world. Language employed in Communion must strongly facilitate movement in this latter sense. The service of Communion is to move with swift, dramatic force, unimpeded with lengthy devotional comment and interludes,[70] and the dismissal of the communicants in particular should be abrupt, unprotracted by music or speech.

[69] Von Allmen, *Worship: Its Theory and Practice*, p. 278.
[70] See Massey H. Shepherd, Jr., *The Reform of Liturgical Worship* (New York: Oxford University Press, 1961), p. 93.

The Principle of Rhythm

Vitality of language can also be expressed in rhythm, another principle liturgy can appropriate from art. Rhythm is movement particularized, accented. Music is sound and silence heard at prescribed intervals. Poetry moves at a certain metre. The fenestration or colonnades of a building rhythmically moves the eye to points of particularity. The dance is executed at a certain pace. The importance rhythm holds for liturgy is evident in the relation of the word "rhythm" to the word "ritual." The Greek *arithmos* and the Latin *rhythmus* underlie both, and rhythm actually is the most primitive form of liturgical expression. The dance, as we have noted, is the oldest liturgical form, and the drum, interestingly, is the most primitive liturgical instrument. Understood in this sense, rhythm also is an expression of the principle of unity in that it channels vitality into form. But in another sense—the sense in which we are now thinking—rhythm is the sheer naked force of vitality itself, though measured. And liturgy shares with art the understanding that biologically and psychologically rhythm is deep in man's nature.

But again, the meaning of rhythm needs to be reconceived theologically. Will it seem strange to say that such restatement may well start with the impression which the cycle of the seasons and the hours made upon Jesus' mind, and with his vision of the rhythms of nature and time as signs of the divine vitality; with his understanding of the rhythms of man's engagment with the world and withdrawal from it; with his vision of the dialectic of self-denial and self-fulfillment as the axis of man's moral life; and especially with his vision of dying and rising as the inmost motif of the life of faith? But the theological meaning of rhythm for liturgical language inheres not only in Jesus' understanding of life; it inheres also in our understanding of him. As the Word he is both human and divine, we have said; he holds both historical and trans-historical meaning; his action has both a "once-for-all" and an "ongoing" reality; he morally judges and he mercifully saves; the life he gives is both worldly and otherworldly; he offers life now, he promises life to come. Such deep Christological meanings as these are to inform liturgy with rhythm and govern its language.

To illustrate, the rhythm of readings from both Old and New Testaments can mark the historical character of the Word as rising out of the matrix of Jewish history and its eternal character as fulfilling and transcending history. The dialectic of confession and absolution can convey the judgement and mercy of the Word. The rhythm of processional and recessional can signify the ascent of the people unto the heavenly temple and their return to their worldly life. Especially, the rhythm of the action of the Lord's Supper is to inform liturgical language. Language here not only recapitulates

Jesus' action in general; it above all restates his action rhythmically. The sequence runs: (1) "He took bread, (2) and when he had given thanks, (3) he broke it, (4) and gave it to them saying, 'Do this in remembrance of me.'" Four points punctuate the rhythm of eucharistic action which the language of speech, ceremonial, architecture, music, posture is to mark: offering, thanksgiving, fraction, communion. In its broadest sense this rhythm is normative for all worship, far more so than the trifold rhythm of Isaiah 6, for example, whose pattern of vision, contrition, and commission has almost become a liturgical cliché.

In summary, vitality in liturgy becomes authentic when kindled by movement and rhythm as these are redefined by the Word which gives and sustains life.

The Principle of Concreteness

One further insight illumining the meaning of vitality lies in the importance art assigns to concreteness. When most vital, art disavows abstraction and presses for particularity—what Wallace Stevens has called "The Vulgate of Experience." When Robert Frost wishes to express estrangement, he speaks of a "Wall." When Cézanne wishes to convey the presence of nature's space and form, he paints a "Large Tree." When Tchaikovsky wishes to portray heroic patriotism, he writes an "1812 Overture" and explodes Russian cannon. This is to say, art uses the concrete "thingness" of the world to kindle and convey vitality. A critic puts the point well in speaking of "Expression and Individualization" in poetry:

Expressing an emotion is not the same thing as describing it. . . . If you want to express terror which something causes, you must not give it an epithet like "dreadful." For that describes the emotion instead of expressing it, and your language becomes frigid, that is, inexpressive. . . . The reason . . . is that description generalizes. . . . Expression, on the contrary, individualizes. The anger which I feel here and now, with a certain person, for a certain cause, is no doubt an instance of anger, and in describing it as anger one is telling truth about it; but it is much more than mere anger: it is a peculiar anger not quite like any [other] anger. . . . The poet, therefore, in proportion as he understands his business, gets as far away as possible from merely labelling his emotions . . . and takes enormous pains to individualize them by expressing them in terms which reveal their difference from any other emotion of the same sort. . . . *The artist proper is a person who . . . does not want a thing of a certain kind, he wants a certain thing.*[71]

Now the minister as artist likewise is one who does not want a thing of a certain kind; he wants a certain thing. But as a special kind of artist he wants a certain Christian thing. It is the particularity of the Word and the

[71] Collingwood, *The Principles of Art*, pp. 111-14. Italics mine.

particularity of life illumined by the Word he is after; and these require that the language he uses be different from any other language of the same sort. Language appropriate to worship understood merely as an expression of religion and not of the Gospel, for example, or conceived within the category of "worth" or understood only as the abstract "celebration of life" will not do no matter how artistically proper it may be; for this is to generalize, not individualize.

Lest this seem a restrictive way of thinking, let it be remembered that the power of biblical worship lies precisely in this quality of concreteness. When the Jew wanted to declare the saving nature of God, he did not generalize about the attributes of the deity but re-cited a concrete event, the Passover or the crossing of the Red Sea (see for example Deut. 26:1-11). When the early Christian wanted to tell of his thankfulness for God's grace in Jesus Christ, he did not indulge in abstractions; rather, he retold a particular story about a manger in Bethlehem when Herod was king of Judea, or about a certain hill named "Golgotha," or he performed an act in which his consciousness was bound to a certain "night in which the Lord was betrayed" and to palpable things whose concreteness he could not escape— a cup and bread and wine. The Hebraic-Christian instinct was always for concrete realities; and the mark of worship expressing this instinct was always that it did not so much embody a thing of a certain kind but a certain thing.

Concreteness in this sense is to be normative for worship. Indeed the incarnation does not permit anything else. On the deepest level such concreteness requires language to recapitulate the salvation history of the Word because the concreteness of this history is fateful for man's life precisely because it is different from any other history. Thus the call to Christian worship, for example, is to be a "Christian call," not just a religious call. It is to convey the action of the God who called his people out of Egypt, who called his prophets, who called through the call of Christ to the disciples on the lakeshore, and who calls now. The Christian Creed, likewise, is not first to be a statement of abstract dogma to which the believer assents but a recapitulation of God's unique action in Jesus Christ which the worshipper joyfully acknowledges. The Christian "Amen" to be said by all the people is similarly an act in which the believer ratifies the particular history of Jesus Christ as decisive for his destiny. Especially, observance of the Christian Year makes for vitality in that it concretizes the history of the Word and enables the worshipper to relive it in a mythic way. With a certain arbitrariness it confronts him with concrete events in which God has acted toward him in a way in which he has acted nowhere else; and with the worshipper's response to this unique action, liturgy declares, his destiny is bound.

288

To be sure, psychological and cultural factors also affect the observance of the Christian Year. The Christian cycle, for example, to a degree parallels critical moments in the life cycle of every man. The feast days of Jesus—his conception and foetal life which parallel the experience of all men, Jesus' birth, naming, circumcision, and his death and resurrection as these become expressed in Baptism, Confirmation, marriage, death—correspond to rites of passage all men know. As such they make an archetypal appeal to man's genetic memory which is a condition of his life generally and of his ritual life in particular. Man is a creature of time and matter; his life is an experience of successiveness and finiteness; and he depends on reiteration and reification to furnish meaning to his existence. Indeed from the viewpoint of psychology, the question is not whether we shall have a liturgical year embodying structures of memory; the question rather is by what kind of year men shall live.

Of course the life-styles, rhythms, and dominant moods of culture also affect the meaning of the structure of memory which Christian liturgy proposes, and the Church must take these into account. Civil and commercial meanings, even those of sport and carnival, affect if they do not actually displace the religious meanings of traditional structures. Likewise the ethos of a culture as it affects man's sensibilities influences both his psychic and religious calendar. It has been suggested, for example, that the preoccupation of modern man's consciousness with his physical environment, with physics and mathematics, and with the exploration of space and heavenly bodies disposes him to appreciate the doctrine of creation more than the doctrine of redemption, and that accordingly it would be wise to revise the liturgical year to include a Festival of Creation—perhaps in the autumn—to precede the festival of Advent and Christmas. The Church must keep her worship sensitive to cultural and psychological realities and constantly strive to state sacred history in secular ways.

Nevertheless her language cannot yield up the substance of that sacred history in which she finds her very identity, nor the concreteness of that history she holds to be fateful for human life. Accommodation to culture must stop short of sacrificing the salvation history which the liturgical year sets forth in the great cycle of Easter, Ascension, Pentecost, Trinity or Kingdomtide, Advent, Christmas, Epiphany, Lent, Passiontide, Good Friday. This cycle, to be sure, holds many other values. It communicates the fullness of the Word. It provides variety and balance at the same time that it distinguishes importance of meanings. Its symbols splendidly teach and proclaim. The art and craftmanship with which the Church adorns her festivals profoundly speak to man's hunger for the wedding of the holy with the beautiful. But these values are secondary to the shattering claim the Christian

Year embodies, that the God of eternity once acted toward man in history in a way he has acted nowhere else, and gave life to the world in a revelation whose finality and fullness we cannot imagine to be surpassed. In short, nothing less than the integrity of the Gospel is at stake in the concreteness of the language with which the Church worships in her observance of the Christian Year.

But "concreteness" as we have theologically redefined it means not only the historical particularity of the Word; it also means the particularity of human life within light of the Word. The functional source of particularity in this sense is the mode of presence of the Word we have spoken of as the Holy Spirit; and consequently the pastor is to be sensitive to the Spirit's action as it interprets to his mind the particular life-situation of his congregation in their place and time. The Spirit, we have said, is the Word present here and now with immediacy and power, and the pastor must trust its power to enable him to identify liturgical possibilities in their concreteness and ways to fulfill them. His own imagination and sensibilities will not suffice. Of himself, he will lapse into well-meant generalizations, and life in its particularity will not be grasped.

Prayer so often fails in worship, for example, precisely because it is insensitive to concrete life-situations. Intercession, especially, fails to name names, events, concerns, causes. Petitions and thanksgivings likewise do not seem to rise out of the lived experiences of particular individuals in a particular congregation.[72] The rites of the Church likewise need to concretize meaning with "hereness" and "nowness" for the particular people involved. It is all very well to say conceptually, for example, that Baptism is the engrafting of the life of the baptized into the Christian community. But how much better to provide in the order of service a charge to the congregation to accept its responsibility for Christian nurture, to arrange for laymen to participate in the ceremony with the minister, perhaps even manually participating in the actual pouring of water, and to gather before the font lay representatives of various groups in the congregation to which the baptized person and his family may be related. Or in the funeral service, the theological and psychological finality of death against which the Christian hope of resurrection is set is best concretized by the scattering of real earth by the minister, not flowers, over the casket as he speaks the words: "Earth to earth, ashes to ashes, dust to dust." As Calvin remarked, in the funeral service we need "some honest show."

---

[72] Parenthetically, concreteness in the very style of prayer makes for concreteness of substance. Concrete nouns are preferable to abstract, concrete symbols to propositional and descriptive statements, and active verbs to passive. Free prayer often succeeds in this respect where set prayer fails.

But concreteness as particularity means above all that the language of worship embodies meanings from man's daily life in the world and from the history through which he is living in common with all men of his time. Because the historical nature of the Word requires man to live a historical existence, worship is vital only as its forms are resonant with the questions and agonies, the raptures and the burdens, that make up the "vulgate" of that existence. One could describe such concreteness as a kind of Christian "realism," and its affinity with the rebellion of artists today against every kind of angelism and false spirituality is too evident to go unmarked and unappropriated. Respect for what has been called "the stubborn whatness of things," so characteristic of art, surely finds echo in liturgy. With art, liturgy understands how life for every man is made up not of things of a certain kind but of certain things—an election to be voted in, a child to be raised, a job to be done, a law to be obeyed or disobeyed, a marriage to be saved, a wrong to be made right, a peace to be won. Such "things" liturgical language must concretely name in their "whatness," for these are the vital realities by which men live and die. Norman Brown has cryptically written: "All knowledge is particular, goes into the natural man in bits, a scrap here, a scrap there. Food taken in bites. Bread broken to feed five thousand." [73] The bread of the Word feeds liturgically only when it is broken into pieces of particularity.

In the last analysis, then, man's worldly life is to be the dictionary of concreteness from which liturgy takes its language. To be sure, its language comes from another world as well. Yet, to use the term so increasingly important for liturgy today, liturgical language must rise out of the Church's "mission." Only as we know what it is to be sent into the world can we know the language the Church must speak as she gathers from the world. The concreteness of the apostolic life bestows concreteness upon her cultic life. Liturgical action in the world is of a piece with liturgical action as we worship. And to this sovereign question of action we now turn in our concluding essays.

[73] *Love's Body* (New York: Random House, Vintage Books, 1966), p. 189.

VII

The Nature of Liturgical Action
Part 1: The Context of Culture and Psychology

It is fitting that an inquiry into the nature of liturgical action should conclude these essays in that integrity of worship is finally defined in terms of what God and man do. Christian worship is mandated by a Gospel that itself is essentially Act; man apprehends the reality of this Gospel only as he acts; and the question of action must therefore be expected to be the crowning question. "Worship is a transaction in which will answers will," [1] and only as liturgical practice and theology obey this mandate do they possess integrity. Sadly, however, it must be confessed that the Church's obedience has often resembled the behavior of the son in Jesus' parable who was commanded to go to work in his father's vineyard: " 'I go, sir,' he said, but went not." The Church usually means well and speaks obediently, but her failure liturgically to convert intention into deed falsifies her life.

Hopefully the evil of this contradiction is beginning to be brought home to us. Biblical study has recovered the meaning of "liturgy" as so essentially act that we now understand the phrase "liturgical action" itself to be redundant, in that to speak of liturgy at all is to speak of an act. [2] The Christian life in its totality is also understood as a liturgical life: the cultic action of the congregation and their apostolic action in the world are the same action

---

[1] William Ernest Hocking, *The Meaning of God in Human Experience: A Philosophic Study of Religion* (New Haven: Yale University Press, 1912), p. 341. Hocking adds: "Worship . . . in some way . . . enacts the presence of God, sets God into the will to work there."

[2] The term "liturgy" is a compound word formed from *laos* meaning "people" and *ergon* meaning "work." (From *ergon* also derive such words as "en-ergy" and "erg," a term used in physics as a unit of energy.) It should also be noted that the word "cult" probably derives from the Latin *colere*, meaning the attention and care given to a thing or enterprise, as tilling and cultivating the fields, or as directed to the gods. However, in the New Testament the verb *colere* (in the Vulgate) is preferred to denote pagan idol worship. Peter Brunner comments that "the basic meaning of the word 'cult' is indeed unsuited to express the essence of the worship of the Christian Church." *Worship in the Name of Jesus*, trans. M. H. Bertram (St. Louis: Concordia Publishing House, 1968), p. 20.

292

performed under different modes. The liturgical movement, likewise, has searched the Church's history and made clear how domination of worship by the clergy is an aberration, that the action of worship belongs to all the people. Secular influences also, such as the civil rights movement with its rallies, freedom songs, and ritualized marches, or the emphasis on involvement in the arts as we have noted, expose by contrast the lifelessness of much conventional worship today. Light cast by the social sciences upon the dynamics of personality and upon cultural influences conditioning man as agent have similarly raised radical questions for the Church. "How is the basic liturgical act constituted?" asks one scholar. "How are its demands related to the make-up of the modern man?" He continues:

Is not the liturgical act . . . so bound up with historical background—antique or medieval or baroque—that it would be more honest to give it up altogether? Would it not be better to admit that man in this industrial and scientific age, with its new sociological structure, is no longer capable of the liturgical act? And instead of talking of renewal, ought we not to consider how best to celebrate the sacred mysteries so that the modern man can grasp their meaning through his own approach to truth? [3]

And running through all is the anxiety of the pastor, and to a degree the desire of the layman, to rethink worship as action. Next to the concern for relevance, clergy today are probably more concerned for congregational participation in worship than anything else. In short, we now understand "lethargy and liturgy" to be a contradiction in terms.

INADEQUATE ANSWERS TO THE QUESTION OF ACTION

Given these challenges, one would have expected the response of the Church to have matched their gravity, but on the whole our analysis of the problem has been shallow and the remedies proposed only more or less helpful. Sir William Osler once said that in curing illness it is more important to know what sort of patient has the disease than to know what sort of disease the patient has; and because we have focused on symptoms more than we have analyzed the patient, prescriptions have been ineffective.

One common response has been to blame the clergy, and the degree of truth this prescription holds only makes harder an assessment of its value. Certainly control of worship by the clergy and the centrality of preaching in much of Protestantism—together with the vanities of ministerial human nature—justify this response. Yet one feels that the wholesale charge of

[3] Romano Guardini, quoted by Clement J. McNaspy, S.J., *Our Changing Liturgy* (Image Books; Garden City, N. Y.: Doubleday & Co., 1967), pp. 13-14.

clericalism, taken by itself, is too simple. The obverse of clericalism of course is the vesting of the action of worship—including much of its conduct —in the laity, and theological principle amply supports this approach. Yet, just to detach the conduct of worship from the clergy and mechanically shift some of its performance to selected laity hardly assures that authentic congregational action will take place. As Martin Thornton once remarked, an orchestra is not created just by handing out instruments to the audience. We shall return to this point presently.

Another prescription equates authentic action with physical activity and would provide much more of it, even to turning worship into a "celebrative kick." It is assumed that passivity can be overcome by bringing people to participate physically in unison prayers, litanies, responses, to say the "Amens" and to sing more hymns, to engage in bodily movement such as walking, touching, clapping, swaying—in short, by engaging man's body. In an important sense this assumption is sound in that a congregation is composed of flesh-and-blood beings, and action is grounded in physical presence. The Church has not sufficiently understood this and too long has taught people to be afraid of the body in worship as elsewhere, as we shall explain presently. Nevertheless, to equate liturgical action too simply with physical activity can be sterile. Such reductionism can let the worshipper off too easily and defend him from reality. Indeed, **on important levels of his being, indiscriminate physical action can reinforce passivity.**

Authentic action, it must be remembered, is as much inward as outward.[4] It is subconscious and conscious. It is attitude as well as behavior. Liturgical action can be real when physically unexpressed, as it can be false when a worshipper is outwardly "going through the motions." In a service of liturgical dance, for example, while the people sitting in the pews seem only to be spectators, actually they can be deeply involved.[5] Or in the silence of a Quaker meeting, one does not doubt but that behind physical passivity action of a most real kind can take place—what Friends speak of in a revealing phrase as "the work of worship." Again, emotion can be action as we have noted,[6] and it is false to set these against one another. To belittle

[4] C. F. D. Moule has written that "the whole history of worship might be written round the fascinating and difficult question of the relation between the outward and the inward." *Worship in the New Testament* (London: Lutterworth Press, 1961), p. 12.

[5] See Margaret Fisk Taylor, *A Time to Dance* (Philadelphia: United Church Press, 1961), p. 9.

[6] See ch. V. Emotion can also be an act of knowing, a cognitive participating in a knowledge of reality. In illustrating this point, Susanne K. Langer reminds us that musicians' emotional experience of musical reality is "the prime source of their mental life." *Philosophy in a New Key: A Study in the Symbolism of Reason, Rite, and Art* (New York: New American Library, Mentor Books, 1948), p. 93. Similarly, one could say that the emotional experience of musical reality for many people in the Church is the

"going through the emotions"—we may say—is as much of a mistake as to belittle "going through the motions." In worship as elsewhere, often "feelings are too deep for words." The emotional act of penitence, for example, or the time-transcending act of "remembering," or the yearning, eschatalogical act of hope—these may be entirely silent and internal.[7]

Again, there is such a thing as "passive action." Sometimes more effort is required to be still than to act, to receive than to give. "In Baptism we are washed because we are unclean; and in the Sacrament of the Altar we are fed, because we are famished. In both cases . . . our action is passive action." [8] Perhaps our tendency to subsume worship too simply under the category of "expression" or "offering" misleads us here. We forget that authentic action is as much impression as expression, as much man's receiving of what God offers as it is man's offering of what God receives, that indeed God's offering precedes man's offering. To slip into thinking of action only as our expression can turn the Gospel upside down and substitute human works for divine grace.[9]

Another simplistic prescription for dealing with the problem of lethargy views the spoken word with great suspicion and would reduce the place of

---

prime source of their theological life; through emotion fostered by music, especially by the tune, they actually know the Divine. The poet Robert Bridges has said that "the enormous power of the tune" to create emotion is thus "the one invaluable thing of magnitude which overrules every other consideration." Bridges' comment is reported by John Bishop in his volume, *Methodist Worship: In Relation to Free-Church Worship* (London: Epworth Press, 1950), p. 21. Bishop also records the judgement of Sidney Dimond, who, in a study of the psychology of the Wesleyan Revival in the eighteenth century, wrote of the Wesleyan hymns: "Their power of suggestion, their educational value, and the effect of the music with which they were associated, contributed in a marked degree . . . to the permanent influence of the religious ideas and impulses which were the psychological centre and soul of the movement" (p. 141). Accordingly, the greatest attention should be paid to the emotional character of hymns sung in worship. The pastor is not always the foremost expert in hymnody, but it is his duty to identify emotion as a form of action and revelation. The Episcopal Church is probably right in regulating the place of music in worship by placing final responsibility in the hands of the minister in order to protect the doctrinal and devotional integrity of the rite. See *The Oxford American Prayer Book Commentary*, ed. Massey H. Shepherd, Jr. (New York: Oxford University Press, 1950), pp. 72-73.

[7] Clement J. McNaspy, S.J., reports a San Francisco newspaper poll of the reactions of Roman Catholic communicants to new forms of the Mass, in which 53 percent of the people replying objected to having to participate in responses and prayers. The chief reason given was that such participation "intruded" upon their habit of "personal, silent prayer and worship." This reaction can be interpreted as a mistaken protest against the corporate participation which worship by definition requires. Or, it can be interpreted as a rightful protest against enforced physical action that deprives the worshipper of inward action he feels to be true. See *Our Changing Liturgy*, p. 16.

[8] Walter Lowrie, *Action in the Liturgy* (New York: Philosophical Library, 1953), p. 103.

[9] See S. F. Winward, *The Reformation of Our Worship* (Richmond: John Knox Press, 1965), p. 51.

295

preaching and give more place to the sacraments, especially Holy Communion. Worship transacted as speaking and hearing is felt to foster passivity, and participation in the Sacrament is equated with action: "Worship is always inadequate if it is merely seen or heard," it has been typically said; "true worship is always something we do." [10] Or again, "when worship is something *said*, the congregation comes to hear; . . . when worship is something *done*, the congregation comes to *take part*." [11] Even a statement of the Consultation on Church Union slips into this oversimplification: "Preaching is the gospel in the form of a message; Baptism and the Eucharist proclaim the gospel in the form of an action." [12] Now often this suspicion is justified, but not always. Liturgy as so heavily oral speech must of course be rethought in our multi-medial age, but surely integrity requires that we not be thrown off balance and maneuvered into opposing speech and hearing to action.

A common complaint made by free-church laymen about the service of Holy Communion in contrast to a service of preaching, for example, is that it is "boring because nothing happens." Theologically speaking, of course, the layman could not be more wrong, for if the Sacrament is anything it is an act. But practically speaking, the layman may be partly right, for he is implying that he finds speaking and hearing to be an act; and he has considerable psychological, historical, and theological support. From infancy on, so the social scientists tell us, words are active forces whose authority and power we never outgrow, and all through our lives they function as doors to the all-important world of relationships. Historically, we recall Augustine's phrase, "the ministry of the tongue," and his injunction to "recognize Christ's voice in our voice." The Reformation understanding of preaching as a sacramental event requiring the most strenuous action on the part of preacher and congregation also cannot be forgotten. "Faith," said Luther, is "an acoustical affair," and preaching is "a sacrament of sound waves" [13] able to convey and enlist action as vital as any other form of action. To be sure, cultural developments altering man's sensitivity to the spoken word require us to qualify Luther's aphorism. And it will always be fatally easy "to separate . . . God's dealing with our ears from his dealing

---

[10] Millard Schumaker, "First Steps in Liturgical Reform, *Reformed Liturgics*, III (Spring, 1966).

[11] Kenneth G. Phifer, A *Protestant Case for Liturgical Renewal* (Philadelphia: Westminster Press, 1965), p. 133.

[12] *Digest*, III (Princeton: Consultation on Church Union, April, 1965), p. 30. Even such an able interpreter as John A. T. Robinson also understands "the Liturgy of the Word" as "not that of action." See *Liturgy Coming to Life* (Philadelphia: Westminster Press, 1960), p. 17.

[13] Martin E. Marty, *Second Chance for American Protestants* (New York: Harper & Row, 1963), p. 159.

296

with our entire lives." [14] But any simple answer to the question of liturgical action which unbiblically opposes deed and speech and which flies in the face of our own experience of the power of words is hardly credible if one is concerned for liturgical integrity.

Another prescription which often ends up abortive consists in arbitrarily structuring worship to force action and to categorize its character—what we have previously called the absolutizing of structures.[15] Action is delineated within preconceived categories and everything done in a service is assigned a conative value. Hymns are always "praise," for example. "Offering"—despite its many layers of meaning—is always "dedication." "Commitment" always comes at the end of a service, and "confession" is always placed at the beginning. And so forth and so on. One common device divides the service into "revelation" and "response," and every act is mechanically designated one or the other. Now certainly these categories constitute a basic theological dialectic. They also denote a certain functional rhythm and underscore the priority of divine action. But "revelation" and "response" so interfuse that the attempt to force action to correspond to them becomes absurd. The revelatory action of God cannot be confined to the opening part of a service as is often supposed, nor can the responsive action of man be restricted to the concluding prayers, offering, hymn, and perhaps creed. "Response" in a spoken "Amen" or hymn can actually be a form of revelation. The Psalter can be both proclamation and prayer, both God's word to man and man's word to God. Or the lessons, while nominally revelatory, can be responsive praise. Failure to perceive the aspects of simultaneity and dynamic these categories hold, coupled with the attempt to trap the congregation into maneuvered postures, often renders action spurious.

A more positive answer to our problem arises out of a renewed sense of history and selects forms recovered from the Church's tradition to involve the people. Worship in the apostolic and patristic ages, we now know, was much more what we today would call multi-medial, and its actional and pentecostal character was much more prominent than we had understood. Ecstatic singing and speaking with tongues, the loud crying of the "Amen," antiphonal responses by the congregation, the laying on of hands, the sacramental eating of salt, fish, and honey as well as bread, the drinking of water and milk as well as wine, the tactile exorcising of demons, the waving of banners, signing with the cross, robing with the white vestment of Baptism, the processional at the offertory, the lighting of tapers, the dramatic opening

[14] Amos N. Wilder, *Otherworldliness and the New Testament* (London: SCM Press, 1955), p. 56.
[15] See ch. I.

and closing of doors—such actions are part of the Church's liturgical heritage. Certain elements from this heritage are being reintroduced, such as the "kiss of peace" transposed into the clasping of hands with one's fellow worshipper, the making and use of banners, the bidding of intercessions gathered up into a collect-type prayer to which the people respond with "Amens." When interpreted to the people, these actions can contribute much; indeed their naturalness makes one wonder why we have been so slow to appropriate them. Yet, helpful as they are, one feels that this approach does not get to the root of the matter. To know what sort of patient suffers from the disease of passivity, as well as what sort of disease the patient has, clearly requires much more than recovering a few forms from liturgical tradition.

The best point of departure for dealing with the question of liturgical action, we suggest, lies in focusing first on the deeper context out of which action rises—or fails to rise—rather than upon action or inaction itself. This context consists, first, of the worshipper's existence in its total range and depth, and secondly, of the action of Jesus Christ toward his people out of the fullness of his life. On the one hand, the worshipper's ability to engage in liturgical action is conditioned by many influences beating upon him which must at least be identified. Man is the same agent in worship he is elsewhere, and his action and inaction must be viewed in depth within the constellation of forces converging upon his being. In important ways, the question of action is an anthropological and sociological question, and man's consciousness and all that conditions it is first part of the context.

On the other hand, the Christological nature of action—what we have called the "properties of the Light"—is finally decisive if one is inquiring into *Christian* worship. Just any form of action will not do, no matter how well attuned to man's consciousness it may be. Certain avant-garde experiments in liturgical action on university campuses and amongst youth cultures, for example, are well attuned to the sensibilities of the modern man, but their fidelity to the liturgical action of Jesus Christ is another matter. One feels that *lit-orgy* is sometimes confused with *lit-urgy*, and that action lacks integrity because the Christological nature of action is not kept sovereign. In short, the context out of which action—or inaction—arises must be seen dialectically as embracing both the nature of man and the nature of Jesus Christ.

Accordingly, in this chapter—part one of our inquiry—we focus predominantly (although not exclusively) upon the context of culture and psychology in which the question of action is to be set. In the following chapter—part two—we look more directly at the context of the believer's life in the Church and at the theological meaning of the Word.

ILLUSTRATIVE ANALYSIS OF CULTURAL INFLUENCES CONDITIONING MAN AS LITURGICAL AGENT

Certain cultural influences conditioning man as agent have previously been identified in these essays, especially the influence of secularization, which we shall assume in turning now to examine the nature of the man who worships. We need always to remember, however, that the question of liturgical action must be dealt with in relation to the medium in which it is being asked—to paraphrase Kierkegaard. That medium is man's liturgical behavior as it embodies and reflects his life in his culture; and the very passivity we deplore is man's way of putting the question. His reluctance to participate in worship is the means by which he registers the contradiction he feels between the way he is expected to deal with reality in worship and the way he experiences reality elsewhere. The "feeling for life" the Church customarily expects from him in worship does not match up with the feeling for life he brings to other realms of his existence, and he can only react with disinterest. Man's liturgical behavior, in short, is the medium through which the question of action in relation to culture is being asked, and correspondingly this relation is to be borne in mind in trying to provide an answer.

To illustrate, the depressing solemnity of much free-church worship today must be expected to frustrate the man who trusts the vitalities of his personality elsewhere. Participation in the statements of faith which liturgy inevitably makes can hardly be other than reluctant for the man who has had no part in formulating them. The rigor mortis encasing liturgical forms will inevitably offend a temperament which elsewhere delights in what is plastic and open. The programmatic nature of liturgy grates on a consciousness conditioned to openness and spontaneity. The propositional abstractions of worship go against sensibilities trained to function empirically. And a somber spirituality which does little more than foster a sense of guilt for loving God through the things of this present world will hardly engage a secularized consciousness.

When his nature is thus contradicted, the modern man may be too polite or frustrated to voice his resentment and can only covertly act it out; or he may repress it and conceal it from his conscious self. In any case, his inward life does not cease being what it is nor does his outward world cease being what it is. And the result is the passivity we deplore, the smiling or sullen boredom we so often find, and disengagement from the action of worship—or even from the Church itself. In short, man's passivity is the question of liturgical action being culturally and psychologically asked.

Now let it be said that the accommodation of liturgy to man's consciousness—what we have elsewhere called relevance—can be purchased at too high a price, and man's sensibilities in dealing with the question of action are not the last word. Moreover, the phrase "the modern man" is an abstraction. Not every man is "modern," and "man" must be translated as "men" with individual "street addresses," as we have remarked. Further, ambiguity and paradox must restrain one from trying to get things too clear, and psychological considerations also merge with cultural ones. Nevertheless, four observations on the cultural conditioning of man's consciousness may illumine the question of action and illustrate the kind of sensitivity the pastor is to bring to it.

The Paradox of Man's Heightened and Problematic Sense of Self

First, man's consciousness seems to reflect simultaneously a heightened sense of self and a problematic, if not a lost, sense of self. On the one hand, man's sense of self seems to have displaced all other centers unifying his existence in a way that was hardly the case until, let us say, the eighteenth century. Many historical developments and movements of thought reflect— if they have not caused—this displacement. The physical sciences, technology, and the *Weltanschauung* accompanying them rest on man's confidence in his own senses and mind; man is no longer nature's servant but master. Revolutionary political movements likewise have as their first axiom the human individual and his sense of his place in history and in the political process; Marxism, for example, locates all meaning in man and his own history. Likewise, the social sciences have fostered in man an unprecedented preoccupation with his own psychological existence and declare his self to be the source of all his social values. In existentialism, reality is defined and evaluated in terms of man's personal "I" and is said to be apprehended by putting forth the self in decision. What have been called "mood theologies," such as the death-of-God theology or more recently Dionysian theologies, take man's sensibilities as the starting point for thought and as the end point of decision on metaphysical questions. In saying these things we simply mark the obvious: ours is an era of humanism in which man arbitrates all questions out of his own selfhood. Man's vision has turned in upon himself as the first point of reference for all reality. Man has profoundly become Subject spelled with a capital "S."

Yet at the same time, forces are at work weakening his sense of self and disabling his will, if not actually destroying his identity and autonomy. The mobile nature of our society and the absence of stable social groupings is one such force, as we have noted. The multiplicity of stimuli drawing man in different directions, disorienting him and rendering his sense of self mercurial —the "damnation by distraction" we have mentioned—is another. Likewise technology flattens and collectivism smothers man's sense of personhood, reducing him to "one-dimensional man" and extinguishing his capacity to perceive difference in himself from others, with the result that the initiative to engage his self with reality other than himself becomes liquidated. Indeed, contemporary man impresses one at times as being crippled as an individual becomes crippled who has psychologically been unable to cope with the changes bound up with the stages of life through which he passes from childhood to adulthood, and whose ego remains undifferentiated. He remains amorphous as a person and hence incapable of that authentic intimacy or distance which normally enables one to see another as other and to react to it in terms of reality. In this sense man becomes disabled as agent, as doer, unable to commit himself to, or to assert his self against, another reality. Because his selfhood has caved in, if it was ever formed, he is not capable of the decision for encounter which is at the heart of liturgical action. The "I" has become "problematical" as "the acknowledged center" of personality,[16] and so far from being Subject who acts, man has become object that is acted upon.

Man as Both Free and Imprisoned

Secondly, man's consciousness reflects an understanding of himself as both free and imprisoned. On the one hand, he feels "he is on his own in history," as Langdon Gilkey has described him, and that he can freely fashion for himself the meaning of his life. Technology has freed him from the confines of space to travel at 25,000 miles an hour. Industrialization frees him to move to a new job or a new home, or from a lower to a higher income tax bracket. Electronics frees him to turn a dial and enter into a multitude of life experiences other than his own. Education frees his mind—and in many respects his conscience. Medicine frees him from disease; psychiatry and chemistry free his emotions. Music and art free his imagination. Government—at least in theory—frees him for political decision. A thousand tyrannies in both his inward and outward life have been broken, and man today has rightly been called *homo perturbatus*, restless man intoxicated with such freedom as he has never known before.

Yet, mingled with his freedom is a sense of being bound, even at times of imprisonment. The man who travels at 25,000 miles an hour has a nervous breakdown. Affluence and poverty, each in its own way, lock him in. Television captures his sensibilities and homogenizes his tastes. Education becomes a "treadmill." Vogues in art fasten on the public consciousness, and three

---

[16] J. C. Hoekendijk, *The Church Inside Out*, ed. L. A. Hoedemaker and Peter Tijmes, trans. Isaac C. Rottenberg (Philadelphia: Westminster Press, 1964), p. 57.

million people buy the same novel. Drugs "enslave"; wars become stalemated"; diplomatic negotiations become "deadlocked." The "system" or "establishment" constricts; anarchy irrupts, and law answers with repression. "Determinism" is still a reality-term in psychologists' lexicons, and death still lies at the end of life. "Fate seems to ride into history on the back of human freedom as easily as it did on that of ancient authorities," Gilkey adds;[17] and what has been called "the night-side of human life," [18] man's bondage to sinister forces greater than himself, is still real. The terror of his bondage often is too great to be acknowledged. Repressed in the subconscious mind, its effect is to immobilize; and what we suppose to be apathy is man's escape valve for handling fear that would otherwise be intolerable. Hence, in the life of the Church, what seems on the surface to be liturgical passivity is often, if we have ears to hear, "the scream of a trapped animal." [19]

Man's Consciousness as Both Sensate and Sacral

Thirdly, the consciousness man brings to liturgy is both sensate and sacral; or, to name analogous polarities, it is both secular and spiritual. To be sure, this use of terms may state the situation falsely in that the sacred can be thought of as manifesting itself in the sensate, and the spiritual in the secular. Yet, the truth of the term "sensate" applied by Pitirim Sorokin to western culture years ago still stands as demonstrable, and the term itself as useful. "Sensate" denotes that aspect of culture internalized within man's consciousness whereby man determines value in terms of physical reality perceived by his senses rather than in terms of spiritual reality perceived by religious faith. Man's fascination with *matter* in myriad ways—his concern for his body and senses, especially his sexuality, his dependence upon profit as the mainspring of his economic order, his fascination with space and objects in space, his passion for science and technology, his pride in making and transporting things, his delight in controlling nature, his empirical and quantitative modes of thinking—these express his material sensateness. Likewise, his concern with *time*—his calendars and datebooks, his timetables and up-to-the-minute news, his time clocks and time-studies, his deadlines and production schedules, his business cycles and his fiscal years, his rejection of past history and immersion in the "now," his adulation of youth

---

[17] "Unbelief and the Secular Spirit," in *The Presence and the Absence of God* ed. Christopher F. Mooney, S.J. (New York: Fordham University Press, 1969), p. 65.
[18] Peter L. Berger, *A Rumor of Angels: Modern Society and the Rediscovery of the Supernatural* (Garden City, N. Y.: Doubleday & Co., 1969), p. 93.
[19] Hoekendijk, *The Church Inside Out*, p. 50.

and his neglect of the aged, his New Year's Eve hilarity and his alleged disinterest in immortality—these mark the temporalization of his consciousness.

However, beside man's sensateness persists a feeling for the sacral, and disavowed divinities seem more alive—at least subconsciously—than man admits. While often dispensing with religious language, poets still write poetry and affirm a world of the spirit over against the world of matter. Millions throng church and synagogue when a president is assassinated. Wonders revealed through microscope and telescope bring religious language instinctively to a scientist's lips. The existence of unidentified flying objects from heavenly spheres is debated in national magazines. Departments of religion burgeon in colleges and universities. Certain "signals of transcendence" a sociologist speaks of still seem to be heard: the play and sport in which man so avidly engages, for example, are found meaningful because they enable him to transcend ordinary structures of consciousness and to enjoy "a beatific immunity to time." [20] Again, man's fascination with the occult, with astrology, with thought forms and art forms of the Orient, even with witchcraft, reveals his capacity for the sacral; driven underground here, it deviously re-emerges there. The Church surely must read the sensate-sacral ambivalence of man's nature perceptively, and as we shall note shortly, rethink action to correspond to it.

Man as Both Amoral and Moral

Lastly, man's capacity for liturgical action is affected by a strange combination of a moral insensitivity—or an amorality—and a moral sensitivity, co-existing alongside one another. On the one hand, it is commonplace to say that man no longer depends on ethical absolutes; morally, he is a relativist and pragmatist. Or, it is felt that he is so amoral that he is no longer capable of guilt before God, and that the assumption that religion can grasp man at the point of conscience is false because he has no conscience. Certainly, only amoral man could be capable of a Belsen or a Hiroshima or a My Lai. Only a fatal mutation of man's moral sense can explain an Eichmann or a Stalin, or genocide, or the pathological savagery directed at oppressed peoples today.

Yet, one feels that this is not the whole story. Aside from a residual ethic still practiced by many people in their personal day-to-day affairs, man's moral sense also operates subconsciously in cryptic ways. The catastrophic social sins he has committed, for one thing, have wounded his conscience in

[20] See Berger, *A Rumor of Angels*, pp. 72 ff.

ways which still exact a subterranean toll. It is strange that liturgical theology has not understood this, for Jesus' command to be reconciled to our brother before we bring our gift to the altar is an image of social as well as one-to-one relationships, and of large-scale as well as small-scale historical time sequences. It may seem a far cry from the nuclear destruction of Hiroshima to the passivity of a Sunday morning congregation, for example, but the two may be not unconnected. For whether he is conscious of it or not, the modern man bears in his being the legacy of guilt flowing from that apocalyptic event. In its flash was concentrated the reality of the diabolic whose irruption into history and whose savage grasp on his socio-psychic life man cannot escape. His individual, conscious memory of that event may be short, but his racial, subconscious memory—through which judgement is transmitted from one generation to another—is long, and the moral toll levied by that event will not be denied. Or rather, only by repressing the guilt under which he lives and by concealing from himself the fate toward which his evil bears him can it be denied. Transposed into the sphere of religion, the form his repression takes is nothing less than disablement for engagement with the holy, and what appears to be apathy is the behavioral device with which he dulls an intolerable wound to his moral sensibilities and hides from himself the apocalyptic judgement history may hold in store for him.

To be sure, one would not draw such conclusions from man's general behavior. He talks loudly and heartily—too heartily, one feels—about his coming of age. As in the days of Noah and Lot, he feasts and dances, buys and sells, plants and builds, marries and gives in marriage. But in his subconscious life he cannot rid himself of the evil he has done, and does. He has tasted of an apocalyptic end, and his being is poisoned with a perverse eschatology. As he worships, he does not cease being the historical, moral, psychological creature he is elsewhere; and the price exacted by his unexorcised guilt and unidentified despair is just his inability to bring his gift to the altar. Bonhoeffer put it well once by saying that only he who has cried out for the Jew has the right to sing the Gregorian chant. The modern man subconsciously knows that he has not cried out for the Jew, the Oriental, the Negro, that he is involved in their destruction. And that is why he cannot sing the liturgical song.

Such observations as these on the conditioning of man's consciousness are not to be taken as thoroughgoing analyses; rather, they are impressions, if not speculations. But they are meant to suggest the deeper context in which the question of liturgical action is to be set. In light of them (and of other observations from previous essays), what insights can help us deal with the question of action in the medium in which it is being asked?

Some Implications of Cultural Analysis for Liturgical Action

For one thing, because inaction reflects the ambiguity of man's predicament, he should not be overwhelmed with frontal demands to act. The patient beset with the disease of apathy is both sick and well, both crippled and able; and simple, brutal prescriptions will not do. Just to hustle him into overt action, rudely bombarding him with multi-media, jazzing him up here and electrifying him there, may only reinforce his apathy. Shock therapy may please the doctor, but it does not necessarily cure the patient, at least not permanently.

Secondly, speaking tactically more than theologically and acknowledging the risks involved, liturgy is wise to reach out to man's selfhood and experience as the genetic dynamic. In an era of humanism, liturgical action is to be humanized, and liturgy may best start with man where he is. Or, in the idiom of an earlier essay, subjectivity can rightly ground objectivity. The vital points in man's being and experience—his preoccupation with himself, his fascination with matter and time, the forces both liberating and imprisoning him, his play and his empirical facts, his guilt and his hope, his faith and his unfaith—such existential points are the grid along which the current of action will likely flow. Our era requires what has been aptly called "Socratic evangelism," and all the ways in which man asks the question of his own humanity can be grasped as handles with which he can be brought to ask the question of God.

To be sure, risks inhere in such an approach. Humanized liturgy may attribute to the man with a crippled sense of self more initiative than he is capable of. Or addressed to the autonomous man-come-of-age, it can foster a kind of titanism which, if theologically uncriticized, can result in the overstatement that worship must be "shorn of its sacral, religious character so that it is recognized as a fully human activity as part of the world and *not divine in any sense.*" [21] Or, addressed to the moral-amoral man, humanized liturgy can end up as only a summons to moral athleticism driving him into deeper despair; anxiety over moral problems may so overpower him that the sense of the sacral never comes through.

Yet, at stake is a certain resonance with the human tone of man's lived world which liturgy must embody if the worshipper is to act with integrity. Similarly, despite the ambiguity of man's moral predicament, the moral tone with which his world still vibrates must also be evoked if liturgy is to be truthful. One critic has described this resonance as knowing when to change

[21] Howard Moody, "Worship as Celebration and Confrontation," in *Multi-media Worship*, ed. Myron B. Bloy, Jr. (New York: Seabury Press, 1969), p. 87. Italics mine.

the emphasis "from divine gift to human task." [22] Only when "tasks" from his everyday world are set before him which he can identify as needing his moral action is the current of liturgical action likely to flow. Delivering men from poverty, assuring the right to a job regardless of race, working for prison reform or mental health, problems of population control and environmental improvement—against such palpable realities man's problematic self can at least try itself out. They also can engage the imprisoned man if for no other reason than that they may enable him to name some of his captives with their true names. Such humanized liturgy also accepts man's sensateness with a wise realism but reaches beyond it to what may be his sense of the sacral under the mode of the ethical as it meets him in his space-time world. Such liturgy can also draw lines of moral difference against which both the moral and amoral man can measure themselves and discover how moral or amoral they really are. In a word, when liturgy connects up with human experience man feels to be important, and truthfully identifies the moral tasks claiming his action in his real world, authentic liturgical action is likely to take place. While allowing for its overstatement, one can understand the truth of a sentence of J. DeWitt: "We start with life, not liturgy. Roots of liturgy are in society, rather than in the Church." [23]

Thirdly, authentic action is likely to take place when liturgy appeals to man's multi-dimensional sense of time and engages him with past, present, and future. To be sure, man's sensate obsession with time "now" would hardly lead one to expect this insight to apply, and much liturgical renewal today assumes that because the modern man is predominantly a time-oriented, present-tense person, the contemporary must be sovereign. As a young woman exclaimed in protesting "ordered" liturgy: "You can't program now!" Perhaps not, if "now" is all there is in man's liturgical consciousness; and tactically, liturgy may well take man's "now" as the starting point. Yet, man's consciousness in its totality is more than a "now" consciousness. In an earlier essay a statement of Mircea Eliade was quoted to the effect that the modern man is determined to regard himself as a purely historical being, but that the extent to which he has succeeded in his resolve is an open question.[24] We posit the answer to this question to be "no." Man still seeks immunity to time in too many ways, and he is simultaneously too much a creature of the past and too much a person of the future for his obsession with history "now" to be taken at face value; and only as the

[22] Tony Stoneburner, "Emotional Resonance and Life Change in Worship," in Bloy, *Multi-Media Worship*, p. 136.

[23] Quoted by John Gordon Davies, "The Missionary Dimension of Worship," *Studia Liturgica*, VI (1969).

[24] See ch. III.

action of liturgy engages all three dimensions of man's being will it touch his deepest vitalities. Psychologically, it must be remembered, people's time perspectives vary greatly; each individual has his own, as we have observed.[25] Further, while culture may seem to orient man's consciousness to time, his subconscious transcends time and craves more than just to feed on time. And theologically, liturgy cannot forget a harsh passage from St. Paul on "unbelieving minds," "blinded by the god of this passing age" (II Cor. 4:1-6 NEB).

Action must be conceived to appeal to man's sense of time past, for one thing, because man cannot live—as we have noted earlier—without a ritualized structure of memory.[26] If not the Christian Year, then he will have a "civil" or "academic" or "business" or some other kind of "year" because ritual recall of the past is essential to the rhythm of his being. Again, he needs tradition in its function of simultaneously stabilizing him in time and detaching him from time.[27] Further, action must refer man to his moral—or should we say, immoral?—past (as for example in the act of confession cited in the preceding essay); until he faces his past through real confession precipitating real conflict, he is left split apart; he is not in touch with all the parts of his self. He does not know how imprisoned or free he is, nor does he know how moral or amoral he is. In short, to recall his moral past is an act of "self" discrimination. Only thus is the full self realistically identified, freed for engagement and made available to act toward the present and future. This is to say, man's sensate obsession with time present must be both negated and affirmed if he is to act from the depths of his being. To be sure, action engaging him with the past risks corrupting liturgy into the backward-looking fundamentalism or the neurotic retreat from reality against which we have warned. But this risk can be accepted if liturgy is theologically anchored to the historical nature of the Word, as we shall explain presently.

In its triple time-orientation, action must similarly take into account man's orientation toward the future. The man who feels himself imprisoned yet strains toward the possibility of liberty. The moral/amoral man hopes for a redemption. The sensate man is not totally bereft of some expectation of sacral meaning; despite his obsession with time, he is still "frightened of going down the drain" and asks the question of immortality in terms of the question of his own identity. The man of problematic self teeters between closed and open possibilities. And despite the convulsions in the social existence of the secularized man, hope under such metaphors as "The

[25] See ch. V.
[26] See ch. V.
[27] See ch. II.

American Dream" or "One World" or "2001" still mingles in his consciousness with his fears. In short, only as action engages man's attitudes toward the future as part of his *humanitas* will it correspond to what he feels with his full being to be real.

Lastly, liturgical action in the gathered assembly will be authentic when it is reinforced by liturgical action elsewhere in the form of disciplined prayer. Admittedly, such a recommendation goes against the advice currently given us by certain secular theologians who urge us to throw in the towel, allow the modern man to abdicate the discipline of prayer and seek the sacred only when he spontaneously feels like it. But the truth is that people will find liturgical action to be real when they gather as congregation only if they have regularly engaged in the action of prayer in their personal life. On this point, so far from yielding to cultural conditioning, the Church must resist its pressures and desist from so cheerfully letting people live as "practical atheists." We shall examine this principle more fully in inquiring into the relation of cultic action to the congregation's total life. Here, as illustration, we cite a phrase used by teachers of the life of prayer: "remote preparation." This phrase conveys the truth—as Friedrich von Hügel once remarked—that reality in prayer is determined by one's life prior to the act of prayer, that prayer does not take place in isolation but must be prepared for by reading and contemplation, that man on his knees is pretty much the same man he has been or failed to be elsewhere. Analogously, action in the Church's public prayer will seem real only to the man who has faithfully knelt elsewhere. His liturgical behavior in church is of a piece with his liturgical behavior outside the church. And if in concession to his secularity the church has let him only "run with Jesus" occasionally in subway train or discotheque, then subway and discotheque will be more real than encounter with Jesus Christ in the gathered congregation. A very wise minister once said: Men complain that because God is not real to them, they do not pray, whereas it would be truer to say that because men do not pray, God is not real.[28] The degree to which the Divine seems real in the action of prayer of the gathered community is in ratio to the perseverance with which secularized man has been challenged to practice the discipline of prayer elsewhere.

ILLUSTRATIVE ANALYSIS OF PSYCHOLOGICAL FACTORS CONDITIONING MAN AS LITURGICAL AGENT

Such, then, are some of the cultural influences affecting the worshipper's existence and constituting the context in which the question of action must

[28] Harry Emerson Fosdick. See *The Meaning of Prayer* (New York: Association Press, 1951), p. 34.

be set. However, we have inevitably crossed over into a consideration of psychological factors which also bear on man as agent. Some of these are visible and factual—psychological "givens" we might call them, which often one can only accept, learn from as one can, and only more or less change. Others are less tangible and more problematic, but perhaps more within our power to do something about. One "given" is the psychological effect of church architecture and appointments upon the consciousness of a congregation. A Lutheran writer has said that most congregations walk into "liturgical prisons" each week which instantly determine them to inaction. "The nave, instead of a place of action, is usually designed to contain suppressed spectators." Chancel furnishings are "permanently nailed to the floor." The altar is immovably fixed against a wall as far away from the people as possible. "The pews, set so rigidly and formally, immediately determine the role of the congregation as a quiet, watchful audience, with no assignment but to be reverent.[29] The point is perhaps overstated, but often what we like to think of as "the house of God" is psychologically unsuitable for the liturgical action of man. The problems involved in altering architecture and appointments are so complex that obviously no prescription will fit all congregations—the substitution of movable chairs for fixed pews, for example. But surely pastor and laymen would profit much from rethinking this whole matter together.

The Relation Between Minister and Congregation

The psychological relation between the minister and the congregation, indeed their total life together, also affects the people as agents. Clericalism in worship usually signals clericalism elsewhere, and an autocratic attitude on the part of the minister is bound to condition the people liturgically. Of course, church polity also operates, and the degree of responsibility assigned to the laity generally conditions them liturgically. Yet, one suspects that the authoritarianism of the minister psychologically undercuts the liturgical ministry of the laity more often than the handbook on polity. The pastor's ministry of education—is its style dialogical or didactic? His pastoral care— is it sensitive or mechanical, permissive or coercive? Experiences of parish fellowship for which he is responsible—are they vital or formalized? The emotional tone of parish administration—is it democratic or dictatorial? Surely the layman cannot be blamed for not participating in worship on Sunday if he has been railroaded into decisions at the session meeting on Tuesday. And he can hardly repeat the Creed enthusiastically if his religious education has only piped information into him and not helped him to work

[29] Ralph R. Van Loon quoted in *The Christian Century*, May 7, 1969.

out his own creed existentially. Other correlations could be cited. The sloth of the congregation is often in ratio to the authoritarianism of the minister.

But not always! It also may spring from the minister's indifference to his liturgical responsibilities. When he takes these carelessly, the congregation absorbs his insensitivity and does likewise. Indeed the minister's indifference may reflect an uncertainty about, if not an actual denigration of, his own professional identity.[30] He has not determined in his deepest self what being a minister really means, or he has not had the courage to come to terms with his role as priest and his undefined identity crops out in weak liturgical leadership. This may especially be the case today, when Protestant understandings of ministry are so fluid.

Further, the ambivalence which congregations bring to changes in worship may complicate the situation. The minister may misread attitudes, take the congregation's conservatism at face value and weakly surrender to it; or he may ally himself with the avant-garde as a way of proving to his shaky self that here at least he knows who he is and where he stands. Such pitfalls can be avoided if the minister has emotionally come to terms with his own selfhood and role, if he has studied the psychological problems bound up with changing people's attitudes toward liturgical change,[31] and if he has worked out with his people the implications for liturgy of the doctrines of the ministry of the laity and the priesthood of all believers, as we shall need to understand presently. Clearly, these require the recognition that worship belongs to the local congregation, not to the pastor, and that he conducts worship only as their delegate.[32] They also require that changes be based on knowledge, be preceded by mutual learning and instruction, that decisions be democratically and not autocratically arrived at, and that a certain openness to liturgically learning-by-doing be preserved. Above all, changes in liturgy are to be made in love. "Love is the first commandment for those who attempt to change the order of worship in their church," it has been written, because anything else contradicts the commandment of the risen Christ whose presence finally controls all form and order.[33]

[30] See Paul W. Pruyser's essay, "The Master Hand: Psychological Notes on Pastoral Blessing," in *The New Shape of Pastoral Theology*, ed. William Oglesby, Jr. (Nashville: Abingdon Press, 1969).

[31] See the article by Raymond Menne, "Psychological Aspects of Liturgical Renewal," *Worship*, XL (Mar., 1966).

[32] See the essay by A. T. Hanson, "Shepherd, Teacher, and Celebrant in the New Testament Conception of Ministry," in *New Forms of Ministry*, ed. David S. Paton (London: Edinburgh House Press, 1965).

[33] Dietrich Ritschl, *A Theology of Proclamation* (Richmond: John Knox Press, 1960), p. 108.

The Overall Tone of a Congregation's Life

However, while awareness of the psychological relation between minister and congregation is crucial, it is only part of the overall "tone" of a congregation's life. This tone will need to be analyzed theologically, but one must also be sensitive to it psychologically. To illustrate, the instinct of gregariousness is obviously an important psychological "given" in church life. A congregation is made up of social beings, and their action in liturgy must be viewed in relation to their experiences of fellowship elsewhere. *Koinonia* is many-sided and many-layered, and the meaning people find in acting together at any one place is colored by the meaning their actions together have held for them elsewhere. A congregation's experiences of play, its committee meetings, its suppers and breakfasts, its task forces and service groups, its study groups and art exhibits, its choir practices and concerts, its bazaars and Christmas tree sales—such experiences constitute a web of relationship whose dynamic inevitably carries over into liturgy. Any one type of corporate action holds psychological fallout from all other kinds of corporate action, and action is likely to be vital in liturgy only when people have acted together in healthful and satisfying ways elsewhere. Hence, announcements of mundane events in the congregation's life which we once were so fastidious in eliminating should probably have place in worship—though with taste. Psychologically, they symbolize the matrix of congregational life and can evoke a certain security of belonging which, as an emotional purchase point, can free the worshipper to give himself to the action of worship. The nerve of liturgical action has been maimed if connections are not made between what a worshipper does with his fellow worshippers on Sunday and what he does with them at a task force committee meeting on Wednesday.

The Factor of Sexuality

The factor of sexuality, another psychological given, must also be recognized; although to what extent and in what way it affects the action of worship, no one knows with certainty because so little research has been done in the field. The question of action, however, is doubtless tied up with the demonstrable fact that women attend church in larger numbers than men.[34]

[34] A poll taken in the 1930's reported a ratio of 2 to 1. A study of 27 Lutheran congregations in 6 midwestern states in 1958 revealed that 38 percent more women than men attended church. A Gallup poll in 1959 found the ratio to be 55 percent women and 45 percent men. A survey of Augustana Lutheran congregations in the Minneapolis area reported by the (Methodist) *Christian Advocate* in 1962 indicated an attendance of 57 percent women, 43 percent men, following closely the membership ratio of 56 percent and 44 percent, respectively. The *Advocate* added that the survey was prompted by a report that an Episcopalian congregation in Washington, D.C., had a male attendance of 19 percent.

Is this because the female finds more or less passive worship appealing, while the more aggressive male finds it dull and so—physically or psychologically —stays away? Or, is it because the structures of worship have an objective, bracing character which complements the feminine psyche and hence is found attractive? Is it to be explained by the fact that the leader of worship is almost always a male and that an unacknowledged eroticism operates? One critic relates the preponderance of women and the absence of men to the moral shame felt by men caught in the compromises of business and public life. Another explains it by the attachment women feel for their place of constant psychological residence—their domestic community symbolized by the local church. A psychiatrist conjectures that the minority of male worshippers can be explained by the predominance in Protestant thought and devotion of the masculine conception of God as Father and by the absence of an accompanying female deity.[35] A psychologist correlates the predominance of women with the differences in attitudes of boys and girls in the oedipal stage of development which in turn influence their understanding of God.[36] The boy feels an ambivalence, if not predominantly a hostility, toward his father; girls, on the other hand, see the father more in terms of love; and both project onto God their emotional reaction toward the human father. Accordingly, there is less fear and more love of God in women, more fear mingled with admiration in men; and barriers to be overcome in worshipping God are less difficult for women than men. Such analyses may seem strained to us, and one is not quite sure what to do with them. But they at least alert us to dynamics deeper than we commonly perceive.

Man's Physical Body and Senses

The chief "given," however, is the fact of man's physical presence as he worships and the grounding of liturgical action in the body as the matrix of personality; and in this important sense the question of liturgical action is indeed an anthropological question. While authentic action is not to be equated with physical activity, man's bodily being nevertheless grounds his personality and experience: "the living organ of experience is the living body as a whole."[37] Indeed, "man does not have a body, he *is* a body."[38] His

[35] See Ernest White, *Christian Life and the Unconscious* (New York: Harper & Bros., 1955), pp. 188 ff.

[36] See R. S. Lee, *Your Growing Child and Religion* (New York: The Macmillan Co. 1963), pp. 62 ff., 97-98; and Lee's *Psychology and Worship* (New York: Philosophical Library, 1956).

[37] Alfred North Whitehead, quoted by Norman O. Brown, *Life Against Death* (New York: Random House, Vintage Books, 1959), p. 314.

[38] John A. T. Robinson, *The Body: A Study in Pauline Theology* (London: SCM Press, 1952), p. 14.

bodiliness is his self real and present, and, as William Ernest Hocking once remarked, worship is too spiritual a process to dispense with the physical.

In understanding the body as the liturgical "organ of experience," we need to remember certain insights of psychology reported in earlier essays: the unity of man's being and the connection between the body and all the faculties of personality; the importance of man's emotional life; his nature as *animal symbolicum* and the relativity of language to personality structure; the pervasive reality of the subconscious; and the power of sensuous stimuli to concretize meaning transformingly. Further, we need to understand that man's physical senses are the most primitive thing about him, and that there seems to be a hierarchy of effect whereby one sense exerts more power than another, although effect depends on other factors also. Normally, the meaning of a thing thought is less powerful than the meaning of a thing heard, which in turn is less powerful than the meaning of a thing seen as well as heard. In turn the meaning of a thing heard and seen is less potent than meaning kinetically conveyed or grasped, i.e., through bodily motion. Meaning apprehended through touch and taste is still more vital than meaning kinetically or audibly experienced. (In this respect we apparently do not outgrow the instinct of infants to put objects into their mouths to evaluate reality.) And lastly, meaning involving several senses is obviously more vital than meaning involving only one.

Such an understanding explains why religion was danced long before it was said or sung, and why the touching and tasting of objects have always possessed psychological and numinous power. In Scripture, we recall, David dances and Ezekiel eats the scroll. The eating of manna is associated with divine providence, and of milk and honey with divine deliverance. John baptizes with water; Jesus heals with clay and spittle; and Thomas must touch the wounds of Christ. The breaking of bread and drinking of wine are set at the center of the early Church's devotion, and apostles are commissioned by the laying on of hands. Still today, motion, touch, and taste are powerful carriers of numinous meaning: the fingering of a rosary or a cross, the carrying and kissing of the Bible, wearing special clothes, kneeling, standing, walking, the clasping of hands in reconciliation and fellowship, inhaling incense, bathing with water, signing with the cross, beating of the breast, the thumbing of oil and ashes upon the forehead, and others. Psychologically speaking, man's bodily senses are decisive for his apprehension of numinous meaning.

But clearly, here again the data of psychology answer to the claims of theology. While we may be troubled lest the sensateness of modern man has run away with him, this is not to say that man as he worships must be less sensate than God has made him. "God likes matter; he created it,"

313

C. S. Lewis once said; and surely we are not wrong in believing that God likes man to be a body because he created him a body. The Church's suspicion of the body and its emphasis upon the dualism of body and spirit is essentially a heresy; and it derives from hostility toward the body absorbed by Christianity from Orphism and Neo-Platonism, not from its own heritage. Luther once made the perfect comment on the liturgical importance of the body in saying that God has given man five senses with which to worship him and that it would be sheer ingratitude to use less. Above all, the truth of the incarnation validates the office of the body, as we have frequently observed in these essays. The words of a Latin nativity hymn by Tomas de Victoria to the Virgin Mary read: "*O beata virgo, cuius viscera menuerunt portare Dominum Jesum Christum. Hallelujah!*" Surely it is significant that even in its tenderest moods Christian devotion does not hesitate to speak of the "viscera." And despite our criticism in an earlier essay of vitalism for the sake of vitalism, it is not wrong to think of Christianity as a visceral religion and of worship as a visceral matter.

It hardly needs to be pointed out that failure to grasp this psychological and theological truth explains the sickness of passivity in many Protestant congregations today. We have not understood that liturgically man is a visceral, breathing, heart-beating, secreting animal, as Gerald Heard once remarked, and that without the body as acolyte the soul's worship is so much the less. Misled by its own heresies, the Church has taught the worshipper only too well to be afraid of his body and has restrained him from employing in liturgy the very senses with which he delights to express his being and to experience meaning elsewhere.[39] Consequently, because the worshipper has been required to be something other than he really is, he has had no alternative but to turn passive and withdraw from an experience that contradicts the vital instincts embedded in his nerves and tissues. Given this situation, a certain liturgical unlearning or re-education is called for to enable people to appreciate the use of the body in worship.

To be sure, the misunderstandings and inhibitions people bring to using the body must not be underestimated. Especially, touching the bodies of others may evoke latent erotic and sexual fears—justified or unjustified; and for this reason also people should not be abruptly manipulated into tactile action or overwhelmed with experimentation. Interpreting to them historically the liturgical use of the body together with theological explanation

---

[39] It has been observed that in most mainline Protestant congregations today, the characteristic posture—especially at Holy Communion—is sitting with folded hands, head slightly bowed, arms kept close to the body, and that not surprisingly "the basic feeling tone" is one of "depression." See Pruyser, *A Dynamic Psychology of Religion* (New York: Harper & Row, 1968), pp. 36, 165-66, 187.

may help up to a point. But attitudes toward the body are shaped emotionally and pragmatically more than rationally. Here peculiarly one learns by doing, and here accordingly lies the rationale for experiments in multimedial and multi-sensuous worship, and for experiments in sensitivity training—borrowed from the human potential movement—as preliminary to worship.

In any case, the imagination of pastor and layman should be put to work to reconceive familiar actions and to invent fresh ones to involve the body and senses. For example, why cannot the pastor clasp the hands of the people in greeting as they come to worship rather than as they leave, and the people similarly greet one another in the pews? Cannot the equivalent of "friendship circles" be restored, perhaps around the table at Communion or while the prayers are being prayed? At Communion, the laymen can serve the bread and wine to one another rather than being served directly by the clergy. In congregations where children do not receive Communion, they nevertheless can come forward and, while standing or kneeling with their parents, be blessed by the pastor or layman with a brief sentence, and the hand placed on their heads or the cross signed on their foreheads. Likewise, at confirmation and reception of new members, laymen can share in the laying on of hands as well as in extending the right hand of fellowship. At Baptism, representative laymen can join with the pastor and parents in clothing the newly baptized—especially a child—with a white gown or robe to signify the new life. On Maundy Thursday, the Last Supper and Foot Washing can be re-enacted as in the East Harlem Protestant Parish in New York City: after a fellowship meal, hymns, biblical readings, the congregation come forward in groups of eight and while the people stand in the chancel, the clergy kneel and symbolically wipe the shoes of each person with the ends of their stoles. Services of commissioning similarly lend themselves to tactile action. And at weddings, after the statelier parts of the ritual, why cannot a more or less ritualized dance, in which the wedding party join hands, conclude the ceremony? To this day what is called "the Dance of Isaiah" is often performed at Greek Orthodox weddings in which the bride and groom are guided by the priest in circling the altar in a dance to express their joy while rose petals are rained upon them.[40]

But other forms of physical action may well be rethought also—kinetic, mimetic, and even gustatory actions. Processionals and parades, and outside the church building as well as within, at festive services and on high days

---

[40] Theologians and clergy similarly ought to learn to dance a bit more! Even today the ritual dance of Isaiah is performed in the ordination service of priests in the Greek Orthodox communion. And we are told that as late as 1700, it was the custom in Germany at the presentation of a degree by the theological faculty, for the Dean and professors to perform a dance around the newly invested *doctor theologiae*.

315

such as Easter, Pentecost, and Epiphany, with banners, symbolic tokens, singing and chanting, are surely appropriate. On these occasions, material from the Bible can also be dramatized with the congregation participating, such as the narrative of Jesus' passion and trial from St. John's gospel on Palm Sunday or in Holy Week, with the congregation taking the part and reading the words of the populace. At ordinary services, instead of the sermon a play performed in the chancel can present the message from the Gospel with congregational discussion following. Liturgical dance can be employed in the same way, though sometimes the drama or dance is best left to make its own impact because discussion can make the congregation more conscious of their own reactions than of the meaning of the liturgical act itself. Agape meals, such as breakfasts and suppers, similarly provide for gustatory action, either directly or indirectly in connection with Communion. The service of Communion itself, for example, may well be shortened and incorporated into a congregational supper on Maundy Thursday or the first Sunday in Advent. Similarly, vocational or "craft" Communion breakfasts can be held on designated Sundays or on weekday mornings. In medium-sized or large congregations, all the members engaged in the healing or teaching professions, for example, can be invited to come together for breakfast at which religious or ethical questions arising out of their professional life are discussed; and then, while still seated around the breakfast table, Communion can be briefly celebrated as a sign and pattern of their Christian vocation in the world. In a different vein, a service of Baptism or confirmation and reception can be followed by an informal gathering in the narthex or by a social hour at which symbolic food is served and eaten, such as bread and milk and honey signifying the new life into which the believer has been received. And at wedding receptions, surely the wedding cake and punch are to be thought of and can be interpreted as having quasi-sacramental meanings.

The Theological and Psychological Importance of Impression vis-à-vis Expression

It is crucial to understand, however, that integrity of liturgical action can only be ensured when re-education is *not* based on the assumption which seems widely to underlie such efforts at reform, namely, that physical action is mainly to be thought of as man's expression of his self and his devotion. While it is natural for reflection upon liturgical action to begin first with ourselves, the category of expression taken by itself is the wrong point of departure theologically, and it may well be a dubious point of departure psychologically. Theologically, impression is prior to expression because God is prior to man and because his action is liturgically prior to man's response.

Psychologically, likewise, impression is as important as expression because the realities which act upon man are as decisive for his selfhood as his action upon them. And unless the mind holds the categories of impression and expression in this dialectic in reflecting upon bodily action, thought cannot be true and worship risks losing integrity.

Now it is to be understood that in speaking in this way we are speaking conceptually more than functionally. Functionally, impression by divine reality can only take place through some form of human action. Man's action is the field in which divine impression occurs. But it is essential conceptually to keep the priorities clear. When, for example, expression is taken as the starting point for stating the meaning of physical action, worship can quickly lose integrity because expression for the sake of expression becomes an end in itself. It is forgotten that Christian worship is expression of a certain kind evoked by certain realities, and that the meaning these realities hold must in some way be impressed if expressive action is to be authentic. Liturgical action has been defined as taking up a position vis-à-vis the divine, but it is exactly the nature of "the divine" that is vital for the nature of the "position" taken up. The nature of the God worshipped determines the nature of the action with which man physically worships. If the divine is zodiacally conceived as a luminous tract of sky, let us say, liturgical action may well consist in taking a drug that will fill the worshipper's vision with all the colors of the spectrum and drive him to sit on a mountain at four o'clock in the morning. Or if the deity is conceived as divine energy vibrating at the heart of things, action may appropriately consist of attuning man's body to waves of the cosmos. On the other hand, if the divine is conceived as a personal Father whose glory has shown before men in the face of Jesus Christ, and whose judgement and mercy have acted to reconcile man to himself on a cross, appropriate action will likely be a bowing or kneeling as a bodily *miserere*, and a standing or even dancing as a *sursum corda* of the body in adoration and thanksgiving. In *Christian* worship just any kind of physical action will not do. Expression follows upon and is to be congruous with impression.

But psychologically also, we need to think of physical impression as preceding physical expression far more than we do. To be sure, the dynamic of simultaneity operates here as elsewhere. To paraphrase a sentence Walter H. Frere wrote years ago concerning the reciprocal relation between ceremonial and doctrine: Bodily action (such as ceremonial) serves at the same moment both to convey doctrine (impression) and to evoke man's response (expression).[41] (And as we have observed, one cannot rigidly

[41] *The Principles of Religious Ceremonial* (New York: Longmans, Green, & Co., 1906), p. 13.

structure "revelation," i.e., impression, and "response," i.e. expression.) Yet, worship easily becomes mired in self-generated sentiments when man's expression of his own inward states is made the spring of action. One may make tactical concessions here, as we have suggested in pressing the wisdom of humanizing liturgy, but always with risk and only if one has theologically gotten his priorities clear. But even in terms of tactics, of psychologically getting a purchase upon man's inward experience, often it is the case that inward states are more powerfully affected by bodily action evoked by external stimuli than by spontaneous expression of the inward states themselves. A certain psychological discontinuity between what the worshipper is experiencing and the realities encountering him, and a certain psychological priority to his inward states of these realities and the action appropriate to them, may provide the greatest purchase upon his being and most intensify his action.

It was something of this truth that William James was getting at in his study of religious experience when he maintained that our bodily actions determine our emotions more than our emotions determine our bodily actions. We do not cry because we are sad, for example; rather, we are sad because we cry.[42] James's theory doubtless is oversimple and to a degree perverse; and abundant data to the contrary make the point questionable— the literature on psychosomatic illness, for example. Yet, a modern psychologist has argued that the language available to a man determines his thought more than his thought determines his language.[43] And the principle of action therapy referred to earlier, which holds that it is easier to act one's way into a new way of feeling than to feel one's way into a new way of acting, surely speaks truth to liturgy. It is interesting, parenthetically, how this principle was anticipated many years ago in the oft-quoted words of Friedrich von Hügel in illustrating the action with which man liturgically offers his love to God: "I kiss my child not only because I love it; I kiss it also in order to love it." [44]

The importance of impression is also verified by the associational or recall power of liturgical stimuli as they evoke action. The power of ritual (as we observed in a preceding essay) partly lies in its ability to reawaken,

[42] Noted by E. R. Micklem, *Our Approach to God* (London: Hodder & Stoughton, 1934), pp. 19-21.

[43] Noted by Pruyser, *A Dynamic Psychology of Religion*, pp. 110, 115. The poet Mallarmé once remarked that one does not make a poem first with ideas but with words. The externality of language acts upon the mind to foster internal genesis of meaning. One also remembers A. E. Housman's aphorism, that poetry is not the thing said but a way of saying it.

[44] *Essays and Addresses on the Philosophy of Religion, First Series* (New York: E. P. Dutton & Co., 1921), p. 251.

even reinstate emotional attitudes once experienced but presently lost. For many people the feeling-tone of certain bodily acts associated with experience identified as religious in the past has become part of the psychic complex which constitutes their religious sensitivity.[45] Actions such as kneeling, bowing of the head, repeating words or songs familiar from the past, can induce attitudes not initially present. Feelings are seldom under the control of the will, but actions are; and to perform acts that in the past have been useful associates of feelings can evoke attitudes that go with them.[46] Of course, such recall power can be used for good or ill. But its reality must not be underestimated.

Still further, action fostered by external impression speaks to the common problem of inattention and verifies the didactic potential of worship. People's minds, we have said, are usually distracted and slow-moving, and concentration is difficult. A poll of members of a Lutheran congregation, for example, reported that 65 percent of the people had trouble concentrating on the service. Inattention of course is due to many factors, and especially to the failure of worship to make connection with what the worshipper is inwardly thinking and feeling. Yet, it may be that the worshipper's random flow of consciousness is best countered and grasped when it is not left to itself but is invaded by objective forms, and the didactic power which liturgy at its best exerts is partly to be accounted for on this basis. As prayed doctrine, liturgy can be a powerful catechetical agent precisely because it confronts man with a certain objectivity, even at times with discontinuity. Holy Communion in particular has been described as the Christian Creed in sensuous form, and in summoning the whole man to act, its objectivity teaches through grasping the senses as well as the mind. In this respect, the physical action of eucharistic worship has probably done more than anything else to save Christianity from becoming mere intellectualism. In being physically summoned to act out faith in his nerves and joints and tissues, man existentially learns faith.

Thus with sure instinct and in countless ways the Church has affirmed the liturgical importance of impression vis-á-vis expression. While it has not—at its best—belittled man's inward vitalities, it wisely has not located the source of liturgy in them nor defined the integrity of worship only in light of them. Rather, the Church has conceived the springs of worship as in a sense independent of man's sensibilities. The Church has sometimes carried this insight to extreme, but it has not been wrong either theologically

[45] See James Bissett Pratt, The Religious Consciousness (New York: The Macmillan Co., 1921), pp. 281-82.

[46] See J. Alan Kay, The Nature of Christian Worship (London: Epworth Press, 1953), p. 69.

or psychologically in understanding that men are more likely to be devout because they are made to pray, than to pray because they feel devout. A beautiful prayer from an Armenian liturgy reads: "Have mercy on this people, which, bowed down adore Thy Godhead. Keep them whole, and *stamp upon their hearts the posture of their bodies,* for the inheritance and possession of good things to come." [47] Surely this is a liturgical paradigm of unfailing truth. It not only rebukes the pride which leads men in every generation to reduce liturgy to self-expression. In understanding the power of objective realities to impress man's body and being with meaning, it also offers healing to our disease of liturgical passivity. For if men do really bring on their own illnesses as medical and psychological evidence increasingly suggests, if "a man dies of his own character," then we are most likely to be healed when worship rises out of something more than ourselves. Liturgically, our health and our salvation would seem to be bound up with the grace of that divine Word which is always "there" before we are, and which, when men truly bow down in adoration, will not fail to stamp upon their souls the posture of their bodies.[48]

Bodily Action as Declarative, Interpretative, and Reflexive

A fuller analysis of impression and expression at this point would extend our discussion into the theological context of liturgical action which we reserve to the following essay. However, bearing in mind the dialectical relation between impression and expression, clearly bodily action can powerfully express the vital elements of man's nature which we commonly name will, emotion, and thought. Actions which typically embody these—the offering as the expression of the will, for example, the creed as the assent of the mind and heart to salvation history, singing as the expression of the emotions—have previously been cited. What is not so self-evident is the

[47] Quoted from The Armenian Liturgy by Kay, *The Nature of Christian Worship,* pp. 70-71. Italics mine. Similarly, the Constitution on the Sacred Liturgy of the Roman Catholic Church enjoins the priest to exhort the people "to attune their minds to their voices" in praying the daily office. See par. 90.

[48] I may also cite here a crucial incident in the life of the late Bishop Eivind Berggrav of Norway, who was imprisoned during the Nazi occupation of his country. During his imprisonment, the Bible was his constant companion. But crises of despair came when "the book seemed to give me no solution, no hope. In such a black mood one day I got the idea to read aloud. Seemingly no effect at all! But one hour later I noticed how my mood had changed. The confidence had returned, I was again myself. God had visited his weak son! Why aloud? I don't know. But I think that the sound of the voice was something like the incarnation of the printed word *and* that I had physically *acted* in faith." The italics are Bishop Berggrav's. See his article "What the Bible Means to Me," in *Christianity and Crisis,* Nov. 28, 1955.

variety of functions which expression performs and the variety of effects it achieves. These need to be discriminated.

For one thing, bodily expression is *declarative*. In acting with his body a man exposes and declares his "self." In moving from one stance to another he risks a new relationship with reality and becomes liable to a commitment that was not there before. So far from being felt as a threat, however, actually declarative expression is probably welcomed by most worshippers. Psychologically, man's need to assert his "self" is a fundamental drive of his being. Moreover he usually lives a pathetically bottled-up life; he constantly seeks some reality to which he can open and give himself; and he needs physical ways to concretize his commitments. Hence his salute to the flag, his standing with his hat on his breast for *The Star-Spangled Banner*, his handshake to seal an agreement, his bestowing of a ring at marriage, his writing of his name on a contract. Such bodily acts are intrinsically satisfying. They also can be more unequivocal and less liable to distortion than other expressions of commitment.

The Church of course has long understood this. Altar calls, invitations to discipleship, presentation at Baptism, walking to the Communion rail—all the ways the Church has asked people to "stand up for Jesus" come to mind as illustrations. But surely liturgy can provide for much more declarative expression that is at the same time informed with theological integrity. While local custom and tradition also enter in, may not such traditional actions as kneeling, standing, walking, gathering, signing with the cross, genuflecting be rethought and reappropriated in our ecumenical time by free-church congregations? "There is a *kerygma* in kneeling," it has been said. "When a man is on his knees, then God is not far away!" A real bending of the knees, not merely what we may call the free-church crouch, can declare the bending of the soul.

Yet, standing was by far the most common form of physical action in the early Church, especially to receive the bread and wine. In fact the Council of Nicaea forbade anyone to kneel on Sunday, the Lord's Day, and at Eastertide, because only standing could declare the Christian's faith in the victory of the Resurrection. The same mighty act of God which "raised up Jesus" raised up the believer also. Indeed, standing was "a paschal sign." Thus, standing to declare one's readiness to receive the call to worship or the invitation to Communion would seem to be essential. Standing to receive the elements of Communion—as in Orthodox and certain Lutheran congregations today—can also declare the individual's priesthood with all believers, especially when his fellow believers stand gathered with him around the altar or table and share with one another the bread and the cup. Standing as part of the ceremonial of confirmation may also need to be rethought. It has been suggested, for example, that it is appropriate at confirmation for each confirmand to stand, walk to the communicants' rail, kneel to receive the laying on of hands, and then return to his former place, in order to avoid only passively receiving the blessing and in order to act out the decision the confirmand has made. Especially, standing to hear the reading of the Gospel [49] (and to receive the benediction at the close of the service) can declare the believer's decision to take into his life Christ the Word. It also signifies the believer's readiness to live out the Gospel in obedience. It is as if the *miles Christi* comes to attention, salutes, and accepts the commands of the Captain of Salvation.

To identify such meanings as these that bodily action can declare is not to say, of course, that they will automatically come to pass. Always other factors operate that are beyond anyone's control; and even when faithfully performed, bodily actions can seem wooden. Yet, liturgy errs when it overlooks the reciprocal relation between the body's action and the soul's faith. Through physical action, commitments can be made, vows registered, and the risks of faith accepted. In short, through them the Christian man can declare himself.

Secondly, bodily expression is *interpretative*. One may say of expression in this sense what Scott Francis Brenner has said of ceremonial: It is "a living commentary upon the Gospel." [50] Such commentary of the body affects the worshipper himself; it affects his fellow worshippers—hence the power of corporate physical action; it affects any "outsider" who may be present, as St. Paul well knew; and we may believe that it affects God. If the voicing of truthful prayer by the tongue and vocal chords, or even the thinking of truthful prayer by the brain cells, affects the divine, as these surely must if God is as Jesus Christ reveals him to be and if prayer itself is not an illusion, then other physically grounded actions must be thought of as efficacious.

Accordingly, great care must be taken that at any given moment, bodily action as part of the language of worship interpret truthfully the Christian nature of man's relation to God and God's relation to man. When, for example, the worshipper sits to hear the Gospel read, his posture of passivity belies the action of really hearing which the Gospel is calling for; the body's commentary is at cross-purposes with the Gospel itself. Similarly, the interpretative effect of the minister's bodily action is vital. There is much to be said, for example, for the pastor coming down from the chancel and

[49] Standing for the Gospel was ordered at least as early as the fourth century.
[50] *The Art of Worship: A Guide in Corporate Worship Techniques* (New York: Macmillan Co., 1961), p. 21.

standing amidst the people to read the Gospel, to signify that the "Gospel of grace" comes down amidst men. Or, if it is felt that the Word does not so much "come down to" as "rise out of" man's world, then let the Gospel be read by someone who rises out of the congregation to do so. It is not too much to say that the interpretative effect of bodily action can make or break the integrity of a service, or that it can convey—or fail to convey—an entire theology of worship. John A. T. Robinson has written, for example, that the "eastward" position the minister often takes in celebrating Communion, with his back to the people, pictorially focuses attention upon a point "out there" toward which the people's worship is conducted. The effect of the "westward" or "basilican" position, on the other hand, with the minister facing the people, focuses attention upon "a point in the middle" where Christ comes to stand among his people as the divine host. The former position interprets the Eucharist more in terms of transcendence, the latter more in terms of immanence. While "no one is to say that the one is right and the other is wrong" in that "each is complementary, and a useful corrective, to the other," [51] in any case physical expression powerfully interprets spiritual meaning.

Lastly, the *reflexive* effect of bodily expression must not be underestimated. As we have noted, it can happen that the worshipper will undertake an action he does not feel like engaging in at the moment, but the meaning implicit in the action bends back upon his being through nerves and tissues to effect an inward state that was not there before. Illustrations again quickly come to mind. Singing a hymn of praise when we do not initially feel joyful can reawaken joy. Declaring the Creed when our spirits are low and our faith is dim can rekindle faith. To be sure, such reflexive effects do not always happen. Sometime a hymn of praise begun in the doldrums ends there too; and to declare faith when faith is dim may foster guilt more than it bolsters belief. Yet, people cannot be left merely to their own passing feelings, important as they are, for deeper, longer-range effects are at stake. Actions repeatedly engaged in over a period of time can react upon man's inward life to build a structure of kinesthetic certitude that stabilizes him amidst fluctuations of faith and feeling. Physical actions also can foster motor carry-over into man's moral life. Indeed, as agents of transformation, they also can react upon man's subconscious life. Each action—in a figure of Douglas Steere—can be thought of as resembling the effect of a stone dropped beneath the surface of the waves in constructing a jetty at the seashore. Taken by itself, any one action is not too important; but while invisible to the eye and forgotten by the conscious mind, the effect of

[51] *Liturgy Coming to Life*, p. 27.

repeated actions becomes cumulative. An interior bulwark only partly visible can fortify the inward life. Tides are less violent. The power of the shifting winds is mitigated. Erosion is halted and reference points for navigation are preserved. A worshipper may bring more courage to the threatening changes of history if he has regularly knelt—as Luther advised us to do—at the words of the Creed marking the invasion of the Divine into history: *homo factus est.* He will face the prospect of death with less fear if he has sung again and again the "Gloria": 'is now and ever shall be, world without end. Amen." He can appraise both the good and the evil of secular influences hourly beating upon his consciousness if he has regularly signed his existence with the sign of the cross. And he may more likely stand for the Gospel in the ambiguous ethical decisions he must make in his life in the world if he has stood for the Gospel in his worship.

Such, then, are some of the realities conditioning man as liturgical agent in whose light the question of action must be viewed—the influences of culture, and the psychological and physical nature of man's being. Important as they are, however, the nature of liturgical action is finally to be understood within the context of the worshipper's life in the Church and within the light of the Word. To these we turn in the concluding part of this essay.

VIII

The Nature of Liturgical Action

Part 2: The Context of Church and Word

While the question of liturgical action in important ways is an anthropological question, it is finally a theological question. Its decisive context is the action of Jesus Christ amidst his people, and ecclesiology and Christology become the ultimate frame for thought. Therefore—to revert to our earlier metaphor—to know the kind of patient we are dealing with as well as what kind of sickness the patient has, one must look empirically at the patient's life in the congregation. One need not be cynical in saying this for always the Church is both sick and well, *simul justus et peccator*; but diagnosis requires us to view the patient in his ecclesiastical environment as well as his cultural environment and try to observe its effect upon him.

Our task is not made easy by the lip service paid by churches to the importance of action. A reading of almost any up-to-date denominational statement on liturgy would lead one to think that the action of the congregation is well understood and adequately provided for. The trouble is, however, that ecclesiastical definition is one thing; what the laity actually experience the Church's worship to be is another. And what ecclesiastical statements usually ignore is the reciprocal relation between liturgical action and the total life of the cult community. The congregation's entire life grounds the dynamics of liturgy, and the question of action cannot be dealt with in detachment from that life. The community's life is an unceasing commentary upon the integrity with which people and pastor have engaged in liturgical action, as their liturgical action in turn validates—or fails to validate—their congregational life.

ILLUSTRATIVE ANALYSIS OF THE WORSHIPPER'S LIFE IN THE CHURCH

We may call this relation *the principle of correspondence: authenticity or inauthenticity of action at one place makes for authenticity or inauthenticity at another.* The action of the congregation in relation to the Word in worship and their action in relation to the Word elsewhere condition one another. Indeed in the last analysis these are one action, and integrity in worship—as the word "integrity" signifies—consists exactly in understanding and preserving these as one. The interrelation of three Greek categories derived from the New Testament can be employed to state this truth: *leitourgia* meaning liturgy, *koinonia* meaning fellowship, *diakonia* meaning service or ministry. These three expressions of congregational life condition one another. The measure of reality which a congregation finds in the action of *leitourgia* depends on the reality they have experienced in the action of *koinonia* and *diakonia*.

Liturgical Action and Congregational Discipline

This insight can be verified by inquiring into the correlation between worship and congregational discipline. Broadly speaking, "discipline" may be thought of as the concerned, loving confrontation of the members of the *koinonia* by the ministry of the congregation—both lay and ordained—to inquire into the congregation's Christian faith and discipleship, and into their commitment to the worship and ministry of Christ's Church. Warrant for the exercise of discipline goes back to the New Testament itself, in which it is implied throughout that one can be part of the Church's worship—in particular, eucharistic worship—only on profession of faith in Jesus Christ, Baptism in his name, and obedience to his lordship. The necessity of discipline was reaffirmed by Calvin and the Puritans in the familiar metaphor of the sinews of the body which knit the members together, and was regarded as being as vital to the body of the community as the worship which gave life to the community's soul. Protestantism has generally disavowed the ultimate form of discipline, excommunication. But in our day it also has largely abandoned any norms for determining the grounds on which the layman participates in the Church's worship, and it inquires only perfunctorily into the congruity of his cultic life with his life elsewhere. The effect upon liturgy of the collapse of Church discipline has been incalculable. In allowing the relation between the action of worship and the worshipper's action elsewhere to be severed, the nerve of integrity has been cut. And we can only expect it to be restored when the layman is made to understand that the action he is expected to put forth in worship is of a piece with the action he is expected to put forth elsewhere.

An insight from the history of worship can instruct us here. In his study of early Christian worship, Oscar Cullmann remarks upon the stereotyped usage in a number of writings of the Greek verb *koluein* meaning "to hinder." [1] For example, a candidate for Baptism would be asked: "What doth hinder thee from being baptized?" The frequency of such usages, together with their stereotype character, testifies to the care with which the Church related discipline to liturgy. One was unthinkable without the other, and on the deepest level this must always be the case. This is to say, *the question of liturgical action must be seen as an ethical question.* In a phrase of Paul Lehmann, the "ethical reality of the *koinonia*" conditions the integrity of *leitourgia*.[2] Liturgical action can be authentic only as the Christian man is claimed to live out the commitments that illumine its meaning.

When the relation of discipline to liturgy is recognized and transposed into the life of the modern congregation, a number of questions follow—questions admittedly easier to state than to answer but which must nevertheless be asked. What thought is given to, and what provision is made for, the exercise of discipline in the structures of congregational life? Is the constraint of baptismal vows taken once in years long past lifted up and re-pronounced? Do pastor and people warn confirmands and new members of the moral meaning of their liturgical vows, and how can this be done with love, without legalism, and yet forcefully? What moral preparation for worship must the congregation be taught to undertake? How can the ethical ambiguity of their worldly life be recognized, and yet moral claims be identified and announced? How can the pastor teach the people the discipline of self-examination and renunciation of sins that render unworthy their hearing of the Lord's word and the eating of his bread and drinking of his cup? To what brother must they be directed to be reconciled and what penance must they practice? [3] What vows must be renewed? What

---

[1] *Early Christian Worship* trans. A. Stewart Todd and James B. Torrance (London: SCM Press, 1953), p. 25.

[2] See Lehmann's *Ethics in a Christian Context* (New York: Harper & Row, 1963), p. 103.

[3] Free-church Protestantism would do well to learn from the Roman Catholic Church and find its own equivalent of penance which, as a form of discipline, can replace flabbiness with sinew. To object to penance as "salvation by works," aside from being a misapplication of the phrase, blinds us to the relation between the moral work of the Christian life and the "work" of "liturgy," a word whose very root means "work." In speaking of the observance of Lent, the Constitution on Liturgy of Vatican II states that its purpose is to encourage a penitential spirit in the faithful "so that the joys of the Sunday of the Resurrection may be visited on uplifted and responsive spirits." "The role of the Church in penitential practices is not to be passed over," and "penance should not be only internal and individual but also external and social . . . according to the possibilities of the present day and of a given area, as well as of individual circumstances." *The Documents of Vatican II*, ed. Walter J. Abbott (New York: Guild Press, America Press, Association Press, 1966), p. 170. The relation of the "joys of the Resurrection" to a "penitential spirit" is a paradigm of all worship in its soteriological character, not only of Lent and

deaths must a congregation die and to what new life would it be resurrected? Where must the people fast and watch in order to pray, and how
can fasting be redefined for today? [4]

Liturgical Action and the Discipline of Prayer

Indeed, part of the discipline of the congregation's life is the discipline
of prayer, as we have observed; the sense of reality felt by the congregation as
it acts to pray when gathered is conditioned by the members' faithfulness in
prayer when dispersed. Prayer is a total dimension of the life of the *koinonia*
and it is as much an ethical as a liturgical claim. Only as the congregation has
performed its duty to confess, give thanks, and intercede when dispersed
can its prayer be real when it gathers. In this respect the people's action of
prayer simultaneously sustains the Church and is sustained by the Church.
The Christian man both prays for and is prayed for.[5] The prayers of the
individual influence the prayer of the Church, and the prayer of the Church
affects the prayers of the individual. Indeed, in an ultimate sense the prayer
of the *koinonia* is part of the prayer of Christ himself. His words at the tomb
of Lazarus, "thou hearest me always," may be figuratively interpreted to
mean that our prayer is not our own; it is part of the eternal, living intercession of our Lord himself. And by as much as the congregation does not
fulfill the discipline of prayer, Christ's action is hindered.

Given this understanding, the more that the prayer of the *koinonia* when
dispersed is joined to their prayer when gathered, the more vital the action
of worship can be expected to be. Intercessions in public worship, therefore,
should rise out of intercession in the people's daily life. Events and things
for which they are thankful elsewhere should be named as such when they
gather. Correspondingly, the concerns of the Church, local and universal,
should be impressed upon the people to be remembered in prayer in
private. Names of individuals, movements, causes, organizations, needs—

Easter. And only as Protestantism devises a relevant form of penance can liturgical action
be grounded in ethical reality.

[4] On the relation of fasting and prayer, Alex C. Vidler writes: "Have you reflected on the
fact that in the New Testament the duty of praying is generally married either to the duty
of watching or to the duty of fasting? 'Watch and pray.' 'Prayer and fasting.' The Word
of God has joined these duties together; it is men, and especially modern men, who have
put them asunder. In the modern church we are often urged to pray; but hardly ever
urged to watch or to fast, or told how we should do so. And that may be one of the
reasons why the modern church is a weak church." *Windsor Sermons* (London: SCM
Press, 1958), p. 104.

[5] Dietrich Bonhoeffer writes: "The first condition, which makes it possible for an
individual to pray for the group, is the intercession of all the others for him and his
prayer. How could one person pray the prayer of the fellowship without being steadied
and upheld in prayer by the fellowship itself?" *Life Together,* trans. John W. Doberstein
(New York: Harper & Bros., 1954), p. 63.

and, not least, thankful remembrance of the dead—might well be printed in weekly or monthly cycles and distributed to the people. Also, intentional prayers of the congregation for their services when they gather should be solicited. One clergyman asks members of his congregation in turn to gather on Saturday evening for intercession for the services on the next day. The deacons of Reformed and Presbyterian congregations similarly gather on Sunday for prayer before the service. The discipline of prayer can mightily weave the fabric of a congregation's liturgical life. And liturgy in turn can be to the people a "school of prayer" and a "school of fellowship" in their congregational life.

Liturgical Action and Love in the *Koinonia*

But discipline is ultimately to be gathered up in love. Only love in the *koinonia* can render the action of *leitourgia* authentic, as love manifest in worship can alone make authentic the life of the community. The model for thought in grasping this truth must surely be the mind of St. Paul as he deals with worship in the eight through the fourteenth chapters of the First Epistle to the Corinthians. At the very heart of his discussion, it will be remembered, Paul places his matchless hymn on love, as if to say that from love everything liturgically flows and to it everything aspires. The early Church bodied forth this truth in various ways, most notably in the sign of the holy kiss through which—in the words of St. Cyril—"souls are mingled together"; and correspondingly its common life so shone forth with love that the reaction of the unbeliever—in the legendary words—was to marvel, "See how these Christians love one another."

Here lies the core of the relation of congregational life to the action of worship: love visibly enacted in worship is the source of the members' love for one another elsewhere, and their love for one another elsewhere conditions their action in worship. The fountain of this love is always the Christ whose Presence is nothing other than his love in action we speak of as grace. The milieu of his love, however, is the people of the congregation. His action is manifest in theirs, and anything that violates the spirit of love in worship contradicts the essence of the action of worship. Competitiveness between the choir and clergy, the vanity and exhibitionism of ushers, intolerance on the part of critics, monopolizing of the service by the minister or the musicians, insensitivity to the needs of the people, scorn for people's ignorance, favoring one group over another, failure in intercessory prayer to reach out to the world, preaching that is harsh and unloving in tone— such denials of love disable the action of worship at its source and extend over into the congregation's common life.

Especially, bitter quarrelling over changes in worship vitiates action. Always of course the constraint to speak the truth in love, operates. Love does not mean, in the words of Peter Brunner,

that the form of worship must conserve spiritual faults. Whoever construes love as an accommodation to existing conditions misunderstands its essence. It would be veritably loveless, if love were to assent to any existing perversion. It cannot be denied, for instance, that the obscurity to which the celebration of Holy Communion is often relegated as an adjunct to worship for individual members of the congregation poses a great spiritual blemish. . . . The demand that the form of worship be subject to love must not, under any circumstances, be construed to mean that the congregation dare not be roused from its false contentment with any perversion in its life of worship.

Yet,

without love, the church's liberty is not the eschatological liberty in the Spirit. Love, which rules all charisms, . . . also rules the form of worship in that broad and free area between the forbidden and the commanded. . . . Only that form of worship that is ruled by love builds the congregation. Love beholds the brother. . . . Love is endowed with a long life. Love can afford to wait. Love is paired with wisdom. Love does not force a certain form of worship on the congregation. With patience and wisdom love . . . waits until, in the spontaneity of spiritual insight, that which is appropriate in the form of worship is apprehended in liberty and realized in liberty.[6]

Similarly, insofar as jealousy, grudges, complacency, deceit, an unforgiving spirit, which wound the congregation's common life, are not set within the claim of love, liturgical action is hindered. The members are separated from one another. Each is driven in upon himself; he is not freed to act and to do what worship requires. To speak of love in this way of course is not to romanticize the congregation and pretend that people are other than they are. People come to worship precisely to get rid of the sin of lovelessness that disables them for worship. The Church is always *peccator*, and the pastor must not maneuver the people into impossible attitudes in the manner of the clergyman who listed as No. 1 of "10 Rules for Worship": "I will leave at home all things and thoughts unbecoming to the house of God, . . . hates, grudges, frettings, worldly cares, sinful thoughts." Such unrealism falsifies the action of worship at the outset. Rather, sins and sinfulness are to be recognized as such but always set within the constraint of that love which flows from the presence of Christ among his people. Very simply, only as the members of the congregation are claimed to love one another as Christ has loved them, to love one another as themselves, to care for one another costingly, in all things to strive to bring a will that is good and a heart that

[6] *Worship in the Name of Jesus*, trans. M. H. Bertram (St. Louis: Concordia Publishing House, 1968), pp. 232-33.

reconciles and is reconciled, can liturgical action become true. The congregational participation so many ministers profess to desire will only come to pass when both pastor and people are willing to bear the liturgical command addressed by Paul to the Church in every generation: "Put love first" (I Cor. 14:1 NEB).

The Congregation's Ministry in the World

The community's life, however, includes *diakonia*—their "ministry" or "service" as well as their fellowship. The Church's very being, we have said, consists in its apostolic nature, and the principle of correspondence requires one above all to inquire into the relation between worship and the congregation's ministry in the world. Here this principle operates in the Church's life with something of the ruthlessness with which Jesus joins together the first and second commandments on which hang all the law and the prophets for liturgical theology as for all else. In fact, while we have named this relation with the colorless term "correspondence," we are dealing here with nothing less than the integrity of worship as the wholeness of the Christian life in its cultic and apostolic aspects, as the love of God and man, and in the relation of *leitourgia* to *diakonia*, of liturgy to service, lies the main key to the question of this essay. While the relation between liturgy and ministry—or alternatively, of worship and mission—ultimately inheres in the nature of Jesus Christ, their mutuality is also to be understood ecclesiologically. And in order to determine the authenticity of liturgical action, one must inspect how a congregation sees itself as Church, and in light of its self-image what its operating as well as its theoretical doctrines of liturgy and ministry really are.

In light of this approach it becomes clear that the passivity we deplore —probably more than anything else—is due to a congregation's restricted self-understanding as "Church" as largely the assembly for worship, and of worship in turn as something detached from their ministry in the world; and given the realities of parish life for many congregations, they can hardly be blamed for this misunderstanding. The grip of inverted, static parish structures upon the layman's consciousness, for one thing, inevitably carries over into his understanding of "Church" and of "worship," both psychologically and theologically; for it is through parish structures, be it always remembered, that the layman experiences the Church as Church. The theological definition of "Church" in his denomination's articles of faith is not half as decisive for what he feels the Church to be as the bulletin he reads with its listing of organizations and activities, the church mail he receives, the committee meetings he attends, the impression of the church building, and the appeals the church makes for his money and time. For him the nature of the Church is what the nature of empirical structures tells him it is. And clearly, when structures organize the congregation's life by the imperative "come" to the exclusion of the imperative "go," when "Church" is understood as something to be withdrawn into rather than as something sent, when such terms as "membership," "churchmanship," "worship," "service" hold primarily in-group meanings, or when threats to a congregation's security have bred a rigid defensiveness—the layman can hardly be blamed for misunderstanding the Church as something gathered from rather than as dispersed into the world. Further, when imagination has broken down and inertia prevails, and misconceived structures have become ossified and idolized, fixity of structures will beget fixity in attitudes. It may not be straining things to say that the congregation which conceives its structures "according to the book" or conducts its organized life according to *Roberts Rules of Order* is likely to rigidify worship in the same way.

Materials commonly used in worship reinforce this inversion and edify the congregation in a bad rather than in a good sense. Many church rites, prayers, responsive readings, invitations to worship, Sunday school worship materials, printed materials distributed by denominational bureaus, consolidate a conception of the Church as an institution more than as an expedition and reinforce a congregation's preoccupation with itself. An analysis made by J. G. Davies of the eighty-six collects used in the Book of Common Prayer illustrates this tendency. Eighty-two collects, Davies found, are concerned solely with the Church and its members, and only four have any reference to the world.[7] Invitations to worship widely used in thousands of Sunday bulletins similarly reveal a corrupting self-image. The following is typical: "This church seeks to give rest to the weary, comfort to the troubled, hope to the downcast, and the Christ-like strength of a quiet mind to all who come within these portals. Worship begins as you enter here, and a reverent silence is requested as you depart from the sanctuary. Leave not without a prayer for yourself, for him who ministers, and for all who have worshipped with you." One can only conjecture as to the effect of such an invitation upon a congregation's mind week after week! When the Church is conceived as mainly retreat, and worship is understood to take place only within its portals; when the layman is conceived as a passive vessel come to be filled, and when ministry is interpreted as confined to the clergy, the wholeness of the Christian life as both cultic and apostolic has probably been ruptured and authentic liturgical action rendered all but impossible.

To be sure, what appears on the surface to be liturgical action may be going on. Given an inverted understanding of itself as Church, a congrega-

[7] *Worship and Mission* (London: SCM Press, 1966), p. 151.

tion may well find forms of worship which consolidate its self-image congenial and actively participate in them. The congenial, however, is by no means authentic, and participation for the sake of participation can be demonic.[8]

In a different vein, the boredom which many free-church laymen find the service of Communion to hold can be equally revealing. While boredom may reflect an appreciation of the preached Word as an event that truly involves, more likely it betrays the Church's failure to press home upon the layman the connection between his liturgical action in Communion and his diakonal action in the world. The intention of Communion, as the term "Mass"—deriving from the verb *mitto* meaning "to send"—suggests, is to send the layman in Christ's name into the world. The bread and wine through which Christ's presence is made known are symbols of the world. But because the layman's consciousness has been corrupted by a congregational ethos and by congregational structures which detach him from the world, he is disabled for finding meaningful the sacrament of God's love for the world. Because the Church has failed to teach him to relate reality in worship to reality elsewhere, he can only react to Communion as something foreign to his real life: his boredom confesses that the meaning of his worship and the meaning of his ministry have not been existentially made one. That which God has joined together the Church has put asunder.

If there be truth in this analysis, then it becomes clear that the question of liturgical action can only be answered by restating the theological relation between *leitourgia* and *diakonia* in ways the layman can empirically grasp. The layman will get a true understanding of the relation between worship and service in the same way he has gotten a false understanding—by being exposed to this relation through concrete experiences whose impact he cannot escape. This is to say, an unlearning of the *esse* of the Church as only cultic and a *relearning of the esse of the Church as also apostolic* may need to be the first order of business, and in very practical ways. This may require for one thing a change in strategy whereby the pastor reconceives his priorities, first sensitizes the layman to experiences of ministry in the world, and

---

[8] The results of a psychological survey of the meaning which worship held for a well-educated, white, upper-middle-class congregation in the upper South are enlightening. On the one hand, the congregation experienced worship—on their terms—as "a vital source of strength for Christian living" in that it strengthened family life, provided "a sense of fellowship" and of "growth" through the teaching impact of preaching. On the other hand, the congregation felt practically no need for relief of guilt through confession of sin in weekly worship; the desire to thank God for his blessings was acknowledged by few; and the offering of self and gifts to God was consistently ranked the least helpful element. Significantly, among 12,000 responses given on 167 returned surveys, only 15 were negative in any way. See Harold L. Wahking, "Why Do People Go to Church?" *Pastoral Psychology*, XVII (Feb., 1966).

then works inductively into the meaning of liturgy. And as long as liturgical action is understood as having integrity only insofar as it embraces both, and as long as the presence of Christ is understood as the source of the life and the shape of the mission the layman lives out in the world, such an approach may be indicated. Another way to describe this strategy is to say that the pastor's first duty may be to think through with his people what it means to be a missionary congregation, to train them to become a lay apostolate, and then to consider together how worship rises from mission as well as leads into mission. Or again, pastor and congregation may need to learn together how social action can be a form of liturgical action; how the congregation's witness in the world and their service to God when gathered is the same action moving in different directions; how the Gospel is "celebrated" in both social action and cultic action.

Indeed, liturgical action may need to be related to, if not transposed into, political action in particular, not merely into social action in general, if it is to be real. The congregation may need to think through what has been called "the political hermeneutics of the Gospel"; and despite the controversy this process may provoke, the pastor may have no alternative if the action of *leitourgia* is to be related to the action of *diakonia* and worship is to possess integrity. The truth of any theological concept can be experienced as real by most people today only insofar as it is related to action involving human relationships, and in our time the collective relationships that matter are nothing if not political. Politics is the battleground of salvation today, it has been said, the place where the very meaning and destiny of human life are being determined. At the same time, Christian liturgy itself is nothing if not political. It rises out of a political and sacred history so intertwined that one can hardly turn a page of that history without running head on into political realities. And this history comes to focus in an eschatological event whose very name is political: "Jesus came into Galilee proclaiming the Gospel of God: 'The time has come; the *kingdom* of God is upon you.'" (Mark 1:14 NEB). In that event was announced "the immediacy of that political reality of power in which liberation was possible and offered: the kingdom of God. The Gospel is thus the annunciation of the historical reality of the ongoing politics of God." [9] Liturgy contradicts itself if in one way or another it does not mark the meaning of human life with the light of this political Gospel. Thus all movements in the congregation's worldly life which seek to liberate men from poverty, from oppression, from ignorance, from discrimination, from war, from pain—in these the layman can be trained to identify the political and liberating power of the Kingdom at

[9] Rubem A. Alves, *A Theology of Human Hope* (Washington: Corpus Books, 1969), p. 92.

work. And in these spheres likewise the layman can be trained to identify the political nature of the principalities and powers that hold men captive as well.

When liturgical action is reconceived in this way, as the intersection of cultic action and social action, worship can take on the character of the truly "public" worship to which we have referred. Practical means may have to be devised to provide for this intersection and to enable the congregation both to recollect and to anticipate the meanings of service, fellowship, and liturgy as they interfuse. For example, J.-J. von Allmen has said that "the Eucharist is the point from which all the income and expenditure of the Church should be controlled." [10] Is it farfetched to suggest that discussion be held and decisions be made as to the claim of social needs upon the congregation's funds right in the Communion service and in light of its meaning? Again, it has been said that only those who obey the command of Christ to "go" have the capacity to know what forms of worship the community should use when it obeys the command to "come." [11] Should not the form of preaching, accordingly, even the substance of preaching itself, the kind of music sung, the nature of the prayers offered, the symbols and ceremonial used, be shaped by those engaged in the congregation's mission in the world? And might not the controversy this would likely precipitate be made part of the discipline of the congregation of which we have written?

Indeed, cannot the service itself be redesigned to include preparation in the form of discussion of vital social and political questions in light of the Bible, perhaps by discussion task forces organized in advance, and then to include reports from these? For that matter, the "reporting" itself of members' experiences of ministry could constitute part of the materials of worship, perhaps tape recordings, the reading of important newspaper and magazine articles, statements of concern, and announcements and interpretations of significant events.[12] When these acts and elements are set within the context of Bible, song, prayer, sacrament, worship may become changed into a kind of holy town meeting and take on a vitality that comes in no other way. The people can unaffectedly express their secularized consciousness and need not feel embarrassed in doing so. Similarly they can find themselves apprehended at points in their life they know to be important and hence feel worship to speak to them with truthfulness. The gulf between clergy and laity can also be overcome. The minister still functions as the responsible

[10] *Worship: Its Theology and Practice* (New York: Oxford University Press, 1965), p. 296.
[11] "The Congregation for Others," *Study Encounter* (Geneva: World Council of Churches, 1967), III, 101.
[12] An order for this type of service could be: Gathering; Concern; Word; The Answer of Faith; The Form of Obedience; Sending.

leader, but he is no longer identified as having the answers and the laity the questions; rather, both participate together in asking the questions and discovering the answers. Most of all, the doctrine of the Church can become lived doctrine. The people can learn the full meaning of the Church through being the Church: *leitourgia, koinonia, diakonia* become one.

Liturgical Action and the Priesthood of Believers

But while the congregation's life consists of *koinonia* and *diakonia*, its *esse* consists not least of *leitourgia*, and once more theological priorities must assert themselves. The Church is a distinctive community, and its worship is to declare this: the Church is liturgical event. It is not first a society for self-nurture nor an organization of men of political concern and social goodwill. Rather, the Church is a dynamic reality which comes into being through the action of Jesus Christ forming himself in his people. The Church is also a charismatic community of divine grace even as it is a human community. It is not first a multitude of human individuals voluntarily coming together but a unity of persons who know themselves to be objectively grasped by a divine life. Especially, it is a corporate community whose members are so "changed into one another" through their participation in Christ—in Luther's words—that only such metaphors as "one bread," "one body" can convey the ontological nature and cohesion of their life together. Such corporateness is not to cancel out the worshipper's personal identity; but understood as the congregation's common life in Christ, it is both the ground and the goal of liturgical action, and its reality alone guarantees the authenticity of action as *Christian* action.[13]

Perhaps the most helpful thought-form with which the Church has conceptualized this liturgical self-understanding is that of the priesthood of believers. Because the living, interceding Christ is the true agent in liturgy,

---

[13] See ch. II. Herman A. Preus quotes a moving passage from Luther to portray the depth of corporateness: 'If anyone be in despair . . . or have any other burden on his heart, and desire to be rid of them all, let him go joyfully to the Sacrament of the altar and lay down his grief in the midst of *the congregation* and seek *help from the entire company of the spiritual body.* . . . Therefore, the immeasurable grace and mercy of God are given us in this Sacrament, that we may there lay down all misery and tribulation and *put it on the congregation, and especially on Christ,* and may joyfully strengthen and comfort ourselves and say: 'Though I am a sinner and have fallen, . . . I will go to the Sacrament to receive a sign from God that *I have on my side Christ's righteousness,* life and sufferings, *with all holy angels and all the blessed in heaven, and all pious men on earth. If I die, I am not alone* in death; if I suffer, *they suffer with me. I have shared all* my misfortune *with Christ and the saints,* since I have a sure sign of their love toward me.' Lo, this is a benefit to be derived from this Sacrament, this is the use we should make of it; then the heart cannot but rejoice and be comforted." Jaroslav Pelikan, Regin Prenter, and Herman A. Preus, *More About Luther* (Decorah, Iowa: Luther College Press, 1958), p. 149. Italics mine.

and because he has promised to be present in each member as well as collectively in the community, all act as priests and celebrants with him. Today as in the early Church, experience teaches us that the congregation can act effectively only if leaders are elected or appointed, but this does not mean that the leaders' action can be substituted for the members', that special grace is conveyed through their leadership, that they are to act as intermediaries, or that they are to perform functions which each person does not have the right himself to perform. All the people minister liturgically as otherwise, and the work of liturgy—as we have noted—properly belongs to all

To work out the implications of this ecclesial understanding may be the first step for pastor and people in dealing with the problem of inaction. The doctrine of "priesthood" may or may not be named as such, but straightforward, even didactic instruction in its truth may need to be the first order of business. Given capable leadership and well-chosen materials, there is no reason why laymen cannot be interested in a study of New Testament worship in this sense—for example, of such biblical key words as "minister," "laity," "church," "presbyter" (the word "priest" derives from the biblical word "presbuteros" via the old English word "préost"), "deacon," "liturgy," "service," and so on. Similarly, worship historically and ecumenically understood as the people's worship can be brought alive. Confirmation classes, occasional sermon series, forums, lectures by guests from other traditions, worship workshops and retreats—perhaps using a full day and involving families and children, with congregational meals and fellowship—distribution of printed materials, discussion at stated board and committee meetings —these offer obvious opportunities. "Instructional" or "commentary" or "narrative" services are also appropriate: before a service begins, or as an opening part of the service itself, a teacher can take the congregation and informally explain the rationale for their participation, interpret the meaning of elements in the service, and even rehearse the people in their parts.

In this respect, a cardinal rule employed by the Roman Church applies to Protestant congregations also: "No legislation without formation." That is, people's attitudes and understandings must be formed before liturgical decisions are made and functions defined. Indeed, often education best takes place through involving the laity in liturgical revision, and so far from fearing, the wise pastor will welcome their involvement. Any new or "correct" order imposed without their involvement is a contradiction in terms if one really believes that worship belongs to the people; and their uncertainties or protests may actually be nearer to an authentic conception of action than the determination of the minister to do what he thinks is best. At least the laity are saying, "This is our worship, this is our service," and in this respect they are right.[14] Moreover, if the laity are left passive in changing worship they will probably remain passive in living out the meaning of worship: whatever they fail to be in worship, they will fail to be in the world, it has been rightly said.[15]

Most of all, involvement of the laity in preparing and conducting worship can help them empirically learn theological doctrine: the concept of the priesthood of all believers will come alive when liturgy is the people's work not only in the sense that they perform the action of worship, but also in the sense that they do the work of studying and planning for worship as well. Teams or committees should be formed to work with the leader of worship perhaps on a weekly or monthly cycle, and the pastor may well reallocate the time he would normally devote to "his" sermon and service to working with them on their service—on the order, music, readings, proclamation, experimental innovations, even ceremonial and physical and artistic arrangements. Particular attention should be paid to providing opportunity for improvisation and spontaneity that involve laymen in the service. One is rightly suspicious of rigged "happenings," but opportunity can be provided for them genuinely to occur; and no one will know better how to do this than the laymen themselves. In this connection certain characteristics of the layman's liturgical consciousness we have identified should be borne in mind: the vitalities of his nature he trusts elsewhere, his pleasure in the plastic and empirical, his insistence that he have part in shaping statements of faith, the ecstatic element that is deep in us all and that needs to be brought to expression.

Within this theological understanding also, much, if not most, of the service can be conducted by the laity. In the early Church, we know, a deliberate effort was made to divide up the functions of worship among as many people as possible;[16] and if the people are theologically instructed and not just mechanically used, there is no reason why services today cannot be similarly conceived. In fact, while in most congregations the pastor will continue to be nominally responsible for worship, he may well reconceive his liturgical ministry as that of coach or equipper of the laity in their liturgical ministry as well as in their ministry in the world. Actually, it is

[14] See the article by James Whyte, "Liturgy, Laity, and Architecture," in *Church Service Society Annual*, May, 1962.

[15] See Davies, *Worship and Mission*, p. 148.

[16] See A. G. Hebert, *Liturgy and Society* (London: Faber & Faber, 1935), p. 75. Even in the Middle Ages, when worship is commonly supposed to have been dominated by the priest, the laity participated in substantial numbers. Walter H. Frere writes that in a medieval Sarum rite for matins on Christmas Day, for example, nearly fifty persons were required to conduct the service. *The Principles of Religious Ceremonial* (New York: Longmans, Green & Co., 1906), p. 279.

hard to think of any part of the service which laymen cannot be trained to conduct. And even in the denominations which restrict certain acts to the ordained clergy—the words of institution or the prayer of consecration in Communion, for example—cannot lay deacons or their equivalent take the rest of the service?

As noted in an earlier essay, music especially belongs to the people, and theologically the burden of proof rests on those who support the case for a choir separate from the congregation. *The congregation is the true choir, and all music should be conceived within this principle.*[17] "Let the people praise thee, O God; let all the people praise thee" is the proper rubric for musical action. This rubric can allow that a group of people within the Christian community who with faith, humility, and self-effacement undertake to voice the proclamation and prayer of the congregation musically can be designated to represent the congregation as *choros.* It also allows that the congregation can be thought of as involved in the action of music even though they appear only to be passively listening. But this rubric also requires us never to forget that all liturgical music is ultimately to be thought of as Christian prayer and Christian proclamation; that those who minister musically perform a sacrificial and sacramental function; that their action participates in the action of Christ and is to be the means of his presence to his people. Choir—as well as clergy and congregation—are bound by no less high a claim than this.

However, this rubric may well mean also that anthems and solos be abolished and more hymns used instead so that the people can physically participate in the action of music; or that if an anthem is sung, it be in the spirit of a true "anthem," that is, an "antiphon" in which the people and choir join.[18] This rubric may also mean that instead of weekly rehearsals of special music to be sung by a choir at the people, periodic rehearsals be held for the congregation to train them to sing as the people—in responsive singing, chanting, new hymn tunes, folk music appropriate for worship, etc. In fact, such rehearsals can also be conducted in place of the "prelude" music before the service.

Similarly, the substance and much of the conduct of proclamation and prayer belong to the laity. Sermon seminars in which laymen work with the pastor to prepare the sermon, dialogue preaching, preaching as congrega-

---

[17] See the passage quoted in footnote 85, ch. I., pp. 102-3 from Olof Herrlins' *Divine Service: Liturgy in Perspective.*

[18] The word "anthem" is an Anglicized form of "antiphon." It is noteworthy that the first song of praise mentioned in the Bible, the Song of Moses, bears this character: "Then sang Moses and the children of Israel . . . unto the Lord . . . and Miriam . . . and all the women . . . answered them" (Exodus 15, KJV). See also I Chron. 15: 16-25; 25:1-8; Neh. 12; and of course the Psalms.

tional "conversation about the word of God," talk-back services and coffee hours—in such ways the laymen can be involved.[19] Especially, prayer is to involve the laity as priests in that it uniquely embodies corporate action.[20] The vicarious character of action hardly comes to focus anywhere else so clearly, especially in the intercessions. If the pastor prepares and offers the prayers, he should take the greatest of pains to be sure that their content reflects the life of the people. Prayer will be more than this, to be sure; it will minister divine grace to the people as well as speak relevantly for the people. But it will be the people's prayer. The minister's freedom here is uniquely the "bound freedom" of which we have written. That is, in his prayers he is bound to serve the people and at all costs to avoid that subtle clericalism whereby he uses prayer "to wrestle with his own theological problems, to scold the people from behind the Lord's back, or to summarize succinctly the points of his sermon." [21] If he is wise, he will also solicit the congregation's help in preparing the prayers and in offering them, perhaps in asking for "biddings" or topics of thanksgiving or intercession,[22] or by asking laymen themselves to prepare and offer the prayers.

The priesthood of the people can also become real when the pastor teaches them how to engage in physical action appropriate to theological reality; and here the declarative and interpretative nature of physical action as we have described it especially applies. For only as action declares and interprets theological intention is it more than physical activity. In prayer, for example, the people may well be taught to stand for the intercessions—the custom in the early Church—as a way of physically declaring their part in the Church's act of caring for others. Likewise the theological importance of saying the "Amens" should be interpreted to the people; otherwise the "Amen" is likely to be only a verbal activity. The Christian "Amen," as we have said, is most essentially an eschatological act: through it the believer joyfully ratifies the decisiveness for his own destiny of the Christ-Event through which he has passed from death into the life of the New Age.[23]

[19] See Ian Fraser, *Bible, Congregation, and Community* (London: SCM Press, 1959); Reuel Howe, *Partners in Preaching: Clergy and Laity in Dialogue* (New York: Seabury Press, 1967); Dietrich Ritschl, *Theology of Proclamation* (Richmond: John Knox Press, 1960). The Lutheran conception of preaching as "mutual consolation of the brethren" has been imaginatively reconceived in one congregation in which the traditional sermon is dispensed with on certain Sundays. In its place, each person is invited to write on a card his most serious personal problem, signing his name or not, as he wishes. The cards are then gathered and redistributed, and each person comments on the card that comes to him, out of his own Christian faith and obedience.

[20] See chs. II, III.

[21] Howard G. Hageman, *Pulpit and Table* (Richmond: John Knox Press, 1962), p. 38.

[22] See ch. III.

[23] See ch. II. In the early Church the "Amen" accordingly held great theological and

In this sense it is an existential act of which the people should not be deprived; it possesses a certain fatefulness, and to participate in it is to perform a faith commitment. Other meanings are also implicit in the "Amen" but none more vital than this. Father D. Mathieu, in writing of the "Amen" in Catholic worship, surely gathers up its meanings for Protestants also:

The priest is encouraged to go on; he is not alone. The faithful declare themselves to be in union with the priest in the presentation of mankind's prayer to the God of majesty. More than an element of dialogue between priest and people, the Amen is a manifestation of mutual support between the celebrants in an audacious and perilous action. Moreover, the Amen varies from one celebrant to another; it is both a communal and a very personal expression. My Amen is filled with anxiety, with joy, with the activity of my own life. The Christian is no more or no less than his Amen. There are as many Amens as there are celebrants. And yet the communal Amen binds all these personal attitudes together into one unique acclamation. The quality of our Amen is an indication of progress in our role as liturgical celebrants.[24]

The interpretative character of physical action applies to the people's priesthood in other ways also. The faithful dead, for example, surely are to be recognized as one with the worshipping community, and Protestant revolt against abuse of Masses for the dead should not be permitted to cancel out the theological meaning of the great Tersanctus: "Therefore with angels, archangels and *all the hosts of heaven*, we laud and magnify thy holy Name." But cannot action other than occasional singing of this chant be conceived to mark the unity of the faithful—such as the reading by a layman while the congregation stands of the names of members who have died, or brief testimonies by members of the congregation to the life and faith of the dead? In a different vein, the action of laymen at the Communion service in carrying in the offertory procession a common loaf from the neighborhood market can declare the relation between Communion and the laymen's weekday life. The carrying of a Bible during an entrance hymn and placing it on the table or lectern by a layman can symbolically "enthrone" it in the congregation's gathered life. Similarly at Baptism, processions of the baptized's family, sponsors, and representative laity, provision for the congregation to stand and in well-chosen words—printed in the order—renew their own baptismal vows, the placing and lighting by a child's parents of a candle on the altar on the yearly anniversary of his baptism—such actions reinforce theological meaning. And at weddings, why cannot the congrega-

liturgical importance. Jerome reports, for example, that in Roman basilicas the people's "Amen" resounded "like heavenly thunder." A functionary or deacon was commonly appointed to stand where all might see him as he waved a banner to signal the proper moment to cry out the "Amen."

[24] "All Are Celebrants," *Worship*, XXXIX (June, 1965).

tion participate in hymns, responsive readings, prayers, and why cannot the parents of the bride and groom, or other relatives or friends, offer prayers or read appropriate scriptural lessons?

In these ways and others, the action of worship can be set within the doctrine of the Church and related to the priesthood and ministry of the laity. And here, once more, the minister has a unique opportunity to function as a liturgical theologian and as a theological pastor. It is within his power to make doctrine come alive for his people in an existential way and to gird the congregation's empirical life with theological truth. In relating the action of worship to the life of the community as a *Christian* community, he is dealing with the heart of liturgical integrity.

LITURGICAL ACTION IN LIGHT OF THE WORD

Important as the doctrine of the Church is, however, the nature of liturgical action is finally to be understood within Christology, and the properties of the Light are to be sovereign over empirical study of the eye. Knowledge of the patient and his illness will always be necessary, but the action of the man who worships is ultimately to be defined in light of the Word through whom he worships. The fullness of that Word, we have said, consists of its incarnational character, its eventful character, its historical and trans-historical character, and its ontological, soteriological, and eschatological character.[25] While all these meanings speak to the question of action, the incarnational, ontological, and eventful meanings emerge as decisive for thought, for liturgical Christology can say nothing more fundamental than that Jesus Christ supremely makes himself known through what he does. The deed of Jesus Christ reveals the nature of Jesus Christ. Thus, on the one hand, the ground of liturgical action is always an ontological ground in that action rises from Christ's mystical presence in his people. On the other hand, Christ's being is "being in action." The presence of Christ is declared in the action of Christ, and in this sense the ground of liturgical action is event as well.

The Liturgy of Jesus Christ: Action as Sacramental

The paradigm for the mind's reflection in this sense must always be some such image as that with which St. Luke pictures Christ in relation to the disciples at Emmaus after the resurrection: through Christ's *action* in taking, blessing, breaking, and giving the bread, his *being* is known and his *life* is received. *In fractione panis eum cognoverunt:* "they recognized him"— not in the bread, not in conversation before he broke the bread, not in the

[25] See ch. II.

342

table bearing the bread, but—"*in the breaking* of bread" (Luke 24:30-32, 35 KJV). Divine "being" is known in human "breaking." The presence of the Word is the act of the Word.

But liturgical theology is drawn to such an image not only because of the Emmaus incident in itself. Even more, this image summarizes the meaning of the total Christ-Event liturgically understood. The action of Jesus Christ in taking, blessing, breaking, and giving the bread at Emmaus only epitomizes all other actions through which the mind of the Church had known Jesus Christ as Life. Thus it is said that the disciples *re*-cognized, not merely "cognized" him, as it were. They knew him again only as they had known him before. His liturgical action at the table at Emmaus was one with the liturgical action of his life. Of virtually any action Jesus performed, it could be said that he made himself present in what he did. In reading from the prophet Isaiah in the synagogue in Nazareth, in conversing with a Samaritan woman at the well, in teaching and preaching from the mountainside, in healing a demoniac, in cleansing the temple, in washing the disciples' feet, in bearing his cross and dying his death—in all these a liturgy was done and an epiphany took place. The liturgical action of breaking the bread at Emmaus is but Christ's signature to the liturgy of his life; and in that liturgy, ontology and event are finally one.

For the mind's reflection upon worship as for the experience of worship itself, this insight underlies everything else, first in the sense that Christ's liturgy is the ground of our liturgy and that his liturgical action precedes ours. From the mystery of his presence acting toward us derives our ability to act. In the poetic language of the Emmaus story: only because he breaks the bread and acts can we act. Or in the drier language of theology: liturgical action inheres in prevenient grace. Or in the philosophical language of the schools: Christ's liturgy is both the "final" and the "efficient" cause of our action. Or in the metaphorical language of Judaism: through the living priesthood of Jesus Christ we are able to act as priests. Or in the language of pneumatology: we do not know how to worship as we ought, but the Spirit makes intercession for us. But however it be said, it is Jesus Christ who liturgically holds the service. He is the true Celebrant, and our action is grounded in his. This is to say, we can think theologically on the question of liturgical action only in the same manner in which we engage in the action of worship itself: through Jesus Christ our Lord.

Restated as a conceptual principle, this insight requires, first, that action be thought of as sacramental, but "sacramental" understood not as referring to a particular rite but to the initiatory action of divine grace coming to us from outside as well as within our existence. In this sense, the term "sacramental" is to be referred to the liturgy of Jesus Christ as that in which the

Divine as other than man yet gives itself in service to man; and worship possesses integrity only as its action is sacramental in the sense that it provides for Christ's offering himself to us before we offer ourselves to him. It is this fundamental truth which the Church especially needs to remember as it undertakes to rethink action in our day, a truth which under varying thought-forms and in different categories we have affirmed again and again in these essays—in asserting the priority of impression to expression, in yoking "irrelevance" with "relevance" as essential to liturgical integrity, in understanding objectivity as the ground of subjectivity, in borrowing from art the principle of vitality, restating it Christologically and saying that we know the Word to be Act when its action moves us with the movement of God. Ultimately, these are only different ways of stating that truth which the apostle far more simply and profoundly laid down as the deepest truth of the Gospel for liturgy as for all else: we love because God first loved us.

However, the sacramental nature of action needs to be thought of not only conceptually but functionally as well. And functionally—as we have said—the action of the Word can only take place through man's action. The congregation is the field of Christ's action, and his action becomes real only through what man does. Thus, we have said, the congregation are priests to one another. Or in Luther's bolder metaphor: they are "Christs to one another." Functionally, their action is mimetic action in the sense that they reach into the liturgical event of Jesus Christ and re-enact it to one another. In this sense, congregational action goes beyond the formula with which we commonly describe it: revelation and response. In its deepest meaning it is revelation itself. To cite Lutheran categories described earlier: divine action occurs "in," "with," and "under" human action. Alternatively, we may say that through the congregation's action the "mystery" of Christ takes place. Or again, through the congregation's action a miracle occurs whereby past, present, and future time is transcended and what we can do no better than to speak of as "eternity" becomes eschatologically present. In a word: through the action of ordinary, weak, sinful, flesh-and-blood people, nothing less than the action of incarnation again takes place.

On no less deep a level of understanding are the practical forms of action to be conceived and employed. To our shame, we often forget the revelatory function of language in this deep Christological sense, but it is the pastor's duty to remember and teach it to the congregation. To be sure, pastor and people will not make the mistake of assuming that in order to be sacramental the forms of action must necessarily be unhuman or esoteric. To think in this way would be to violate the incarnational nature of the liturgy of Jesus Christ as human as well as divine. From one point of view, the language of worship cannot be too human, as all the illustrations of this truth cited in these essays testify. However, ultimately, the sacramental nature of action is probably best conveyed through human language that is yet informed with a "mysterious density." To be sure, tactics will vary. And sensibilities will vary also. Yet, as at Emmaus, the human liturgy of Jesus Christ ultimately bestows its Life out of his divine mystery and the forms of congregational action are to convey this. St. Theresa of Avila, it is said, always spoke of the Christ of the Supper as "His Majesty." And once the majesty of his liturgy is dissolved in forms too earthly and too transparent, his action no longer can tell us who he is. "Great action demands great language," it has been said, "and here is the greatest action of all." [26]

The Liturgy of Jesus Christ: Action as Ethical

The Christ-Event understood as a liturgy also determines man's liturgical action to be *ethical*. Inevitably, we have anticipated this meaning in inquiring into the worshipper's life in the Church, and much of our preceding analysis applies to the ethical nature of action understood within the context of Christology. The correspondence between the worshipper's life in the *koinonia*, the fellowship, and his *diakonia*, his service in the world, we have said, is vital: the ethical reality of *koinonia* and the ethical character of *diakonia* determine the integrity of *leitourgia*. However, as the action of the Word constitutes the Church, not vice versa, so Christology is sovereign over ecclesiology for understanding action as ethical. And again, the starting point for thought lies in the relation in the Word between ontology and event. The action of the Word declares the nature of the Word, and the core of its action is exactly liturgy in the strict sense of the term—the work of a man serving man. Correspondingly, the congregation's action is defined by and resituated in this action. The congregation's action is human not only in the functional sense that their humanity is the field of Christ's action, but also in the ethical sense that their action—as his—is to be directed toward their fellowmen.

To describe the congregation's action as "ethical" in this sense may at first sight seem a restricted way of speaking, and alternate terms could be employed. One could denote the "manward" character of the congregation's action as "apostolic" or "missionary," or as "worldly" or "secular," or as "human" or "historical." These are not synonyms, but they sufficiently point to the same reality so that we have not hesitated to use them almost interchangeably in these essays. Yet, in choosing terms the decision must lie with that category which emerges as ultimate under which other meanings

[26] Irene Marinoff, "The Erosion of the Mystery," in *New Theology* No. 7, ed. Martin E. Marty and Dean G. Peerman (New York: The Macmillan Co., 1970), p. 27.

can be subsumed. In writing on the relation between incarnation and redemption, P. T. Forsyth once said that Christ came to redeem, which he could only do by his incarnation; he did not come to be incarnate and incidentally to redeem.[27] In somewhat the same way one feels that ultimately the action of Jesus Christ is not ethical in order to be missionary but missionary in order to be ethical; that it is not ethical in order to be secular but secular in order to be ethical. The ultimate thing to be said about the liturgy of Jesus Christ is that it is service and love toward men. And in this conceptual sense the congregation's action is ontologically ethical.

A paradigm for the mind's reflection here can be the image of Jesus' action in washing the disciples' feet (John 13: 1-17), the Johannine addendum to the synoptics' narrative of the Last Supper, and as such a liturgical and eucharistic narrative.[28] The divine aspect of Jesus' liturgy of course is marked by John in the introductory words: "Jesus, knowing that the Father had given all things into his hands, and that he was come from God and went to God, riseth from supper, and laid aside his garments, and took a towel" (vss. 3, 4 KJV). But the inmost truth of the narrative lies in the human and servant character of Jesus' action evident throughout, that is, in its ethical character. Symbols having a more "servant" meaning cannot be imagined—water, a basin, a towel—and action having a more "servant" meaning likewise cannot be imagined—the human hands of Jesus taking and washing the soiled feet of men. Similarly, language which more forthrightly lays upon men the ethical nature of action cannot be conceived: "Do you understand what I have *done for you?* . . . I have set you an example. You are to *do as I have done for you.* . . . If you know this, happy are you if you *act* upon it" (vss. 12-17 NEB). Further, the mind can hardly conceive an image which more fully gathers up the totality of meaning of Jesus' life and death. As with the Emmaus image, the liturgy of the foot washing epitomizes the spirit of service evident in every aspect of the Christ-Event. Indeed, the author of the fourth gospel presents his narrative as exactly this—as a summary paradigm of the liturgy of Jesus: "He had always loved his own who were in the world, and now he was to show the full extent of his love" (vs. 1 NEB).

Again, one hesitates to wrest theology from poetry, but liturgy as conceptualized ethically here can mean nothing other than that worship is

[27] See *The Church and the Sacraments* (London: Longmans, Green & Co., 1917), p. 184.

[28] See William Temple, *Readings in St. John's Gospel: Second Series* (New York: The Macmillan Co., 1940), pp. 207 ff; Edwyn Clement Hoskyns, *The Fourth Gospel*, II, ed. Francis Noel Davey (London: Faber & Faber, 1940), pp. 510-19, and especially Hoskyns' note, "The Liturgical Use of the Pedilavium or the Washing of the Feet," pp. 520-24.

always to be shot through and through with the claim to love and to serve. Worship whose action does not announce that commandment which crowns all ethics, "Love one another as I have loved you," which does not pronounce the fatefulness of man's moral life for his personal and social destiny, which does not engage him with time and history as the matrix in which he is ethically to live out a liturgical life, contradicts itself. And this is the truth, once more, which in numerous ways has been the burden of these essays— in understanding worship as missionary, as intercessory, as relevant, as worldly and historical, as human, as subjective, as prospective and recollective, as occasioned, as public, as social and political action, as both the Mass of the altar and the Mass of life. Let it be clear once and for all that the congregation can partake of the action of Christian worship only as they act ethically toward their fellowmen, and that they can partake of the reality of Jesus Christ in worship only as they partake of the reality of the world.[29] If worship is to possess integrity, its action must be held within this truth as in a vise.

We have previously explored the implications of this understanding, and we shall not repeat. It will suffice to say that they are as broad as the range of human life and as practical as the smallest detail. On the one hand, liturgical action will have as its reference every personal and social situation of men; action will raise the question of what Christ's love commands in each situation; and action will claim the worshipper to be present in that situation with a presence incarnating the love of Jesus Christ. The ethical action of the congregation when gathered, organically determines the ethical character of their action when dispersed. In both, action is to be ethical in a Christological, a liturgical, indeed, even in an eucharistic sense. The ground, the motive, and the shape of ethical action inhere in the liturgy of Jesus Christ: "If I, your Lord and Master, have washed your feet, you also ought to wash one another's feet. I have set you an example: you are to do as I have done for you (John 13:14-15 NEB).

To be sure, there is also what we may speak of as anonymous Christian action—that is, ethical action unnamed or unknown as Christian. We do not forget that in the parable of the last judgement, the righteous do not know or name their ethical action as Christian: "Lord, when was it that we saw you hungry and fed you, or thirsty and gave you drink? . . . And the king will answer, 'Anything you did for one of my brothers, however humble, you did for me' " (Matt. 25:37-40 NEB). But normatively—and abundant New Testament evidence confirms this—man's ethical action arises from the consciousness of Christ's action toward him, and it is the task of worship

[29] See Dietrich Bonhoeffer, *Ethics*, ed. Eberhard Bethge, trans. Neville Horton Smith (New York: The Macmillan Company, 1955), pp. 61-62.

to bestow this intentional character. While the use of cultic terms to describe ethical action in the New Testament reveals how fluid the boundaries are between worship and service in the world,[30] nevertheless worship is not dissolved into ethical obedience. Worship holds a certain priority, and the congregation's assembly for worship in Christ's name rules and sustains their ethical life in the world in a way that their life in the world does not rule their worship.[31] In short, "obedience and service that are not rooted in worship are as unthinkable in New Testament terms as worship that does not issue in obedience and service. . . . There is but one Christian liturgy, focalized in Word and Sacrament, continued in mission and service." [32]

At the same time, action is ethical not only in the sense that its reference and content are man's moral life; the attitudes one brings to the experience of worship itself and the practical decisions one makes about it are also to be viewed ethically. The problem of relevance, for example—and all the decisions bound up with it—is finally to be seen as an ethical as well as a theological problem: worship whose action does not meaningfully engage the people is immoral simply because it disserves them and disables them for serving others. Similarly, practical judgements on how worship is to edify the congregation are an ethical and not merely an ecclesial matter. Likewise, the language of worship in all its range is to be tested ethically: all forms, symbols, media are to serve the worshipper and enable him to perform his liturgy for others. And not least—and once more this may be a hard saying— all the insights that art and psychology and culture can provide are to function in Christian worship as a basin of water and a towel. Lastly, all efforts at liturgical reform are to be interrogated as to their servant character. Whether it is a local congregation arguing out the touchy question of "experimental" versus traditional forms, an ecumenical convocation grappling with the problem of secularization and liturgical renewal, a denominational commission preparing a new service book, or a seminary teacher trying to think through thorny questions of liturgical theory—all are subject to the same ethical test that must apply to the action of worship itself: "I have set you an example: you are to do as I have done for you."

The Liturgy of Jesus Christ: Action as Sacrificial

The liturgy of Jesus Christ, finally, determines the action of worship to be *sacrificial* in the sense that it is the action of man offering himself to God.

---

[30] See ch. I.

[31] See notes 13 and 14 to the Introduction to Peter Brunner's *Worship in the Name of Jesus*, pp. 314-15.

[32] Howard G. Hageman, *Pulpit and Table*, p. 130.

Whatever else one may say of the liturgy of Jesus Christ, one must at all costs say that it is service to God. Not to say this is to deny the Reality of the divine in whose light his human liturgy takes on its full meaning and becomes Light to men. Only as the Godward direction of Jesus' action is understood as polarizing other aspects of his action can his liturgy declare the fullness of who he is. That liturgy, to be sure, is also a liturgy of God serving man and of a man serving man, but its sacramental and ethical character is ultimately gathered up in a fullness exceeding even these. The "lodestar" that clarifies with ultimacy all other meanings Jesus holds for men is the divine Reality he names "God"—the Reality for whom he lives, toward whom he acts, unto whom he dies, and into whose hands he commits his destiny. The metaphor with which Jesus conceptualizes the claim upon his consciousness of the ultimacy of divine Reality is the "kingdom of God" (or "my Father's kingdom") and correlatively the "will" of God—supremely a metaphor of ontology, of sovereignty, of action and volition. The kingdom of God is the very presence and life of God; it is also the rule of God; it is the activity of God; and it is the claim upon man's will of the Reality of God. And as this Reality so claimed the human life of Jesus as to transform its every act into a sacrifice, so the Reality of God is to transform into a sacrifice the action of those who worship in his name. This is the truth St. Paul transposed into what is perhaps the Church's most memorable definition of worship: "Therefore, my brothers, I implore you by God's mercy to offer your very selves to him: a living sacrifice, dedicated and fit for his acceptance, the worship offered by mind and heart" (Rom. 12:1 NEB). The sacrificial action enjoined in these words is both ethical and cultic. But it is not least cultic. And its nature is to be understood in light of the Reality of God that governs the liturgy of Jesus Christ.

The paradigm for our thought here can hardly be other than the narratives of the institution of the Lord's Supper given us in the synoptic gospels, typically in St. Matthew's words: "And he took the cup, and gave thanks, and gave it to them, saying, 'Drink ye all of it. For this is my blood of the new testament which is shed for many. . . . I say unto you, I will not drink henceforth of this fruit of the vine, until that day when I drink it new with you in my Father's kingdom'" (26:27-29 KJV). Jesus' words, "my blood shed for many" (Luke uses the direct vocative "for you"), partly illumine the profoundly sacrificial meaning of action. In these words, on the one hand, Jesus' mind conceives sacrifice as sacrifice for men; the cross of which the wine is a symbol can mean nothing less. But even more, on the other hand, his mind eschatologically conceives sacrifice as offered to God. That which he does on earth, he says, is consummated in eternity. The fruit of the vine he drinks now has its counterpart in the wine of the Kingdom. The supper he shares in an "upper room" foretells a banquet in heaven. "The hour" in time when "he sat down, and the twelve apostles with him" (Luke 22:14 KJV) presages "that Day" in eternity when he shall drink "anew" with his own in the "Father's kingdom." Controlling Jesus' consciousness is a realm of Reality other than man, far transcending the human reality of those with whom he drinks and eats and for whom he will lay down his life. Without this dimension of the divine, his action in drinking and eating with his friends at a last supper would indeed be a moving act of pathos and love, and the death it prefigures a noble deed that would ever bring tears to men's eyes. But such action would hardly be different from all other acts in which good men have sacrificed themselves for other men. What makes the action of Jesus Christ different is exactly that which makes it more than ethical even as it is supremely ethical—the passion with which he offers himself in his living and in his dying as a sacrifice of love unto God, and the faith with which he believes his sacrifice to avail at the heart of the universe. That which with ultimacy defines the action of Jesus Christ as sacrifice, in short, is that while it is done *for men*, it is offered *to God*.

Now again, terms other than "sacrificial" might well be used to convey this truth. Broadly construed, such terms as "eucharistic" or "otherworldly" or "eschatological" mark somethnig of the same meaning. "Eucharistic" as meaning "thankful" would denote the character of liturgcial action as expressive of man's grateful love of God in response to God's love for man; it would affirm the otherness of the divine Reality with which man feels himself engaged; and it would mark the direction of action as "Godward," as it were, rather than "manward." "Otherworldly" would similarly mark the distinction between human and divine Reality, between historical and trans-historical reality, and it would distinguish meanings of time from meanings of eternity. Perhaps the term "eschatological" comes closest to denoting the truth we conceptualize as "sacrificial." "Eschatological" signifies the eternal, qualitatively different realm of Reality the man of faith is claimed by in Christian worship; yet it affirms the presence of this Reality to his historical consciousness. It also signifies the essential mystery of worship as embracing past, present, and not least the future—the hereafter that is yet here. We cannot forget, parenthetically, that eschatology is the dominant mode of New Testament worship and the key that unlocks its normative meaning.

Yet, in reflecting upon worship as *action*, the term "sacrificial" can include the meanings denoted by the terms "eucharistic," "otherworldly," and "eschatological," and at the same time go beyond them in marking the costly putting forth of man's will, the thrust of his selfhood toward the eternal, and the passionate commitment of his being to God. But by whatever term it be denoted, action possesses integrity only insofar as man's consciousness is claimed by a divine Reality other than himself, and insofar as he is summoned to offer his entire being—heart, mind, soul, and strength —in love to God.

This is the truth, again, which like a theme with variations has sounded throughout these essays—in our critique of the corruption of worship into humanism, in understanding the full dialectic of the incarnation as fulcral, in emphasis upon the ontological and soteriological meaning of the Word, in understanding worship as an end, and irrelevance as disengagement from the world, in defining the liturgy of Jesus Christ as a liturgy of eternity as well as of time, in affirming objectivity as the ground of subjectivity, in analyzing psychologically the mystery of liturgical time, in describing the function of liturgical language as negating as well as affirming culture, in understanding man's nature as sacral as well as sensate. The great *cantus firmus*, the deep, beating affirmation which in one way or another must sustain both worship itself and reflection upon it, is nothing other than the affirmation of divine Reality as the polar reality for man's life and destiny.

The sacrificial nature of action understood in this deep sense thus holds a certain ultimacy for the theology and practice of worship which other ways of thinking do not hold. The ultimate question to be asked about all worship is whether its decisive referent is the Reality of God and whether its action possesses the character of offering to God. But such a question can be a meaningful question only if our liturgy—as the liturgy of Jesus Christ— is understood as shot through and through with a consciousness of God as Reality other than man. This to say, the question of action finally becomes the question of God and of the transcendence of God. In speaking of divine transcendence in relation to evolution, Teilhard de Chardin once said that God must be independent of the collapse of the forces with which evolution is woven, that "while God is the last term *in* the series, He is *yet outside* all series." [33] The action of worship is to be conceived within this truth and informed with this mood. One may state its meaning and transpose it into liturgy in any one of a number of ways. The transcendent Reality toward whom man acts can be conceived as a Heavenly Father, as the Unconditioned, as Above or Beyond or Ahead, as the Future, as the Encompassing Whole, as the Ultimate Power or Dynamic Process urging human life to a richer harmony—or as the God in whose will lies man's destiny and in whose Kingdom he shall drink the wine of heaven. But the action of worship possesses integrity only when it is boldly offered to the

[33] Quoted by Christopher F. Mooney, S.J., "Teilhard de Chardin on Belief in God," in *The Presence and the Absence of God*, ed. Christopher F. Mooney, S.J. (New York: Fordham University Press, 1969), p. 41.

Reality Jesus Christ names "God"—a Reality strangely "outside" man's action even as it claims man's action.

But one cannot ponder the meaning of action in this ultimate sense without having to mark, lastly, its character as transfiguration—or one might say, as transformation or transposition. Such ways of speaking may seem strange to us, but somehow they become unavoidable when one contemplates the liturgy of Jesus Christ as the form of our liturgy. For in our worship as in his, man offers not only *things* to God; he offers not only *action* to God; indeed he not only offers *worship* to God. Above all he offers his "very *self* a living sacrifice" to God, his "mind and heart" (Rom. 12:1 NEB). And while it is God's grace, not man's act by itself, that transfigures man's being in the way we have chosen to speak of in these essays as ontological,[34] surely one cannot but believe that in "sacrificing" his "very self" man's life is grasped and transformed by divine Reality.

It would be germane to observe here that the word "sacrifice" derives from the Latin *sacer* meaning "sacred" and from the verb *facere* meaning "to make," and that "sacrifice" literally means to make or to be "made sacred." Given our modern aversion to the sacred, we may not find such etymology persuasive, but the liturgy of Jesus Christ will not let us speak of worship as less than "sacrifice" in this sense and of its action as other than dying and rising to a transfigured quality of life. These realities are written too deeply in the Church's mind and rise too profoundly from her prayer to allow us to speak otherwise. Nor can liturgical theology finally evade the meaning of Jesus' use of the very word "new" as he mystically speaks of the act he does and its consummation in eternity. Always his liturgy will require us to think of worship as transforming men into "newness" of life, whether in drinking the cup of the New Covenant, or hearing the Word that gives life, or in being washed with the water of Baptism. We may, if we wish, interpret this transfiguration as future, and worship does indeed fail if its action does not somehow turn men in hope toward that "Day" when they shall inherit a Kingdom prepared from the foundation of the world. Whether conceived as the Parousia at the end of history when the Son of Man shall come to judge the quick and the dead, or as one's personal destiny in which one is changed from glory unto glory, the action of worship is to transfigure man's vision and open to him the prospect of a Reality beyond that in which he now lives.

But even more confidently we may understand transfiguration as present. Gregory Dix, in speaking of the eucharistic prayers of the early Church, writes in a memorable phrase that their language strikes upon the ear as "the

---

[34] See ch. II.

language of *achieved triumph*." [35] The transfiguring character of action is like that. Through the liturgical sacrifice of his self gathered up into the sacrifice of Jesus Christ to God, the Christian man knows himself to have been transposed into an imperishable Life that has met and triumphed over the last enemy—death—and the language of his prayer and song cannot but say this. In worship he knows his mortal life to have put on immortality. Here, as Bonhoeffer has written, "the life of Christians together under the Word has reached its *perfection*. . . . United in body and blood at the table of the Lord, so will they be together in eternity. *Here the community has reached its goal*." [36] Christian worship claims man for no less a destiny. It promises to transfigure his life in no less ultimate a way. Hence its action will always summon him to his sacrifice with no less ringing a cry than that with which the Church triumphantly calls to those who worship in Christ's Name: "Lift up your hearts! We lift them up unto the Lord!"

VII   pp. 292-353

Leitourgia means liturgy. Liturgical action must be seen as an ethical question. Part of the discipline of the congregation's life is the discipline of prayer. But discipline is ultimately gathered up in Love. Love manifest in worship can make the life of the community authentic. The community's life includes service. The priesthood of believers is a thought form in which the Church has conceptualized its self-understanding. The nature of liturgical action is finally to be understood within Christology. The liturgy of Jesus Christ requires the action of worship to be sacrificial. It is man offering himself to God. Gregory Dix says that the language of early Christian eucharistic prayers is the language of achieved triumph.

---

[35] *The Shape of the Liturgy* (Westminster: Dacre Press, 1945), p. 265. Italics mine.
[36] *Life Together*, p. 122. Italics mine.

INDEX

Diakonia, 32, 54, 110, 130, 136, 184-85, 186, 206, 306, 326, 331-36, 343-53. *See also* Action; Ethics; Koinonia; Leitourgia; Mission

Dialectic. *See* Theology, dialectical

Discipline of congregation, 28, 57-59, 103-6, 326-31, 346-48

Divine initiative. *See* Christology; God; Expression-impression; Response; Sacrament-sacrifice

Drama, worship as, 46 *n*, 247, 271, 315-17

Ecumenism, 16, 26-27, 82, 89, 135, 157, 186, 327 *n*. *See also* Church; Tradition

Edification of congregation, 27-30, 58-59. *See also* Action; Church; Congregation; Corporateness; Discipline; Koinonia; Love; Mission; Pastoral liturgy; Pathological worship; Subconscious; World

Education, 29-30, 294-95 *n*, 309, 310, 314-16, 337-42. *See also* Church; Congregation; Cultural influences; Emotion; Man; Psychology; Rationality; Renewal; Theology

Emotion, 194-95, 196, 199-206, 209-13, 232-33, 294-95, 318-24. *See also* Existential character; Experience; Man; Psychology; Subconscious; Symbol

End and means, worship as, 25, 28, 31, 52-55, 152-156, 175-76, 206, 209, 351-53. *See also* Ethics; God; Historical character; Objectivity-subjectivity; Relevance-irrelevance; Social action; Mission; Theology, dialectical; World

Errors, 34-44. *See also* Corruptions

Eschatology, 28, 65, 119, 131-32, 134, 141, 143, 182-84, 246-47, 258, 264, 270, 271, 282, 284, 349-50, 352-53. *See also* God; Historical character; Hope; Future; Time-eternity; Transcendent; World

Eternity. *See* God; Historical character; Time-eternity; Transcendent

Ethics and worship, 30-31, 54-55, 68,

Ethics and Worship–*cont'd*
72-75, 171, 187-88, 303-6, 327-28, 333, 345-48. *See also* Christology; End and means; Historical character; Mission; Social action; World

Eucharist. *See* Holy Communion

Evangelism, 28, 57-59. *See also* Conversion; Ethics; Historical character; Mission; Salvation history; Soteriology; World

Event of Christ. *See* Christology; God

Evil. *See* Demonic

Existential character, 13, 49-50, 52, 57, 65, 70, 73-74, 88, 92, 141-42, 145-46, 152-53, 177-84, 187-88, 189, 197-203, 206, 208-10, 229-31, 236, 243-47, 281-82, 298, 300, 304-8, 341. *See* also Cultural influences; Experience; Incarnation; Objectivity-subjectivity; Psychology; Relevance-irrelevance; Soteriology; Time-eternity

Experience, worship as, 24-25, 40, 44-46, 63, 87-88, 104, 155, 171, 194, 209-13; 265-66. *See also* Existential character; God

Experimental worship, 25, 34, 45-46 *n*, 171, 264-66, 277, 285, 305-6, 310, 314-15, 348. *See also* Action; Art; Corruptions; Cultural influences; Language; Music; Psychology; Relevance-irrelevance; Secularization

Expression-impression, dialectic of, 43, 55-56, 204, 268, 295, 316-24, 343-44. *See also* Action; God; Objectivity-subjectivity; Relevance-irrelevance; Response; Sacrament-sacrifice; Theology, dialectical; Tradition

Fatefulness. *See* Existential character

Forms, 40-44, 97-98, 176-77, 216-19, 242, 247, 282-83, 297-98. *See also* Art; Expression-impression; Freedom; Language; Myth; Psychology; Symbol

Free churches, 15

Freedom, 51-52, 56-58, 83-84, 117-18, 126, 175, 216-19, 256, 301-2, 340. *See also* Expression-impression;